CANADA

THE STORY OF A DEVELOPING NATION

SENIOR AUTHORS

Elspeth Deir
Elementary Social Studies Curriculum Professor, Faculty of Education, Queen's University, Kingston, Ontario

John Fielding
History and Contemporary Studies Curriculum Professor, Faculty of Education, Queen's University, Kingston, Ontario

AUTHORS

George Adams
Teacher, Notre Dame Secondary School, Brampton, Ontario

Nick Brune
Teacher, Iroquois Ridge High School, Oakville, Ontario

Peter Grant
Writer, Victoria, British Columbia

Stephanie Smith Abram
Writer, Toronto, Ontario

Carol White
Teacher, Calvin Park Public School, Kingston, Ontario

McGraw-Hill Ryerson Limited
Toronto   Montréal   New York   Burr Ridge   Bangkok
Bogotá   Caracas   Lisbon   London   Madrid
Mexico City   Milan   New Delhi   Seoul   Singapore
Sydney   Taipei

McGraw-Hill Ryerson Limited

A Subsidiary of The McGraw·Hill Companies

Canada: The Story of a Developing Nation

ISBN 0-07-560738-7

http://www.mcgrawhill.ca

1 2 3 4 5 6 7 8 9 0 GTC 0 9 8 7 6 5 4 3 2 1 0

Printed and bound in Canada

Canadian Cataloguing in Publication Data

Deir, Elspeth, date
  Canada: the story of a developing nation

Includes index.
ISBN 0-07-560738-7

Canada – History –1763 – 1867 – Juvenile literature. 2. Canada – History – 1914-1918 Juvenile literature. I. Fielding, John (John F.). II. Title.

FC170.D433. 2000   971   C99-932897-2
F1026.D433 2000

PUBLISHER: Patty Pappas
ASSOCIATE EDITOR: Jenifer A. Ludbrook
SENIOR SUPERVISING EDITOR: Nancy Christoffer
SUPERVISING EDITOR: Crystal Shortt
FEATURE WRITER: Dyanne Rivers
COPY EDITOR: Geraldine Kikuta
PERMISSIONS EDITOR: Jacqueline Donovan
PRODUCTION CO-ORDINATORS: Yolanda Pigden, Susanne Penny
EDITORIAL ASSISTANT: Joanne Murray
INTERIOR DESIGN: Word & Image Design Studio Inc.
ELECTRONIC PAGE MAKE-UP: Word & Image Design Studio Inc.
INTERIOR MAPS AND ILLUSTRATIONS: Deborah Crowle, Paul McCusker
COVER DESIGN: Greg Devitt

Front Cover Credits

Centre Glenbow Archives, Calgary, Canada, Glenbow poster design by Dennis Budgen;
top left NAC/C-097750; **bottom left** NAC/C-018734; **right** NAC/PA-009256

Back Cover Credits

Top left Courtesy Rogers Communications Inc.; **top right** Provincial Archives of BC/A-05056;
bottom left Courtesy General Motors of Canada; **centre left** NAC/C-029977

REVIEWERS

Patrice Baker
   Teacher, Elora Public School, Elora Ontario

Susan L. Lawrence
   Teacher, Jacob Beam Public School, Beamsville, Ontario

William Trezise
   Retired teacher, formerly of Queen Elizabeth Park School, Oakville, Ontario

Jennifer Watt
   Curriculum Co-ordinator, Social, Canadian and World Studies, Toronto District School Board East,
   Scarborough, Ontario

CONSULTANT

Brenda Ahenakew
   Director of Education for Saskatoon Travel Council, Saskatoon, Saskatchewan

Acknowledgements

To the Deirs, who supported me in this project: Paul, Andrew, Matthew, Peter, and Emily. To my parents, Melba and Bill McKay, who taught me that Canada's history begins with stories of the everyday people who built our country. To all the teachers and students who make Canada's stories come alive in their minds, hearts, and lives. And to my colleague and friend, John Fielding, whose passion for history and sense of fun makes "work" play.

— *Elspeth Deir*

To Dianne for her patience as I embarked on another project. To Ellie Deir, with whom I have co-authored since 1991 — a funny and fine person to work with. To Grade 7 and 8 teachers, who may have the toughest job in education but are great to work with because they always seem ready and willing to learn.

— *John Fielding*

Thank you to Patty Pappas for her confidence in us and for letting us build into the texts much of the kind of learning we know works for students. Thanks to the author team, Stephanie Smith Abram, George Adams, Nick Brune, Peter Grant, and Carol White for working within the parameters we created for the texts. Thanks to Jennifer Ludbrook for performing the difficult role of editor with good humour, skill, and patience, and to Crystal Shortt and Jacqueline Donovan for their efforts to get these texts into the hands of students. We are also grateful to our reviewers: Patrice Baker, E. Jane Errington, Susan Lawrence, William Trezise, and Jennifer Watt.

— *Elspeth Deir and John Fielding*

Contents

A Tour of the Text		**vii**
A Tour of British North America, 1860		**2**
The Royal Tour		4
Rupert's Land		17

Unit 1 **Toward Confederation** **24**

Chapter 1	**Growth and Change**	**26**
	The Great Migration	28
	Boom, Bust, and Boom Again	37
	The Industrial Revolution Begins	43

Chapter 2	**Political Deadlock**	**52**
	The Changing Political Scene	54
	Deadlock Sets In	58
	The End Draws Near	68

Chapter 3	**The Path to Confederation**	**72**
	The Talks Begin	74
	The United States: A Nation Divided	79
	The Québec Conference	83
	The Confederation Debates	87

Chapter 4	**Building Confederation**	**100**
	Decisions in the Atlantic Colonies	102
	Westward Expansion	106
	The Island Reconsiders	111
	Territories into Provinces	113
	Newfoundland and Labrador Join At Last	118

Unit 2   **The West**   **124**

Chapter 5   **Settlement at Red River**   **126**

The Fur Trade   128

Red River Settlement, 1811 to 1820   132

Living at Red River, 1820 to 1849   137

The End of Isolation   143

Chapter 6   **King-George Men Move In**   **154**

Europeans on the West Coast   156

The North West Mounted Police   161

Treaties with the Aboriginal Peoples   167

Building the Great Railway   172

Chapter 7   **Settlers, Rebellion, and Gold Again**   **182**

Looking for Settlers   184

Settlers from Many Cultures   186

Hard Times for Prairie People   191

Klondike Gold, 1896   201

Chapter 8   **A Home in the West, 1896–1914**   **208**

The Work of Our Own HAnds   210

Working Off the Farm   223

Communities in the West   228

Unit 3   A Changing Society   236

Chapter 9	**An Era of Change**	**238**
	Toward Canada's Century	240
	We Have the Technology	252
Chapter 10	**The Working People, 1867–1920**	**264**
	The Workplace	266
	Workers Organize	279
	Winnipeg General Strike	283
Chapter 11	**The Struggle for Rights**	**290**
	The Good Old Days?	292
	Women's Struggles	294
	The Changing Role of Children	302
	Aboriginal Struggles	306
	Choosing Immigrants	311
Chapter 12	**Canada at War, 1914–1918**	**316**
	The Road to War	318
	The Battlefield	325
	Crisis at Home	335
	The Story Today	**344**
	Aboriginal Peoples	346
	Diversity Encouraged Here	350
	Canadian Technology	352
	How Canadian Is Canada?	355
	One Nation — Or Many?	358
	Glossary	**364**
	Credits	**368**
	Index	**371**

A Tour of the Text

Welcome to *Canada: The Story of a Developing Nation*. This textbook introduces you to stories of the recent past that will help you understand Canada today. It first describes how people in four British colonies united in Confederation, and how other territories in British North America joined them until the nation stretched "from sea to sea," linked by a great transcontinental railway. You will read about immigrants who came to settle the West, and the impact of their settlement and government policies on the Aboriginal Peoples. At the same time new inventions altered the ways people travelled, communicated over long distances, and worked. You will read about the effect these changes had on peoples' lives, and the impact of the first global war, World War I, on Canadians.

UNIT 2

The West

CHAPTER 5

Settlement at Red River

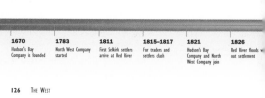

1670	1783	1811	1815–1817	1821	1826
Hudson's Bay Company is founded	North West Company started	First Selkirk settlers arrive at Red River	Fur traders and settlers clash	Hudson's Bay Company and North West Company join	Red River floods wi out settlement

126 THE WEST

Unit Opener

- *Canada: The Story of a Developing Nation* has three units.
- A large illustration that is representative of the unit sets the scene for the story to come.
- The Big Picture provides a list of topics you will read about in the unit.
- A unit time line shows the important dates and a pictorial representation of what happened then.

Chapter Opener

- Each chapter opener includes an illustration that is representative of the chapter.
- An overview of the chapter content is presented under the heading Setting Our Focus.
- Previewing the Chapter lists the specific topics you will be learning about in the chapter.
- Key Words is a list of the important words in the chapter. The words are introduced in boldface type the first time they appear in the text, where they are also defined. They are also collected and alphabetized in the glossary at the back of the book.
- A time line displays the important dates and events highlighted in the chapter.

Biographies

- Three biographies, one of a famous person and two of less well-known people, appear in each chapter. All the people are important players in the story of Canada's past.
- At the end of the biographies is a list of other people who also had a part in the story. Their names are provided for you to do further research if you wish.

Reflections

- In these journal activities, you have an opportunity to think about a particular historic event and record how you feel about it.

Web Connection

- These computer research activities occur in every chapter.
- By following the directions given, you can use the Internet at school or at home to find a history topic that is related to what you are learning about in the chapter.

SETTING OUR FOCUS

It is 1840, and the people in the painting are on their way to their annual summer buffalo hunt with their dogs, horses, oxen, and Red River carts. They are Métis hunters, farmers, and traders from the settlement at Red River. For the next two months they will work together to gather buffalo hides, fat, and a huge supply of buffalo meat for making pemmican.

They travel under a wide Prairie sky, at home in the grasslands and parklands of the western plains. Within a few years of this painting, many of the Métis will have moved again, this time to escape the rapid changes that are overtaking them. In the meantime, put yourself in the picture. Will you ride in a cart? That's a very noisy and bumpy ride, for sure. Soon it will be time to take the tent poles off the carts and make camp for the evening. Enjoy your ride.

PREVIEWING THE CHAPTER

In this chapter you will learn about these topics:
- the fur trade rivalry between North West Company and the Hudson's Bay Company
- the reasons Europeans came to Red River early in the nineteenth century
- some of the problems the fur trade rivalry caused for the early Scottish settlers
- the daily life of these settlers and other people at Red River
- the struggle of the Métis and other people in the West to assert their rights as their community became Manitoba, a Canadian province

KEY WORDS

amnesty
crofters
merger
middlemen
pemmican
provisional government
resolutions
squatters

1861	1867	1868	1869	1870
Settlers arrive at Red River from the Canadas	Confederation of the Canadas, Nova Scotia, and New Brunswick	Canada sends out surveyors	Métis set up provisional government at Red River	• Scott is executed • Manitoba joins Confederation • Riel leaves Red River

Snapshot

- This feature explores an event, person, or invention that is not part of the central story but was an interesting piece of news at the time.

The Evidence Behind the Story

- In each chapter, an item of historical evidence is presented for you to consider.
- Questions and activities are provided to assist you in your assessment of the historical value of the material provided in this feature.

Stepping Into the Picture

- Two large pictures are presented in each unit. You are asked to step into the role of a person in them and imagine what it would be like to be part of the scenes.

The Pictures Behind the Story

- In this pictorial essay, you will learn more about transportation and communications innovations after 1867 through illustrations, photographs, and captions.

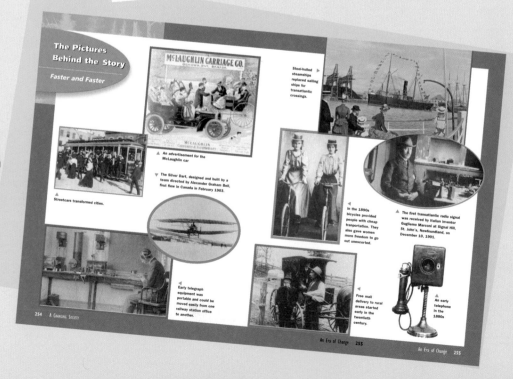

The Story So Far...

- Throughout each chapter, questions and activities are provided to help you recall and explore some of the people and events presented in a section of the chapter.
- The activities are designed to include different learning styles.

Enemy Aliens

In 1914 the Canadian government passed the War Measures Act. This Act gave the government sweeping powers to protect the lives of Canadian citizens. In response to public opinion–some even called it hysteria–the government began to take action against individuals with German, Austro-Hungarian, and other "enemy" backgrounds, who were considered a threat to the war effort. By the end of 1915 over 7000 men were locked away in 24 camps.

Another 80 000 people, all from Central Power nations, were classified as **enemy aliens**. Many lost their jobs. They had to report regularly to the police. Their foreign language newspapers were suppressed and censored and were forced to print bilingual columns. Their language schools and some of their churches were closed. Any who had become citizens of Canada after March 1902 lost the right to vote, and others were also denied Canadian citizenship until after the war ended.

The Story So Far . . .

1. Imagine you are a young person in Canada in 1914. Discuss in a report what factors would influence your decision on whether or not you should join the Canadian Expeditionary Force heading for Europe.
2. Create a recruiting poster to attract young men to join the Canadian Expeditionary Force.
3. Create a political cartoon to show that even in times of war some Canadians were not treated fairly.
4. What extra powers did the government assume when the war started? Discuss whether these powers were needed.

Canada at War, 1914–1918 **321**

Snippet

An Independent Decision

The council of the Six Nations Reserve on the Grand River in Ontario refused to join the war effort. The reason? As a sovereign nation, their Chiefs said, the Iroquois were not bound by Britain's declaration of war. They would enter the fighting only at the request of the British King. Despite this official stand, many residents of the reserve contributed to the war effort and many young men enlisted in the Canadian forces.

The internees were forced to construct camps if they did not exist. They also built roads, cut wood, cleared land, and built railways.

Snippet

- Every now and then this feature appears in the margin of the text. It presents interesting bits of historical information that are relevant to the content.

Chapter Closer

- At the end of each chapter, there is a brief summary of the major events in the chapter under the heading Sum It Up!
- A number of questions and activities appear under the headings: Thinking About Your Learning, Applying Your Learning, and Using Key Words, where you can put into practice what you have learned from the chapter.
- From these activities, you and/or your teacher can choose which ones to complete individually or in a group.
- The activities take different learning styles into consideration.

SUM IT UP!

In this chapter, we learned how rivalry between the North West Company and the Hudson's Bay Company was focused on events at Red River. Conditions in faraway Scotland had a big impact on the Canadian West when Lord Selkirk sponsored Scottish settlement around the Red and Assiniboine rivers. Families whose ancestors were Aboriginal and French or Aboriginal and Scottish joined these settlers. During the 1860s, the Hudson's Bay Company gave up control of Rupert's Land. A new country, Canada, declared an interest in adding the area to Confederation. When Canadian officials failed to consult the people who lived at Red River, residents of the colony resisted the Canadian takeover. In 1869 Métis leader Louis Riel and his followers formed a government at Red River and negotiated with Canada about joining Confederation. A peaceful settlement was upset when Métis guards executed Canadian Thomas Scott. Nonetheless, after tireless negotiations, Manitoba became Canada's fifth province.

THINKING ABOUT YOUR LEARNING

1. Why was there conflict at Red River in the early years of the Selkirk settlement?
2. Why did this conflict end with the merger of the HBC and the NWC?
3. List the groups at Red River in the 1840s. Describe how they made a living.
4. Why was the colony's isolation a problem?
5. What events outside Red River made change there inevitable in the 1860s?
6. Why did the Métis have the most to fear when Canadians began to move to Red River?
7. What actions did the Métis take to protect their claims?
8. Why might some historians consider Riel's execution of Scott a terrible mistake?

APPLYING YOUR LEARNING

1. This chapter includes many dramatic moments. Choose one and create a one-minute performance to tell the story. You will need to write a script, find actors, make some props, and put together some costumes. Record your minute on video, or present it to your class. Suggestions: Lord Selkirk's representative inviting Scottish settlers to join him; Colin Robertson persuading the settlers to return to Red River; Louis Riel and his followers stopping the Canadian surveyors.
2. Do some research to find out
   - what happened to Lord Selkirk
   - the state of the fur trade in Canada today
   - the state of the Hudson's Bay in Canada today
3. Name a person from the chapter would like to meet. Explain your

152 THE WEST

1. How did the travellers secure their horses?
2. How do you know this painting shows Métis?
3. From what you have learned in this chapter, how is this painting a valuable historical document?
4. Imagine you are one of these travellers. Write a letter or journal entry to describe what it is like to travel and camp on the prairies.

Paul Kane (1810–1871), Camping on the Prairie, 1846, oil on paper; 8¼ x 13¼" (20.4 x 34.0), Stark Museum of Art, Orange, Texas.

Paul Kane painted this picture, Camping on the Prairies, in 1845.

5. Develop a set of interview questions to ask Chief Peguis, Louis Riel, or Marie-Anne Lagemodière.
6. Write a newspaper account of fur trade rivalry between the HBC and NWC.
7. Create your own artwork to show fur trading between Aboriginal Peoples and HBC or NWC traders; the work of the voyageurs; or the buffalo hunt.
8. Make a model of a Red River cart or make a mobile to show who is at Red River in

USING KEY WORDS

Write your own definition, using examples, for each of the following:

- pemmican
- merger
- resolutions
- provisional government

Unit Closer

- At the end of each unit, there are two pages of activities called Connecting Your Learning. These encompass Understanding Concepts, Developing Research Skills, Communicating Required Knowledge, Applying Concepts and Skills, and Creating A Mind Map.
- You and/or your teacher can choose which ones you will complete individually, in small groups, or in large groups.
- These activities will allow you to apply your learning in a number of ways.

UNIT 3

A Changing Society

CONNECTING YOUR LEARNING

UNDERSTANDING CONCEPTS

1. Create a poster to show how one group or one individual contributed to the development of Canada between 1867 and 1920.
2. Choose the invention you think changed Canadian society the most between 1867 and 1920. Create an advertising campaign to promote the invention. Make sure you include its significance to the development of Canada.
3. Write a newspaper article to explain how social changes affected Canadian society between 1867 and 1920. Remember to include information about individuals who contributed to these changes.
4. Create a hanging mobile to illustrate the major conflicts and changes in Canada from Confederation to 1920. Each element of the mobile should include an illustration and a few words to identify the conflict or change.

DEVELOPING RESEARCH SKILLS

1. Choose one of the individuals mentioned in this unit and explain how that person contributed to change in Canada or the world.
2. Form a group in which some members act as workers in an enterprise such as a mine, a forestry company, or a factory in the late nineteenth century and three members act as owners. The workers and owners should present their priorities and concerns in a public meeting.
3. Take on the role of one of the following in World War I: a soldier, a fighter pilot, a female ambulance driver serving overseas, a nurse serving overseas, a farmer, a Ukrainian interned in a prison camp, a factory owner, a woman working in a munitions factory, a school child, a wife waiting at home. Research to find out more about the impact of the war on your character. Be prepared to share your findings with your classmates.
4. Choose a topic in this unit that you would like to learn more about. Make a list of questions you could use in researching this topic. Include factual, comparative, and speculative questions. Then use these questions as a research guide to discover more about the topic.

342 A CHANGING SOCIETY

COMMUNICATING REQUIRED KNOWLEDGE

1. Imagine you were ten years old in 1867. In 1920 you are being interviewed and asked to talk about the changes you have seen in your everyday life? In society? In transportation and communications? In the workplace?
2. Design a web site or other computer-generated project to teach other students about the Women's Rights Movement in this period. Some topics you might include are inequalities in the work; force; inequalities in the home; actions by the movement leaders; personalities of the movement; significant changes.
3. Role-play a conversation between a government official who is putting in place the federal policy of assimilation of Aboriginal Peoples, residential schools, and the banning of traditional Aboriginal ceremonies and Frederick Loft.
4. Prepare an audiotape of a news report on one of the following events in World War I: internment of "enemy aliens"; the awarding of the Victoria Cross to Thomas Ricketts; the federal election campaign of 1917 and the issue of conscription; the Battle of Vimy Ridge.

APPLYING CONCEPTS AND SKILLS

1. Make a list of how technologies described in this unit changed peoples' lives. Then write an opinion paper to discuss the effects of changes in technology in your lifetime and on Canadian society today.
2. List the rights of workers today that workers in the late nineteenth and early twentieth century did not have. How did the efforts of individuals in this period help gain those rights?
3. As a class create a personality gallery of Asian and non-European immigrants who have made a significant contribution to Canada.
4. Why is it important to a historical inquiry to consider different viewpoints? Choose a local issue that is of concern in your community. Describe the different viewpoints held by various community members.

CREATING A MIND MAP

For each category in the mind map list statements that show what role the topic played in change in the period from 1867 to 1920.

Canada at War, 1914–1918 **343**

A Tour of British North America, 1860

SETTING OUR FOCUS

Here is a scene familiar to Canadians: a royal visit. The year is 1860. The most important royal person ever to visit this part of the world has just arrived in Halifax, Nova Scotia. Albert Edward, Prince of Wales, the eldest son of Queen Victoria, the reigning British monarch, is just 18 years old. Edward will one day be King of England. Like his mother, he will become ruler of British North America and the vast territories that stretch away to the Pacific and Arctic oceans.

As a student of history you have a special pass to join Prince Edward's two-month-long Royal Tour of British North America to inspect the state of his mother's colonies and territories. You will visit some of the larger cities in British North America and learn about the different people living in the regions that make up Canada today.

PREVIEWING THE CHAPTER

In this chapter you will learn about these topics:
- **the chief places visited by the Prince of Wales during the Royal Tour**
- **some of the issues that caused conflicts in British North American society in 1860**
- **some of the major industries and export trade**
- **the extent of British North America in 1860**
- **documents, artifacts, and community resources that historians use to understand the past**
- **the research skills you will develop in studying the story of Canada's development**

KEY WORDS

archives
census
charter
citadel
heritage building
Lieutenant-Governor
Legislative Assembly
Métis
monopoly
motion
primary document
responsible
    government
Rupert's Land
shipway

1860

July 24
Edward, Prince of Wales, arrives in St. John's, Newfoundland

August 26
Edward opens the Victoria Bridge in Montréal

September 1
Edward places the cornerstone of the new government buildings in Ottawa

September 7
Edward arrives in Toronto

September 20
Edward departs Canada from Windsor

THE ROYAL TOUR

Newfoundland

Fog and rain often blanket St. John's, Newfoundland, even in summer. On July 24, 1860, the bad weather did not prevent almost the entire town from going to the docks to greet the royal visitor. Prince Edward had arrived after a two-week journey across the Atlantic Ocean. Near the wharf, islanders had built a big arch of wood and decorated it with garlands. On the harbour side of the arch, people had carved and painted the words, "Welcome Prince."

Finally, the clouds lifted, and a barge left one of three British ships. After stepping through the arch and exchanging greetings with the **Lieutenant-Governor** of Newfoundland, the royal visitor and his large party climbed into open carriages. A tall, bearded gentleman could be seen talking with the prince at every turn. This was the Duke of Newcastle. He was Prince Edward's guardian during the tour. As Secretary of State for the Colonies, he was responsible for all the affairs of British North America. The crowds cheered and waved flags as the carriages drove through the winding streets of Newfoundland's capital.

At the time of the Royal Visit, most of Newfoundland's 130 000 inhabitants were fishers, living in tiny settlements along its rocky coast and returning every night with their catch. The British population was increasing, especially with the arrival of immigrants from Ireland. Newfoundlanders had begun to have some control over their own affairs in 1832. They elected representatives who soon demanded that their decisions, not those of the men chosen by the British governor, should guide the government. This was called **responsible government**. At the time of Edward's visit, responsible government had been in place in Newfoundland for five years.

Nova Scotia

Prince Edward's next destination was Nova Scotia. Near Sydney, on Cape Breton Island, coal miners greeted Edward. Their ancestors had mined coal there since the late eighteenth century. He also visited a village of the Mi'kmaq nation.

Nova Scotia's population was concentrated on the coast. Shipbuilding was the major industry. Nearly every town had a **shipway** where tall-masted sailing ships were built of old-growth softwood and rolled down to the water. Locally designed ships were famous around the world.

Parishes, cultural groups, businesses, and workers' associations built arches along Edward's route in each city he visited to show their loyalty. After the visit, the arches were dismantled.

USING HISTORICAL PICTURES TO UNDERSTAND HISTORY

The picture at the beginning of this chapter appeared in *The Illustrated London News* in 1860. The artist drew it to give readers an idea of the Prince's landing in Halifax, Nova Scotia. Photography was in its early days, so sketch artists made drawings of important events for newspapers.

QUESTIONING THE EVIDENCE

1. How do you know which figure in the drawing is Prince Edward?

2. He is being greeted by Lieutenant-Governor Lord Mulgrave. Identify this man.

3. Describe the other groups in the picture.

4. Prince Edward came on the battleship *Hero*. How were the ships in the background different from today's warships, and why?

5. How valuable is this picture in helping you imagine the event?

6. Do you think the artist exaggerated or changed any parts of the scene? Explain your answer.

7. What does the picture tell you about British North America in 1860? Make a list of the things you know about it so far.

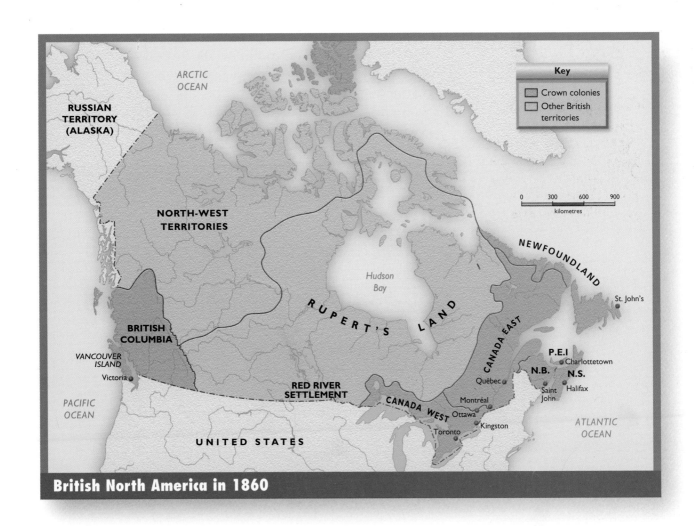

British North America in 1860

When Prince Edward visited Halifax, the capital of Nova Scotia, he gave a speech to the members of the legislature. Many of Halifax's 30 000 residents were members of the British armed forces, stationed at the naval base and garrison. In 1853–1856 some of these men had served for the British in the Crimean War. He referred to them in his speech when he said:

Most heartily do I sympathise in the pride with which you regard the laurels won by the sons of Nova Scotia, and the affection with which you honour the memory of those who have fallen in the service of my country and yours.

New Brunswick

Prince Edward's entourage travelled across Nova Scotia from Halifax to Windsor on a recently opened railway line. Then they crossed the Bay of Fundy by ship, and visited Saint John, the oldest and largest city in New Brunswick. With a population of 30 000, Saint John was a bustling port and centre of both the timber trade and the wooden shipbuilding industry.

Next Prince Edward took a trip up the Saint John River to Fredericton, the capital of New Brunswick, on a railway line that had opened only days earlier. All along the river, loggers were working the evergreen forests. The timber trade was the colony's biggest employer. Huge white pine logs were floated to Saint John for export to Britain by the shipload. In Fredericton Edward helped to mark the establishment of the University of New Brunswick.

William Hall, the son of slaves who escaped to Nova Scotia, was the first African Canadian to win the Victoria Cross. A Royal Navy sailor, Hall earned the Empire's highest award for bravery in 1857 after serving in India. He was aboard Hero during the royal visit.

1 Suggest why the Aboriginal Peoples were not included in the census.

2 Rank the populations for the areas from highest to lowest.

** This table shows the population of British North America, according to the **census** of 1860–1861. Newfoundland was not included in the census, nor were the Aboriginal populations.*

Population of British North America in 1861*	
Area	**Population**
Nova Scotia	330 857
New Brunswick	252 047
Prince Edward Island	80 857
Canada East (Québec)	1 111 566
Canada West (Ontario)	1 396 091
British Columbia	51 524
North-West Territories	6 691
Total	3 229 633

LEARNING FROM GRAPHS

This line graph shows the rise and fall of the wooden shipbuilding industry in the Maritime colonies. The graph is made from information collected by a researcher.

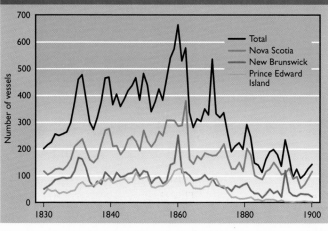

Number of Vessels Built and Registered in the Maritimes 1830–1900

Legend:
- Total
- Nova Scotia
- New Brunswick
- Prince Edward Island

y-axis: Number of vessels (0, 100, 200, 300, 400, 500, 600, 700)
x-axis: 1830, 1840, 1860, 1880, 1900

QUESTIONING THE EVIDENCE

1. a) How are the years marked?
   b) How is the number of ships built each year shown?
   c) Which line shows the total number of vessels built in the Maritime colonies?
2. About how many ships were built in the Maritime region in 1860?
3. Which area produced the most ships in 1860? About how many ships did this area produce?
4. What was the peak year for shipbuilding in the Maritimes?
5. Speculate about why there was a sudden growth in shipbuilding in the 1860s.
6. Research to find out why the wooden shipbuilding industry declined after that.
7. Make a list of the work that a researcher would have to do to collect this kind of data.

This picture of a Mi'kmaq wigwam near Sydney appeared in one of the many books published about the Royal Tour. What does this picture tell you about the lifestyle of the Mi'kmaq people? For example, how big was the wigwam? What materials were used? Why do you think tour organizers took Edward to visit the Mi'kmaq village?

LEARNING ABOUT HISTORY FROM BUILDINGS

You can learn about the history of a community by looking at the buildings, historic markers, and monuments.

The war memorial in Confederation Square, Ottawa. Like all war memorials, it commemorates those who died in war.

QUESTIONING THE EVIDENCE

1. Most Canadian communities have war memorials and historical plaques. Locate one near you and visit it. Make notes on its design, decorations, and inscriptions.
    a) Which wars does it commemorate? From which war do the most names appear?
    b) What can you learn about different wars from a memorial?
    c) What does a war memorial tell you about your community?

2. Are there any designated **heritage buildings** in your community? If so, locate one and find out its history, including how and why it came to be designated, and by what agency. If you are unable to locate a heritage building, check this web site:

    http://www.saintjohn.nbcc.nb.ca/~Heritage/index2.htm

    It has information about the courthouse, King's Square, and other Saint John heritage sites. Choose a heritage building and find out what you can about it.

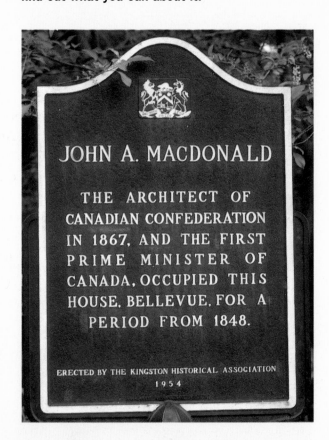

Buildings that are of special historical interest are sometimes preserved as heritage buildings and marked by plaques. This one identifies a house once occupied by Sir John A. Macdonald.

In 1860 there were no overland links between New Brunswick and the Province of Canada. Prince Edward's entourage returned to Nova Scotia before crossing Northumberland Strait to the island that bore his grandfather's name.

Prince Edward Island

Prince Edward made a brief stop in Charlottetown, which was the capital of Prince Edward Island. The city had a population of 7000. Farming, shipbuilding, and fishing were the little island's biggest employers. The Prince attended a reception at Fanningbrook, the home of the Lieutenant-Governor. In the days when the Queen's representative was the ruler of the colony, this was the decision-making centre of the government. After the beginning of responsible government in 1851, the Lieutenant-Governors' duties were limited to representing the monarch.

Canada East

Prince Edward's convoy steamed out of Charlottetown harbour, bore north and entered the Gulf of St. Lawrence. After passing the Gaspé Peninsula, the ships turned west and entered the broad mouth of the St. Lawrence River. Prince Edward was now in the Province of Canada.

The 1841 Act of Union had joined Lower Canada and Upper Canada. The two parts were now named Canada East and Canada West. The **Legislative Assembly**, or law-making body of elected representatives, had two leaders, one from each part.

© Canada Post Corporation, 1860. Reproduced with permission. NAC/POS 149

In 1860 Charles Connell, New Brunswick's postmaster, was in charge of issuing a new series of postage stamps. He put a picture of himself on the five-cent stamp! Connell had to resign, and most of the stamps were destroyed. The few that survived are now worth about $6000 each to collectors.

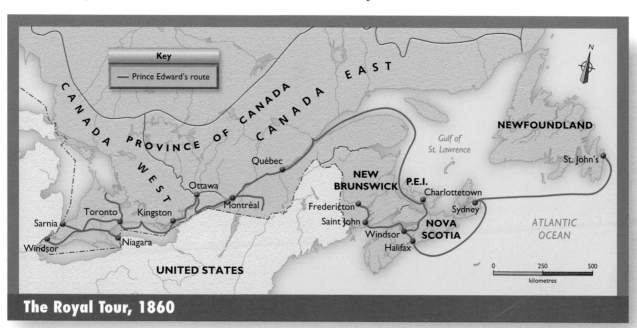

The Royal Tour, 1860

This was because each part had distinct cultures and laws. Canada East was the homeland of the French Canadians, while people in Canada West were mainly English-speaking. At the time of Prince Edward's visit the co-premiers were George-Étienne Cartier from Canada East and John A. Macdonald from Canada West.

The warships slid past the farmlands that lined the banks of the St. Lawrence River. On August 18, they anchored off Québec City. Guns boomed out a welcome from the **citadel**, or fortification, high atop the rock on which the walled city was built.

Québec City was the heart of French-Canadian society. After the fall of New France in 1759, the city became the capital of British North America. By the time of the Prince's visit, however, Québec City had lost its standing as the largest city and chief port and would be the capital for only a few more years. Most of its 59 000 residents were French-speaking, but an English-speaking minority held key positions in industry, trade, and commerce. Its chief industry was the handling of timber. Squared timbers from the Ottawa Valley were floated down the St. Lawrence to Québec to be sawn into lumber or loaded whole onto ships for export to Britain.

Many French-Canadian people demonstrated their loyalty to the British monarchy by putting up arches along the route of his procession. French Canada was strongly Roman Catholic, and the first group Edward received in Québec was the bishops in their purple robes. Edward also visited the nuns in the Ursuline Convent in the heart of the old city.

Squared logs were loaded into the hulls of ships at Québec City and exported.

I-76323, Loading ship with deals through the bow port, Québec City, QC, 1872. McCord Museum of Canadian History, Montréal.

INTERPRETING HISTORIC SETTLEMENT MAPS

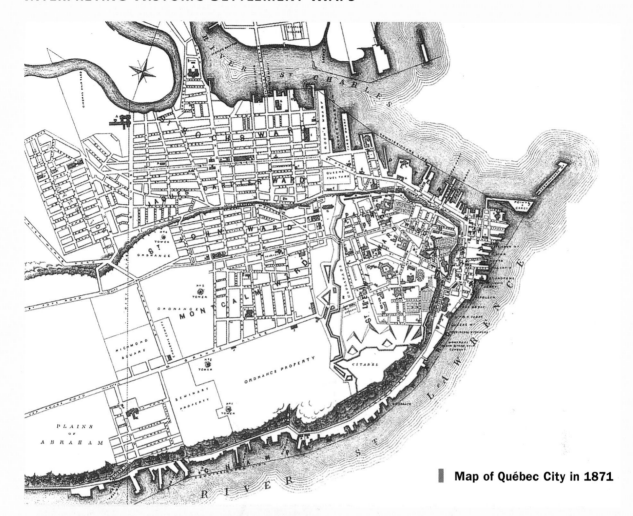

Map of Québec City in 1871

QUESTIONING THE EVIDENCE

1. Most maps have common symbols that help the reader to interpret the information. Look in the top left corner for a compass that shows the orientation, or direction. Which side of the map is north?

2. Study the map and decide how these features are represented and identified:
   a) rivers
   b) docks
   c) forested cliffs
   d) the walls of the old city
   e) the citadel
   f) streets
   g) important buildings

3. What is the difference in the shapes of the streets inside and outside the walls? How would you explain this?

4. Find an old map of your community or of the nearest large settlement.
   a) Is the pattern of streets in the oldest district different from areas built later? If so, how would you explain the difference?
   b) Do the street names have the same names today?
   c) Who or what were the streets named for?
   d) How does this map help you understand the history of the community?

Soon it was time to board another steamer. The royal party sailed up the St. Lawrence River, arriving in Montréal on August 25. With a population of nearly 100 000, Montréal was British North America's most important city. Its harbour was crowded with ships and its shoreline with factories. Most of its residents were English-speaking.

Everywhere Edward turned, he was barraged with the wealth and finery of Montréal society. A ball for 6000 people was held in a pavilion built especially for the occasion.

In a special ceremony the Prince drove the last rivet on the newly opened Victoria Bridge across the St. Lawrence River. The bridge stretched for more than 2 km. For decades the only way people and goods had been able to reach the Great Lakes region was by the St. Lawrence and Ottawa rivers. Starting in 1818 people began building an expensive system of canals to improve transportation to the Great Lakes. When the Grand Trunk Railway was completed in 1859, an era of rapid development began. The railway, the longest in the world at the time, stretched from Sarnia, Canada West, to Rivière du Loup, Canada East, with a branch line to the American all-season ocean port of Portland, Maine. The railways helped to create more trade with the United States.

The footings of the Victoria Bridge were built to withstand the pressure of the frozen St. Lawrence River in winter and were high enough to allow sea-going ships to pass underneath.

ll-477427 Victoria Bridge, Montréal, QC, painting, 1878. McCord Museum of Canadian History, Montréal.

Canada West

Prince Edward next journeyed on a steamboat to Ottawa, Canada West. Less than 36 years before, the city had been just a construction camp on a bluff overlooking the Ottawa River. In 1826 Colonel John By started building the first locks on the Rideau Canal. The waterway connected the river with Lake Ontario. The camp evolved into a rough-and-tumble logging centre called Bytown. Renamed Ottawa, the city was chosen to become the permanent capital of the Province of Canada. How did history and geography influence this decision? Here is a clue: Ottawa was farther from the border with the United States than Toronto, Kingston, or Montréal.

Ottawa's new government buildings had started to take shape. On September 1, 1860, the Prince of Wales laid the cornerstone for the buildings, which dwarfed all others in the growing city of 15 000 people.

The loggers of the Ottawa Valley staged several impressive shows for Prince Edward. They demonstrated their practice of riding a timber raft through a chute bypassing the Chaudière Falls. In those days, loggers cut the huge white pines, shaped the trunks into squares with axes, and lashed them together in rafts. They floated these rafts down the river to tidewater, where the rafts were broken up and the timbers loaded aboard ships for export. Edward astonished the newspaper reporters by jumping on a raft for the ride through the chute.

1 How big is the raft? What is the clue to its size?

2 How is the raft decorated?

3 How is the chute constructed? Why was a chute needed?

4 What can you tell about the setting of the city?

The Prince of Wales on the raft in the chute bypassing the Chaudière Falls.

EXAMINING HISTORICAL DOCUMENTS

This piece of paper is a **primary document**. It is a part of the daily record of debate in the Legislative Assembly of the Province of Canada for 1860. It is stored in the National Archives of Canada in Ottawa. **Archives** are like museums, preserving documents of historical value rather than artifacts.

This document records a proposal to amend, or change, a **motion** that was on the floor of the Assembly. George Brown, a member of the Legislative Assembly for Toronto, proposed the amendment.

At the time, the Province of Canada faced an uncertain future. There was widespread talk of ending the union of the Canadas. There were too many differences between the English- and French-speaking people. Brown proposed a new kind of relationship between the two. His party, the Clear Grits, proposed a federation where each of the Canadas had its own government for "local and sectional matters," with a "general government" for "subjects of national or common interests." Historians see this simple proposal as the beginning of our nation's federal government.

A primary document

1. a) **Read the document. Why was it handwritten?**
   b) **Work with a partner to write out what the document says. Use a dictionary to look up the meaning of any words you do not understand.**

2. **How would historians use this document? Would they consider it an accurate record of the proceedings in the Legislative Assembly?**

3. **Why is it important that documents like this are kept for the public to read?**

4. **The records of debate in our democratic legislatures are known as the Hansard. The complete verbatim (word-for-word) proceedings of each day's debates in Canadian legislatures are published and distributed by the beginning of the following day. Research the history of Hansard. Why was it so named?**

5. **You may have a public archive in your community. If so, arrange to visit it and find out what is there. Why would people seeking information about their family's history visit an archive? What kinds of documents would they look for?**

The Prince's entourage boarded a special railway train for a short trip on the Ottawa & Prescott Railway. When they reached the St. Lawrence River, they transferred to the steamer *Kingston*. The plan was to stop at several cities along the Lake Ontario shore. Thousands of people turned out at the city of Kingston on September 4. The *Kingston* anchored overnight, but the Prince did not leave the ship. Protestant Irish Canadians in a society known as the Orange Order had put up arches, assembled bands, and marched through the streets of Kingston, dressed in the costumes of their society. One banner proclaimed, "Our God, Our Country, and Our Queen." The Duke of Newcastle refused to allow the Prince to recognize the Orangemen by walking through their arches. In Britain the Orange Order was outlawed. Members of the Orange Order were bitterly opposed to the Roman Catholic Church, and the Order was believed to stir up religious hatred and violence.

John A. Macdonald tried to convince the Duke of Newcastle to visit Kingston. He argued that the city, not the Orange Order, had invited Prince Edward to visit. Besides, Orange lodges were legal in British North America, where they had first appeared in 1830. The Prince had given the Roman Catholics plenty of recognition, beginning in Halifax, when he had walked through an arch that the Catholics had erected. He had also lavished attention on the Catholic bishops and nuns in Québec. But Edward stayed on board and the *Kingston* steamed away. The same thing happened in Belleville. The people were disappointed.

McCord Museum of Canadian History, Montréal. I-8561.0.1, Albert Edward, Prince of Wales (Edward VII), copied 1863, *photograph (detail)*

When Prince Edward was in Montréal, William Notman took this portrait of him. The prince was about 170 cm tall.

On September 7, Prince Edward arrived in Toronto. One American eyewitness gushed that "the magnificence of the celebrations in Toronto is admitted to have surpassed every thing else of the kind that has ever been seen since the Prince arrived." Huge crowds turned out to greet his procession, and arches loomed at every turn, proclaiming unbounded loyalty. The Orange Order caused a sensation by disguising an arch until the moment the Prince's party passed through it, when the coverings were pulled away!

In 1860 Toronto was the third largest city in British North America, with a population of 44 000. Toronto was growing faster than Montréal. Canada West was changing: although farming and lumbering were still the most important activities, manufacturing and trade were growing rapidly.

The rest of Prince Edward's stay in Canada West was a busy round of parties, receptions, tours, and openings. The young Prince took a train to Collingwood and back, and then another train to Sarnia, with stops along the way in Guelph, Berlin (now Kitchener-Waterloo), Stratford, and London. The return trip took the royal party to Niagara Falls. Edward watched the Great Blondin walk a tightrope on stilts across the Niagara River. When Blondin offered to carry the Prince across the gorge, Edward expressed an interest, but declined. In Hamilton, Edward opened the annual agricultural exhibition and the new steam-powered pumping station, which provided the city with running water. In Windsor, Edward left Canada and crossed the Detroit River to begin a tour of the United States.

We now say goodbye to Prince Edward and board a different kind of vehicle for the rest of our tour of British North America. Beyond the head of Lake Superior there were no roads or railways to connect the tiny settlements. To cover the vast territories that stretched away to the west and north, we will have to use our imaginations and a bit of advanced technology—a steerable airship.

The first dirigible, or steerable airship with steam-powered propellers, was built in 1852 in France. Such an aircraft might have been suitable for travelling across Western North America, although it is not recorded that anyone actually made such a trip.

RUPERT'S LAND

In 1860 all the territory that drained into Hudson Bay was called **Rupert's Land**. It totalled about 4 million km² (about two fifths of the present area of Canada). In 1670 the King of England had granted the Hudson's Bay Company (HBC) the rights to trade with the Aboriginal Peoples in Rupert's Land. The Company had **monopoly** rights, which meant it was the only company that could trade there. In 1860 Rupert's Land was still under the control of the company, even though its **charter,** or agreement that gave it the right to trade, expired in 1859.

First we will travel north across Lake Huron and pass over Sault Ste. Marie. In 1860 this town, the gateway to Lake Superior, was the westernmost community in the Province of Canada. Soon our airship takes us over Fort William, the old Northwest Company headquarters on Lake Superior, now one of a network of HBC trading posts stretching as far as present-day Alaska. We may be able to catch a glimpse of Captain John Palliser and his expedition, just returning from their fourth and last summer exploring Rupert's Land for the British government and the Royal Geographic Society. Palliser's expedition examined the old canoe routes west from Lake Superior to see if settlers travelling west could use them. They studied the soils under the prairie grasses to see if they could support agriculture. They surveyed six passes or narrow passages through the Rocky Mountains to see whether a railway line could be built to the Pacific Ocean.

Red River

Soon we are floating over the multicultural settlement of Red River. Started in 1812 with an area of 300 000 km², this struggling colony is home to several groups of Aboriginal Peoples, two communities of mixed-race people (the **Métis**), the British remnants of the original colony, and a community of retired HBC employees and their families. About 7500 people live at the settlement. The largest single group are the French-speaking people who are descended from Aboriginal mothers and French-speaking voyageurs and fur traders. Their chief way of making a living is by hunting buffalo for their meat and hides.

By 1860 the steamboat *Anson Northrup* was used on the Red River to improve transportation to the south.

The buffalo herds are already declining in number. Across the West, Aboriginal Peoples are suffering as European diseases sweep through their lands. In the United States, the government is beginning a war of conquest in the Western plains that will see entire Aboriginal nations wiped out. Just south of the Red River colony is the new state of Minnesota, with nearly 175 000 residents. Red River would soon turn into a powder keg.

The North-West Territories

Now we will detour far to the north. Arctic North America was occupied by Inuit Peoples but claimed by Britain. American whaling ships made seasonal visits to the Arctic Ocean. As late as the 1850s British interests still hoped to find a Northwest Passage connecting the Atlantic and Pacific oceans.

Sir John Franklin had departed from England in search of the Northwest Passage in 1845. His well-equipped party was last seen that July. For years search parties braved the twisting channels of the Arctic Archipelago in search of Franklin's lost expedition. THis is a painting of Dr. John Rae at Pelly Bay learning of Franklin's fate from Inuit.

A group of Inuit playing their national ball game in 1865 at Little Whale River in what is now the province of Québec.

Bearing southwest, we float across the northern treeless tundra. Soon we can see stunted stands of spruce, willow, and birch trees. Lakes both large and small are everywhere. We are now within the vast drainage area of the Mackenzie River. The occasional Aboriginal settlement appears. This is the traditional domain of the Dene (DEE-nee) people, who follow huge herds of caribou on their migrations.

British Columbia

When the snowy crags of the Rocky Mountains loom ahead, we have to drop some weight to make sure we can get over the highest peaks. Soon we are crossing the Fraser Plateau in the colony of British Columbia. We spot cowboys herding cattle across the grassland ranches of the dry plateau. Farther east, miners are busy panning for gold in creeks flowing into the Cariboo River. The gold rush began in the canyons of the lower Fraser River in 1858, when 30 000 miners flocked to southwestern British Columbia.

Most of the miners at Rock Creek, near the US border, are American, and they make no secret of their intention to take the "British" out of British Columbia. Unruly American miners rebelled against the law requiring them to buy mining licences. They drove a visiting gold commissioner out with a hail of stones. Governor James Douglas, based on Vancouver Island, made a tour of the gold fields in the summer of 1860. He reached Rock Creek on September 25. He put on his ornate governor's uniform and bravely faced a crowd of 300 miners. Douglas promised he would have a road built into the area; he also threatened to return with the Royal Marines if the miners refused to take out mining licences. The miners applauded his speech, and every one of them cheerfully shook his hand. Douglas was tough as nails and was not shy about using force to maintain law and order.

The first Chinese miners arrived during the Fraser River gold rush.

These African Americans came to British Columbia during the gold rush. In 1860 they formed a militia regiment, the Victoria Pioneer Rifle Corps, to help keep the peace while thousands of gold seekers flooded into Victoria.

Vancouver Island

Our final destination is the colony of Vancouver Island. James Douglas, in 1843 when he was an officer with the Hudson's Bay Company, established Fort Victoria. Vancouver Island became a colony in 1849, and Douglas soon became its governor. The colony prospered and grew with the gold rush. By 1860 there is a tiny legislature, although Douglas blocks any suggestion of responsible government.

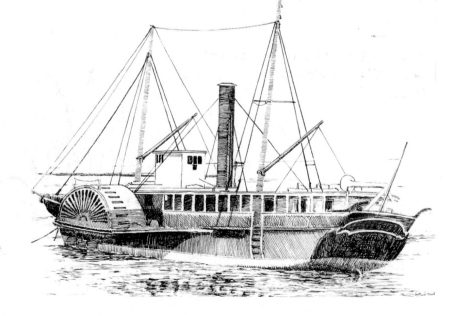

SS *Beaver* was the first steam-powered vessel on the Pacific Coast of British North America. The little ship helped the Hudson's Bay Company open up the vast Pacific Rim to trade.

INTERPRETING DATA

Across the harbour from Fort Victoria was the Coast Salish village of Songhees. About 600 people lived there in the winter. Every spring visitors from up the coast paddled into the harbour in big canoes. In April 1859, the police commissioner ordered a count of these visitors and their habitations. The count was summarized in the *Victoria Gazette*.

Aboriginal Nation	Number of Dwellings	People
Haida	32	405
Tsimshian	34	574
Stikine	17	223
Ducash	9	111
Bella Bella	11	126
Charcheena	4	62
Kwakiutl	4	44
Total	111	1545

By the time the count was published, another 690 Aboriginal people had arrived at Victoria harbour.

QUESTIONING THE EVIDENCE

1. Consult a map that shows the territory of Northwest Coast Aboriginal nations. Where did each group originate? About how far had each group travelled? (The Stikine people were of the Tlingit Nation; Ducash and Charcheena may represent groups that no longer exist, or their names may have been garbled in the writing.)

2. a) On average, how many people lived in each dwelling?

   b) Choose one of these groups and find out more about their housing and social organization. How could the information in this chart be used by a historian to illustrate this organization?

3. Find out what you can about the seasonal migrations of these Aboriginal Peoples. Why did they migrate? What kinds of goods would they have wanted to obtain in Victoria? What would they have offered in trade?

4. What do you think was the reaction of the European population to the yearly arrival of the Aboriginal Peoples?

Web Connection

http://www.school.mcgrawhill.ca/resources

Go to web site above to see photographs of British Columbia in the 1860s, including a photograph of Victoria from the Songhees village. Go to History Resources, then to *Canada: The Story of a Developing Nation* to see where to go next.

SUM IT UP!

Edward, Prince of Wales, made a tour of British North America in 1860. He visited Newfoundland, Nova Scotia, New Brunswick, Prince Edward Island, and the Canadas. All had achieved responsible government — that is, they were self-governing in their own affairs.

People were using the resources of the land to make a living. They cut and sold timber, built ships, and constructed railways to improve transportation. The largest city in British North America was Montréal. It was the centre of a transportation system that included canals and railways, which were gradually overcoming the obstacles of geography.

British North America included the colonies of Red River, British Columbia, and Vancouver Island, as well as Rupert's Land and the North-West Territories. The total population of what is now Canada was a little more than 3 million at the time. The future nation was already racially diverse, with Aboriginal Peoples, Métis, Chinese, African American, and Europeans living here.

THINKING ABOUT YOUR LEARNING

1. Write a brief account of the Royal Tour that answers these questions for readers of a foreign newspaper:
   a) Who was Prince Edward?
   b) Why did he visit British North America?
   c) What is British North America?
   d) How long did he stay?
   e) What was his route?
   f) How did he travel?
   g) Why was his visit important?

2. Compile a list of ten important things to know about British North America in 1860. Rank them in order of importance.

3. a) What conflicts have you learned about that were present in British North America in the 1860s?
   b) List other conflicts that can you foresee from what you have read.

APPLYING YOUR LEARNING

1. In groups, make a heritage map of your street, neighbourhood, or part of your community. Locate and identify historic places and buildings.

2. Research to find out what the Prince of Wales would have seen in 1860 if he had visited the area where your community is today. If there was a settlement, who would have greeted him and what sights would he have been shown?

3. Royal Tours have always been popular in Canada. Research and report on the media coverage of one day's events in one Canadian Royal Tour.

4. Role play a conversation between John A. Macdonald and the Duke of Newcastle in which Macdonald tries to persuade the Duke to allow the Prince to visit Kingston.

5. Research the styles, designs, or fashions of 1860 — in clothing, building, or behaviour.

6. Create a map of British North America in 1860 with visuals to give an overview of the people and how they lived.

USING KEY WORDS

Match the words with their definitions.

Legislative Assembly	something written or printed that gives a first-hand account of some fact
primary document	a place where public documents and historical records are preserved
responsible government	a group of elected representatives who represent the voters in the law-making body of the government
citadel	a form of government where the people making decisions are chosen from elected members of the Legislative Assembly. They are answerable for their decisions to the Assembly
census	the right granted to one person or body to control trade exclusively
archives	people of mixed European and Aboriginal descent
Métis	the area of land that is drained by rivers flowing into Hudson Bay. The monopoly rights to trade in this area were granted to the Hudson's Bay Company in 1670.
monopoly	an official count of the population
Rupert's Land	a fortification

1850 1864 1867

Toward Confederation

THE BIG PICTURE

These are some of the stories you will read about in this unit:

- the immigration of the "famine Irish" and fugitive African-American slaves to British North America
- the effect of free trade in Britain on people in British North America
- the impact of the railway building age in the British colonies
- why there was political deadlock in the Province of Canada before Confederation
- why the Province of Canada suggested that other colonies join them to make a new nation
- events in the United States that pushed the Province of Canada and the colonies of Nova Scotia and New Brunswick to unite
- the people who worked together to make an agreement on Confederation
- why the new nation chose a federal system of government
- how the West and Prince Edward Island became part of the new nation
- how Newfoundland joined Confederation in 1949

1949

CHAPTER

1

Growth and Change

1840
- Great Migration starts
- *Britannia* crosses the Atlantic on her maiden voyage
- Golden Age of shipbuilding begins in the Maritime colonies

1846
British government repeals the Corn Laws

1847
Timber and wheat trades decline

26   TOWARD CONFEDERATION

SETTING OUR FOCUS

You can hardly wait! You hear its whistle and bell as your father reins the horses to a stop at the station. You jump down from the carriage and run to the station as fast as you can. There it is! The sun bounces off its red and black metal. Look at the size of this "Iron Horse"! You are going to visit your aunt, uncle, and cousins in the big city of Toronto. The last time you saw them was three years ago at your grandmother's funeral. That trip took several days. Now the train will get you there in a few hours. Down the platform, the Royal Mail is unloaded and loaded. You see the bundles of *The Globe* newspaper being carted off. Some local farmers are loading their fresh vegetables on to a freight car so they can be sold at the St. Lawrence Market in Toronto. What a difference the railway has made!

As you and your family prepare to board the train, you have to wait for hundreds of people to leave the train. They speak English, but their strong Scottish accents make their words difficult to understand. The train conductor mentions that these people are immigrants who have bought tracts of land near Lake Erie. They will make the rest of their journey on foot and by wagon.

It reminds you of the trip your parents made from Ireland in the mid–1840s, when you were just three years old. How life has changed since then in British North America.

PREVIEWING THE CHAPTER

In this chapter you will learn about these topics:
- **the experiences of the famine Irish and African-American fugitive slaves in the Great Migration**
- **the main industries and exports of British North America between 1840 and 1860**
- **the effects the Repeal of the Corn Laws had on people's lives in British North America**
- **how the Reciprocity Treaty helped British North America**
- **how the Industrial Revolution was affecting British North America**

KEY WORDS

abolitionists
cash crop
Corn Laws
free trade
Industrial Revolution
navvies
preferential tariffs
quarantine station
reciprocity
tariffs
timber ships
Underground Railway

1850	1851	1854	1856	1859
Traffic on the Underground Railway increases	St. Lawrence and Atlantic Railway is started	Lord Elgin signs Reciprocity Treaty with Americans	Montréal-Toronto section of the Grand Trunk Railway is completed	Grand Trunk Railway is completed to Sarnia

THE GREAT MIGRATION

The immigrants to this country, we did the dirty work that made it live and grow. We worked where there was something to be done...we did everything in our day. I'm not kiddin' you.

Alfred, a logger

The 1840s to the 1860s were years of dramatic change for the British colonies in North America. Tens of thousands of Scottish, English, Irish, and Welsh people emigrated from Britain. African-American slaves escaping from the United States also came. These added their language, customs, and beliefs to those of the Aboriginal Peoples, French Canadians, and British settlers already living in the colonies.

1 Rank the areas by population from largest to smallest in 1861.

2 What do you think was the effect on Canada West of the huge growth in population between 1841 and 1851?

Population in Areas of British North America, 1841–1861			
Area	**1841**	**1851**	**1861**
Canada	**1 149 000**	**1 832 000**	**2 508 000**
Canada East	717 000	890 000	1 112 000
Canada West	432 000	942 000	1 396 000
New Brunswick	154 000	194 000	252 000
Newfoundland	NA	102 000	122 000
Nova Scotia	NA	277 000	331 000
Prince Edward Island	50 000	70 000	80 000

The Famine Irish

The Irish made up the largest number and were the most desperate of the immigrants. The potato was the basic crop or staple food of poor Irish farmers. It required little attention when growing, but it did not store well and was vulnerable to diseases. In 1845 and 1846, a blight turned the potato crop into a mushy waste. The results were disastrous and deadly for the starving population. A relief worker wrote in a letter:

The population were like walking skeletons, the men stamped with the livid mark of hunger, the children crying with pain, the women [were simply] too weak to stand.... All the sheep were gone, all the cows and all the poultry killed.

The famine and diseases like cholera and typhus turned villages into ghost towns. Facing starvation and disease, the "famine Irish" who could raise the cost of the passage emigrated to North America. Many boarded **timber ships**, which were ships built to carry timber from the colonies to Britain. The *Thomas Gelston* was a typical timber ship. It carried over 500 passengers in its holds for its nine-week crossing. The living quarters were cramped beyond belief, and the passengers did not have enough food or water. A government inquiry reported:

> *There was only a passage of just less than a metre between their berths…. The passengers were thus obliged to eat in their berths…. In one were a man, his wife, his sister, and five children; in another were six full-grown young women, whilst that above them contained five men, and the next eight men.*

One journalist, Steven de Vere, wrote of his trip:

> *Hundreds of poor people, men, women, and children…huddled together, without light, without air, wallowing in filth… sick in body, dispirited in heart…washing was impossible… the voyage took three months.*

Reflections

Imagine you are an Irish immigrant in 1847. Write a letter to family members left in Ireland. Decide before you start to write whether you want to encourage them to come to North America.

Web Connection

http://www.school.mcgrawhill.ca/resources

Go to the web site above to read about how orphaned Irish children were cared for in Canada at this time. Go to History Resources, then to *Canada: The Story of a Developing Nation* to see where to go next.

Immigrants were crowded below decks without enough berths for every person. When a storm struck, or infectious diseases broke out, the crew was ordered to keep everyone below decks.

Death at Sea

In 1847 and 1848 vessels carrying Irish immigrants to North America came to be called coffin ships or fever ships. One of the most notorious was the *Looshtauk*. Of this ship's 458 passengers, 117 died while crossing the Atlantic Ocean. Of a 13-member crew, 11 fell sick. At Middle Island, a quarantine station on the Miramichi River near Chatham, New Brunswick, another 100 people died.

Snippet

Deadly Disease

Known as ship fever or "the fever," typhus is carried by lice, which multiply quickly in dirty, crowded places. When a louse bites a typhus-infected person, it carries the disease in its digestive system. Other people are infected when they scratch a disease-carrying louse — or its feces — into their skin. Symptoms start with headaches, backaches, and coughing. These are followed by a high fever, red spots on the skin, and extreme weakness. At one time deadly, typhus can now be cured by antibiotics.

After the long voyage, every ship had to stop at a **quarantine station** where passengers were checked for sickness. Immigrants who entered at Québec City or Montréal had to stop at Grosse Île near the mouth of the St. Lawrence River. In May 1847 alone, 36 ships with 13 000 passengers waited to be inspected by the health inspectors. Of the 89 738 immigrants who entered at Québec City in 1847, 5293 died in the passage and almost 5000 died in quarantine on Grosse Île.

A painting by twentieth-century artist, William Kurelek, of the immigrant quarantine sheds at Grosse Île.

Jane White

When the *Eliza Morrison* arrived at the inspection station at Grosse Île in June 1849, 18-year-old Jane White and her parents breathed a sigh of relief. The perilous eight-week voyage from their home in Belfast, Ireland, was over.

During the crossing, the ship had been pummelled by storms. All the passengers had feared for their lives, and many had been terribly seasick. The Whites were comfortable compared with the penniless immigrants who were crammed into steerage, the cheapest accommodation in the hold of the ship. They had been able to afford a cabin — and to bring along a servant.

For the steerage passengers, the trip had been miserable. Crammed together in filthy conditions, some had come down with typhus and smallpox, dread diseases that often killed. In the 1830s cholera epidemics had swept through ships arriving from Ireland. Thousands of people had died. The memory of this horror was strong. This is why all ships carrying Irish immigrants were required to pass through an inspection station.

When the *Eliza Morrison* dropped anchor at Grosse Île, a doctor came aboard to inspect the immigrants. Discovering that some of the steerage passengers were sick, he ordered them to the hospital sheds on the island. Even the healthy passengers were quarantined aboard the ship, which was not allowed to leave its anchorage.

The cabin passengers escaped the worst of the quarantine. They could leave the ship — but not the island. One day Jane, her parents, and two friends packed a picnic lunch and went strolling through the woods on the island. The people in quarantine must have envied them this brief taste of freedom.

The picnic provided a welcome break from the boredom of waiting for the ship to be cleared to travel upstream to Québec City. Another break came when a steamship carrying people on a holiday excursion stopped near the island. "[The boat was] full of people gaily dressed," wrote Jane in a letter to a friend. "They stopped here and came past our ship. They were accompanied by a band and played 'The Troubadour,' 'Garry Owen,' and other tunes. It was a very handsome sight."

Still people grumbled. They wanted to start their new lives in Canada. Perhaps they did not understand the horrors that might have awaited them. "I assure you the passengers all feel very discontented at being kept here," wrote Jane.

When the passengers of the *Eliza Morrison* were finally allowed to leave, Jane and her family made their way to Goderich, the small town on Lake Huron that was to be their new home. For them, the quarantine on Grosse Île had been nothing but an irritating inconvenience.

More people you could research are

James Croil

Timothy Eaton

Casimir Gzowski

Father Pernard McGavran

Jane White

Snapshot

No names mark the graves of the typhus victims buried in the cemetery on Partridge Island in the harbour of Saint John, New Brunswick. Conditions were so desperate at this quarantine station in 1847 that no records were kept.

The previous winter people had talked of a coming flood of Irish immigrants. Despite these warnings, no one was prepared for what lay ahead. Only one doctor was assigned to the station's hospital. By early June, 2471 deathly ill people were crammed into every corner of the building, which was equipped to handle only 100 patients. More sick and dying lay outside. Extra hospital sheds were thrown together and tents were quickly pitched. Two more doctors were persuaded to help, but they, too, came down with the fever. Once again, a single doctor was caring for thousands of sick and dying people.

As rotting corpses began piling up, the only choice was to bury them in mass graves. The horror grew even worse when heavy rains washed away the thin layer of dirt that had been hastily shovelled over the bodies.

That summer, which became known as Black '47, more than 12 000 immigrants landed on the rocky, barren island. About 600 — no one is sure of the exact number — never left. Their hopes and dreams, and even their names, were buried with them in the island's mass graves.

Immigrants came by steamers, like the one shown at the dock, from Québec City to Montréal. The trip took 20 to 30 hours. This picture shows the dockside at Montréal in 1850.

The Story So Far . . .

1. What type of person do you think would be most likely to survive a trip across the Atlantic Ocean in a "coffin ship"? Explain your answer.
2. Why were the timber ships used to bring people to North America?
3. Grosse Île has been made a national historical site. Do you agree with the decision? Explain your answer.

The Underground Railway

For some people living in the United States, the Promised Land was north of the border. These people were African-American fugitive slaves from the Southern states. Between 30 000 and 40 000 slaves risked their lives to escape the shackles of bondage.

Africans had first been brought to America to work as slaves in the seventeenth century. In the mid-nineteenth century slavery was the foundation of the way of life in the Southern United States. Workers picked the cotton that was sold by plantation owners to the clothing factories in Britain. With the invention of the cotton gin, 200 times more cotton could be cleaned per day. More and more workers were needed.

In the "free" Northern states, slavery was regarded as an evil practice. An antislavery movement emerged in the early 1800s with the aim to abolish or get rid of slavery. A number of **abolitionists** worked to set up the **Underground Railway**. This was a secret network of safe houses or "stations" that were used to help slaves reach the province of Canada and freedom. The fugitive slaves would travel at night following the Big Dipper and the North Star. During the day, they hid at safe stations as they made their way to freedom. The trip could take days or months and was full of danger. Professional bounty hunters stalked the runaway slaves like animals, even into Canada West. There were dangers for the "station agents" as well. The 1850 Fugitive Slave Act in the United States required any person who knew of the whereabouts of any runaway slaves to turn them in, or face severe penalties, including imprisonment.

Follow the Drinking Gourd ★

So long old Master,

Don't come after me,

I'm heading north to Canada

Where everyone is free.

★ *The name escaping slaves gave to the stars of the Big Dipper or Ursa Major*

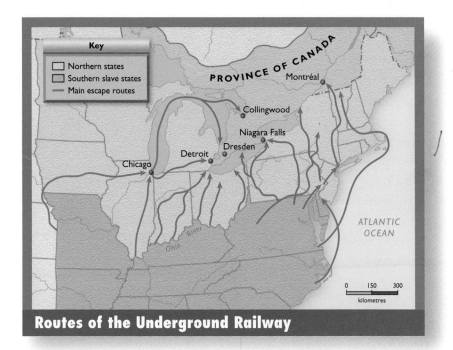

Routes of the Underground Railway

Eliza Parker

ACCUSED OF TREASON

Turkey with all the trimmings! This was not the kind of Thanksgiving dinner Eliza Parker had expected in jail. She was facing a charge of treason and her trial would start in a few days.

Abolitionists had delivered the dinner to the prison near Christiana, Pennsylvania. It lifted Eliza's spirits. Maybe there was a chance that she, and the 29 other prisoners facing the same charge, would be found not guilty.

The trouble had started early on a September morning in 1851. Slavecatchers brandishing guns had forced their way into the house where she and her husband William had been living since escaping from slavery. With the help of the Underground Railway, the Parkers had come to Christiana because slavery was against the law in Pennsylvania. This did not mean they were safe. The Fugitive Slave Act gave slave owners the right to track down runaways anywhere in the United States. The fugitives could then be returned to their owners in states where slavery was legal.

The uproar had drawn neighbours to the scene. Soon about 50 people had gathered. They were determined to help the Parkers. Outnumbered, the frustrated slavecatchers had fired their guns at the crowd. As panic-stricken people scattered in all directions, some of the defenders had fired back. One of the slave owners was killed, and several people were wounded.

The incident sparked an outcry. People who favoured slavery called it the Christiana Riot; abolitionists referred to it as the Christiana Resistance. In the days that followed, a posse hunted down anyone suspected of helping the Parkers. Eliza Parker was one of 30 people — 27 Black and 3 white abolitionists — caught in the roundup.

All were charged with treason for using force to defy the Fugitive Slave Act. If convicted they faced the death penalty. For Eliza, the only bright spot was that William had escaped to Canada West. Using his contacts in the Underground Railway, he had made his way to the Elgin Settlement, a community of fugitive slaves near Chatham.

Abolitionists used the incident to step up their campaign against the Fugitive Slave Act. They hired first-rate lawyers and worked hard to swing public opinion in favour of the defendants. When the trials were held, all were found not guilty.

When she was set free, Eliza joined William at the Elgin Settlement. There they raised their family and celebrated when Pennsylvania barred slave catchers from hunting fugitives in the state. When slavery was finally abolished years later, William returned to the United States. Eliza Parker did not go with him. She chose to remain in the adopted country that had become her home.

More people you could research are

Charles and Nancy Alexander

William Hall

Josiah Henson

Eliza Parker

Harriet Tubman

Many of the fugitives went to the Dawn settlement (in present-day Dresden), which had been started by a fugitive slave, Josiah Henson. The settlement was well established by 1842 and had a school, the British-American Institute, where former slaves could be educated. The settlement included farms, a gristmill, and a sawmill. Abolitionists in the United States gave money to support the Dawn settlement, but after slavery was ended in 1863, many of the fugitives drifted back to the United States.

The African Americans were not always accepted in the society. "There is much prejudice here against us," commented one man. He tried to register at a hotel and was told "the hotel is full." Some local parents would not send their children to schools that accepted African-American children.

Despite the dangers and hardships of the trip, most who came had no regrets. Canada West was indeed their Promised Land. The words of the fugitives speak for themselves.

I look upon slavery as I do upon a deadly poison...

My feet were frostbitten on the way North, but I would rather have died on the way than to go back.

I want to say to the coloured people in the United States:...if you wish to be free men, I hope you will all come to Canada.

I came in without a shilling. I now own a house and one hundred and one acres [40.9 ha] of land.

Josiah Henson escaped to Upper Canada in 1830 with his wife and four children. He died at Dresden, Ontario, in 1883.

Web Connection

http://www.school.mcgrawhill.ca/resources

Go to the web site above to read about the experiences of other fugitive slaves who used the Underground Railway. Go to History Resources, then to *Canada: The Story of a Developing Nation* to see where to go next.

The Story So Far . . .

1 a) How did the Fugitive Slave Act result in many African Americans coming to Canada West?

  b) What does the Underground Railway tell you about the conditions of slavery?

2 Research one of the settlements that were set up by the fugitive slaves. Make a list of questions to guide your research. For example: How did the settlers make a living? What happened to the settlement after slavery was abolished in the United States?

3 What is the difference between a *riot* and a *resistance*? How did a person's choice of what to name the Christiana incident reveal their bias?

Occupations of Immigrants Landing at Québec and Montréal, Selected Years				
Occupation	1846	1854	1856	1858
Labourer	6 733	10 448	4 338	1 593
Farmer, farm worker	4 831	5 632	2342	1 651
Carpenter, joiner	162	617	308	205
Smith, blacksmith	61	370	234	85
Merchant, clerk	–	156	104	192
Shoemaker	87	358	227	52
Tailor	84	433	206	94
Total	**12 366**	**19 466**	**8 769**	**4 442**

The table shows information that was collected at the ports of Montréal and Québec City in given years. Historians can use this information to learn about the immigrants who came to the Province of Canada. These figures show only the chief occupations.

Labourers were needed to clear land, work in forests, and for construction of canals and railways.

QUESTIONING THE EVIDENCE

1. a) Which two occupations had the most immigrants in these years?
   b) How would you explain this?
   c) Work out the percentage of the total immigrants that these two occupations filled for each of the given years. Brainstorm explanations for any changes you see.

2. Use a reference source to find out more about the type of work for any of the occupations that you do not understand. What does this tell you about this period?

3. Do you think it would have been easier for a merchant or clerk to find work in 1846 or in 1858? Explain your answer.

4. How would these figures have been collected?

5. How are they useful in helping you understand this period in history?

6. Summarize in a few sentences what these figures tell you about the Great Migration.

BOOM, BUST, AND BOOM AGAIN

The British North American colonies had a special trading arrangement with Britain in the 1840s. At the time, the British government collected **tariffs**, or taxes on goods that were imported by business people. Britain charged lower taxes on goods imported from British North America than it did on imports from other countries. This was known as **preferential tariffs**. In return the colonies shipped most of their raw materials to Britain. These lower taxes meant products from the colonies could be sold in Britain for a lower price than products from other places. This was particularly true for the two chief exports, wheat and timber. As a result of the preferential tariffs, the colonies prospered and expanded as their goods were in demand in Britain.

The Preferential Tariff	
Baltic Log	$1.00
British Duty	.20
Cost	**$1.20**
Canadian Log	$1.10
British Duty	.05
Cost	**$1.15**

Good Times

In the 1840s there was a dramatic change in the pioneer way of life in the Province of Canada. Early pioneer farming families had struggled to make a living. They grew crops to feed themselves, selling what they could for cash. Many farmers had to work off the land in the forests to survive. Now the growing numbers of people in Britain needed Canada's wheat. More and more fields were cleared and planted with grain. Workshops making farm machinery were started, many using designs of machines made in the United States. For many people, farming became a full-time occupation. Wheat was a profitable **cash crop**, a crop that farmers grew for sale. More gristmills sprang up along the St. Lawrence and other rivers to process the wheat into flour. Between 1839 and 1841 exports of wheat and flour increased fivefold. By the end of the decade, that amount skyrocketed another sevenfold. Even American farmers were having their wheat milled in Canada so they could sell it in Britain at the special rate allowed by the preferential tariffs.

Mills were built wherever running water could be used to turn the waterwheels. Gristmills ground grain into flour.

A Logger's Song

"I see that you are a logger

and not just a common bum

For nobody but a logger

stirs his coffee with his thumb."

Growth and expansion in the timber trade mirrored the booming wheat trade during the 1840s. While more people farmed wheat than harvested trees, wood accounted for two thirds of the value of exports to Britain in 1841. The demand for lumber in Britain was so great that trees in the colonies were harvested year-round.

The main centres for the timber trade were the Ottawa Valley and St. Lawrence in the Province of Canada, and the Saint John River Valley in New Brunswick. Before the 1840s part-time, independent loggers cut wood and sold it. After the 1840s more and more workers became full time employees for logging companies, such as J. R. Booth's company in Ottawa.

Lumber gangs camped out in forests in the winter. Life in the camps was tough and strenuous. One preacher complained that being out in the wilderness for so long "encouraged profanity, Sabbath-breaking, gambling, and drinking." Each gang in the Ottawa Valley cut about 400 white or red pines a season. In the forest they cut the logs into squares lengths, called "sticks," then used horses or oxen to haul the logs to a nearby stream. In the spring the log drivers moved the trees downstream. Sometimes the logs jammed, bringing the log run to a quick halt. It was the loggers' job to break the jam as quickly as possible. Otherwise other gangs would get their logs to market first and receive the best price. At the end of the drive, loggers always heard that some driver had been crushed and drowned. As the stream widened into rivers the logs were corralled and tied together in great rafts. The men poled, or their horses pulled, the great rafts down to waiting harbours.

The rafts were broken up at Québec and loaded on to waiting ships. This photograph was taken in 1872.

I-76310 Timber Coves from Spencerwood, Québec City, QC, 1872. *McCord Museum of Canadian History.*

The main ports for export were Québec City in Canada East and Saint John in New Brunswick. Here the rafts were torn apart and loaded on to timber ships. These ships were built in the colonies and shipbuilding was another important industry in the Maritimes and Québec.

The Golden Age of shipping in the Maritimes began in the 1840s. The industry had started soon after the timber trade, with ships being built to carry the logs from the forests to Britain. By the 1850s Nova Scotia, New Brunswick, and Prince Edward Island were the fourth in the world in the amount of tonnage of ships that they owned and operated. Only Britain, France, and the United States were ahead of them. There were hundreds of small shipyards. At the time both banks of the Miramichi River were lined for 20 km by shipyards. The largest shipyards were at Saint John.

The *Marco Polo*, built in New Brunswick in 1851, was called the "Fastest Ship in the World" when she completed the round trip from England to Australia in less than six months.

By the mid-nineteenth century, Saint John was a major shipbuilding centre, building over 100 ships a year. This engraving shows the shipyard with a ship being built in the foreground.

The shipbuilding industry was based on the plentiful supply of wood from the forests for building the ships and the skill of the workers. Usually the builders were part owners of the ships with the merchants who ran them. Few wooden sailing ships that were used as merchant ships lasted more than 15 years, so there was a steady demand for them. The industry boomed when ships were needed to carry people and supplies to the gold rushes in California in 1849 and Australia in 1851, and to the Crimean War in 1854. One ship, the *Marco Polo*, was called the fastest ship in the world when it made the voyage from England to Australia in record time.

The Story So Far . . .

1 a) What trading advantages with Britain did the colonies have?

   b) What advantage was it for Americans to send their wheat to Canada to be milled in the 1840s?

   c) Why did Britain want raw materials from the colonies in North America at this time?

2 Why was timber such an important resource in the mid-nineteenth century? List the industries that you know depended on wood.

3 Draw a flowchart to show how the shipbuilding industry grew up in the Maritime colonies.

Special Treatment Ends

Since the end of the eighteenth century, Britain had been caught up in the whirlwind of the **Industrial Revolution**. Beginning with the invention of the steam engine and other machines, the Industrial Revolution changed how people worked and lived in Britain and in the rest of the world. Mechanized power replaced muscle power. Gradually, working in factories replaced working on farms for most people. Living in cities replaced living in the country.

By the mid-1840s British factory owners were putting pressure on their government to introduce **free trade**. In free trade there are no duties or taxes put on goods that are imported or exported. The industrialists wanted the cheapest materials for their factories, the cheapest food for their workers, and the largest markets for their products. This meant the end of preferential tariffs for the colonies.

In 1846 the British Parliament passed a bill for the Repeal of the **Corn Laws**. The Corn Laws had guaranteed that no cheap wheat (called corn in Britain) would be imported to compete with British farmers. Now this protection was gone. The cancellation of the other special import taxes for the colonies followed one after the other. Free trade ruled in Britain.

The effects of the Repeal of the Corn Laws came at the same time that the Irish famine victims started to flood into British North America. Many farmers, unable to compete with cheaper wheat from Europe on the British market, simply abandoned their farms and moved south to the United States. The timber from the forests of the Province of Canada and New Brunswick could not compete on the British market with timber coming from the Baltic Sea area. Sawmills and flour mills stood idle. To make matters worse, the American government allowed grains and other materials from British North America to be exported duty-free through American ports, such as New York and Boston, so that ports in the colonies lost business.

Lord Elgin was made Governor General of the Province of Canada in 1846 and stayed in office until 1854.

Reciprocity to the Rescue

The merchants in the Canadas faced financial ruin. Lord Elgin, the Governor General of the Province of Canada, reported to the British government in 1848 that, "three quarters of the merchants in Montréal faced bankruptcy." The merchants felt betrayed and abandoned. There was even talk of joining the United States.

Snapshot

The Heroine of Long Point

When the cold fall winds started blowing, the settlers of Long Point, Canada West, knew there would be shipwrecks. The shifting sandbars around the long, narrow peninsula jutting into Lake Erie were notorious. Ships often ran aground in the shallow, treacherous waters.

In November 1854, 24-year-old Abigail Becker was home alone when a vicious storm blew up. Her husband Jeremiah, a hunter and trapper, was away buying their winter supplies. Worried, Becker braved the storm and made her way to the shore. She hoped to spot Jeremiah on his way home. Instead, she saw a heart-stopping sight.

Just offshore, a schooner had foundered on a sandbar. Eight sailors were clinging to its frozen rigging as huge, icy waves crashed over the wreck.

Becker knew she had to do something. Unable to swim, she waded as far as she could into the cold, roiling surf. She knew the waters well and beckoned to the exhausted sailors. One by one, they followed her directions and made it to safety.

The grateful sailors eagerly spread word of Becker's bravery. She was showered with honours, including a letter and £50 from Queen Victoria. This rescue was not to be her only heroic act. She later helped six other shipwrecked sailors and saved a boy who had fallen down a well.

Early Photographs

In 1839 Louis Jacques Mandé Daguerre announced the invention of the daguerrotype. The process marked a giant leap forward in the art of photography — and it became popular right away. Within a year, the first daguerrotypists had opened studios in Montréal and Québec City. Their early clients were called "patients," perhaps because creating a likeness took so long. Subjects had to remain completely still as the camera slowly recorded their image on a silver-plated copper plate.

Lord Elgin believed that the British colonies in North America needed free trade with the United States if they were going to prosper. American politicians did not think **reciprocity**, or free trade in some items, with British North America was an advantage to their citizens. Lord Elgin would not give up. In 1854 he went to Washington to carry out negotiations himself. His personal charm, persistence, and diplomatic skills won over the Americans and the Reciprocity Treaty was signed. Grain, timber from New Brunswick and the Province of Canada, coal and fish from Nova Scotia, and potatoes from Prince Edward Island could all enter the United States duty-free for the next ten years. British ships could sail on Lake Michigan, and the Americans could use the St. Lawrence waterway. Most important for the American politicians, their fishers could drop their nets in the British waters off the Atlantic coast.

Good Times Return

The 1854 Reciprocity Treaty with the United Stated helped to fuel an economic boom during the 1850s. The value of exports from the Province of Canada alone doubled from $8 million in 1853 to $16 million in 1855. The value of fish, timber, and other exports from the Maritimes experienced a similar growth. Britain needed wheat from the colonies when the 1854–1856 Crimean War with Russia cut off its usual supply of grain from Ukraine. Britain still remained the main market for colonial products, but the 1854 Reciprocity Treaty broadened the market for British North America. The agreement established a north-south pattern of trade with the United States, a pattern that would grow and expand in the future.

The Story So Far . . .

1 a) What advantages did the British gain by introducing free trade?
   b) What effect did this have in British North America?
2 Imagine you were a merchant in Montréal when Britain cancelled the preferential tariffs. Present an argument for joining the United States (population 23 million) at this time.
3 How did the Reciprocity Treaty help bring prosperity to British North America?

THE INDUSTRIAL REVOLUTION BEGINS

Improved Transportation on Water

By the 1840s the Industrial Revolution was starting to transform the way of life in British North America. The first impact was in transportation and communications. The great rivers and waterways were the arteries for trade in British North America, and it was natural that the first improvements were made along these waterways. The Lachine Canal was built to bypass rapids on the St. Lawrence in 1823. Six years later the Welland Canal bypassed the mighty Niagara Falls. The government of the Province of Canada believed canals were needed for progress and was prepared to raise money to help pay for them. In 1841 Governor General Lord Sydenham arranged for a £1.5 million loan to pay for canal construction by private companies. Up to 10 000 workers, called canal **navvies**, many of whom had immigrated from Southern Ireland, worked on this construction,

Snippet

The Welland Canal

An engineering marvel when it opened in 1829, the Welland Canal is the only canal still used for commercial shipping. Now part of the St. Lawrence Seaway, the canal has been rebuilt and expanded four times over the years. It takes lake freighters and ocean-going ships about 12 hours to make their way through the eight locks of the 42-km canal linking Lake Ontario and Lake Erie.

The Rideau Canal was an engineering marvel when it was built between Kingston and Ottawa to guard against an American invasion. It was never a commercial success.

Snippet

An Expensive Waterway

Not all canals were a success. In Nova Scotia an ambitious plan to build an 85-km canal between Halifax and the Bay of Fundy faced setbacks from the beginning. The Bay of Fundy's high tides caused problems. The locks heaved in winter and a dam collapsed. Started in 1828 the Shubenacadie Canal was not finished until 1861. By then the era of canals was long over. Railways had made canals obsolete.

digging, hauling, and quarrying stone for $0.50 a day. By 1850 the canal navvies had built a network of canals that linked the main waterways. Steamboats could travel from the Atlantic coast to the head of the Great Lakes.

Steamboats had become the new workhorses of the Great Lakes. Steam engines, the new invention that powered Britain's textile mills, were used in the Great Lakes paddlewheelers. John Molson owned the first steamboat, *Accommodation*, which first travelled the St. Lawrence waterways in 1809. By the 1840s steamboats were the preferred method of transportation in the Canadas. The trip upstream from Montréal to Kingston took only 19 hours compared with the seven-day journey by road. It took only five days to travel from Niagara to Kingston, Brockville, Preston, and back to Toronto. The steamers provided fast, regular service for people and goods, at least until freeze up.

The new steam engines also powered the ships crossing the Atlantic Ocean. The *Royal William*, a sail-equipped paddlewheeler, made the first crossing using steam power in 1833. Seven years later, the *Britannia*, owned by "Steaming Sam" Cunard, took an amazing 12 days to make the crossing. These passenger liners provided two types of accommodation. Steerage, the cheapest accommodation, cost $25. The cabin rate, which included a room, meals, and a better location on the boat, was between $60 and $80. As well as the profit from carrying people and cargo, Cunard's government contract for carrying Her Majesty's Royal Mail brought him prestige and profit.

The Story So Far . . .

1   a) Why are transportation improvements important for increasing trade?
    b) How did the canals affect the transportation of products in the 1840s?
2   Imagine you lived in a community where the steamboats docked. Give an account of how the steamboat changed your community.
3   Explain how faster travel across the Atlantic Ocean would change life in British North America. Describe how it could affect trade in goods and everyday lives of people.

Samuel Cunard
KING OF THE NORTH ATLANTIC

By 1838 Samuel Cunard had achieved success. The 51-year-old Halifax businessman had built up the timber business started by his father and invested in whaling, iron, coal, and sailing ships. He was a wealthy man who could relax.

But Cunard was not ready to retire. He had watched with interest as steamships had started transporting passengers, mail, and goods on lakes and rivers. These vessels travelled much faster than sailing ships. Still, they had not been used for ocean crossings. They could not carry enough coal — the fuel used to power the engines — for the long voyage. Their engines also broke down frequently.

Then, in 1838, two specially built steamships successfully repeated the *Royal William*'s 1833 crossing of the Atlantic Ocean. Cunard sensed that these ships were the vanguard of a revolution in travel — and he wanted to be part of it.

Yet he was cautious. In 1839 he saw his opportunity. A method of prepaying postage with an adhesive stamp was being tried in Britain, and the British Admiralty had invited shipping companies to bid for the contract to carry mail by steamship across the Atlantic. The trip was to take place once a month.

Cunard decided to make a bid. First he hired Robert Napier, a leading marine engineer, to oversee the building of three steamships "of the very best description." Cunard liked Napier's ideas. To eliminate delays caused by engine breakdowns, Napier said that ships should be equipped with a workshop and spare parts. The crew should include a mechanic to carry out repairs.

With his ships under construction, Cunard won the mail contract. He did it by promising to carry mail across the Atlantic *twice* a month, a stunning improvement in service.

The *Britannia* was the first ship built by his company, the British and North American Royal Mail Steam Packet Company, which became known as the Cunard Line. A packet is a ship that carries mail and passengers. On July 4, 1840, the sidewheeler steamed out of the harbour in Liverpool, England, on her maiden run. She arrived in Halifax 12 days later — two days earlier than expected!

By the time Cunard retired in 1848, his company's steamships were providing weekly mail and passenger service between England and North America. He became Sir Samuel Cunard when Queen Victoria made him a baronet.

When Cunard died in 1865, family members carried on the business. For more than 100 years the Cunard Line operated some of the world's most famous passenger ships. These included the *Lusitania* and the *Mauretania*, the fastest ships of their day, as well as the luxury liners *Queen Mary* and *Queen Elizabeth*.

More people you could research are

Hugh Allan

James R. Booth

Samuel Cunard

Alexander Galt

Allan MacNab

Hart Almerrin Massey

The Railways

The first railway in Britain was built in 1830, and it started a new era in transportation. There had been some early lines built in British North America to link waterways, but it was not until the 1850s that railway building really began in the colonies. Railways could solve several of their transportation problems. Waterways froze in winter, but the railways could operate all year if the tracks were cleared. At the time overland transportation by road was slow and unreliable. Railways could reach areas that were not accessible by water.

Railway-building fever took hold in British North America in the 1850s. Construction was expensive, so most entrepreneurs who were building the lines needed government support.

The first railway line of any length, the St. Lawrence and Atlantic Railroad, ran from Montréal, Canada East, to Portland, Maine, and was completed in 1853. Alexander Galt was the chief promoter in Canada. He believed the line would take grain-exporting business away from Montréal's chief trade rival, New York City.

A Grand Trunk locomotive about 1860. Wood was used for heating the water to produce steam.

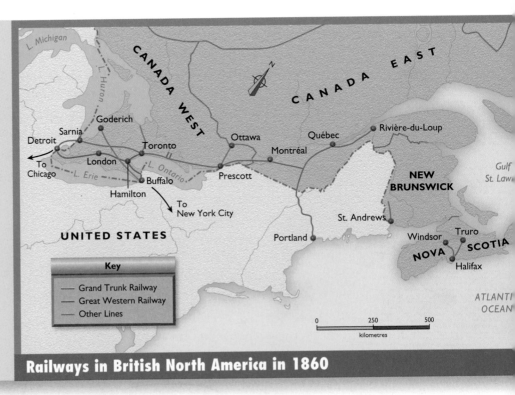

1 Why do most of the lines link with American rail lines?

2 Toronto's growth challenged Montréal's after the railways were built. How does this map help explain this?

Key

— Grand Trunk Railway
— Great Western Railway
— Other Lines

Railways in British North America in 1860

There were several accidents on the railways in the first years of their operation. The disaster pictured here happened at the Great Western Railway bridge over the Desjardins Canal in March 1857. The train crashed through the bridge and plunged into the canal below, killing 59 people.

Imagine you were one of the onlookers at this scene. How would you feel about train travel? What do you think could have caused the disaster? What can be done to help the people who have been hurt? As a group, role play a conversation with people around you.

As early as 1851, politicians and Montréal business interests were talking about the need to build an east-west railway line to link Halifax and Windsor. This line could be used to ship grain from Chicago to Montréal for export. It would also develop intercolonial trade with the Maritime colonies. The plans for the Maritime section failed when New Brunswick and Nova Scotia could not agree on a route. However, the section of the Grand Trunk Railroad in the Canadas was started in 1852.

First the Grand Trunk leased the St. Lawrence and Atlantic Railroad link to Portland, Maine, so that it had a winter terminal on the Atlantic coast. British investors and contractors agreed to build the Toronto-Montréal section of the line; the Toronto-Sarnia section was to be built with Canadian money. The directors asked the Canadian government to lend them money, and since six of the directors were cabinet ministers in the government this was not a problem. The engineering costs for building the line went over budget, and the Canadian government went more deeply into debt as it loaned the Grand Trunk more money. The Toronto-Montréal section of the railway was opened in October 1856. There were parades, speeches, and lavish parties in both cities.

The next year, news of political scandals filled the newspapers. Some politicians, including Prime Minister Francis Hincks, had received kickbacks from the Grand Trunk and other railways. The whole project was out of control. By 1858 the public debt had reached $54 million because of the railway costs and corruption. The government raised more money by taxing imports. Municipalities raised property taxes to pay off their bad railway debts. In 1859 the Grand Trunk was completed to Sarnia. It was the longest railway in the world at the time, stretching from Sarnia in Canada West to Rivière du Loup, Canada East, with a branch line to Portland, Maine. By the end of the 1850s, the Canadas had over 3000 km of railway. It also had a huge debt to repay.

Snapshot

Businessman-politician

Among railway promoters Sir Allan MacNab was the master of mixing politics with railways. A hero in the War of 1812, MacNab sat as the member of Parliament for Hamilton. He was a government minister in the 1840s and served as Prime Minister of Canada in 1854. While holding these political offices, Sir Allan was also the president of three railways, chairman of one other, and director of two more at various times. MacNab was accused of profiting from his position and taking cash payments from railway companies. When asked to explain how he could be so closely involved with the railways and be in politics, MacNab replied, "Railroads are my politics."

Like many wealthy entrepreneurs of the time, Sir Allan MacNab lived in an impressive home. This was his 72-room mansion, Dundurn Castle, in Hamilton.

The Impact of the Railway

The railway age transformed life in British North America. People could travel hundreds of kilometres in one day. The isolation of winter and living in the bush was broken. People could work in one town and live in another. Fresh produce was delivered to stores every day.

Railways influenced where people lived. Settlements that were bypassed by the railway stagnated and eventually disappeared. A city served by the railway, such as Toronto, grew because it was a railway hub. Port Hope, a town of only 4000 people in Canada West, borrowed $740 000 to invest in a railway line so that trains would stop there. Railways created other businesses and industries. Bridges had to be constructed. Machine shops repaired train engines. Steel foundries rolled out the iron and steel for the rails. Factories crafted the engines. Passenger cars had to be built. Wood had to be cut to fuel the engines. Engines and tracks had to be maintained. Telegraph lines followed the tracks and telegram offices were set up at railway stations.

Railways also changed how governments saw their role. They understood that they had to invest public money to support private ventures because of the small populations. Because railways and canals brought so many permanent and profound benefits, governments had to support them.

Railway companies were one of the largest employers in the colonies by the end of the 1850s. The railway shop workers belonged to "brotherhoods." These early unions provided insurance, sickness, and death benefits for their members.

Reflections

Imagine you are living in a village that has been linked by rail to other settlements. Write a letter to a friend to describe how this has changed your life

The Great Western Railway workshops in Hamilton, Ontario, in 1863. Railway stock was repaired and locomotives built at this site.

The Story So Far . . .

1. Prepare an advertising brochure selling shares in the Grand Trunk Railway. Use a map to show where it will run, and explain why it is a good investment.
2. Explain why having a railway station would cause a settlement to grow.
3. Create a flowchart to show how the building of a railway could cause other industries to be established.

SUM IT UP!

In this chapter we learned about the impact of the Great Migration on British North America. We traced the experiences of the famine Irish and the African-American fugitive slaves as they made their way to British North America. The 1840s saw the commercial development of the wheat and timber trade. The Repeal of the Corn Laws in 1846, however, brought economic hardship. The 1850s witnessed an economic boom, which was helped by the signing of the Reciprocity Treaty with the United States.

By the 1850s the Industrial Revolution had started to transform people's lives in British North America. A network of canals helped move goods to markets. Steamboats travelled the Great Lakes and crossing the Atlantic Ocean became routine for ocean liners. Railways were changing the whole way of life. Goods could be moved faster and trade improved. Cities grew more quickly. Railways linked people and set the stage for the political changes in the 1860s.

THINKING ABOUT YOUR LEARNING

1. Why did many Irish emigrate to British North America and then move to the United States?

2. What risks accompanied someone trying to escape on the Underground Railway? Why would a person take those risks?

3. What changes took place in the wheat and timber trade during the 1840s?

4. Why did many people feel abandoned after the Repeal of the Corn Laws?

5. As a 13-year-old, explain how your life would have improved in British North America from 1840 to 1860.

6. How did the Industrial Revolution affect transportation in British North America?

7. Why might historians say that 1840 to 1860 was a crucial time in our history?

APPLYING YOUR LEARNING

1. Create a Heritage Minute about *one* of the following stories: the trip across the Atlantic Ocean with Irish immigrants; stopping at Grosse Île; escaping on the Underground Railway.

Year	Number of Immigrants
1844	2 605
1845	6 133
1846	9 765
1847	14 879
1848	4 141
1849	2 724
1850	1 838
1851	3 470
1852	2 165
1853	3 762
1854	3 440
1855	1 539
1856	708
1857	607
1858	390
1859	230
1860	323

2 The figures in the table show the number of immigrants who arrived in New Brunswick between 1844 and 1860.

a) Draw a graph that shows immigration between 1844 and 1850. Decide whether to use a bar graph or line graph. Label the graph and give it a title.

b) Write a short paragraph to explain the graph to someone who has not read this chapter.

c) List possible reasons why the number of immigrants to New Brunswick fell from 1854 to 1860 even though thousands of immigrants were coming from Europe to North America.

3 Research and write a letter, or draw a picture, about working as a logger in the bush, or taking the logs downstream for shipping.

4 Write a newspaper article commenting on the Repeal of the Corn Laws.

5 Draw a poster or write an advertisement for a trip on a steamboat or on one of Samuel Cunard's passenger liners.

6 Record the names and lyrics for songs about railways.

7 Prepare a presentation on locomotives or rail passenger cars used in the 1850s.

8 Create a telegram. Remember that each word costs money. Research the proper telegram format to ensure your telegram is historically accurate.

USING KEY WORDS

Explain the role these terms played in this chapter.
quarantine station
reciprocity
timber ships
Underground Railway
preferential tariffs

Political Deadlock

McCord Museum of Canadian History, Montreal.
MII588 Attributed to Joseph Légaré, The Burning of
the Parliament Building in Montreal, ca. 1849, oil on
wood, McCord Museum of Canadian History

1849

Legislative Assembly of the
Province of Canada burns

1851

Robert Baldwin and Louis-
Hippolyte La Fontaine retire

1853

Francis Hincks retires as Prime
Minister

1856

Liberal-Conservative Party led
by John A. Macdonald is created

SETTING OUR FOCUS

The scene is Montréal; the date April 25, 1849. Governor General Lord Elgin has just signed a bill into law. It allows the government to give money to citizens, mainly French Canadians, for losses they suffered during the 1837–1838 Rebellion. A mob chases Lord Elgin's carriage when he leaves his office, pelting it with stones and rotten eggs. Then the mob barges into the Assembly chambers, makes kindling out of the wood furniture, and rips the fine curtains. A gas lamp ignites and sets the whole structure on fire. The fire department of the city arrives, but the crowd will not let the firefighters through. If you look carefully at the painting you will see one person carrying part of a fire hose, cut by protesters.

The burning of the Parliament buildings of the Province of Canada was a dramatic end of an era. Lord Elgin had signed into law a bill that he did not want, and the mob of protestors did not agree with it either. He signed it because the majority of elected representatives had voted for the bill. At last the Province of Canada had responsible government.

Over the next 15 years, the representatives became divided and unable to agree. Governments gained power only to lose it in weeks and even days. How did this happen? What solution was there to break the political deadlock?

KEY WORDS

Clergy Reserves
coalitions
Constitution
conventions
federal system
la survivance
non-sectarian
   school
party platform
political deadlock
political parties
populist party
representation by
   population
   (rep by pop)

PREVIEWING THE CHAPTER

In this chapter you will learn about these topics:
- the different views held by political parties in Canada East and Canada West in the 1850s
- how these differences led to political deadlock in the Province of Canada in 1864
- how the politicians proposed to end this deadlock
- the politicians who shaped these decisions

1857
New Clear Grit Party led by Brown is formed

1859
Ottawa is chosen as capital of the Province of Canada

1862
George Brown marries Anne Nelson

1864
Great Coalition is arranged

Left: Robert Baldwin, leader of the Reform Party in Canada West. His father, William, pressed for responsible government in the 1830s.
Right: Louis-Hippolyte La Fontaine, leader of the Reform Party in Canada East, spoke French in the Assembly, which was contrary to the law. His leadership caused the British government to change the clause in the Act of Union that said French was not to be used officially in the House.

THE CHANGING POLITICAL SCENE

The achievement of responsible government in 1849 was a personal victory for two men — Robert Baldwin and Louis-Hippolyte La Fontaine, leaders of the Reform Party. In some ways the two men were alike — they were both lawyers, wealthy and clever. They became great friends after 1841, when Baldwin helped La Fontaine get a seat in the Legislative Assembly.

La Fontaine worked for *la survivance*, or the survival of French Canadian culture. He believed that French Canadians had to vote together as a bloc in the Legislative Assembly and support the same party in elections. If they worked with the party that had the largest number of seats in Canada West, they could ensure that the laws passed protected their interests and culture. In 1850 his friend, Robert Baldwin, led the main party in Canada West. La Fontaine strongly supported the use of the French language in the legislature.

Baldwin and La Fontaine brought in a variety of reforms before they both retired in 1851. It looked as though the colony was entering a time of progress and success. Instead opinions were soon so divided that between 1854 and 1864 there were ten governments, with one government lasting only two days. When you consider that nowadays most governing parties in Canada stay in power for between four and five years, you can see how unstable the governments were. What were the issues and opinions that divided people?

Divisions in Opinions

One issue raised in the legislature was the question of **representation by population**, or, as it was known *rep by pop*. Rep by pop meant that each politician in the legislature represented the same number of people. The 1841 Act of Union said that Canada East and Canada West were to have an equal number of representatives in the Legislative Assembly. At that time, there were more people living in Canada East than in Canada West. By 1851 that had changed. The people of Canada West felt that they were being controlled by voters in Canada East, especially as they tended to vote in a bloc. Some people went so far as to call for "one man, one vote."

Some people wanted an American-style government, where all the officials, including judges, were elected. They wanted to get rid of the parliamentary system of government and have a republic, with a president instead of the British monarch as the head of state. Party members would choose their leaders at **conventions**. The people who supported these ideas were called radicals. In Canada East they supported Le Parti Rouge; in Canada West, they voted for the Clear Grits candidates although not everyone in these parties agreed with these ideas.

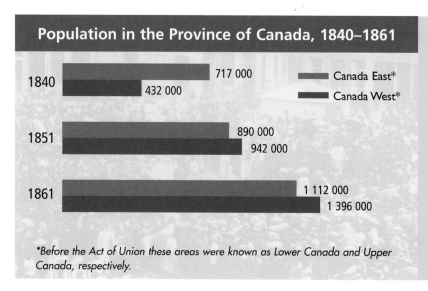

Population in the Province of Canada, 1840–1861

	Canada East*	Canada West*
1840	717 000	432 000
1851	890 000	942 000
1861	1 112 000	1 396 000

*Before the Act of Union these areas were known as Lower Canada and Upper Canada, respectively.

1. From what you already know, how do you explain the growth in the Province of Canada between 1840 and 1851?

2. If there had been rep by pop in 1840, which area would have had more representatives, Canada East or Canada West? In 1850, which area would have had more representatives?

Snapshot

Elections in the 1840s–1860s

Voting at this time was quite different from voting today. Women could not vote. Men could only vote if they owned property. The property had to produce an income of £12 if it was in the country or £5 if it was in a town. This meant most men could not vote either. There was one voting station in each district. These districts were called *ridings* because the only way people could reach them was by riding on horseback.

Voting was not secret. This led to election corruption. People would try to buy votes with money or a meal, or use threats to influence the voting.

Because voting took place over several days men could vote more than once by going to different ridings. One of the most corrupt elections took place in 1841, during which gang fights left several men dead. The following year laws were passed to deal with election corruption.

It was not unusual in election campaigns for fights to break out. In 1861 the supporters of John A. Macdonald had to barricade themselves in the upstairs of a schoolhouse to beat back his opponent's supporters, and a fight broke out between the two sides after one meeting. Elections in those days were often "fought" in the true sense of the word.

C. W. Jefferys (1869–1951) used eye-witness accounts of the election of 1841 to paint this scene. Here, armed men around Montréal threaten and drive away French-Canadian voters.

Religion also divided people at this time. It is very difficult for most people today to understand why people became so upset about religious issues in the 1850s. We live in a country that is made up of many religious, ethnic, language, and racial groups. Canada in the 1850s was different. Most immigrants came from a world where religious conflicts and wars had been ongoing for centuries. Western Europe was divided between Roman Catholics and Protestant groups that had broken away from the Roman Catholic Church in the early 1500s. Many newcomers brought their religious intolerance and hatred of other groups with them. In fact, there were a number of religious conflicts that involved Protestants killing Roman Catholics and Roman Catholics killing Protestants.

The religious divisions in the province came to be centred around two issues: what should be done with the *Clergy Reserves*, and whether the money from the province should be used to set up schools that were run by religious groups.

Governor John Graves Simcoe had set aside the **Clergy Reserves** in Upper Canada in 1791. They amounted to one seventh of all the land. The sale of this land was to help the established Protestant church, which was the Anglican Church or Church of England. By the 1830s the Presbyterian and Methodist churches, which had more members than the Anglicans, demanded a share of the monies. Others wanted the tracts of land sold and the money given to the local governments. There was a powerful group that did not want the government to give money to any "religious sect" or church. They wanted **non-sectarian schools**. Schools paid for by public money would not be run by religious denominations. Any religious group that wanted separate schools would pay for them themselves.

In Canada East, the Roman Catholic Church played an important role in welfare, education, and other services like hospitals. Many people supported the church in this role. In Canada West.

By the 1850s new **political parties** were forming as people with similar ideas united to get their ideas adopted. By 1855, just four years after Baldwin and La Fontaine retired, these divisions were beginning to affect government. As well there were many representatives who sat in the legislature as independents. These members, called "loose fish," did not belong to a political party and so were free to vote on issues as they wished. Their votes sometimes caused governments to fall.

The Story So Far . . .

1 a) What signs were there at this time that the Province of Canada was going to be difficult to govern?
b) How did the Act of Union contribute to this problem?

2 What was *la survivance*? What role did this idea play in politics at this time?

3 The "loose fish" could vote according to their consciences or what they thought the voters wanted. They did not have to vote with a political party unless they agreed with its views. What do you think is the advantage to the voters in having a "loose fish" representative? What would be the disadvantages?

Snapshot

The Gavazzi Riots

Religion and politics were already a volatile mix when Alessandro Gavazzi arrived in Canada and stirred things up even more. An Italian patriot and former friar who had turned against the Roman Catholic Church, Gavazzi gave two lectures in Toronto on May 31 and June 1, 1853. His message? Down with the Pope, the leader of Roman Catholics around the world. Gavazzi's Toronto audiences cheered his words. Canada West was a Protestant stronghold. Many people liked the idea of overthrowing the Pope.

Then Gavazzi headed for Canada East, where Catholics formed the majority. Not surprisingly, Catholics in Montréal did not welcome Gavazzi. When an angry mob gathered outside the Protestant church where he was speaking, things quickly turned ugly. The police lost control. The mayor called in troops to put down the riot, and someone gave the order to fire. In the mêlée, 10 Protestants were killed and 50 more were wounded.

This did not end the incident. Rampaging gangs continued to smash the windows of Protestant churches and attack Protestant ministers. It was a sign of how fanatical people could become over religious differences.

A painting showing the riots in Montréal that followed Gavazzi's preaching.

Francis Hincks

DEADLOCK SETS IN

Irish-born Francis Hincks took over from Baldwin in 1851 as leader of the Reform Party. When Hincks arrived with his new bride in Upper Canada in 1832, he rented a property from Baldwin's family. The two men became friends. Hincks was against radical reform and rebellion but supported change in the government. In 1838, he started a newssheet. Its masthead read "Responsible Government."

Hincks realized that Upper Canada and Lower Canada had to work together for change. In 1839 he had contacted La Fontaine and persuaded him to work with Baldwin. So it is not surprising that in 1851 Hincks worked with Auguste-Norbert Morin, the new leader of the Reform Party in Canada East as co-premier.

George Brown — Man with a Mission

By 1851 Hincks was already in conflict with George Brown, another newspaper publisher turned politician. Brown was from a strict Scottish Presbyterian family that had immigrated to North America in 1837. He was an energetic, clever, and ambitious man with firm opinions. Brown was what people of the time called "a man of righteous principle." He had started the Toronto paper, *The Globe*, in 1844. It soon became the newspaper read by the educated and business people in the province. In less than ten years, Brown's paper had one of the largest circulations in British North America. In 1852 Brown was elected to the Legislative Assembly.

Brown resented what he called "French Catholic domination" of Canada East over Canada West. This "injustice" had to end. There had to be rep by pop. In his mind, the French Canadians, because they voted as a bloc, were making decisions for Canada West. He was also strongly anti-Catholic — he thought Roman Catholics were mistaken in their beliefs, and the church and its leader, the Pope, were evil and corrupt. It is not surprising that he saw any plan to extend public support to Catholic schools in Canada West as a conspiracy. Brown was a strong believer in the church and state being completely separate, so he was very much opposed to public money going to schools run by religious groups. He agreed that the money from the Clergy Reserves should go to the local governments. Brown had some supporters among the Clear Grits. The Grits were given their nickname because people said they were like fine sand or grit — hard, single-minded, and persistent.

Snippet

The Battle of the Titans

The 1851 by-election in Haldimand County, at the eastern end of Lake Erie, was a battle of the titans. George Brown and William Lyon Mackenzie were squaring off. Pardoned for his role in the 1837 Rebellion, Mackenzie was running under the Clear Grit banner. After a hard-fought campaign, Mackenzie defeated Brown, who was running as a Reformer, ruining the newspaper publisher's first attempt to win a seat in Parliament.

Snapshot

Newspapers were very important in the 1850s. There were 200 in the Province of Canada alone. The papers were simply one sheet of paper folded in two. The outer pages were covered with advertisements. The two inside pages had news, reports on what was happening in the legislature, and the all-important editorial. Far fewer people could read than today, but that did not mean that the contents of the four-page broadsheets were not talked about, debated, and questioned. They were the only form of media available for spreading opinions and ideas; there was no television, radio, film, or Internet.

This is why many of the politicians of the day published their own papers. It was the easiest and cheapest way for them to communicate their ideas. The opinions in the editorials were their views on the issues of the day, and the readers knew this. The most well-known politician-publisher in the 1850s was George Brown, but he was not the only one. Among others, Francis Hincks, Thomas D'Arcy McGee, Augustin-Norbert Morin, and Joseph Howe in Nova Scotia all started or wrote broadsheets.

This is the printing press used by Joseph Howe to print his newspaper.

They wanted to overhaul the whole political system. The Clear Grits was a "grass roots" or **populist party**, a party that had the support of ordinary people. The Grits were opposed to any group receiving special treatment or privileges from the government. To them the government should represent all of the people. It is not surprising that they supported rep by pop. They felt that the people of Canada West were being treated unjustly because they had the same number of representatives in the Assembly as the voters of Canada East.

The Story So Far . . .

1 Explain how religion played a different role in Canada in the 1850s and 1860s compared with today. Think of reasons why there is this difference.

2 a) What words do you think we would use to describe Brown and his views?

b) Why is it unwise for historians to judge the actions and views of a person from the past by present-day standards?

3 List the advantages to a person who wanted to run for political office in the 1850s of having a background in journalism.

Mary Ann Shadd
BLAZING TRAILS

Mary Ann Shadd was upset. Her enemy, Henry Bibb, had gone too far. In his newspaper, the *Voice of the Fugitive*, he had called her and others who shared her views "half-cracked hotheads."

Bibb's attack was the latest attack in a war of words the two had waged since Shadd had come to Windsor, Ontario, from the United States. A teacher, her goal was to set up a school that would welcome the children of African-American people who were fleeing slavery in the United States. She believed, however, that the school should also accept children of other races. Bibb said that the school should be for African-American children only. Shadd and Bibb had also clashed over the way Bibb was using money collected to help fugitives slaves start new lives in Canada West.

The name-calling in the *Voice of the Fugitive* was not unusual. Balanced journalism was rare in British North America. People started newspapers to promote political opinions.

Shadd's problem was that those who disagreed with Bibb had no forum where they could express their ideas. The solution? Start her own newspaper. In March 1853 the first issue of the *Provincial Freeman* appeared, making Shadd the first African-American woman newspaper editor in North America.

Knowing the idea of a woman editor would shock readers, she persuaded Reverend Samuel Ward to list his name as editor. Later, Shadd's name did appear, but only the initials of her first name were printed. She did not want to broadcast the fact that a woman ran the *Provincial Freeman*.

The ruse failed. When word got out, subscriptions dried up. To save the paper, Shadd and her sister, who had started helping her, stepped down so that a man could take over.

In Shadd's final editorial, she wrote bitterly that people found her and her sister "offensive" because they were "editors of the unfortunate sex." Still she urged other African-American women to follow in their footsteps: "To coloured women, we have a word — we have 'broken the editorial ice,' whether willing or not, for your class in North America; so go to editing, as many of you as are willing and able."

Her experience at the *Provincial Freeman* did not silence Shadd's voice, however. She married Thomas Cary and eventually returned to the United States, where she continued working for her people, and later helped to win the vote for women. In 1883 when she was 60 years old, she became the first woman to earn a law degree from Howard University, and the second African-American woman in North America to receive a law degree.

More people you could research are

Julia Hart

Rosanna Leprohon

Susanna Moodie

Mary Ann Shadd

Catharine Parr Trail

Brown's Opponents

By 1855 two other men who were to shape the future of Canada had been elected to the legislature. In Canada East George-Étienne Cartier followed the path laid out by La Fontaine before him. He worked for French-Canadian interests within the British parliamentary system. To do this he entered **coalitions**, or alliances, with politicians in Canada West.

Cartier had trained as a lawyer. He had supported the 1837–1838 rebellion in Lower Canada and fled to the United States to avoid prison and exile. Later he returned to his law practice. Cartier became leader of La Fontaine's party, now called Le Parti Bleu. It helped that he got along very well with the English-speaking business community. He encouraged commercial development in Canada East, as well as the railway boom, and he acted as a lawyer for the Grand Trunk Railway.

In Canada West John A. Macdonald, a young lawyer, was first elected to the legislature in 1844 at the age of 29. Macdonald was born in Scotland and at the age of five immigrated to Kingston with his parents. He left school at age 15 to work with a lawyer in Kingston and learned so quickly that he ran his own office when he was 19 years old. By 1855 he was a skilled and respected politician.

Snapshot

French Canadians Giving Voice to History

François Xavier Garneau, the author of *Histoire du Canada depuis sa découverte jusqu'à nos jours*, has been called French Canada's "first national historian." Garneau originally trained as a lawyer, and in 1842 he became the French translator in the Legislative Assembly. That gave him access to its rich library holdings as well as time to read and write.

Garneau was incensed when Lord Durham wrote in 1839 that French Canadians were a people without a history or a culture. He set out to show that French Canadians indeed had a rich, diverse, and unique history, literature, and culture. The culture had evolved through relationships with other cultures, with Aboriginal Peoples, then with Anglo-Americans, and finally, with English Canadians. His history of the French in Canada was enormously popular when it was published between 1845 and 1852. It helped to instill a powerful and lasting pride and sense of community.

François-Xavier Garneau is considered the greatest writer of nineteenth-century French Canada.

Macdonald was a Tory supporter. Tories favoured business and the railways, as well as the Anglican Church. They were loyal to the British connection and heritage. It was Tory supporters who had burned the Parliament buildings in 1849 because they were incensed at "rebels" being paid compensation for their losses. The party died out in Canada East soon after this, but in Canada West it survived. Macdonald realized that the Tories in Canada West had to work with politicians from Canada East. After the election of 1854, he set to work to persuade supporters of Hincks, now called Liberals, to join with his party and Cartier's Bleus in Canada East. With Macdonald and Cartier as its leaders the new Liberal–Conservative Party started in 1856.

By 1856 Brown took up another issue that interested the voters in Canada West far more than the people of Canada East. The Hudson's Bay Company's lease for Rupert's Land expired in 1859. Brown wanted the Province of Canada to purchase the rights to this great tract of land. The Northwest would provide new land for cultivation and settlers, as well as new markets for Canada West's businesses.

Web Connection

http://www.school.mcgrawhill.ca/resources

Go to the web site above to find out more about Canada's national anthem. Go to History Resources, then to *Canada: The Story of a Developing Nation* to see where to go next.

Snapshot

Macdonald and Brown — Deadly Enemies

Macdonald and Brown were opposites in temperament and political beliefs but the real animosity between them dated back to 1849. Brown was appointed secretary to a commission set up to look into the conditions in Portsmouth prison. The warden, Henry Smith, Senior, and his family were friends of Macdonald. The commission was very thorough. It found Smith neglectful, and he was suspended and faced numerous charges. Smith appealed to Macdonald and said the commission had been secretive and unfair. Macdonald, always a loyal friend, blamed Brown, the writer of the report, for Smith's problems.

The full extent of Macdonald's dislike of Brown was clear for all in the Assembly to see in 1855. In a speech, Macdonald accused Brown of twisting facts and evidence in the prison report. Brown, he said, had intimidated the warden; he accused him of using evidence from criminals to support his report.

Brown, who was known to speak for hours in defence of his ideas, was brief when he rose to reply to the charges. He simply demanded an inquiry. The inquiry found that Brown had been justified in his report, but Macdonald never retracted his charges. For Brown, a man of honour and principle, this was a serious issue. For years after, he did not speak to Macdonald.

John Alexander Macdonald in 1842. At 27 years of age, he was already well known in Kingston and was elected the next year as an alderman.

Calixa Lavallée

THIRSTING FOR ADVENTURE

Fifteen-year-old Calixa Lavallée could not remember a time when music had not been his life. First, his father had taught him to play the piano, organ, cornet, and violin. His obvious talent had caught the attention of Léon Derome, who had become his patron. A prosperous butcher and music lover, Derome had offered the teenager a chance to leave his home in Saint-Hyacinthe in 1855. For two years now, the teenager had lived with Derome's family in Montréal and studied the piano with two European teachers.

Calixa's exceptional musical ability surprised no one. After all, his father, Augustin, was also very musical. A bandmaster, Augustin and his family had moved to Saint-Hyacinthe where he had an opportunity to work for the renowned organ maker, Joseph Casavant. By the time he was 11, Calixa had been playing the pipe organ in the town's cathedral. At the age of 13, he had given a piano recital at the Théâtre Royal in Montréal. It was there that he had met Derome.

Now, in 1857 Lavallée was restless. Bored with formal music lessons, he longed to strike out on his own. He wanted to see the world — and if he had some adventures along the way, all the better. He decided to try his luck in the Unites States. There, he hoped his musical ability would open doors for him. With his parents' blessing, he travelled to New Orleans, where he entered — and won — a music competition. Suddenly Calixa's dreams were coming true. A famous Spanish violinist asked him to travel to South America, the West Indies, and Mexico as his accompanist.

By 1861 he was back in the United States — and about to get all the adventure he could handle. In April of that year, the Civil War erupted between the Northern and Southern states. In a fit of youthful enthusiasm, Calixa became one of more than 40 000 Canadians who fought in the war. In September 1862, when he was just aged 19, he was wounded at the bloody Battle of Antietam. Although his wound was serious enough to earn him an honorable discharge from the army, it was not so serious that it cut short his musical career.

This was fortunate, because Lavallée's greatest achievement lay far in the future. Eighteen years later, he was asked to set to music a patriotic poem written in French by Adolphe-Basile Routhier. When it was performed at an 1880 Saint Jean Baptiste Day celebration on the Plains of Abraham, "O Canada" was an instant hit. A century later, on July 1, 1980, the song — with music by Lavallée, French lyrics by Routhier, and English lyrics based on words penned by Robert Stanley Weir — was officially declared Canada's national anthem.

More people you could research are

Joseph Casavant

Calixa Lavallée

Joseph Légaré

Antoine Plamondon

Adolphe-Basile Routhier

In January 1857 over 150 Clear Grits were joined by former supporters of Hincks and Brown's own followers at the St. Lawrence Hall in Toronto to form a new party. It was still called the Clear Grit Party, but it adopted Brown's ideas. The **party platform** was based on all of his policies: rep by pop, annexation of the Northwest, and a public school system that did not support separate schools for Canada West. Most voters in Canada West supported this party. Macdonald's party, which had fewer supporters in Canada West, could only govern with the support of voters in Canada East. Over the next few years, these divisions made Canada almost impossible to govern.

One example of the **political deadlock** plaguing Canada came in the next year. Since the Parliament buildings were burned in 1849, the capital had alternated between Toronto and Québec City every two years. The politicians could not agree on the site of a new permanent capital, so the matter was referred to a commission. They chose Ottawa. The vote on the new capital site took place on July 28, 1858.

Some members of Le Parti Bleu still wanted Québec City to be the capital. They broke with their party and joined the Clear Grits and Le Parti Rouge in opposing the motion. The motion was defeated, and so was the government of Macdonald and Cartier. They handed in their resignations to the Governor General. He then asked George Brown, as the leader of the opposition, to form a new government. Brown's government only lasted two days before it, too, had to resign. Macdonald and Cartier were back in power. As Macdonald commented about this time period:

Snapshot

From Rowdy Lumber Village to National Capital

In the early 1850s it seemed unlikely that a rough-and-tumble collection of lumber shanties on the Ottawa River would be named the capital of Canada. Other better-established — and more "civilized" — communities such as Toronto, Québec, Kingston, Montréal, and Hamilton were lobbying hard to win the honour. How could Bytown, soon to be called Ottawa, with its reputation as the roughest town in British North America, even be in the running?

Queen Victoria asked Governor General Edmund Head to help settle the question. On a visit to Ottawa, Head was invited to an autumn picnic on a hill overlooking the Ottawa River. His wife painted a watercolour of the beautiful scene. Some people believe that the Queen's advisors saw this picture, and it helped them to choose Ottawa as capital.

In fact there were other reasons for the choice. Ottawa was farther from the American border than the other cities. This was a big advantage at a time when invasion was still a worry. The town was also on the border between Canada East and Canada West. The choice was so surprising that the other cities did not even feel slighted.

We had election after election—we had ministry after ministry [government]—with the same result. Parties were so equally balanced, that the vote of one member might decide the fate of the [government], and [thus] the course of legislation for a year or series of years.

No party could plan on putting their policies into practice because no party could guarantee they would be in power long enough. Governments were reduced to the role of caretakers— just looking after the day-to-day needs of the people. No one could have forseen that George Brown's love life would lead politicians in Canada out of the political quicksand they had created.

In 1859 Ottawa was a logging town at the juncture of the Rideau Canal and the Ottawa River, the waterway that divided the two sections of the Province of Canada.

The Story So Far . . .

1   a) What were the three policies in the party platform of the new Clear Grit Party?
    b) Who would these policies appeal to and why?
2   a) Do you think Brown was justified in not speaking to Macdonald? Explain your answer.
    b) Why do you think Macdonald and Cartier could work together?
3   Explain in your own words why governments at this time did not last long.

George and Anne Brown
NATION BUILDERS

As the train carrying George Brown and his new wife, Anne, chugged into Toronto's Union Depot on the evening of December 26, 1862, it was greeted by a cheering crowd of 5000 people. Bands played and fireworks exploded in the winter sky. Brown gave a short speech of thanks, then joined Anne in the carriage that would carry the couple through the cold rain to their home. The crowd surged around them, lighting the dark streets with burning torches.

For Anne, it was a wild welcome to Canada West. She had known that her new husband was a respected politician who published an important newspaper, but she had no idea that people took politics so seriously.

Anne had grown up in a close-knit, religious family in Edinburgh, Scotland. Her father, Thomas Nelson, was the wealthy founder of a successful publishing company. Intelligent, well-educated, widely travelled and independent, Anne was used to speaking her mind. She had no intention of marrying until she met the right man. That man turned out to be George Brown. Although Brown had gone to school with her older brothers, Anne had been a young girl when he had emigrated 25 years earlier. The two might never have met if Brown had not decided to take a long holiday in Britain in 1862. While visiting Edinburgh, the city of his youth, he fell deeply in love with — and married — the sister of his old friends.

In London, England, Brown had rubbed shoulders with British politicians and listened to the debates in Parliament, the centre of the vast British Empire. The experience changed his attitude toward events in the remote colony that he now called home. Though he was no less committed to the cause of reform, he viewed things more objectively. Quarrels that had once consumed all his energy now seemed like petty bickering.

If Brown's glimpse of British debates had changed his attitude toward politics, his marriage had taught him what was important in life. He felt torn between his desire to spend every spare moment with his much-loved wife and his duty to help change a system of government that he believed was not working. When the first of their three children was born, the pull of family life grew even stronger.

This change in Brown was to have a remarkable effect on the future of Canada. Rather than confrontation, he now chose negotiation. This enabled him to bring together those who would play such important roles in creating Canada. As a result, Brown is known as one of the Fathers of Confederation — and Anne Brown, the woman who transformed and influenced him, is sometimes called the Mother of Confederation.

More people you could research are

Robert Baldwin

George and Anne Brown

James Bruce, Earl of Elgin

Antoine Aimé Dorion

Francis Hincks

Louis-Hippolyte La Fontaine

Love Conquers All

Tired and plagued by poor health, Brown left for a long holiday in Britain in the summer of 1862. While visiting family in Scotland, George met and fell in love with Anne Nelson. George and Anne were married in November and returned to Canada the next month. His marriage brought about profound changes in George Brown's life.

Evidence of the effects of the marriage on Brown showed up in March of 1863. He was running for election. He still had the instincts of a political animal, but he was no longer intent on tearing his political prey apart. Instead Brown was very calm, low-keyed, and even friendly during the campaign. He wrote about his changed attitude in a letter to Anne: "I find a wonderful change in my feeling about all this since the olden times."

After winning the election, Brown made the long, tiring trek to Québec City for the new session of Parliament. He performed his political duties, but gone was the aggressive orator in the debates of the House. Brown confessed to Anne:

> *I hate this parliamentary work because it keeps me away from you. Twenty times a day I fancy myself by your side with our baby on your knee. I put my arm round your neck, and look into your eyes, and kiss you with my whole heart. And then I think what a fool I am to be here.*

Brown was tired of the old politics he had mastered so well. He wanted to go home, to stand over his new baby's crib. Only his Presbyterian sense of duty kept him in Québec City. Now, however, he had a different mission. He would lead the politicians out of political deadlock.

Snippet

A Modern Newspaper

As *The Globe's* circulation skyrocketed, George Brown was able to invest in huge, mechanized presses and hire staff to take over the writing and editing. As a result, *The Globe* became one of the first "modern" journals — newspapers that are more than just platforms for broadcasting the opinions of the editor-owner.

The Story So Far . . .

1 What evidence do you have to show how the marriage to Anne Nelson changed George Brown?
2 Predict how George Brown could break the political deadlock.
3 How much influence do you think women had in nineteenth-century politics? Research the role of one of the wives of the men mentioned in this chapter. Could she be seen as "the power behind the throne"?

THE END DRAWS NEAR

On March 14, 1864, Brown rose in the Assembly to suggest that a committee be set up. The members would look into Canada's **Constitution**, the rules on how the province should be governed. Perhaps a change could break the stalemate. His motion, or proposal for action, did not come to a vote. When the Assembly met again on May 14th, Brown rose to make the same motion. This time it came to a vote and it passed—despite votes against it from Macdonald and Cartier.

The committee recommended a **federal system** of government. In this system there are two levels of government: a national or federal government, and a state or provincial government. Canada today has a federal system of government. As if to show how much change was needed, the government of Macdonald and Cartier was defeated on the same day.

Brown was staying at the St. Louis Hotel while he was in Québec City. Over the next few days Macdonald, his hated opponent, and Cartier, who disagreed with Brown's views, talked to him at the hotel. They wanted him to join them in a coalition government. Together they would create a new Constitution to replace the old Act of Union. At last a deal was struck. Brown would join the coalition. The stage was set for Brown to make one of the most important speeches in his career and in the history of Canada. The official record reads:

> **Hon. George Brown** *then arose, evidently labouring under the deepest emotion, which for a time almost choked his utterance. He said: "...For ten years I have stood opposed to the honourable gentlemen opposite [Macdonald and Cartier] in the most hostile manner it is possible to conceive of....But I think the House will admit that, if a crisis has ever arisen in the political affairs of any country which would justify such a coalition as has taken place such a crisis has arrived in the history of Canada." (The honourable gentleman resumed his seat amidst loud and prolonged cheers from all parts of the House and many members crowded around him to offer their congratulations ...and some French-Canadian members were seen putting their arms around Brown and kissing him.)*

Brown, Macdonald, and Cartier had seized the moment. They all rose to the occasion. Their sense of duty was greater than their party rivalries. As Brown said, "Party alliances are one thing, and the interests of my country are another." The country won. The political deadlock was broken! Confederation was the answer, but could it be achieved?

Reflections

You are an elected member of the Legislative Assembly. Write a letter to your family at home explaining what the Assembly was like when George Brown made his speech on June 22, 1864.

The Evidence Behind the Story

In his address to the Legislative Assembly on June 22, 1864, Brown outlined his reasons for agreeing to enter into the coalition with the other parties. He expressed some of his concerns as well. Brown's letters to his wife Anne provide his personal reasons for being involved in Confederation. Some months after he entered the Great Coalition, Brown wrote these comments to Anne.

Circumstances have separated us very much in the past year, Anne. . . . It was our duty to do it — and perhaps we should be happy that our sacrifices have had much effect on the welfare of half a continent. Is it not so, dearest Anne?. . . Could I possibly have abandoned the trust that has gradually grown up, and now rests upon me? Would you not like that darling little Maggie should be able twenty years hence — when we may be gone — to look back with satisfaction to the share her father had in these great events? For great they are, dearest Anne, and history will tell the tale of them.

QUESTIONING THE EVIDENCE

1 What sacrifices do you think Brown was talking about?
2 What do you think was resting on Brown's shoulders?
3 What does he want Maggie to remember?
4 What does this letter tell you about George Brown as a person?
5 Why are private letters valuable to historians?
6 Do you think Brown was really part of something great?

The Story So Far . . .

1 Why did the politicians think that a federal system could break the political deadlock?
2 Why do you think Brown, Cartier, and Macdonald all agreed to form a coalition?
3 The alliance of Brown, Cartier, and Macdonald has been called the Great Coalition. Suggest why it has been given this name.
4 Canada has had one coalition government since the Great Coalition, and that was during World War I. Discuss why coalition governments are usually formed only in crisis situations.

SUM IT UP!

olitics in the Parliament of the Province of Canada between 1849 and 1864 lurched from triumph to turmoil and triumph again. The 1841 Act of Union set the stage. During the 1840s the politicians in Canada East and Canada West worked together for responsible government. Yet the flames at Les Champs du Mars in 1849 fanned the passions of race, religion, and regional differences that ignited politics during the 1850s. Each of the many political parties had their supporters, but no one party could ever claim to represent all of the people in the Province of Canada.

Coalition governments lasted months and even just days in these years of political turmoil. It was not until one of the key political players, George Brown, had a change of heart that politics in the Province of Canada had a change of direction. It was not until Macdonald, Cartier, and Brown put the interests of the province ahead of personal feelings and political quarrels that the Province of Canada could turn the corner and take the path to Confederation.

THINKING ABOUT YOUR LEARNING

1.
a) What is *compromise*? Explain what this means in your own words.
b) Why was compromise so necessary in the government from 1850–1864?
c) In your view which of the three main politicians compromised the most in 1864? Justify your choice with historical evidence.

2. Why was it so difficult for parties to co-operate through the 1850s?

3. What part did religious divisions between Catholics and Protestants play in dividing Canada East and Canada West in this time?

4.
a) Why is a secret vote needed in elections?
b) Why should elections be held on the same day at the same time?
c) What other measures are needed to make sure elections are honest?

5. What role did George Brown play
a) in creating divisions in this period, and
b) in breaking the deadlock?

6. Why was Anne Nelson called the "Mother of Confederation"? Do you think she deserves this title?

APPLYING YOUR LEARNING

1. Do you think individual people affect events in history? Choose one person in the story in this chapter, and explain how that person may have helped shape events.

2. You are a news reporter. Write a front-page story about one of the following events:
   - the burning of the Parliament buildings
   - Mr. Gavazzi's tour of Canada
   - George Brown's speech in the Assembly on June 22, 1864.

3. Design a political slogan and logo for each of the major parties in the 1850s.

4. Describe the role of newssheets in this period in keeping people informed about events.
   a) List the media that people use now to keep themselves informed about political issues.
   b) Which medium would you use first to find out about an issue?

5. Why is it important for citizens to stay informed about political issues?

6. What concerns that you have learned about in this period are still concerns today? How have they changed?

7. a) Research the present position of the federal Conservative Party.
   b) Do you think John A. Macdonald would be in favour of the party joining a coalition now? Why or why not?

USING KEY WORDS

1. Explain the meanings of these terms in the story of politics between 1849 and 1864:
   coalition
   federal system
   la survivance
   non-sectarian school
   political deadlock
   rep by pop
   responsible government

2. In setting up a school council, why would you need to know the meanings of these words:
   Constitution
   motion

CHAPTER
3

The Path To Confederation

April 1861	November 1861	June 1864	September 1864	October 1864	February 1865
Civil War begins in the United States	*Trent* incident causes Britain to send troops to Canada	Brown, Macdonald, and Cartier form the Great Coalition	Charlottetown Conference is held	• Quebec Conference is held • St. Albans Raid occurs	Confederation debates are held in Canada

SETTING OUR FOCUS

July 1,1867, witnessed a series of parties from the rocky cliffs of Lake Superior to Nova Scotia's sea-swept shores. People were celebrating the birth of the Dominion of Canada. Speeches proclaimed the new nation's praises and parades heralded the country's birth. A northern lights of fireworks exploded in the skies.

Not everyone celebrated. In Nova Scotia flags were flown at half-mast as if a death had occurred. One newspaper carried an obituary: *Died! Last night at twelve o'clock, the free and enlightened Province of Nova Scotia.*

Nevertheless the majority of people regarded the achievement of Confederation as truly remarkable. What the United States had been able to achieve only through the Revolutionary War (1776–1783), Canada had obtained through peaceful negotiations. As you will see in the story that follows, diplomacy, discussion, and compromise were the tools that politicians in British North America had employed to achieve their goal of a federal union.

PREVIEWING THE CHAPTER

In this chapter you will learn about these topics:

- the decisions that were made at the Charlottetown and Québec conferences on Confederation
- how events in the United States influenced Confederation
- how and why the British government supported Confederation
- how the Fenian raids helped supporters of Confederation
- the reactions in the Maritime provinces to Confederation

KEY WORDS

Civil War
the Confederacy
delegates
federal union
Fenians
Manifest Destiny
Maritime union
militia
neutral
per capita grant
secede
the Union

March 1865	April 1865	March 1866	April–June 1866	December 1866	March 1867	July 1867
Voters defeat Tilley in New Brunswick	American Civil War ends	United States ends Reciprocity Treaty	Fenians raid New Brunswick and the Province of Canada	London Conference is held	Queen Victoria signs the British North America Act into law	Dominion of Canada is created

THE TALKS BEGIN

In the summer of 1864 the political leaders of the four Atlantic colonies of British North America wanted to explore the idea of joining in a **Maritime union**. They were arranging to meet for a conference. The leaders of the Great Coalition — George Brown, John A. Macdonald, and George-Étienne Cartier — asked if Canadian representatives could attend the meeting as observers. After some hurried discussions and telegraphs, Charlottetown, the capital of Prince Edward Island, was chosen as the site for a meeting.

There were many issues and concerns to consider before the Canadian **delegates**, the eleven men who were to attend the conference, left for Charlottetown. Would the Great Coalition even last? There were significant political differences among Brown, Macdonald, and Cartier. For example, Brown championed the idea of "rep by pop" whereas Macdonald and Cartier were exceedingly wary of it. There was a major clash of personalities. Macdonald and Brown had not spoken for years. Brown disliked anything to do with Roman Catholicism, while Cartier had been raised a Catholic. Compromise would not be easy.

The Charlottetown Conference

It was the end of August 1864, in Charlottetown. Everyone was excited. All the hotels were packed with visitors. Special steamship excursions arrived with people from as far away as Northern New Brunswick. There had not been as much excitement since the Prince of Wales's visit in 1860. The Slaymaker and Nichols Olympic Circus was performing in town!

In the excitement, the arrival of delegates on the steamship *Queen Victoria* to consider creating a new nation almost went unnoticed. Even Prince Edward Island's government did not seem to take the occasion too seriously. The official greeting committee was made up of one cabinet minister, William Pope. That evening the 15 Maritime delegates invited the Canadians to an evening dinner party at the Lieutenant-Governor's residence.

This painting of the Canadian delegates arriving for the Charlottetown Conference was done in the twentieth century. It shows William Pope rowing to greet the Canadian delegates who are waiting aboard the steamship *Queen Victoria*, which dropped anchor offshore rather than docking.

A written account from the time gives a very different picture of the arrival. Mr Pope was rowed out "in a flat-bottom boat with a barrel of flour in the bow, and two jars of molasses in the stern, and a lusty fisherman as his only companion." Crew from the steamship, led by Pope and the fisher in his flat-bottomed boat, then rowed the 11 Canadian delegates to shore. Then the delegates were driven by horse and carriage to the Colonial Building, the site of the conference and the centre of government for the Island.

QUESTIONING THE EVIDENCE

1. The artist researched his information before painting this picture. What details in the painting match the written account?
2. How would you explain the changes the artist made for his painting?
3. Which do you think is more reliable, the written account or the picture? Explain your answer.
4. How do you think politicians and other people in the news "stage" events today?

George-Étienne Cartier
FROM REBEL TO REFORMER

Any social gathering became livelier when George-Étienne Cartier arrived. The flamboyant politician, who enjoyed good conversation and strong liquor, thrived on the social whirl. He could be counted on to liven up the sometimes dull official functions that punctuated political life in Canada's capital.

Luckily Cartier was a wealthy man who could afford to indulge his taste for society life. Things had not always been this way for him. As a struggling young lawyer, he had taken up arms with the *Patriotes* in 1837. Forced to flee, he had spent a year in hiding before returning to Montréal. The escapade had not harmed his law practice. In Canada East a record as a *Patriote* was a mark of honour that was good for business. And business for Cartier had been good since 1837. His law practice had prospered, especially since the Grand Trunk Railway had hired his firm. With his savings he had bought real estate, which supplied a steady stream of rental income. He had married Hortense Fabre, a young woman from a prosperous family, and the couple had started a family. He had also fulfilled his political ambitions when he was elected to the Legislative Assembly in 1848.

By the 1860s Cartier could afford to turn over the time-consuming details of daily living to an army of hired help. Law clerks and junior partners looked after the day-to-day business of his law practice. An adviser managed his investments. Servants kept his houses in order, and two secretaries helped keep his political life running smoothly.

His personal life was not running so smoothly, though. Cartier's lifestyle did not suit Hortense. A devout Roman Catholic, she was a serious woman who preferred a quiet life and disapproved of her husband's free-spending ways and casual attitude toward religion. As political business kept Cartier away from home more and more, the marriage gradually fell apart. To the delight of gossips in Ottawa and Montréal, Cartier began keeping company with Luce Cuvillier. The daughter of a merchant, Cuvillier shared Cartier's enjoyment of sophisticated conversation and racy French novels. She also wore trousers in the privacy of her home and smoked cheroots, a kind of cigar. This was scandalous behaviour for a woman in the 1860s.

Cartier did not worry about the gossips. Still, he always remained serious about one thing — his commitment to the cause of the French Canadians. The former rebel had come to believe that reform could be achieved peacefully and he worked hard to ensure that this happened.

More people you could research are

George-Étienne Cartier
John Gray
Joseph Howe
Samuel Tilley
Charles Tupper

On the first day of the meetings, September 2, Macdonald and Cartier took centre stage. They had been a team for the past ten years. Each had his own style. Cartier was fiery and passionate; Macdonald was much more low-key. He was not a great formal orator, but his knowledge was impressive, and his personality was outgoing and friendly. He described the powers of the federal government in the system the Canadians had discussed. Then Cartier explained how the provincial governments would protect local interests and concerns. This was very important for the Maritimers. They feared the new Confederation would rob them of their unique heritages, as well as drain them of money.

The Maritimers were impressed. The first day had been a success. After the meeting everyone had an amazing seafood buffet that featured the Island specialities. The evening was spent taking carriage rides in the countryside or boat rides on the bay.

The next day Alexander Galt explained how the central government would take over the debts of the colonies when they joined. He talked about how the federal government would provide **per capita grants**, or payments for every person, every year to the new provinces. The revenues coming in would be divided between federal and provincial governments.

The Conference adjourned. Now the Maritime delegates were the guests of the Canadians. They went out to the *Queen*

Web Connection

http://www.school.mcgrawhill.ca/resources

You can read George Brown's letter to his wife, Anne, describing his arrival at Charlottetown. Go to the web site above, then go to History Resources, then to *Canada: The Story of a Developing Nation* to see where to go next.

Artist Dusan Kadlec, Commissioned by Parks Canada

The painting is an artist's reconstruction of the final evening of celebration by the delegates. Identify Cartier, Macdonald, and Brown. Why did the artist choose to make these men easily recognizable?

Victoria where they were served a sumptuous lunch. The Canadians had brought along cases of champagne to serve their guests. Cartier and Brown made speeches, and soon everyone was talking. Then one of the delegates blurted out, "If any one can show just cause or impediment why the colonies should not be united in matrimonial alliance, let him express it or for ever hold his peace." No objection was raised. The delegates continued to enjoy their newfound friendship at another dinner party hosted that evening in their honour.

On Monday, September 5, Brown rose to speak. He said the federal Parliament would be modelled on the British system. He then talked about provincial governments, and how judges would be chosen. His presentation took the whole day.

On September 7, the Maritime delegates met behind closed doors. They discussed the possibility of three Maritime provinces uniting into one province to be called Acadia. Prince Edward Island refused to give up its independent legislature, which killed any hope of Maritime union. The Maritime delegates then decided to support a union with the Province of Canada if the terms were acceptable. Here was a major breakthrough. They

The delegates to the Charlottetown Conference. Macdonald is seated in the centre on the steps. Cartier stands to his right, facing Brown. In group photographs where do you normally find the more important people? Why? Working with a partner, discuss what elements in this photograph make it a historical treasure.

had all agreed upon the principle of a **federal union**. They would continue their discussions in Québec City.

The final event of the Conference was a grand ball. The delegates partied all night and then sat down to breakfast on the *Queen Victoria* as it steamed its way for Pictou on the mainland. All delegates went on together to Halifax and Saint John. There they explained at public meetings what they had in mind. Of the trip, Brown said, "We have got on very amicably — we Canadians — wonderfully so.... Our expedition has been all and more than we could have hoped."

The Story So Far . . .

1 What decisions did the delegates make at Charlottetown?

2 What evidence is there that people did not think of the Charlottetown Conference as an important event at the time?

3 The delegates probably spent more time entertaining one another than in formal discussions. What role do you think the social events played in the outcome of the Conference? Explain your answer. Do you think social events play the same role today, either in politics or in business? Why or why not?

4 Why do you think the Maritime delegates shelved the topic of Maritime union in favour of a larger federal union after listening to the politicians from Canada speak?

THE UNITED STATES: A NATION DIVIDED

While the delegates in Charlottetown were considering federal union, the **Civil War** was raging in the United States. This war was between the Southern states, **the Confederacy**, and the Northern states, **the Union**.

British North Americans were divided in their views over the Civil War. The majority of the estimated 40 000 to 50 000 British North American volunteer soldiers fought for the Union side because of their hatred for slavery. However, public opinion and most newspapers tended to support the Confederacy.

Snapshot

Manifest Destiny

Over the years, many Americans had come to believe that it was inevitable and right that the United States should take over all of North America. This concept was known as "**Manifest Destiny**." Through wars, threats, and treaties the United States had already taken over the southern half of the continent. As US Secretary of State William Seward preached, "Nature designs that this whole continent... shall be sooner or later within the magic circle of the American Union." It was not surprising that, as the Civil War wore on, some American politicians said the time was ripe to take over the rest of North America. It would be easy for Union troops to march north and invade Canada and the Maritimes.

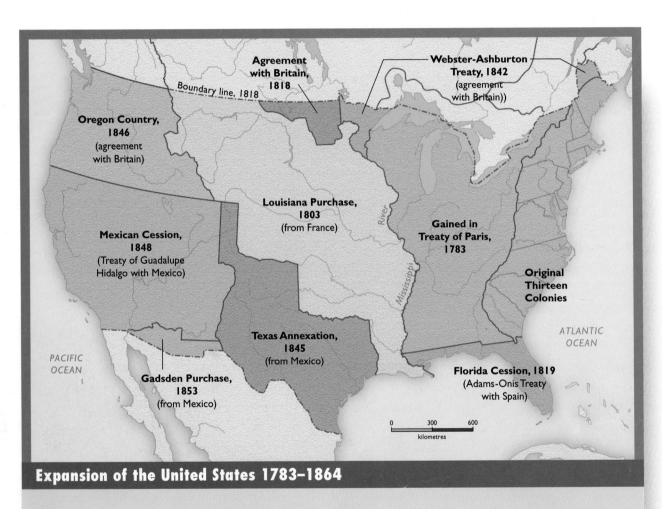

Expansion of the United States 1783–1864

1   Design a time line to show the expansion of the United States from 1783 to 1853.

2   a) Work with a partner and research *one* of the territorial acquisitions shown on the map. Present the results of your findings to the rest of the class.

   b) After the presentations, examine how the United States acquired most of its land. How might that knowledge influence the delegates at Québec City?

The colonies followed the diplomatic lead of Britain, which unoffically supported the Confederacy. There was also the feeling that, if the South lost, British North America could be invaded by the strong army of the Northern states. After all, the Americans had tried to take over the British colonies in the American Revolution of 1776 and during the War of 1812. In the words of Macdonald, "The Americans are now a warlike people. They have large armies, a powerful navy... [and] an unlimited supply of warlike munitions... We ...must put our country in a state of... preparation. We must unite." Confederation would be a powerful defence against the forces of Manifest Destiny.

The *Trent* Incident

Britain and her colonies in North America were officially **neutral**, which means they were not supposed to take sides during the American Civil War. However, there were incidents during the war that could have drawn them into conflict with the North.

In November of 1861, two Southern agents were on their way to Britain to see if the British would recognize the Confederacy as a new country. As the *Trent*, a British steamer, entered the open waters of the Gulf of Mexico, a Union warship seized it. The agents and the documents they were carrying were removed. When the purpose of the agents' trip to Britain was made public in the United States, people wanted Union troops to invade Britain's North American colonies. In response Britain sent over 10 000 troops to guard the Province of Canada's borders against a possible attack. The troops had to make most of the trip from Saint John, New Brunswick, to Canada by sled in the middle of winter, since there was no railway line between the Maritimes and Canada.

The invasion never came and the two agents were eventually released. However, the experiences of the British troops clearly showed the poor state of the colonies' defences. Should the American generals and politicians ever decide to attack British North America, they would have few problems in taking over. What was to be done?

British troops travelling by sleigh to the Province of Canada in 1862. The St. Lawrence River was frozen, so the troops had to travel overland.

The St. Albans raid may have speeded up the Americans' decision to end the 1854 Reciprocity Treaty with Canada and the Maritime colonies. The Americans believed that the colonies benefited much more from the agreement than they did. They wanted the treaty cancelled, believing that it would economically cripple British North America. In the spring of 1866 the United States cancelled the agreement.

Web Connection

http://www.school.mcgrawhill.ca/resources

Go to the web site above to find more information about the *Trent* affair and the St. Albans raid. Go to History Resources, then to *Canada: The Story of a Developing Nation* to see where to go next.

The St. Albans Raid

In November 1863 Southern agents based in Canada started to make lightening raids across the border into the United States. They wanted Union troops to be moved north to defend the border. Perhaps they could cause a crisis that would bring Britain into the war on the side of the Confederacy.

The most famous and dangerous of these raids took place on October 19, 1864, at the time of the Québec Conference. Led by Lieutenant Bennett Young, 21 Confederate soldiers, dressed in civilian clothes, crossed into Vermont. They took possession of St. Albans, robbed the town's banks of $200 000, and killed a person. The raiders fled back over the border into Canada East but were pursued and captured by a posse from Vermont. The captors were then forced to turn the raiders over to the Canadian **militia**, the local troops.

When the raiders were brought to trial, the judge released them because they had done nothing wrong in the eyes of Canadian law. The Americans were furious. The *New York Times* published an article boasting, "We [meaning the Northern forces] were never in better condition for a war with England" on the battlefields of Canada. General Dix of the Union army even told his officers to "pursue any other raiders right into Canada..." and return them "for trial under martial law."

The St. Albans raid played a major role in the Confederation discussions because of its timing. It pointed out the very real threat that the United States posed, and the need for union to improve defences.

The Story So Far . . .

1 Explain Manifest Destiny. To what extent do you think that it posed a real threat to British North America?

2 Could the *Trent* incident have brought Britain into the Civil War? Why or why not?

3 "Timing is everything; in history and in life." Explain why this statement is true as far as the St. Albans raid is concerned. Can you think of important incidents in your own life in which timing played a crucial role?

THE QUÉBEC CONFERENCE

The Maritime delegation arrived in Québec City on October 9. The party of 33 included five wives and nine daughters, who came to enjoy the company, sights, and shopping. While the delegates worked hard during the day, they were wined and dined in the evening. There were several official receptions and balls. A Bachelors' Ball was held to introduce the daughters to the genteel society of the capital.

At Charlottetown the delegates had achieved agreement on the idea of federal union. At the Québec Conference they had to work out the details of the union.

Sir Étienne-Paschal Taché, the premier of the Province of Canada, chaired the conference. However, John A. Macdonald directed the proceedings. He personally wrote most of the 72 Resolutions, which spelled out the details of how the new nation would be governed. They would form the backbone of Canada's first Constitution, the British North America Act, which came to be known as the BNA Act. Macdonald described his crucial role in a letter sent to a friend at the time: "Not one man... has the slightest idea of constitution making. Whatever is good or ill in the Constitution is mine."

Three important decisions were made about the new Constitution.

- The country would have a parliamentary system of government. Elected members of Parliament would sit in the Lower House, the House of Commons. Members of the Upper House, to be called the Senate, would be appointed.

This is Québec City as it would have appeared to the delegates. To the right is Laval University, where the delegates were entertained.

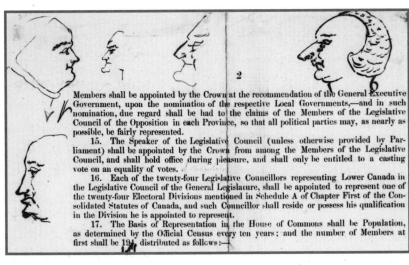

Members shall be appointed by the Crown at the recommendation of the General Executive Government, upon the nomination of the respective Local Governments,—and in such nomination, due regard shall be had to the claims of the Members of the Legislative Council of the Opposition in each Province, so that all political parties may, as nearly as possible, be fairly represented.

15. The Speaker of the Legislative Council (unless otherwise provided by Parliament) shall be appointed by the Crown from among the Members of the Legislative Council, and shall hold office during pleasure, and shall only be entitled to a casting vote on an equality of votes.

16. Each of the twenty-four Legislative Councillors representing Lower Canada in the Legislative Council of the General Legislature, shall be appointed to represent one of the twenty-four Electoral Divisions mentioned in Schedule A of Chapter First of the Consolidated Statutes of Canada, and such Councillor shall reside or possess his qualification in the Division he is appointed to represent.

17. The Basis of Representation in the House of Commons shall be Population, as determined by the Official Census every ten years; and the number of Members at first shall be 194, distributed as follows:—

Macdonald drew these caricatures on one of his draft pages of the Constitution during the Québec discussions.

- The ties to Britain and to the British monarch would remain.
- The state would be a federal union, with a federal or central government to look after larger national issues, and provincial governments to look after local issues.

The delegates wanted to make sure the federal government was strong and would be able to dominate the provinces. They had only to look to the United States to see what could happen when the states had too much power. The federal government in Washington had relatively fewer powers under the American Constitution, and the result had been the Civil War. This is why the delegates limited the powers of the provinces. Cartier knew that several of these, such as power to make decisions on education, civil law, property, and language, were crucial for *la survivance* in Canada East. The provinces could also only impose direct taxes, such as a sales tax or fees for services. Provinces had no right to try to change the Constitution, or to **secede** from, or leave, the new nation.

Some of the Powers of the Federal Government in the BNA Act

- 37 specific powers dealing with important areas such as defence, trade, currency, criminal law, and justice

- Complete control to make laws to promote "the peace, order, and good government" of the new nation

- Unlimited taxing power

- The power to cancel or overrule any provincial law that the central government decided was against the best interests of the country

- The power to appoint provincial officials such as judges and Lieutenant-Governors

The delegates spent a great deal of time deciding on the role of the Senate, and how its members would be chosen. Each of the three regions — Canada East, Canada West, and the Maritimes — was to have 24 senators. Members were to be appointed by the Governor General on the advice of the Prime Minister.

The number of elected members in the House of Commons was to be based on population. Canada East, now to be called Québec, was to have 65 seats in the House of Commons, and all other provinces were to have seats based on their population in comparison with Québec's.

Other decisions were made. The delegates wanted Rupert's Land, Vancouver Island, and British Columbia in the Confederation at some future date. They could foresee a country that would reach "A Mari usque ad Mare"—from sea to sea. They also agreed to build the Intercolonial Railway to link the Maritimes to the Province of Canada.

The Québec Conference ended on October 27. In little more than two weeks, the delegates had agreed on a Constitution for the new country and union between the Maritimes and Canada. George Brown scribbled a note of triumph to his wife. "All right! Conference through at six o'clock this evening — Constitution adopted — a most credible document." Now the delegates had to return home with the proposals and convince their legislative assemblies to approve the 72 Resolutions.

Reflections

You are a journalist covering either the Québec Conference or Charlottetown Conference. You are either to write an editorial, a news story for a broadsheet, or prepare a television newscast on the Conference. Include some personal interviews with key politicians and the wives and daughters who accompanied the delegates.

The Story So Far . . .

1 a) What was the main purpose of the Québec Conference?
   b) How was this different from the purpose of the Charlottetown Conference?
   c) Is it possible to say that one conference was more important than the other? Explain your answer.

2 In what ways did the Civil War in the United States affect the delegate's decisions?

3 What was the main difference between how members for the Senate and members for the House of Commons were chosen. Why do you think the delegates wanted this difference?

Emma Lajeunesse
PRIMA DONNA IN THE WINGS

July 9, 1865, was a bittersweet day for 17-year-old Marie-Louise-Cécile-Emma Lajeunesse. The young singer was eager to stretch her musical wings in Albany, New York, but she was also sad to be leaving Sacré-Coeur Convent. It was the only home she had known for the past eight years.

In 1857, a year after her mother's death, Emma's father, a professional musician, had become the music master at the convent on Montréal Island. Joseph Lajeunesse's job meant that Emma and her younger sister could be educated at the convent. It was the only way he could afford to educate his daughters. Educating his son had already stretched his budget to the breaking point.

Like her classmates, Emma studied subjects like writing, English and French grammar, arithmetic, history, "polite literature," rhetoric and logic, geography, natural philosophy, natural history, chemistry, and botany. As well she learned other skills considered essential for well-educated young ladies — plain and fancy needlework, domestic economy, embroidery, and lacework.

Emma also spent four hours a day practising the piano and singing. It was a gruelling schedule, but her father insisted on it. His daughter had an exceptional singing voice. A soprano, Emma often sang at special events at the convent. The highlight of her musical life so far had occurred when she was just 13 years old. She had performed at a gala concert staged in Montréal to honour the visit of Albert Edward, the Prince of Wales.

If Emma was to have a musical career she would need to train in Europe. Her father could not afford this. Hoping to raise the money, he had organized a concert in Montréal. Although the critics praised Emma's performance, people stayed away. A career as a professional singer was not considered proper for a young lady. Discouraged, the family decided to move to Albany, the capital of New York State. They hoped attitudes would be different there.

Albany residents were wildly enthusiastic about the talented singer. Three years later, they presented her with the money she needed to study in Europe.

There Emma changed her last name to Albani. One of her teachers suggested the name, which belonged to an Italian noble family. He thought it had a more romantic ring than Lajeunesse. Remembering the kindness of the citizens of Albany, Emma was delighted with the idea.

As Emma Albani, the singer would become the first Canadian-born artist to win international acclaim. For more than 40 years she would perform before adoring audiences in concert halls and opera houses throughout Europe and North America.

More people you could research are

Isabella Crawford

Louis-Honoré Fréchette

Emma Lajeunesse

Lucius O'Brien

Anna Swan

THE CONFEDERATION DEBATES

In the Province of Canada the leaders of the Great Coalition spoke in favour of Confederation. The opposition came from Le Parti Rouge and some independent members. They argued that French Canadians in Québec would always be a minority in the new federal House of Commons. Members in other provinces, by acting and voting together, could outnumber the French-Canadian members. Confederation could threaten the French-Canadian way of life.

Supporters of Confederation said the provincial government would help to protect *la survivance*. Cartier saw the new federation as a way of promoting better understanding and co-operation. French Canadians would now have their own province, and they could still work together with the other groups as citizens of this new country.

Supporters Speak Up for Confederation

- We can have a country that will, in time, "extend from the Atlantic to the Pacific."
- We can create a country to "bring to our shores a stream of immigration."
- We can "develop ... the great natural resources... of the northern half of the American continent."
- We cannot "go back to the chronic, sectional hostility...[between] the people of Upper Canada and Lower Canada."
- In the event of war [with the United States] "we can defend [our]selves better."
- We can look forward to having a combined population of "very close to four millions of souls."
- A fresh outlet for our commerce will be opened... We can expect trade barriers among the colonies to fall and the "opening up of the markets of all the provinces."
- We can expect this new union to "inspire new confidence in our stability" from outside investors and "draw capital to our shores."
- We can expect to be the "third largest maritime state of the world."

On March 11, 1865, the vote was taken. The 72 Resolutions passed, with 91 members for, and 33 against the motion. The vote among the French-Canadian members, 27 for, and 21 against, showed French Canadians were deeply divided over joining Confederation.

The Story So Far . . .

1 In your opinion what were the three best reasons for supporting Confederation if you were
   a) French Canadian in Canada East?
   b) English Canadian in Canada West?

2 Imagine that you are one of the delegates attending the Confederation debates. Write and deliver a speech outlining your position regarding the proposed Confederation.

3 Who do you believe took the greatest risk by supporting Confederation? Why?

4 French-Canadian politicians were divided in their opinions about the effect Confederation would have on the survival of the French–Canadian culture. Who do you think was right? Why?

Ottawa in 1866

Edmund and Fanny Meredith
RELUCTANT RESIDENTS OF THE NEW CAPITAL

When Edmund and Fanny Meredith arrived in Ottawa in the fall of 1865, the stench was already unbearable. The smell of raw sewage hung over Canada's new capital, which had no system for getting rid of waste. The Merediths had not wanted to leave Québec City. Life in the backwoods capital was rough and raw compared with the comforts of Québec. The Parliament buildings were still under construction. When it rained, the unpaved streets with their wooden sidewalks became muddy quagmires. Piles of lumber and mounds of sawdust were everywhere, reminders that the city was still a thriving lumber town.

As a senior civil servant, Meredith had had little choice about moving. His job depended on it. "The more I see of Ottawa, the more do I dislike and detest it," Meredith wrote in his diary. Meredith's feelings were shared by many of the other civil servants who were flooding into the city at the same time. Their arrival had caused a housing shortage. Builders could not keep up with the demand for homes. Fortunately the Merediths managed to find a small house for themselves, their four children, and their dog, Rab.

As well, there was a servant shortage. The Merediths' three servants had come with the family from Québec, but they disliked the hardships of Ottawa life and soon returned home. One of the chief hardships was the lack of running water. Twice a week, a delivery cart went door-to-door, selling casks of water. With no running water, it was hard to keep clean. Fire was a constant worry. If a house caught fire, firefighters were often helpless. Even when the city's two hook-and-ladder wagons arrived on the scene, they could do nothing until the delivery carts arrived with water.

Families who wanted fresh milk kept a cow in their yard. Many households also kept horses, pigs, and chickens. There was no garbage collection. Even the most carefully kept homes were often infested with flies and rats. The Merediths worried constantly about disease — and their worries were well-founded. In 1868 their infant son Clarence died of dysentery, a disease caused by unsanitary conditions.

Because life in Ottawa was so uncomfortable, many people believed that the politicians would soon choose a different capital. "I believe now that within five years, Ottawa will have ceased to be the capital ...," wrote Meredith. This prediction proved to be nothing more than wishful thinking. As the city matured, conditions improved and people found that life there could be enjoyable. Still, when Meredith retired, his family had few regrets about packing up and moving to Toronto.

More people you could research are

Charles Baillairgé

Sarah Agnes Bernard

John W. Dawson

Thomas Fuller

Thomas C. Keefer

Edmund and Fanny Meredith

Confederation and the Maritimes

The Maritime delegates returned from Québec City deeply divided over Confederation. The premier of Prince Edward Island, John Gray, was in favour of Confederation, but other Islanders were very upset after the Québec Conference. They thought it was an insult that the Island would receive only five seats in the proposed House of Commons. Why bother with Confederation when there were so few benefits? An election was held in December 1865 and an anti-Confederation party won. Confederation's fate was sealed, at least for now. Prince Edward Island would not be part of Confederation.

Many Newfoundlanders had similar doubts about joining Confederation. An organized opposition circulated a number of rumours: taxes would be increased to pay for Canada's debts; the tax money would benefit the Canadas as they used it to open up the West; Newfoundlanders would be forced to fight for Canada; and their fishers would be forced to serve in the new navy. The decision could wait until an election was held.

The premiers of Nova Scotia and New Brunswick, Charles Tupper and Samuel Tilley, were strong supporters of Confederation. They believed it would promote their economies and protect their borders. The problem for both men was that there was strong, organized opposition in their provinces.

In Nova Scotia Joseph Howe, the former premier and a popular politician, led the anti-Confederation forces. In his newspaper he termed the proposed union, "Confederation-Botheration." Howe believed Confederation would mean higher tariffs and import taxes, so that manufactured goods coming into Nova Scotia would cost more. As well the province would lose its trading link with the New England states. He thought the grant of $0.80 per capita was an insult. "We are," he complained, "being bought for the price of a sheep." He accused the Canadian politicians of trying to use the plan of Confederation to solve their problems. Faced with this opposition, Tupper did not bring the 72 Resolutions up for debate in the Nova Scotia legislature. He decided to wait to see what would happen in New Brunswick.

The population of New Brunswick was uncertain about Confederation. Some agreed with Tilley and saw Confederation as the key to New Brunswick's progress. The Intercolonial Railway would open up new markets for its natural resources. New Brunswick would no longer be a small and isolated colony but part of a great nation whose future was assured. Others thought Confederation spelled disaster for the colony. There

Top: Joseph Howe in later life. He was mainly self-educated, but by the age of 24 he was already publishing a newspaper.
Bottom: Charles Tupper of Nova Scotia went on to become the Prime Minister of Canada in 1896. He served only ten weeks before he was defeated in an election.

would be higher tariffs on goods. There was no guarantee the Canadians would keep their promise about building the railway. It would make better sense to build a railway south to the United States where the market was ten times as large. New Brunswick did not need Canada.

In March 1865 Tilley called an election on the issue of Confederation. He lost to the anti-Confederation forces led by Albert J. Smith. With this defeat it seemed that Confederation was a dead issue. Confederation could not exist if there was no link through New Brunswick.

The Story So Far . . .

1 Why did Tupper decide to delay the debate about Confederation?
2 From the point of view of the Great Coalition, which Maritime province had to join them if Confederation was to succeed? Explain your answer.
3 Copy and complete the chart below into your notebook.

Samuel Tilley was 13 years old when he left school to learn to be a pharmacist. Eventually he became the Lieutenant-Governor of New Brunswick.

Colony	Arguments for Confederation	Arguments against Confederation
Prince Edward Island		
Newfoundland		
New Brunswick		
Nova Scotia		

Britain and Confederation

The British government fully supported the plan of Confederation so it was not pleased with the response of the Maritime colonies. All the Lieutenant-Governors of the colonies were told to promote Confederation.

In New Brunswick, Smith wanted to build a railway to the state of Maine to tap into the rich American markets. When he tried to get financial backing in Britain, the British government told the banks not to help. The only railway the banks were to finance was the proposed Intercolonial Railway, which was part of the Confederation package. As well the United States

The Lieutenant-Governor of New Brunswick, Arthur Gordon, on a canoe trip. He is wearing the top hat. The Colonial Office in Britain ordered him to promote Confederation.

government was not interested in making any special trade deals with New Brunswick or Nova Scotia to replace the Reciprocity Treaty. Cut off from the rich US market, many Maritimers began to have second thoughts about Confederation.

In April 1866 the Lieutenant-Governor forced Smith's government to resign. He then asked Tilley to lead the government. The chances of achieving Confederation were starting to improve. The final push came from a most unlikely band of disorganized radicals called the Fenians.

The Fenians: Outside Assistance

Many of the Irish who came to North America in the Great Migration during the 1840s and 1850s wanted to free Ireland from British rule. One of the secret societies formed to work for this cause was the Irish Republican Brotherhood, or the **Fenians**.

With the end of the American Civil War in the spring of 1865, the Fenians planned to attack the British colonies in North America. Britain would have to take troops out of Ireland to deal with the Fenians. Their Irish brothers in the homeland could then rise up against the hated English and free Ireland.

In January and February of 1866, the Fenians held rallies in towns along the border between the United States and the Canadas. The government of Canada prepared for invasion. They called out 10 000 militia volunteers to guard the frontier.

In April 1866 a group of 500 Fenians set out from Maine to capture Campobello Island in New Brunswick. Only five men managed to cross the border. They threatened an official and captured a Union Jack, the British flag, but withdrew without firing a shot when 5000 Canadian militia and British regulars showed up. The Fenians' first raid had failed miserably.

A second surprise attack, launched from Buffalo, New York, started out more successfully. Although the Fenians scored a victory at the Battle of Ridgeway, this raid floundered too. The Fenians retreated. With 20 000 Canadian militia converging on the area, the raiders knew that they would soon be badly outnumbered.

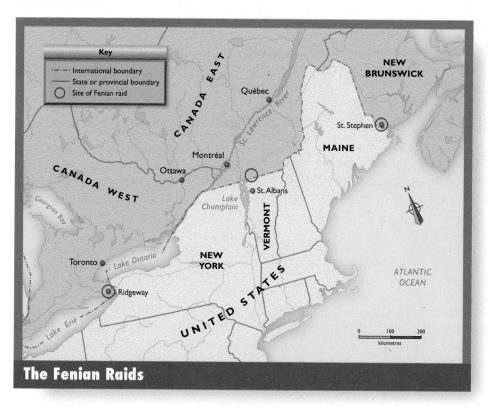

The Fenian Raids

Fenian Marching Song

We are the Fenian Brotherhood,
  skilled in the arts of war,

And we're going to fight for Ireland,
  the land that we adore,

Many battles we have won, along
  with the boys in blue

And we'll go and capture Canada for
  we've nothing else to do.

On May 31, 1866, about 800 Fenians sailed across the Niagara River and easily captured the village of Fort Erie. The news sent the country into a panic. Quickly, militia units grabbed their weapons and started marching to the area.

There, a militia detachment commanded by Lieutenant-Colonel Alfred Booker tried to stop the advance at the village of Ridgeway, about 10 km west of Fort Erie.

Unfortunately, Booker's ill-trained soldiers were no match for the Fenians, many of whom were battle-hardened American Civil War veterans. When the battle was over, nine Canadians lay dead and 38 had been wounded.

This picture shows an artist's idea of the Battle of Ridgeway on June 2, 1866. On the left are the Fenians in their green uniforms, armed with fixed bayonets, and advancing. On the right are the British and Canadian troops lined up in their traditional battle formation. Troops in the front line are firing at the enemy. They will kneel down and the line behind will step forward, take their place, lift their muskets to their shoulders, aim, and fire. You can see two soldiers in the front right priming their muskets to ready them for firing.

Imagine you are in this battle, either with the Fenians or the British and Canadian troops. The noise, the fear, and the excitement make everything a blur, but you want to remember the event to tell your family and friends. What do you hear? What is behind you? What is in front? Are you excited? Frightened? Make some notes of what you will put in your account when you come to write it.

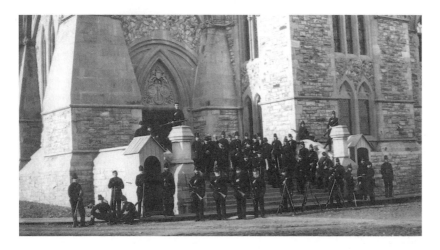

Less than a week later about 1000 Fenians crossed into Canada East and looted villages. Two days later, as Canadian militia rushed to defend the territory, the raiders fled back to the United States. This incident marked the last serious attempt by the Fenians to carry out their plan of holding Canada to ransom for Irish independence.

The Fenians helped the cause of Confederation by making people aware of the danger of invasion from their powerful neighbour. A common, united defence was necessary as the British government had made it clear that it could not be counted on to defend the colonies.

In Nova Scotia Charles Tupper and his pro-Confederation forces won the election in June 1866. Confederation was revived, thanks to the pressures from Britain, the end of the Reciprocity Treaty, and the threat of invasion by the Fenians. Delegates from Canada, New Brunswick, and Nova Scotia set off to London to ask Britain to create the new nation of Canada.

Snippet

On Guard

When word of a possible Fenian invasion reached Ottawa, the city was thrown into turmoil. People talked of little else as they prepared to defend the capital. Militia units were created and soldiers were everywhere. Like many of his fellow civil servants, Edmund Meredith joined a unit called the Civil Service Rifle Regiment. Members of the regiment wore their uniforms to work so that they could leave their desks every day at 9 a.m. and again at 4 p.m. to take part in drills.

The Story So Far . . .

1   How did Britain push the colonies toward Confederation?
2   Why did Smith want New Brunswick linked to the United States?
3   a) What did the Fenians want and how did they propose going about it?
    b) How did the Fenians influence the people in the British colonies?
4   Imagine you are Macdonald or one of the supporters of Confederation. Prepare a campaign poster, campaign literature, or speech using the Fenian raids as an argument for Confederation.

Irish-born Father of Confederation, Thomas D'Arcy McGee, was a fierce opponent of the Fenians. He was assassinated by Patrick Whelan, a suspected Fenian, in April 1868. This is D'Arcy McGee's funeral procession.

Snippet

Wedding Bells

John A. Macdonald had more than constitutional issues on his mind while he was in London. While strolling on Bond Street one day, he met Susan Agnes Bernard, the sister of his former private secretary. The two renewed their acquaintance. Macdonald, who had been a widower for nine years, proposed a few weeks later. In February 1867, while still in London, Macdonald and Bernard were married. Jessie McDougall and Emma Tupper, daughters of two other delegates to the London Conference, were bridesmaids.

The London Conference

The Canadian delegates arrived in London on November 6, 1866. George Brown was not among them. He had declined the Governor General's invitation and resigned from the government. "I do feel so happy to think of it," Brown commented. "I can rejoice at my freedom … from parliamentary responsibilities."

In London, John A. Macdonald was everyone's choice to chair the Conference. The delegates went over each of the 72 Resolutions one more time to ensure that there was complete agreement among all the colonies. A few minor changes and an agreement to pay a little more money to the Maritimes were made. The most excitement took place outside the Conference. Macdonald was reading late one night when his bedclothes and covers caught on fire. His hair was singed and one arm badly burned, but he was back chairing the Conference the next morning.

Joseph Howe had come to London with petitions from Nova Scotians in an effort to break up the Conference. He could not change the opinions of the British members of Parliament.

The one remaining task for the delegates was to decide on the name for the new nation. The popular choice was the "Kingdom of Canada," but there was a problem. Lord Derby, the British Minister of Foreign Affairs "feared the name would wound the sensibilities of the Yankees" as Macdonald explained it afterward. Samuel Tilley came to the rescue. He remembered the lines from Psalm 72: "He shall have dominion also from sea to sea, and from the river unto the ends of the earth." So, on March 29, 1867, after it passed both houses of the British

Parliament with no major changes, Queen Victoria signed the British North America Act uniting Canada, New Brunswick, and Nova Scotia in the new Dominion of Canada.

The original coat of arms for the Dominion was made up of the coats of arms for Canada East, Canada West, Nova Scotia, and New Brunswick.

Snippet

Choosing a Name

As the idea of Confederation took hold, it seemed that everyone had an opinion about what to name the new country. In 1864 the Toronto *Globe* published these suggestions: Tuponia, Albinora, Mesopelagia, British Efisga, Cabotia, and Transylvania.

Few people took these names seriously. Thomas D'Arcy McGee summed up the reaction when he said, "How would you like to wake up one morning and learn that you were not a Canadian but a Tuponian?"

The Story So Far . . .

1 You are Joseph Howe. Write a statement that you will read to the British Members of Parliament to try to get them to support your position on Confederation.

2 George Brown did not choose to go to the London Conference. What can you learn about him from this decision?

3 If the delegates had not agreed on the name "Dominion of Canada," what name would you have suggested for the new country?

4 Design a poster either supporting or opposing Confederation. Give careful thought to your use of colour and words.

SUM IT UP!

The path to Confederation between 1864 and 1867 started as a search for a way out of the political deadlock in the Province of Canada. It led to the Charlottetown Conference, where delegates from the Canadas and the Maritime colonies agreed in principle to a federal union. At the Québec Conference details of the new union were worked out in the form of the 72 Resolutions. However, the government in Prince Edward Island decided not to accept the resolutions. There were grave concerns in Nova Scotia, and in New Brunswick where the pro-Confederation forces lost an election on the issue. Confederation then appeared to be impossible to reach.

At this point, the British government signalled its support of Confederation. It told the Lieutenant-Governors to promote the idea. The ending of the American Civil War brought the renewed threat of invasion from the United States. The Fenian raids and the cancellation of the Reciprocity Treaty only added to that threat. In Nova Scotia and New Brunswick, government leaders accepted the idea of Confederation.

The final destination was reached through a unique combination of the persistence and vision of some remarkable individuals, support and encouragement from Britain, and perceived threats from the United States. On July 1, 1867, the new nation was officially declared. The new Dominion of Canada could now celebrate!

THINKING ABOUT YOUR LEARNING

1 Why did Macdonald, Cartier, and Brown try to make the Great Coalition work? What obstacles and challenges made it difficult?

2 Why do historians consider the Charlottetown Conference important?

3 What did the delegates to the Québec Conference decide about the powers of the federal and provincial governments? Was it a wise decision? What caused many of the delegates to arrive at that decision about the distribution of political power?

4 Do you think Confederation would have happened without the influence of the Americans and the British? Explain your answer.

5 Explain why "timing" was crucial as it relates to the Fenians. Name another historical instance when timing was very important.

6 In achieving some form of consensus in this kind of constitutional conference setting, which factor — personality, argument and evidence, or listening and speaking — is most important? Explain your answer.

APPLYING YOUR LEARNING

1. Organize your class into a constitutional conference. Make a Constitution for your school. Outline the rights and responsibilites of students, teachers, principal, vice-principal, and support staff.

2. You are one of the volunteers on the train going to fight against the Fenian raiders. You are writing a farewell letter to your family— just in case you are killed. You want to explain why you decided to fight the Fenians, your fears, your wishes, and your thoughts about life.

3. Invite a local politician to your class to talk about how the powers of the provincial governments have changed since 1867.

4. Select five or six key events from this chapter and write newspaper headlines for them.

5. Are there any "lessons" from Confederation that politicians of our time should understand? Identify and explain them.

6. Creatively convey what your position on Confederation would have been had you been a Maritimer in the 1860s. You could choose a song, a poem, a skit, an advertising poster, or another form.

USING KEY WORDS

Copy the following sentences into your notebook, filling in the blanks with words chosen from the Key Words list at the beginning of this chapter.

1. After the Charlottetown Conference Nova Scotia, New Brunswick, and Prince Edward Island decided not to join in a _____ _____.

2. Part of the Confederation agreement was that the federal government would pay a ___ _____ _____ to the new provinces.

3. At the Charlottetown Conference the eleven _____ from the Province of Canada and the _____ from the Maritime provinces agreed to explore the idea of a _____ _____.

4. The idea that all of North America would be taken over by the United States was known in that country as _____ _____.

5. The _____ ___ in the United States was a war between the Northern states, known as ___ _____, and the Southern states, known as ___ _____. It started when the Southern states decided to _____.

6. Britain and the British colonies in North America were officially _____ in the Civil War in the United States.

CHAPTER
4

Building Confederation

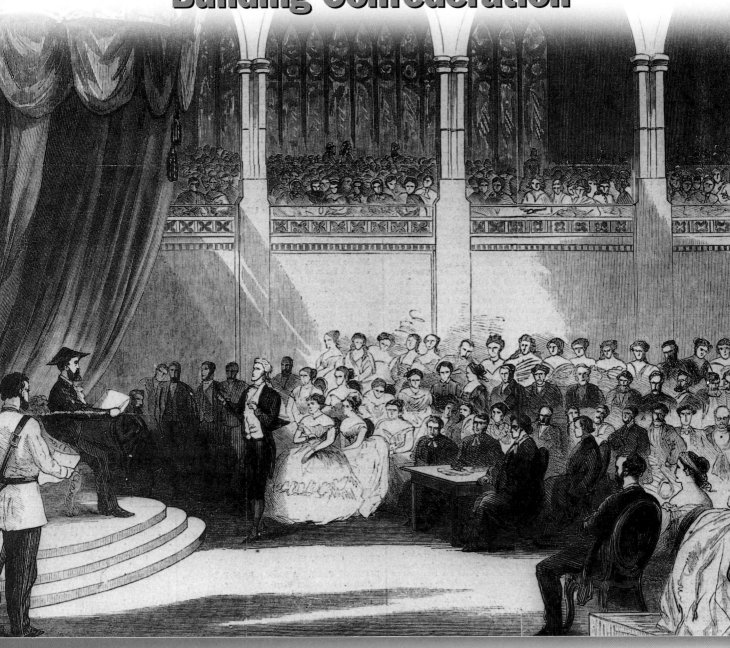

1867

People celebrate
Confederation

1868

Howe accepts Confederation for
Nova Scotia

1869

• Canada buys Rupert's Land
• Newfoundland and Labrador
  reject Confederation

1870

Manitoba joins Confederation

SETTING OUR FOCUS

This is the opening of the first session of the Canadian Parliament after Confederation. Everyone is dressed in fine clothes for this historic occasion. The Governor General is reading a speech describing the plans Prime Minister Macdonald's government has to start building the nation and give it an **identity**.

Identity is an important concept. Many factors, such as your name, your appearance, religion, culture, knowledge, likes and dislikes, make you a unique individual with your own identity. There is no one in the world exactly like you. In much the same way, groups of people, including nations, have their own identity that make them distinctive. History is a part of each country's identity. It provides citizens with a common story about their past, a similar set of myths and heroes, and a shared vision.

As a new nation, Canada's identity began 1867; it continues to grow and change. In this chapter we will look at how the country grew in size as more provinces and territories joined the new nation, and how Sir John A. Macdonald helped shape the early years.

PREVIEWING THE CHAPTER

In this chapter you will learn about these topics:
- **how Nova Scotia tried to separate from the new Confederation**
- **why Newfoundland and Labrador decided not to join Confederation until 1949**
- **how Canada expanded to take in the West**
- **how Canada dealt with Aboriginal Peoples**
- **how Prince Edward Island joined Confederation**
- **how the National Policy shaped Canada's identity**

KEY WORDS

absentee landlords
annexation
cabinet minister
identity
markets
National Policy
Nova Scotia Party
outport settlements
referendums
surveyors
wards

1871	1873	1878	1905	1949
British Columbia joins Confederation	Prince Edward Island joins Confederation	Macdonald wins election on National Policy platform	Provinces of Alberta and Saskatchewan are created	Newfoundland joins Confederation

DECISIONS IN THE ATLANTIC COLONIES

Nova Scotia Wants to Leave!

Nova Scotians did not have an election before they entered Confederation. The supporters of Premier Charles Tupper had passed a motion that agreed to send delegates to the London Conference at a late night session of the legislature. It only passed because most of the opposition members had gone home to bed. Tilley promised Nova Scotians that he would arrange for better terms later, perhaps at the London Conference.

According to the anti-Confederation forces, Tupper had betrayed the people of Nova Scotia when he returned from London. He had sold them out for 80 cents a head, which was the per capita grant. Nova Scotia's economy could be ruined by tariffs — taxes on imported goods that the new federal government could impose. These tariffs would kill their trade with New England.

Joseph Howe led the opposition to Confederation and organized his supporters into the **Nova Scotia Party**. In the election held ten weeks after the Confederation celebrations, his party won 18 of the 19 Nova Scotia seats in the first federal election. A Nova Scotia separatist party was sitting in the House of Commons. In the provincial election of 1868 the Nova Scotia party became the official government, winning 36 of the 38 seats. The voters had spoken very clearly. They wanted to leave Confederation!

In June 1868 Howe went to London again to ask for separation of Nova Scotia from Confederation. Yet again Britain refused. Nova Scotia would have to work with the federal government in Ottawa. Some disillusioned anti-Confederation supporters began to talk about getting the Americans to take over Nova Scotia.

Prime Minister Macdonald understood he must have Howe's support if Confederation were to be accepted in Nova Scotia. He made arrangements to go to Halifax in July 1868. There he met with Howe in secret to talk about arranging better terms for Nova Scotia. Howe knew that his supporters were in an impossible situation. The alternatives of rebellion or joining the United States were unthinkable. After a few months of negotiations, an agreement was made. Nova Scotia would receive more money.

As part of the agreement Howe would be appointed as a **cabinet minister** in Macdonald's government. This meant he

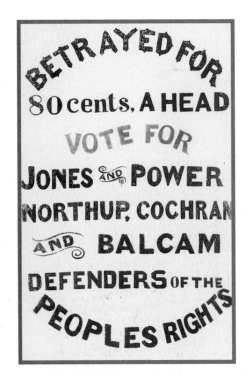

This anti-Confederation banner was made out of a bedsheet and hung in a main street of Halifax in the summer of 1867. What does "Betrayed for 80 cents a head" refer to? What sentiments does the banner appeal to in Nova Scotia?

would be part of the group who made decisions in government. At 65 years of age he had to fight a bitter election campaign to earn a seat in the new House of Commons. It was so hard-fought that he had a physical breakdown and never regained his health. Moreover, some of his old friends were so upset at his turnaround that they would cross the street in Halifax to avoid talking to him. Macdonald had effectively silenced the most vocal and dangerous Maritime critic of Confederation.

Web Connection

http://www.school.mcgrawhill.ca/resources

Go to the web site above and read about Canada's first world champions in a sporting event. Go to History Resources, then to *Canada: The Story of a Developing Nation* to see where to go next.

Halifax in 1870, looking across Halifax Harbour from George's Island.

The Story So Far . . .

1 a) Why did Joseph Howe and his supporters want to opt out of Confederation?

   b) Why do you think Britain was so firm in rejecting Howe's petition?

2 In pairs, write a script that re-enacts the July 1868 meeting between Macdonald and Howe. You might choose to perform your dialogues for the class.

3 Do you think that Howe "sold out" his beloved Nova Scotia or do you think that he obtained the best deal he could? Justify your view with supporting evidence. You might conduct a class debate on the question.

Newfoundland and Labrador Decide

Newfoundlanders had doubts about joining Confederation from the beginning of the discussions in 1864. There was more than the huge stretch of water between the island of Newfoundland and the mainland. Traditions and a way of life set the Rock apart from the rest of the British colonies in North America. The fishing industry was the mainstay. People lived in scattered **outport settlements** nestled around harbours along the rocky shores.

The anti-Confederation song voiced the opposition's fears. Taxes would be increased to pay Canada's debts for its railways, and to cover the cost of opening the Western territories. Newfoundland's sons would be drafted or forced to serve and fight in Canada's defence.

An election was called in 1869 with the decision on Confederation as the issue. Charles Fox Bennett, a 76-year-old merchant and mine owner led the anti-Confederation group. He campaigned along the coast in a small steamer, sailing from outport to outport with his message. He defeated Premier Frederick Carter, winning 21 seats to 9 in the Legislative Assembly. It would take 80 years, a fierce debate, and two **referendums**, or votes by all the people eligible to vote on the question, for Newfoundland to decide to join Canada in 1949.

In 1866 a transatlantic cable was successfully laid between Trinity Bay, Newfoundland, and Valentia, Ireland. This meant that telegraph messages could be sent in minutes across the ocean.

The Evidence Behind the Story

Ye brave Newfoundlanders who plough the
  salt sea,
With hearts like the Eagle so bold and so
  free,
The time is at hand when we'll have to say
If Confederation will carry the day.

Men, hurrah for our own native Isle,
  Newfoundland,
Not a stranger shall hold one inch of her
  strand;
Her face turns to Britain, her Back to the
  Gulf,
Come near at your peril, Canadian Wolf!

Cheap tea and molasses they say they will
  give,
All taxes taken off that the poor man may
  live —
Cheap nails and cheap lumber, our coffins
  to make,
And homespun to mend our old clothes
  when they break.

If they take off all taxes, how then will
  they meet
The heavy expenses on Army and fleet?
Just give them the chance to get into the
  scrap,
They'll show you the trick with pen, ink and
  red tape.

Would you barter the right that your
  fathers have won?
No! let them descend from father to son.
For a few thousand dollars Canadian gold
Don't let it be said that our birthright was
  sold.

This song was popular in Newfoundland and Labrador among people who were against the colony joining Canada.

Read the verses carefully, and discuss the meanings of any words you do not know. *Strand*, for example, is an old English word for the area between the low-water mark and high-water mark along the seashore. You can use a dictionary or exchange ideas to find the meanings.

QUESTIONING THE EVIDENCE

1. **What do the last two lines in the second verse tell you about the anti-Confederates' view of relations with Britain and Canada?**
2. **The third verse uses irony, that is, it says one thing and means another. In your own words, what is the message in the third verse?**
3. **a) Who is meant by "they" in the fourth verse?**
   b) What is the argument against Confederation in this verse?
4. **What feelings of Newfoundlanders does this song appeal to?**
5. **How are the words in this song historical evidence?**
6. **In a few sentences sum up the tone and message in the song. What do you learn about Newfoundlanders' sense of identity from the song?**

WESTWARD EXPANSION

Ten years before Confederation Canada West was looking at the Western plains as an area to settle. By this time, the good farming lands in the Province of Canada had already been settled. The government paid for the 1857–1858 Hind expedition to map the prime farming areas in the prairies and look for possible routes for railways and roads. In 1858 Americans were streaming in thousands to the British territories on the West Coast, looking for gold along the Fraser River Valley and in the mountains. American farmers and loggers were taking over the Sioux lands west of Lake Michigan south of the border. It was only a matter of time before they moved north.

The Hind expedition camping along the Red River, with Métis guides. The expedition took along an official photographer.

The BNA Act had recognized that Canada could stretch from "sea to sea" and included terms for the Western lands to become part of the new nation. In 1867 the Hudson's Bay Company (HBC) still had control of much of the area. The Canadian government reached an agreement with the HBC in 1869. The terms were that the Canadian government would
- pay the HBC shareholders £3 million (about one and a half million dollars);
- grant the HBC thousands of hectares of land around its trading posts;
- give the HBC one twentieth of all the land in the territory.
  In one bold move, Canada had increased its size more than six times.

Manitoba Joins

In 1869 about 12 000 people lived along the Red River Valley in what is now Manitoba, farming, trading, and hunting the few buffalo that were left. Most of these people were Métis. The Canadian government wanted to take possession of the new territories as soon as possible. Macdonald, who usually did not act quickly — his nickname was "Old Tomorrow" — did not waste any time. He did not consult the Métis, the other settlers, or the Aboriginal Peoples before sending out **surveyors** to measure and lay out lots for settlers. The Métis, led by Louis Riel, their fiery and charismatic champion, protested these actions. He claimed that his people were "bartered away like common cattle." As you will read in the following chapter, the Red River Rebellion was short and intense. It ended with the Manitoba Act, which included many of the terms that Riel and the Métis requested. In 1870 Manitoba was created as an officially bilingual province and acquired full provincial status with four members in the House of Commons and two senators.

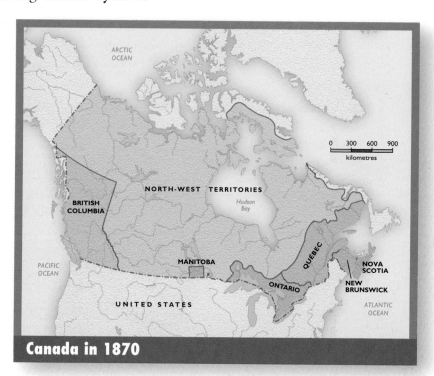

Canada in 1870

The Story So Far . . .

1 Why were Rupert's Land and the Western lands so important to Canada?

2 What do the actions of the Canadian government regarding the Aboriginal Peoples and Métis tell you about the attitudes of the time toward these people?

3 If you were an Aboriginal at this time, what would you think on learning that the HBC had been paid for Rupert's Land? Prepare a speech to deliver to Macdonald to explain your point of view.

No mention was made in the transfer of Rupert's Land of the thousands of people who already lived in the area. No one even knew for sure or bothered to find out how many Aboriginal Peoples or Métis called the area their home. No provision was made for their part in the transfer of the land. A pattern had been set for the way the Canadian government would deal with Aboriginal Peoples. It was assumed that the values, law, and interests of other Canadians would rule in the West. This action of ignoring the Aboriginal Peoples was not surprising. The BNA Act mentioned Aboriginal Peoples only in one section, where their well being was made a federal responsibility. The change that the British North Americans sought for themselves during the first half of the nineteenth century — responsible government — was denied to Aboriginal Peoples. There was no hint that they would be granted equality, partnership, or self-government. Instead, they were made **wards** of the federal government, or people in the care of a guardian. This decision has greatly affected the story of the Aboriginal Peoples in Canada.

A census taker visits a Cree village in 1881. The Canadian government did not know how many Aboriginal Peoples were in the West when they took over Rupert's Land.

British Columbia Joins

Now Canada was bordering British Columbia. The population of the colony in 1869 was a diverse mixture of groups, and, because of the gold rush of the 1860s, there were more Americans there than Canadians. North-south trade between the American states and the British colony was natural. Victoria was closer to San Francisco than to Ottawa. Why would British Columbia choose to join Confederation?

One reason was that the boom times were over. People were leaving. In the gold-rush boom there had been expenses such as roads to be built, and the colony had borrowed money to pay for them. Now the shrinking population could not pay the debt of over $1 million. Half of all the colony's income went to cover the interest payments alone. The government was facing financial ruin.

Some people, particularly merchants, wanted the United States to take over the colony. The American government, however, gave no signals that they were even interested. In 1869 a petition asking for US **annexation** circulated around the parts of the province. It received only 140 signatures. The colony turned to its other major option — joining Canada.

On May 10, 1870, the three delegates sent to Ottawa to negotiate British Columbia's entry into Confederation boarded a ship in Victoria and set sail for San Francisco, California. There, they climbed onto one of the transcontinental trains that had been making regular trips across the United States for a year. After travelling for nearly a month, they reached Ottawa in early June.

A man who called himself Amor De Cosmos, or Lover of the Universe, led the forces in favour of Confederation with Canada. His real name was William Smith, and he came from Nova Scotia. He had worked there as a journalist, and for a time in California as a photographer during the 1849 gold rush. He started a newspaper, the *British Colonist*, and was able to get a number of the colony's newspapers to support entry into Canada. His followers formed the Canadian Party to press for union with Canada.

The issue of Confederation came to a head in the spring of 1870. The motion in the Legislative Assembly to join Canada received unanimous support. A three-man delegation headed off to Ottawa to negotiate the terms.

The delegates got everything they asked for and more. The terms were generous. British Columbia gained provincial status. The colony's debts were to be paid. They were to receive an annual grant and control over most of the public lands. The delegates asked for a wagon road to be built through the mountains. Instead they were promised a railway to be started within two years and built in ten years. Any opposition in the colony to union virtually disappeared and on July 20, 1871, the sixth province was officially welcomed into the fold.

Amor De Cosmos

In 1872 Moodyville, later the site of Vancouver, was already a busy port site for the export of lumber.

The Story So Far . . .

1 Why did Canada want British Columbia to join Confederation?
2 Examine an atlas map that shows landforms in North America. Why did British Columbia want an overland link to Canada?
3 Find out more about Amor De Cosmos, and explain how he influenced events at that time.

Hannah Maynard
THROUGH THE LENS OF HISTORY

Victoria was an outpost when Hannah Maynard arrived there in 1862. Although the port on Vancouver Island boasted 37 brick buildings, Maynard wrote that it was a town of " tents, gullies and swamps and the inhabitants mostly miners." The miners were seeking gold, which had been discovered in the Cariboo. It was gold that drew the family — Hannah, her husband Richard, and their children — to the colony.

Richard, a bootmaker, had already made one successful prospecting trip. Hannah and the children had stayed behind in Belleville, Canada West. This was where she and Richard had settled after emigrating from England. While Richard was away, Hannah had looked after their boot store — and persuaded the operator of the town's photography studio to teach her the new art.

An eager student, she had learned well. When Richard returned home, the couple decided to sell the boot store and resettle in Victoria. There, Richard headed back to the gold fields, while Hannah opened a studio — Mrs. R. Maynard's Photographic Gallery — on the outskirts of town.

In 1863 Richard returned from his prospecting trip. A year later he and Hannah moved the business to a larger building, where they opened a combined boot store and photographic studio. Richard, too, was becoming interested in photography, and Hannah started teaching him how to handle a camera. Soon, the couple closed the boot business to focus on photography. For the next 50 years, the Maynards' studio was a fixture in Victoria. Hannah did most of the studio photography, while Richard travelled throughout British Columbia and beyond to capture outdoor scenes.

In the studio Hannah specialized in photographing people and started experimenting with new techniques. One of these was the "gem," a kind of miniature photographic collage that was popular at the time. Often mounted on rings, pins, or brooches, gems combined several faces in one photograph. While most gems included three or four faces, Hannah took the technique much farther. Her carefully crafted gems included hundreds of faces — all the children she had photographed in a year.

Hannah also experimented with photosculptures, pictures that are manipulated to make people look like statues, and with humorous pictures, often using herself or her children as subjects.

Although Richard died in 1907, Hannah continued operating the studio until she retired in 1912. Many of the Maynards' photographs are now stored in the British Columbia Archives, forming a lasting record of the early history of Canada's Pacific province.

More people you could research are

J. W. Bengough

Ernest Brown

Humphrey Lloyd Hime

Hannah Maynard

William Notman

THE ISLAND RECONSIDERS

The people of Prince Edward Island had rejected six proposals to join the other colonies between 1858 and 1864. After 1867 nothing appeared likely to end their isolation. They had everything they wanted. Reciprocity with the United States brought economic prosperity to the Island's farmers and merchants. They had responsible government after 1854. Why should they join Canada? Their tax monies would be used to open the new lands in the West, which they did not think would bring them any benefits because they were so far away. The financial terms they were offered were not all that attractive, and they regarded the offer of five seats in the new House of Commons as an insult.

Prosperity provides contentment, poverty cries for change. Even though the Americans ended the Reciprocity Treaty in 1866, the Island's farmers and fishers still shipped their produce to the US **markets**. There were even negotiations for an economic union between the Island and the Americans. Those discussions quickly came to an end when this news reached the British. Faced with their disapproval and the continuing economic slump of the 1870s, Confederation looked more and more appealing.

As well, there was the on-going problem of the landownership question. In 1767 the whole island had been divided into 67 parcels of land. These lands had been given to friends of the British government, who did not live on the Island. It was hoped these people would bring over settlers. Instead they became **absentee landlords**, using agents to collect rent payments from tenant farmers, and never visiting the properties. Who was going to buy out these absentee landlords? Britain would not; many of the landowners had friends in the government. The Island did not have the money to pay them. Perhaps the Canadian government would provide the money.

The cost of the Island's railway finally convinced the Islanders to become Canadians. The tidal wave of railway-building mania had reached the Island's shores during the 1870s. In April 1871 the government had approved the construction of a railway from one end of the island to the other. The project was expected to cost $4000 for each 1.6 km. By the summer of 1872 the estimated costs had skyrocketed to $15 000 for each 1.6 km. The Island's debt mushroomed from $250 000 in 1863 to $4 million ten years later.

Snippet

The Secret Ballot

British Columbia spearheaded the introduction of the secret ballot in Canada. Supported by Amor De Cosmos, who had been elected premier of the province, the legislation passed on February 10, 1873. A year later Ontario and the Dominion government did the same. Other provinces, including Prince Edward Island, soon followed suit. Voting in private was not popular in Canada's smallest province, though. In 1879 Prince Edward Island abolished the secret ballot and did not try it again until 1913.

An election campaign in Charlottetown in the late nineteenth century. Who do you think the people on the platform are? What does this picture tell you about people's interest in political events at this time?

What was the government to do? Foreign banks were not going to give loans for such a risky venture. The Island's government was facing bankruptcy and raising taxes to pay off the debt would cripple the economy. Canada was offering a way out of the dilemma. A delegation from the Island went to Ottawa in early 1873. Terms were arranged for Prince Edward Island to join Confederation.

As it turned out, the Islanders did very well. The Canadian government agreed to

- buy out the absentee landlords with a grant of $800 000
- pay the Island's debts and the debts on the railway
- fund a ferry service and telegraph cable to the mainland
- give annual subsidies

There was considerable rejoicing on July 1, 1873, the seventh anniversary of Confederation. Prince Edward Island became the seventh — and smallest — province to join the Dominion.

The Story So Far . . .

1 What were the reasons for the Island's change of heart regarding joining Confederation?
2 Imagine yourself as an Island newspaper editor of the time. Write an editorial either supporting or opposing Confederation.

TERRITORIES INTO PROVINCES

The National Policy

By 1873 the territory of Canada as we know it today was in place, with the exception of Newfoundland and Labrador.

Sir John A. Macdonald was prime minister of the new nation for its first seven years. Then in 1873, a worldwide economic downturn struck. In Canada, businesses went bankrupt, banks failed, farmers could not get good prices for their crops, and thousands lost their jobs. Macdonald had to resign because of a scandal that you will read about in Chapter 6. For five years, the downturn brought the country to a standstill.

In 1878 Macdonald was reelected on a platform called the National Policy. The policy had three parts:
- protection for Canadian industries
- settlement of the West
- completion of the railway to the West

Tariffs were put on goods brought into the country that competed with Canadian-made goods. Canadian-made goods could then sell for the same price or less than American- and British-made goods. As most industries were in Ontario and Québec, the tariffs favoured this part of the country. People moving into the Western plains were expected to buy the farming machinery and other goods that the new industries produced. The railway would link the producers and the market in the West.

The National Policy was in place for decades to come. To the Western farmers it seemed to protect rich industrialists in the East. They would have preferred to buy less expensive American-made goods. In time the policy led to feelings of bitterness in the West.

The Story So Far . . .

1 Imagine you are a Western farmer in 1890. Write a letter to Macdonald to explain how you feel about the National Policy.
2 Why was the railway part of the National Policy?
3 Why do you think Macdonald insisted that the railway be built through Canadian territory even though it cost more than to build part of it through the United States?

John A. Macdonald
LOVING FATHER

When Agnes Macdonald told her husband in 1868 that she was going to have a baby, he was delighted. At 53 years of age, John A. Macdonald had not expected to become a father again.

When his daughter was born in early 1869, he was overjoyed. The birth had been difficult, but both Agnes and the baby had survived. The proud parents named her Mary. As the months passed, their joy was tempered by a growing concern. Mary seemed healthy, but she was not responding the way other babies did. Why was her head so large? Why did she cry so much? Why did she lie so quietly when she was not crying?

Mary's doctors were concerned, too. Finally, a diagnosis was made. Mary's enlarged head was caused by a buildup of fluid around her brain. The condition, called hydrocephalus or "water on the brain," would slow her physical and mental development. The injury had probably occurred during the difficult birth.

The Macdonalds were devastated by the diagnosis. For Macdonald, the news may have been especially hard to bear. His life had already been marked by tragedy. After a long and very painful illness, his first wife, Isabella, had died in 1857. Her death had come nearly ten years after that of the couple's beloved first child — a son named John Alexander, after his father.

Although the couple had a second son, Hugh John, memories of his first-born child always occupied a special corner of Macdonald's heart. For years he kept a box containing a broken rattle, a little cart, and some wooden animals. The toys had belonged to little John A. His father could not bear to part with them.

At first the news about Mary seemed like another tragedy. It did not take long, however, for the Macdonalds to get over this feeling. Although Mary could not walk on her own and usually used a wheelchair, her parents learned to take delight in her achievements — and Mary thrived in the glow of their love. As she grew up, they tried to make her life as normal as possible. Every year, for example, they invited other children to a party celebrating her birthday. Macdonald even had a special balcony built over the dining room of their Ottawa house so that Baboo — his pet name for her — could watch the other children playing.

Mary especially enjoyed listening to nursery rhymes and stories. As a result, her doting father was often seen rushing home after a hectic day in Parliament to read to her. He did not like to disappoint Mary.

More people you could research are

Amor De Cosmos

Frederick Haultain

John A. Macdonald

James C. Pope

Joseph Smallwood

New Provinces in the Prairies

In 1871 the West outside of the provinces of Manitoba and British Columbia was known as the North-West Territories. Not many settlers came to the area because of the economic downturn and because there was no railway. In 1885 about 75 percent of the population were Métis and Aboriginal Peoples.

The government was made up of a Lieutenant-Governor and his appointed council. The people had no representation. Despite requests for land settlements and a voice in the decisions, Macdonald and the federal government were silent. In 1885, as you will learn in Chapter 7, the Métis and some Aboriginal Peoples rebelled to protest the government's neglect.

After the 1885 Rebellion, the North-West Territories were given 4 of the 215 seats in the House of Commons. In 1888 the federal government gave the people an elected Assembly. After 1897 immigrants began to arrive in large numbers and the federal government under Prime Minister Wilfrid Laurier gave the Assembly responsible government. Population in the Canadian West grew at an astonishing rate for the next 15 years. Manitoba's population more than tripled from 152 000 to 554 000 between 1891 and 1914, and the population in what is now Alberta and Saskatchewan mushroomed from under 100 000 to over 1 million. It was time for a new arrangement.

Cree chiefs in Regina after the 1885 Rebellion. Lieutenant-Governor Dewdney is on the left of the chiefs. What does this picture say about the position of Aboriginal Peoples at this time?

By 1904 Winnipeg was already a large centre. With imposing buildings and electric streetcars.

In 1904 the leader of the North-West Territories' government was a lawyer who had come to the West from Ontario in 1884. Frederick Haultain had been elected to the Assembly in 1888 and had pushed for responsible government. He wanted the politicians in Ottawa to create one large province out of the territories. Prime Minister Wilfrid Laurier would not agree to that, fearing that one province might become too powerful. In the federal election of 1904 both national parties promised that two provinces, Saskatchewan and Alberta, would be created. They would run from the 49th parallel to the 60th parallel of latitude. The two provinces were created on September 4th, 1905. Like Manitoba, they enjoyed all the provincial rights, except control over their natural resources. The federal government handed this power over to the three Prairie provinces in 1930.

Frederick Haultain

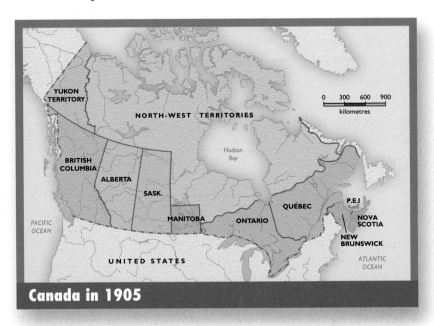

Canada in 1905

The Story So Far . . .

1 Do you think Haultain was right to try to get one province in the prairies? How might Canada be different today if he had succeeded?

2 Why would Laurier oppose this idea?

Maud Montgomery
HOPES DASHED, DREAMS FULFILLED

Sixteen-year-old Maud Montgomery was beside herself with joy. She was a published author! Her poem, "On Cape Leforce," had been printed in the *Charlottetown Patriot*. Maybe her secret ambition of becoming a writer was not foolish, after all.

Maud was especially pleased by her father's pride in her achievement. The only shadow on her happiness was cast by her stepmother, Mary. Her father's new wife sulked when her husband paid attention to Maud. The publication of the poem had simply fuelled Mary's jealousy of her stepdaughter.

The problem was that Mary did not want a stepdaughter; she wanted a servant. Maud found herself doing most of the housework and looking after her young half-sister and new baby half-brother. She was given so much work that she was even forced to miss two months of school that year. Even more upsetting, Mary often went into Maud's room and read her letters. She also refused to let her stepdaughter wear her hair pinned up in the fashion of the day and became angry when her husband affectionately called his daughter Maudie instead of Maud. At her insistence, no one ever called the young woman by her first name, Lucy.

Much as she loved her father, Maud was starting to believe that leaving Prince Edward Island and coming to live in Prince Albert, the raw, young town in the District of Saskatchewan, with her father and Mary had been a bad idea.

She had made some good friends since arriving, but life at home was far from happy. Sometimes she even missed her strict and stern grandparents. They had taken Maud in after her mother died of tuberculosis when she was very young and had continued raising her when her father had left to seek his fortune in the West.

Maud had longed for her father to send for her. Now that this had finally happened, her life was not what she had hoped.

As her dream faded, Maud began to long to return to Prince Edward Island and the home, friends, and family she had left in 1890. Finally, just a year after she arrived in Prince Albert, she climbed aboard a train to start the long trip back to her beloved island.

Although Maud's hopes of finding happiness with her father's new family were dashed, she would realize her dream of becoming a writer. As L. M. Montgomery, she would go on to write some of the best-loved books of all time. The first and most famous of these was *Anne of Green Gables*. Montgomery would write 24 more books — and delight millions of readers.

More people you could research are

Félicité Angers

H. R. Casgrain

Pauline Johnson

Lucy Maud Montgomery

Charles G. D. Roberts

NEWFOUNDLAND AND LABRADOR JOIN AT LAST

Newfoundland and Labrador remained a colony of Britain. By the 1920s the people who made their living from fishing were facing problems making a good living. The colony had fallen so deeply into debt that in 1934 Britain took over the government. The new Commission of Government was made up of a British governor and six people, three of them from Newfoundland.

World War II brought prosperity as the island of Newfoundland was used as a military and naval base for American and Canadian ships crossing the Atlantic Ocean. At the end of the War in 1945, the people of Newfoundland and Labrador were faced with a decision. They had three choices for their future government. The decision was to be made in a referendum. They could

- continue with the Commission of Government
- return to the form of government that existed before 1934 as a self-governing colony of Britain
- join Canada

The British government did not want to continue with the Commission of Government as they did not want the expense. Britain and Canada were in favour of Newfoundland and Labrador joining the Canadian Confederation. The result of the first referendum was so indecisive that a second vote had to be held. This time, there would be only two options: join Canada, or return to being an independent colony.

The forces in favour of joining Canada were led by Joseph Smallwood, popularly known as Joey. Smallwood was a journalist and radio broadcaster. He used his skills to persuade the voters that they would benefit from union with Canada. People would have family allowances and grants that would raise the standard of living. Canada would build and improve roads, ports, and the railway system. It was expected that this would create many jobs for Newfoundlanders.

The result of the second referendum was very close: 52.3 percent voted for joining Canada, and 47.7 voted to become independent. On March 31, 1949, Newfoundland became the tenth province of Canada.

Web Connection

http:www.school.mcgrawhill.ca/resources

Go to the web site above to hear some of the voices in the Confederation debates in Newfoundland and Labrador. Go to History Resources, then to *Canada: The Story of a Developing Nation* to see where to go next.

Joseph Smallwood of Newfoundland signing the Confederation agreement in 1949

Canada in 1949

The Story So Far . . .

1 Do you think that a vote of 52.3 percent of voters was enough for the decision on Confederation for Newfoundland and Labrador?

2 Research to find out how Smallwood persuaded voters to support Confederation. Use what you have learned to debate this statement: Joey Smallwood is an example of one man "making history."

3 Why would Canada want Newfoundland to join Confederation? *Hint:* Think about Newfoundland's role in World War II.

SUM IT UP!

The building of Canada between 1867 and 1949 was a considerable achievement, in some ways as great as Confederation itself. It took wisdom, insight, and persuasive arguments to win over the reluctant and the sceptical Nova Scotians. The move to bring Manitoba into Confederation was taken without consulting the people, which led to resistance from the residents. British Columbia and Prince Edward Island became part of the new nation peacefully with few opponents. As the prairies filled with new settlers Saskatchewan and Alberta were brought into the federation. Only Newfoundland remained on the outside, until 1949. Then a narrow victory by Confederation forces in a referendum made them part of Canada.

One person, Sir John A. Macdonald, steered the new nation through the early years. His achievements and his mistakes have become part of the Canadian identity.

THINKING ABOUT YOUR LEARNING

1. What evidence is there that people in Nova Scotia in 1868 wanted
   a) to break away from Canada
   b) to get better terms for staying in Confederation?

2. Explain why the people of Newfoundland and Labrador rejected Confederation in 1869. Be sure to answer the question in some detail, especially as, apart from Prince Edward Islanders, they were the only group to say "No" to Canada.

3. If you had lived in British Columbia, what factors would you consider in deciding to join Canada or the United States?

4. Make a chart to compare and contrast the reasons why British Columbia and Prince Edward Island joined Confederation. Are those reasons more similar or more dissimilar?

5. From Central Canada's point of view, which of the new provinces was the most important addition for the country's future? Why?

6. Which of the three joining provinces got the best deal? Provide evidence to support your position.

Applying Your Learning

1. If you had been John A. Macdonald, what would you have said to Joseph Howe in order to convince him to keep Nova Scotia in Confederation?

2. Research what happened to Newfoundland and Labrador between their 1869 rejection of Confederation and their acceptance in 1949.

3. In a group discussion, identify significant events in the period covered in this chapter that you think have had a major impact on our country's identity.

4. Write and deliver a realistic speech that Amor De Cosmos might have given.

5. Devise a slogan or logo for both the pro- and anti-Confederation factions in Nova Scotia, Newfoundland, or British Columbia.

Using Key Words

Unscramble the words in Column A, and then match with the meanings in Column B:

Column A

1 beneaste sonllrdda
2 eatixnonna
3 itabecn semitrin
4 ttenydii
5 ilotanna clipoy
6 uprotot stestelmetn
7 yursverso
8 dawrs
9 nufredmeer

Column B

A) a vote by the electors on a single political issue

B) to take over a territory

D) a person in the care of a guardian

E) one of the financial problems in Prince Edward Island before Confederation

F) isolated coastal Newfoundland villages

G) government official responsible for a department

H) the plan for high tariffs, the building of a transcontinental railway, and increased immigration

I) the quality of being distinctive or unique

J) people who measure land for size, shape, and boundaries

Toward Confederation

CONNECTING YOUR LEARNING

UNDERSTANDING CONCEPTS

1. Which of the issues that divided Canada East and Canada West from 1850 to 1867 are still issues in Canada? In other parts of the world? Brainstorm in a group to decide how these issues could be resolved.

2. Imagine yourself in the role of *one* of the political leaders of the 1850s and 1860s in the Province of Canada. Write a speech outlining your party's stand on the major issues of the day and your party's vision for the future. These speeches might then be delivered, in costume, to the class.

3. Explain what is meant by a federal system, and why the Fathers of Confederation decided on a federal system for the new nation.

4. Photographs are an example of a primary source. Choose *one* photograph in this unit that interests you and record the historical information that you learn from the photograph.

DEVELOPING RESEARCH SKILLS

1. Choose *one* of the Fathers of Confederation and make up a list of questions that would explain why he worked for Confederation. Then research to see how many of these questions you can answer.

2. Do you feel, after more than 125 years, that the Maritime provinces were wise to join Confederation? Explain your answer.

3. Canada kept many British institutions and customs in its government. Working with a partner identify as many of those customs and institutions as you can. Then write a summary paragraph to say why you think they chose to keep those customs and institutions.

4. Make a list of the financial help that was promised to persuade each colony to join Confederation.
   a) Why do you think that politicians were prepared to spend this money for Confederation?

b) What do Canadians expect their federal government to spend money on today?

c) Do you think it was a good decision for the colonies to join together in Confederation?

COMMUNICATING REQUIRED KNOWLEDGE

1 In groups of four, make up the inside two pages of a broadsheet paper for the pre-Confederation period, reporting on *one* of the events covered in this unit. Remember that the editorial should have an opinion about the event.

2 Select *one* of the politicians discussed and write a letter to him, explaining what you think about him, his actions, and his policies.

3 Imagine you are *one* of the Fathers of Confederation explaining the new federal system to voters. Write a speech to explain why you think a strong central government is necessary.

4 Prepare a map to show the entry of the various areas into Confederation.

APPLYING CONCEPTS AND SKILLS

1 Working with a partner, creatively devise some alternative ways that might have helped to resolve the political deadlock of the 1850s.

2 Scan newspapers for a week and clip any articles that you think deal with issues related to decisions described in this unit. Explain to the rest of your group how these are related.

CREATING A MIND MAP

For each category in the mind map below list statements that show what role the topic played in the history of Confederation.

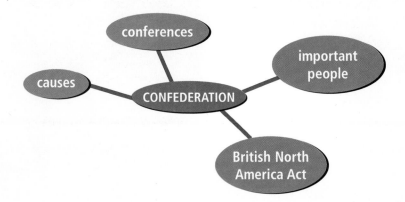

OUNGRE

1812

1871

1885

The West

1900

THE BIG PICTURE

These are some of the stories you will read about in this unit:

- settling the Canadian prairies — who, what, when, where, why, and how this happened
- everyday life of Aboriginal Peoples, Europeans, and Métis
- conflicts and changes involving prairie Aboriginal Peoples, Métis, and the Canadian government in 1870 and 1885
- the early years of the North West Mounted Police
- the building of a great railway across Canada
- the contributions of people from many different cultural groups to the development of Western Canada
- two gold rushes and the stories behind them
- how the prairies became the breadbasket of the world

CHAPTER 5

Settlement at Red River

1670
Hudson's Bay
Company is founded

1783
North West Company
started

1811
First Selkirk settlers
arrive at Red River

1815–1817
Fur traders and
settlers clash

1821
Hudson's Bay
Company and North
West Company join

1826
Red River floods wipe
out settlement

SETTING OUR FOCUS

It is 1840, and the people in the painting are on their way to their annual summer buffalo hunt with their dogs, horses, oxen, and Red River carts. They are Métis hunters, farmers, and traders from the settlement at Red River. For the next two months they will work together to gather buffalo hides, fat, and a huge supply of buffalo meat for making pemmican.

They travel under a wide Prairie sky, at home in the grasslands and parklands of the western plains. Within a few years of this painting, many of the Métis will have moved again, this time to escape the rapid changes that are overtaking them. In the meantime, put yourself in the picture. Will you ride in a cart? That's a very noisy and bumpy ride, for sure. Soon it will be time to take the tent poles off the carts and make camp for the evening. Enjoy your ride.

PREVIEWING THE CHAPTER

In this chapter you will learn about these topics:

- **the fur trade rivalry between North West Company and the Hudson's Bay Company**
- **the reasons Europeans came to Red River early in the nineteenth century**
- **some of the problems the fur trade rivalry caused for the early Scottish settlers**
- **the daily life of these settlers and other people at Red River**
- **the struggle of the Métis and other people in the West to assert their rights as their community became Manitoba, a Canadian province**

KEY WORDS

amnesty

crofters

merger

middlemen

pemmican

provisional
   government

resolutions

squatters

1861	1867	1868	1869	1870
Settlers arrive at Red River from the Canadas	Confederation of the Canadas, Nova Scotia, and New Brunswick	Canada sends out surveyors	Métis set up provisional government at Red River	• Scott is executed • Manitoba joins Confederation • Riel leaves Red River

THE FUR TRADE

The Western plains in 1763 were changing fast. With the fall of New France the fur trade had changed. Traders and voyageurs travelled by canoe over thousands of kilometres of northern and western lands, searching for furs to exchange for trade goods. Soon, two major companies were competing with one another for the furs of the West.

The Hudson's Bay Company (HBC) had permission to trade in all the lands drained by all the rivers that flow into Hudson Bay. The company's purpose was to make money by trading European goods, such as kettles, axes, blankets, and tobacco, for furs to be sold in Europe. Cree **middlemen** traded with other Aboriginal Peoples to collect furs in exchange for trade goods. They then brought the furs to the HBC posts.

By 1773 the HBC workers noticed a huge drop in the number of furs being traded at their posts on the shores of Hudson Bay. Now traders from Montréal were reaching the Aboriginal suppliers first. In response the HBC sent traders and explorers into the interior of the northwest to build trading posts. By 1780 the company was in a desperate trade war with Scottish traders from Montréal.

The men from Montréal joined together in 1783 to form the North West Company (NWC). They followed Aboriginal Peoples' trade routes to link Montréal with the West. Large canoes left Montréal loaded with trade goods in the spring. Paddlers travelled to Fort William at the head of Lake Superior to meet voyageurs coming from the western posts. There they left their trade goods to be taken to the western posts, returning to Montréal with bales of furs. Wintering partners stayed in the West all year to keep up the trade with their Aboriginal allies.

In the 1780s traders and partners raced to find new sources of fur and profits, build trading posts, and defeat their rivals. Relations between workers of the HBC and the NWC often became violent as they competed to get more furs.

Snippet

Fast Food in 1780

You could say the fur trade in the nineteenth century ran on pemmican. The word came from two Cree words meaning "prepared fat." Women cut fresh-killed bison into thin slices and hung the meat on racks to dry. Then they pounded the meat into a powder and mixed it with melted fat in a rawhide bag. For a special flavour they added dried berries. Pemmican kept for years, and 1 kg was the equivalent of 4–8 kg of fresh meat. This was a main food for voyageurs and workers at the posts.

Web Connection

http://www.school.mcgrawhill.ca/resources

Go to the web site above to find out more about the fur trade and the Hudson's Bay Company. Go to History Resources, then to *Canada: The Story of a Developing Nation* to see where to go next.

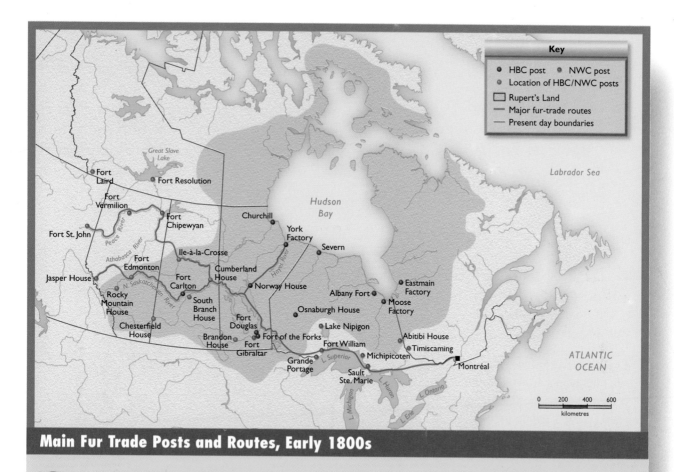

Key

- HBC post
- NWC post
- Location of HBC/NWC posts
- Rupert's Land
- Major fur-trade routes
- Present day boundaries

Great Slave Lake

Hudson Bay

Labrador Sea

Fort Laird
Fort Resolution
Fort Vermilion
Fort Chipewyan
Churchill
Fort St. John
Peace River
York Factory
Severn
Ile-à-la-Crosse
Athabasca River
Fort Edmonton
Jasper House
Cumberland House
Hayes River
Fort Carlton
Norway House
Eastmain Factory
Rocky Mountain House
N. Saskatchewan River
Albany Fort
Moose Factory
South Branch House
Osnaburgh House
Chesterfield House
Fort Douglas
Lake Nipigon
Abitibi House
Brandon House
Fort of the Forks
Fort William
Timiscaming
Fort Gibraltar
Grande Portage
Michipicoten
Montréal
L. Superior
Sault Ste. Marie
L. Michigan
Huron
L. Ontario
L. Erie

ATLANTIC OCEAN

0 200 400 600
kilometres

Main Fur Trade Posts and Routes, Early 1800s

1. Estimate how far the traders travelled from Montréal to reach Fort William.

2. The voyageurs made this trip in six weeks or less. Estimate how far they travelled each day.

3. Compare this map with a map showing cities in Canada today. Which of the cities in the West started as fur posts?

National Gallery of Canada, Ottawa. Rindisbacher, Peter 1806-1834, Canadian. Two of the Companies Officers Travelling in a Canoe Made of Birchbark Manned by Canadians, c.1823. Purchased 1978 with the assistance of a grant from the Government of Canada under the terms of the Cultural Property Export and Import Act.

This painting shows the *canot du nord*, the smaller canoe that carried the furs over the northern rivers to the head of Lake Superior.

English artist Frances Ann Hopkins painted this scene of a *canot de maître*, the canoe used to carry goods from Montréal.

1 How many people are there in the *canot de maître*? In the *canot du nord*?

2 Why do you think the *canot de maître* could not be used to carry the furs west of the head of Lake Superior?

3 Identify the officials of the fur companies in these paintings. How did you know who they were?

4 Why do you think the men in the back of the canoes are standing up?

Reflections

Frances Ann Hopkins made a trip west in a *canot de maître*. On the journey the voyageurs had to carry canoes and equipment over portages; the paddlers rose at three in the morning and paddled until sunset; they camped at night on the shore, with shelters under the upturned canoes. You are taking this trip. Write a journal entry to describe how you felt during and at the end of the journey.

The Cree and Assiniboin supplied food for the voyageurs and traders who lived at the fur posts. Aboriginal women took on important roles in the fur trade. Many married fur traders. They made moccasins and snowshoes; preserved food; harvested fish, wild rice, and berries; made **pemmican**; tanned hides; dressed furs; or sewed seams in canoes to build or repair them. The women's skills as interpreters and negotiators also kept the European and NWC traders in business. Many marriages were arranged "according to the custom of the country," in other words, according to Aboriginal custom.

York Factory was a large,
busy trade centre in 1821.
This painting by 15-year-old
Peter Rindisbacher shows
York boats leaving the fort.

Two sorts of family arrangements developed in the West and
Northwest from these marriages. Families of HBC factors and
their Aboriginal wives lived near the company's posts on the
shores of Hudson Bay, and around the Red River. Some HBC
factors sent their children to schools in Britain, but most
remained in the West. People whose fathers worked for the
NWC and whose mothers were Aboriginal were often French
speaking. People whose parents were a mix of Aboriginal and
European ancestry were called mixed-blood or Métis. Some
called them a "new nation." They would play a huge role in the
history of the West between 1800 and 1885.

The Story So Far . . .

1 Do some research on the Western fur trade. Then create a
comparison chart to note the similarities and differences
between the trading systems of the NWC and HBC.
Categories might include: headquarters, system of trade,
transportation, and others.

2 What did Aboriginal Peoples obtain from the fur trade?
What did Europeans obtain?

3 How was the fur trade a partnership between the traders and
Aboriginal Peoples?

4 Why was pemmican so important in the fur trade?

Snippet

York Factory

Once the gateway to Rupert's
Land, this busy centre was called
a factory because it was home to
the factor, the person in charge
of trading in the area. In the
mid-1800s, York Factory boasted
30 buildings, including
dormitories, a hospital, library,
and warehouses for storing furs
and goods. When the Hudson's
Bay Company started building
inland posts, the importance of
York Factory gradually diminished,
until it was finally closed in
1957.

Snippet

Deadly Scourge

In 1838 a smallpox epidemic swept north from the United States. Luckily, the Hudson's Bay Company had supplied fresh vaccine to many of its posts. At Fort Pelly, trader William Todd started vaccinating visitors right away. He also gave vaccine to Aboriginal leaders and showed them how to inoculate their people. This action saved countless lives. The dread disease spread like wildfire, killing up to three quarters of the Prairie peoples who had not been vaccinated.

In 1810 Thomas Douglas, the Earl of Selkirk had everything a titled landowner in Scotland could want: huge estates, mansions, education, money, and a controlling share of the Hudson's Bay Company. He also had a social conscience. Thousands of hungry and landless **crofters**, or tenant farmers, were being forced to leave the land they farmed. Huge sheep farms were taking the place of the farmers' tiny fields. The crofters were starving, with no hope for work.

Lord Selkirk planned to settle the crofters on the banks of the Red River in faraway Rupert's Land. There he expected them to grow vegetables and provide beef and pork for the Western fur trade posts. He promised them a new life in the land he was granted by the HBC that he called Assiniboia. They would have free transportation there, free farming tools and seed, land to farm, and a job with the Hudson's Bay Company.

The settlement would be built around the forks of the Red and Assiniboine rivers, in the centre of the major transportation and trading network of the North West Company. Nor'Westers, employees of the NWC, did not hesitate to warn the future settlers of the dangers of settling there. The NWC traders saw the Selkirk settlers as serious threats to their fur trading operations.

The first settlers arrived at York Factory, the Hudson's Bay Company post at the mouth of the Hayes River, in 1811; it was too late that fall to travel south to their future farms. They spent a miserable winter in huts and tents.

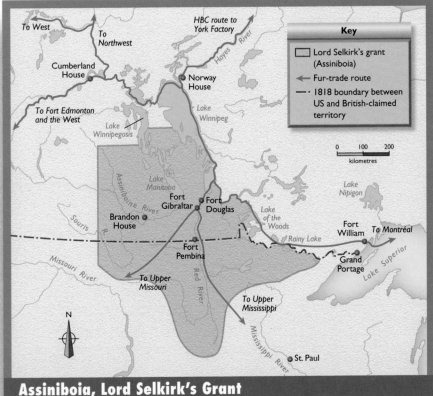

Key
- ☐ Lord Selkirk's grant (Assiniboia)
- ← Fur-trade route
- --- 1818 boundary between US and British-claimed territory

0   100   200
kilometres

Assiniboia, Lord Selkirk's Grant

1 Look at the map on page 129. What main trading routes went through Selkirk's Grant?

2 How was this colony a threat to the North West Company?

Marie-Anne Lagemodière

NINGAH

No picture exists of Marie-Anne. This is her daughter, Julie, with one of her grandchildren.

Marie-Anne Lagemodière of Maskinongé, Québec, knew that tongues were wagging. It was unheard of, the gossips were saying. Respectable women did not travel with their voyageur husbands.

Lagemodière was unfazed. She had married Jean-Baptiste on April 21, 1806, when she was 25 years old. During their courtship, he had often spoken of his days in the West, so it came as no surprise when he confessed that he was longing to rejoin the fur brigades. She wanted Jean-Baptiste to be happy; but she could not bear to be parted from him. The only solution was to go with him. Less than a month later, she was at Lachine, near Montréal, taking her place in a canoe with Jean-Baptiste and nine paddlers.

Paddling at 50 strokes a minute, the voyageurs travelled the rivers and lakes that led west. Lagemodière wasn't expected to paddle, but she made herself useful at portages and when they camped. Finally, they reached a Métis camp near Pembina on the Red River and settled in for the winter.

It was there that the Lagemodières' first child, a daughter, was born on January 6, 1807. The Saulteaux who lived in the area called Lagemodière Ningah, which means mother. The next spring, Jean-Baptiste and Marie-Anne travelled even farther west. A boy, named after his father, was born on this trip. He was the first baby of European parents born in what is now Saskatchewan.

For the next several years, Lagemodière and Jean-Baptiste continued to hunt, trap, and trade. Their third child, a son, was born near Fort Edmonton, becoming the first baby of European parents born in present-day Alberta.

Then in 1811, word came that a colony was being established at Red River. Lagemodière's family was growing and, by this time, she hadn't spoken to another European woman in five years. She and Jean-Baptiste decided to settle down. Arriving at Assiniboia, they found the settlers there completely unprepared for their new way of life. That first winter, Jean-Baptiste's hunting skills helped to keep many of them alive. In 1816, Lord Selkirk rewarded him with a grant of choice land. There the Lagemodières built the house where their family was to live for many years. In 1822 Lagemodière gave birth to her seventh child, a daughter named Julie. Twenty-two years later, Julie became the mother of a man who would have a lasting impact on Canadian history. His name was Louis Riel.

More people you could research are

Janet Bannerman

Thomas Douglas, Lord Selkirk

Cuthbert Grant

Marie-Anne Lagemodière

Miles Macdonell

Peguis

York Boats

When the Hudson's Bay Company started building inland posts, vessels were needed to transport goods along the waterways to and from York Factory. Canoes were not the answer. Company employees, usually from Britain, did not have the skill to build or handle the tricky *canot du nord* favoured by the Nor'Westers. What's more, the materials needed to build canoes were in short supply at York Factory.

The solution? York boats. Named after York Factory, where most of them were built, boats like these had been used for centuries by the people of the Orkney Islands off northern Scotland. In fact, the company recruited Orkney Islanders to build the boats.

Big, sturdy, and stable, York boats were propelled by oars and a square sail. Though less manoeuvrable than the *canot du nord*, they could carry up to three times the cargo. They also required fewer, and less skilled, rowers and lasted several years. The more fragile canoes rarely lasted a year and sometimes did not even survive one trip.

A disadvantage of York boats was their weight. At portages they were too heavy to carry. Instead workers rolled and dragged them across carrying places on skids of green timber. This was backbreaking work that sparked much grumbling among the crews.

Estimate the size of this York boat. Why do you suppose the man in the stern who is doing the steering is standing?

After spring breakup, they embarked on the next 1000-km stage of their voyage, travelling by York boat, portaging, and suffering terribly from insect bites. They arrived too late to build homes or plant seeds that fall.

Peguis, the local chief of the Saulteaux, saved the settlers. The skilful hunters showed them how to hunt buffalo. They kept the newcomers from starving and freezing, providing them with meat, pemmican, snowshoes, tents, and winter clothing.

This first year was the start of many hardships to follow. Drought and grubs destroyed the first harvest. By the winter of 1813–1814, Governor Miles Macdonell was worried about the colonists' food supply. He issued an order, called the Pemmican Proclamation, forbidding the export of any food, including pemmican, from Assiniboia for one year. The NWC fur traders and Métis were outraged. The entire year's fur trade was threatened if they could not supply their forts with food.

The conflict between the settlers and the Métis and NWC fur traders arose from their incompatible goals. The fur trade depended on the buffalo hunt, the production of pemmican and fresh meat by Métis and Aboriginal hunters, and the free movement of furs and food from Montréal to the far northwestern outposts. The settlers were a threat to this way of life. In the face of NWC intimidation, about 140 settlers abandoned the settlement in the spring of 1815. They left in company canoes to settle in far-off Canada. They had had enough.

However, 60 settlers decided to stay at Red River. The Nor'Westers arrested Governor Macdonell and took him to Montréal. Encouraged by the Nor'Westers, Métis horsemen trampled colonists' crops, burned their houses to the ground, and drove the settlers out. The colonists paddled to the HBC post at the north end of Lake Winnipeg, uncertain of their next move. In the spring Hudson's Bay Company special envoy Colin Robertson persuaded the settlers to follow him back to Red River to begin their work again.

The Story So Far . . .

1 Why did the Scottish settlers leave their homeland for Red River?

2 How did Lord Selkirk expect the settlers to make money?

3 Why was the North West Company against this plan?

4 How did Peguis and the Saulteaux help the early settlers survive?

5 a) What did Governor Macdonell hope to achieve by the Pemmican Proclamation?

b) Why were the Métis and fur traders outraged by this decision?

More Disaster: Seven Oaks

As the settlers began to build again in 1816, another group of Scots arrived, led by a new Governor, Robert Semple. The Nor'Westers encouraged the Métis to oppose the settlers. Métis leader Cuthbert Grant believed he had to destroy the colony to preserve the fur trade. In June the Métis under Grant's direction attempted to transport a huge shipment of pemmican out of Assiniboia to the far Western trading posts. They ran into a small force of settlers, led by Governor Semple. In a short battle at

Peguis's Treaty

In 1817 Chief Peguis signed a treaty with Lord Selkirk. In return for 45 kg of tobacco a year, he agreed to let the colonists use land for about 3 km back from the banks of the Red River south of the Forks to what is now Grand Forks, North Dakota. They could also use land along the Assiniboine River to Rat Creek.

Seven Oaks, the Métis quickly overcame the colonists. Semple and 20 settlers died, leaving the remaining colonists in fear and uncertainty. Only one Métis was killed. Lord Selkirk, hearing of the troubles, set off from Scotland to aid the colonists. He arrived in the spring of 1817, along with more colonists and Swiss troops. The settlers returned to their work of building homes, planting crops and establishing farms. During the next few years, fur traders with both companies carried out a violent and ugly trade war in the northwest.

The death of Lord Selkirk in 1820 offered a chance to talk about change. Peace between the HBC and the NWC followed in 1821 with their **merger,** or joining, to form a new Hudson's Bay Company. The merger brought major change to the fur trade, including the move of the company's headquarters to London, England. This ended the huge role played by Scottish business people in Montréal and French-Canadian traders and voyageurs in the fur trade.

This illustration of the fighting at Seven Oaks is by Canadian historical artist C. W. Jefferys.

1 According to Jefferys' picture, which group is the aggressor at Seven Oaks?

2 First-hand accounts say the Métis were not on their horses, and Semple's men fired first. Also, it was not the custom for Métis to wear full-feathered headdresses to transport pemmican. How does this picture show why historians have to use more than one source of information?

LIVING AT RED RIVER, 1820 TO 1849

Peace came to the settlement at the Forks after 1821. Gradually more people settled in the area. Two Métis language groups lived along the Red and Assiniboine rivers close to the Red River Colony. The French-speaking Métis community was the largest single group in the colony. They farmed, fished, hunted buffalo, and traded the pemmican they made to the fur trade companies. English-speaking Métis people whose ancestors had been NWC and HBC traders and Aboriginal women also lived in the area. Red River was also home to Cree, Saulteaux, and Assiniboin peoples who lived by fishing, hunting, trapping, and trading with the HBC.

Europeans were the fourth group. The Selkirk settlers, those stubborn Scots who had refused to give up, lived in farms along the Red River at Kildonan. Over the years retired fur traders and their Aboriginal wives stayed after their service to the HBC was over. They came originally from Scotland and the Orkney Islands. Their families farmed and ran businesses in the community.

Some French Canadians moved in. These were mostly French-speaking farmers who had moved from Lower Canada to the West. They lived at St. Boniface. Their language, added to the many others of the area, created a multilingual and multicultural mix at the Red River Colony. After 1850, English-speaking Canadians began arriving.

The Farmers and Fur Traders

The narrow strips of land that made up the settlers' farms stretched back about 3 km from the riverbank. The soil of the Red River valley was ideal for growing grain and vegetables. Still pioneer farming was difficult. Families worked to break the soil and plant seeds, raise cattle and pigs, and overcome the cold winters, wolves, and insects, as well as harvest grain crops.

Everybody worked to grow, preserve, and prepare the family's food. They ate fish caught in the Red River; dry raspberries, saskatoons, and blueberries; bannock (flat bread made without yeast); oat cakes; pemmican, beef, pork, and dairy products. Sugar and salt were scarce luxuries sometimes bought from the HBC store. Fresh fruit was so unusual that eating an apple was a memorable event.

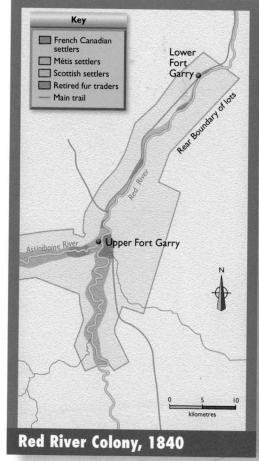

Key

- French Canadian settlers
- Métis settlers
- Scottish settlers
- Retired fur traders
- Main trail

Lower Fort Garry

Rear Boundary of lots

Red River

Assiniboine River

Upper Fort Garry

N

0   5   10
kilometres

Red River Colony, 1840

In 1826 a disastrous flood threatened to wipe out the colony. Retired fur trader Alexander Ross described the scene in his diary:

> While the frightened inhabitants were collected in groups on any dry spot that remained visible above the waste of waters, their houses, barns, carriages, furniture, fencing might be seen floating along over the wide extended plain, to be engulfed in Lake Winnipeg. Hardly a house or building was left standing in the colony. Many of the buildings drifted along whole; and in some were seen dogs, howling dismally. The most singular spectacle was a house in flames, drifting along in the night, its one half in water, and the remainder furiously burning. The water continued rising and extended far over the plains.

In 1852 another huge flood struck the settlement, wiping out homes, barns, fields, and stores.

Ice-fishing at the forks of the Assiniboine and Red River, 1820s, a painting by Peter Rindisbacher. The fort is Fort Douglas, which was later replaced by Upper Fort Garry.

1. What are the people using for transportation?

2. What animals are shown in the picture?

3. Can you tell by the clothing which cultural groups people belong to

4. How is this painting a valuable historical record?

Peter Rindisbacher
BOY ARTIST OF ASSINIBOIA

Peter Rindisbacher was cold, tired, hungry — and very worried. It was November 1821, and the 15-year-old, along with his family and about 170 other colonists, had finally reached Assiniboia. After a gruelling six-month journey, they were eager to start their new lives.

The recruiter in Switzerland had painted a rosy picture of life at Red River. He had not told them about the journey. Their ship was nearly crushed by ice at the mouth of Hudson Bay. Then they had to leave most of their belongings at York Factory because there were not enough York boats to carry them. Seven people died making the treacherous journey up the Hayes River to windswept Lake Winnipeg and on to the Red River. Now the bone-chilling cold, freezing rain, driving sleet and snow made many of them wish they had never left home.

That summer a plague of grasshoppers had destroyed crops at the settlement. The colonists who were already there did not have enough food for themselves. How would everyone make it through the winter? That is why Peter was worried.

Luckily, people shared their homes and meagre supplies with the Swiss newcomers. They killed game when they could and fished through the ice. When things got really desperate, they ate their dogs and horses. Finally spring arrived, and the Rindisbachers were able to start building their own house and planting their own crops.

All the while Peter was sketching the things he saw around him. Since childhood he had loved drawing. He first made a sketch in pen or pencil, then traced a copy, and finished the drawing in watercolours. He drew the settlers, the Métis, and Aboriginal Peoples, who welcomed the friendly young man to their camps. Gradually, his talent came to the attention of Hudson's Bay Company officials. Calling him "the boy artist," they started buying his work and hiring him to create special paintings, usually featuring themselves.

Meanwhile Peter's parents were having little success of their own. After the deadly flood of 1826 the whole family headed south to the United States.

Peter continued to paint, but died of cholera just eight years later. Although his life was cut tragically short, the young artist's drawings have provided historians and geographers with a lasting, vivid and accurate record of life west of the Great Lakes.

More people you could research are

William Armstrong

Henry Hime

William Hind

Frances Hopkins

Paul Kane

Peter Rindisbacher

The pioneer settlers built their houses along the riverbank. Here is what a visitor to a settler's farm home in 1823 wrote:

It is a log cabin with a thatched roof and rough stone and mortar chimney planted against one wall. Inside is but a single room, well whitewashed, as is the outside; a bed is in one corner, a sort of couch in another, a ladder leads up to the loose boards overhead which form an attic; a trap door in the room opens to a small hole in the ground where milk and butter are kept cool. From the beams is suspended a hammock, used as a cradle for the baby. Shelves hold a scanty supply of plates, knives and forks. Two windows on either side, covered with mosquito netting, admit the light. Chests and boxes supply the place of seats, with here and there a keg for an easy-chair. An open fireplace of whitewashed clay gives cheer and warmth and a few books complete the scene.

This 1820s sketch by Peter Rindisbacher shows some Red River colonists — a German in the centre, a Highland Scot seated at the right, and a Métis at the far right. The woman at the left is a Swiss. All wear clothing from their home culture, and moccasins adopted from prairie Aboriginal Peoples.

Schools and churches were important features of life at Red River. Christian religious beliefs were common among the settlers, and religious services were frequent for all.

The Story So Far . . .

1 List the challenges nature posed for the farmers at Red River.
2 Why would retired fur traders settle at Red River?
3 Settlers always had a problem selling their extra farm produce. Look at the map on page 132. Where was the nearest large settlement?

Métis Buffalo Hunters

By 1840 there were about 4000 Métis people at Red River. This was over half the population of the colony. Most Métis settlers were **squatters**, which means they did not hold titles to the lands they used for their homes and fields. Their most important activity was the buffalo hunt. By the 1840s they travelled as far as 400 km from the settlement to find buffalo for pemmican.

Many Métis also worked on the HBC's York boats carrying supplies, food, and equipment from the central post at Fort Garry along the western rivers as far as the Rocky Mountains and Hudson Bay. Farming was less important than hunting and transportation work. After 1850 many Métis men became freight drivers, urging their oxen to pull Red River carts along the rough tracks that joined the Red River Settlement to St. Paul, Minnesota.

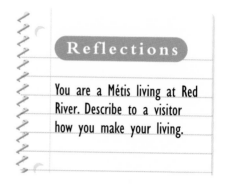

Reflections

You are a Métis living at Red River. Describe to a visitor how you make your living.

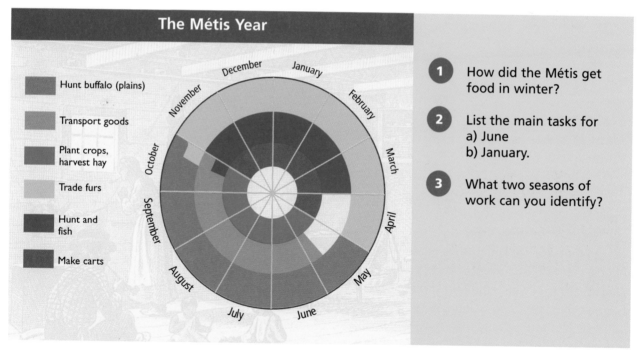

The Métis Year

- Hunt buffalo (plains)
- Transport goods
- Plant crops, harvest hay
- Trade furs
- Hunt and fish
- Make carts

December January February March April May June July August September October November

1 How did the Métis get food in winter?

2 List the main tasks for
a) June
b) January.

3 What two seasons of work can you identify?

Web Connection

http://www.school.mcgrawhill.ca/resources

Go to the web site above to learn more about the Métis way of life in Manitoba. Go to History Resources, then to *Canada: The Story of a Developing Nation* to see where to go next.

The Evidence Behind the Story

Paul Kane accompanied Métis hunters on their spring buffalo hunt in 1846 and created this painting.

In the 1840s Paul Kane travelled across North America by canoe, on horseback, and on foot. He sketched what he saw — people, places, and events. Then he took his sketches back to his studio in Toronto and turned them into large paintings. He wanted to show people in the Canadas what life was like in the West. After all, photography was just beginning, and there were few easy trips to "see for yourself" for most people. Then as now, people relied on artists to help them see the world.

Kane took his job seriously. He wanted to show "Canada" as well as the West, and to show Aboriginal Peoples and their ways of life.

How accurate is Kane's work? One art historian said, "The record he made is outstanding. It's the best Canada has. But he was happy to change the landscape when it suited his purpose. Sometimes he was ethnographically correct [he accurately showed the people and their culture], and sometimes he was way off."

QUESTIONING THE EVIDENCE

1. What strikes you about Paul Kane's painting?
2. a) What elements in the painting do you think might be exaggerated?
   b) Why do you think these elements were exaggerated?
3. How is this picture valuable evidence?

THE END OF ISOLATION

Britain and the Canadas became interested in the lands west of Lake Superior during the late 1850s. Settlers were moving into the American prairies south of the border, and the Hudson's Bay Company lease in the area would soon expire. The buffalo were declining. Hunters were forced to travel farther and farther to find smaller and smaller herds. What was the future for these vast lands?

Residents of Canada West bragged that their country was going to take over the West, starting with Red River, and make it part of the Province of Canada. Some who arrived from the East in the 1860s began to press for a connection with Canada. Most were English-speaking Protestants. They were led by John C. Schultz, a recent immigrant from Canada West. Angry confrontations broke out between supporters of the Canadian party and the Métis, in court, in the newspapers, and in the streets and taverns. Canadians challenged the way of life of the Métis. They seemed to show little respect for the language, culture, rights, and religion of the people of Red River. Like many Protestant people of the time, they were biased against the Roman Catholic Church — the church of many Red River people.

Questions of land ownership became points of concern, since Aboriginal Peoples had not signed any treaties to give up their rights in most of the West. As Canadians moved into the area, they, too, became squatters, settling where they liked. Conflicts over lands became important to everyone at Red River.

A Métis family is shown at home in this sketch from a Canadian magazine in the 1870s. Note the animals, the wood stove, and the baby in the hammock.

This 1870 painting shows a typical settler's house at Red River.

1 Suggest why the settlers fenced the area around their homes.

John Schultz and the new settlers attacked the form of government in Red River. Government was the responsibility of a small group called the Council of Assiniboia, which was made up of HBC officials, headed by a governor. There were no elected representatives. The colony had to find a new system of government; but what would that be?

In 1868 the colony was in crisis. Drought, grasshoppers, and lack of game caused severe food shortages everywhere. The governor appealed to Canada, the United States, and Britain for food aid. Everyone in the colony seemed to be suffering, and a cloud of uncertainty hung over Red River. Decisions had to be made about the future.

Three possible options existed:

- Join the United States. Trade and travel between Red River and St. Paul, Minnesota, was common. Road, river, and later railway links joined the two prairie settlements. Many Americans favoured a union.
- Become a British Crown Colony. This was as unlikely as the British government was not interested in taking control of the Red River colony from the HBC.
- Join the Canadian Confederation. Many Canadians had ties to

the West, since fur traders and voyageurs had travelled there for over 200 years. Joining the West and Canada would help finish the "Confederation Dream" of a country from sea to sea. The idea was popular with many Canadians.

What choices do the people in the Red River Settlement have, according to this cartoon, "The Situation," from a Montréal magazine of January 1870?

The Story So Far . . .

1. How were the people of the Red River area governed before 1870?
2. Why might newcomers from the Canadas be unhappy with this government?
3. List the changes facing the people of the settlement.
4. What choices did the people have for their future government in the 1860s?

Taking a Stand

In December 1867 the new government of the Dominion of Canada passed seven **resolutions** about the West. These were the decisions they made: Canada would pay the HBC for Rupert's Land, build a road between Canada and Red River, and make the West part of Canada. The first Lieutenant-Governor would be William McDougall from Ontario. Nobody had asked Westerners what they thought. Nobody had bothered to consult them. Soon Canadians would learn how the people of Red River felt.

In the summer of 1868 crews of road builders began to push a track east toward Fort William. The next summer the government sent surveyors to the settlement to mark off townships and farm lots.

On October 11, 1869, a small group of unarmed Métis stood on the Canadian survey chains that stretched across a Métis farm. Their message was clear: keep out. You have no right to trespass on our land to do your work. The surveyors left at once. The Métis had made their point. Among the men standing on the chains was Louis Riel.

Louis Riel
FACE TO FACE WITH BIGOTRY

On a warm and sunny Sunday morning in late July 1868, 23-year-old Louis Riel finally arrived at his mother's home in St. Vital on the west bank of the Red River. For the young man who had not seen his family since he was aged 13, it was a joyous moment. One of the people on hand for the happy reunion was his beloved grandmother, Marie-Anne Lagemodière.

For Riel, though, the homecoming was bittersweet. While he had been away studying on scholarship at the Collège de Montréal, his father had died. Jean-Louis Riel's death had left a big gap in the close-knit family circle and his widow, Julie, had struggled to keep going. Things had gone from bad to worse the previous summer when grasshoppers had destroyed crops in the area, forcing the proud family to accept charity.

Riel had spent the past two years working his way home through the United States. At the time this was the route chosen by most travellers to Red River because they could go by train as far as St. Paul, Minnesota, before heading north. Riel had completed the trip in stages. To save enough to pay for the next leg of the journey and to send money home to help feed and clothe his eight younger sisters and brothers, he had paused to work for a time in Chicago, Illinois, and St. Paul.

The troubles faced by his family were not the only reason for Riel's sadness, however. He was still upset over his rejection by Marie-Julie Guernon, the young French Canadian he had fallen in love with in Montréal. He had proposed and Marie-Julie had accepted; but her parents had objected. Their reason? One of Riel's great-grandmothers on his father's side of the family had been Chipewyan. The Guernons would not hear of their daughter marrying someone of mixed ancestry, especially when that someone was a penniless student.

Despite her parents' objections, the couple had continued their courtship in secret. They wrote each other poems and love letters and met whenever they could. Then Riel had landed a job as a clerk with a respected Montréal law firm. Surely, he thought, this improvement in his circumstances would overcome the prejudice of Marie-Julie's parents.

He had been wrong. Once again, the Guernons had angrily refused to allow their daughter to marry a Métis, no matter how bright his future. When Marie-Julie reluctantly bowed to her parents' wishes, Riel was devastated. Angry and bitter, he had decided that it was time to head home to Red River where he could be proud of his Métis heritage.

More people you could research are

Adams Archibald

Simon J. Dawson

William McDougall

Louis Riel

Donald Smith

Colonel G. Wolseley

Declaring a Provisional Government

In 1869 Louis Riel and his followers organized resistance to the plans of the Canadian government. They built a barrier at Pembina to keep Lieutenant-Governor William McDougall from entering their territory. On November 2, 1869, they captured the most important building in the settlement, Upper Fort Garry. Without any violence the Métis walked into the fort and took control. They had captured enough food and weapons to carry out a defence against attack. However, many people in the colony were unhappy with events; would there be violence? Was not capturing the fort a criminal act? Should they admit McDougall and hear what Canada proposed? Were the Métis moving too fast?

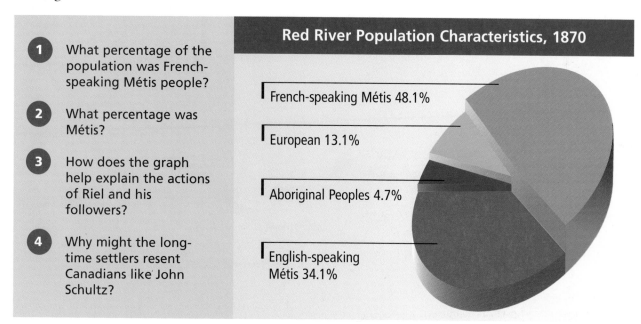

1. What percentage of the population was French-speaking Métis people?

2. What percentage was Métis?

3. How does the graph help explain the actions of Riel and his followers?

4. Why might the long-time settlers resent Canadians like John Schultz?

Red River Population Characteristics, 1870

French-speaking Métis 48.1%

European 13.1%

Aboriginal Peoples 4.7%

English-speaking Métis 34.1%

It was time to calm residents' fears and unite the opposition to Canadian annexation. Riel called for a convention of 12 English-speaking and 12 French-speaking representatives for November 6, 1869.

Why did Riel take this action? Here is his answer:

If a large immigration from Canada were to take place, the Métis would probably be crowded out of a country which they claimed as their own; their wishes had been entirely ignored; they objected to any government coming from Canada without consulting them; they were acting not only for their own good, but for the good of the whole settlement; they did not feel they were breaking any law, but were acting in defence of their own liberty.

Many people in the colony were uncertain about supporting the Métis position. English-speaking colonists changed their minds when they heard Riel's Métis List of Rights.

...nd privileges enjoyed by the people of this Province

...d French languages in the Legislature and in the Courts.

...s familiar with both the French and English languages.

...t who speaks English and French.

...tion as a province.

The members of the provisional government. Louis Riel is seated with his hands on his lap.

On December 7, 1869, the Métis captured the guarded house of Canadian leader, John Schultz, and seized his stored food. This food would have been enough to keep all the Canadians supplied during the winter. The next day, Riel declared a **provisional government**, or temporary government, to arrange an agreement with Canada for the future of the territory.

The provisional government passed a Declaration of the People of Rupert's Land.

- We refuse to recognize the authority of Canada, since we did not agree to the transfer of HBC lands to Canada.
- We have a right to form a government.
- We are ready to confer with Canada to ensure good government for the West.

It was time for the Government of Canada to act. Prime Minister Macdonald sent delegates to the colony to explain that Canada was willing to listen and respect the wishes of the people of Red River. Donald A. Smith, a powerful HBC official, was to negotiate the peaceful transfer of the colony to Canada.

Smith was an experienced negotiator, but he was no match for Louis Riel. He was supposed to make an agreement between the settlement and Canada, and also, secretly, to undermine Riel's leadership. After hard bargaining, Smith accepted Riel's call for a new representative assembly, the Convention of Forty. The men shook hands in front of the cheering crowd of thousands who waited in the clear, sunny cold. Canada and the colony would reach agreement, based on the wishes of the inhabitants and their representatives.

The Story So Far . . .

1 Why did the people of Red River object to the Canadian surveyors in 1868?

2 Why do you think most people in Red River supported the Métis list of rights?

3 What was Prime Minister Macdonald's answer to the provisional government?

Shattering the Peace

Some Canadians did not like the situation at Red River. In February 1870 a group of about 600 decided to attack Fort Garry, release the prisoners taken at the raid on Schultz's house, and possibly set up their own government. They met at Kildonan and milled about. Then most decided to go home. On orders from Riel, Métis horsemen surrounded and captured 48 of the Canadians near the village of Winnipeg. Once again, the Fort was full of angry, chilly Canadian prisoners. Among them was a man who would have an impact on Canadian history for decades. His name was Thomas Scott.

Scott was a 28-year-old labourer from Ontario, well known for his hostility toward French-speaking Roman Catholics. His name would haunt the Métis cause forever. Scott was called "the most hated man in the barracks" for his racist remarks toward the Métis. Guards led by Ambrose Lepine demanded that he be court-martialled for insubordination and striking one of them. He was sentenced to death and executed the next day, March 4.

Historians have wondered why Riel allowed Scott to be executed. Some said Riel wanted to demonstrate to Canadian officials that the convention and its military leaders demanded respect. He may have wanted to speed up the process of joining Canada, or keep order in Fort Garry. Many people were very unhappy with the action, but no one expected the Canadian reaction to Scott's execution.

Snippet

Trouble on the Dawson Road

Surveyed by Simon James Dawson, this trail between Fort Garry and Prince Arthur's Landing, now part of Thunder Bay, Ontario, was an overland link between Canada and the West. When construction began in 1868, one of the crew was a loud-mouthed troublemaker from Ontario named Thomas Scott. Scott was fired but did not go back to Ontario. Instead, he hung around Red River — a fateful decision that would change the history of the colony and Canada.

1   Eyewitness accounts disagree about how Scott was executed. How do you think the artist felt about the execution?

2   This picture appeared in a popular magazine of the time. How could it inflame people's feelings?

In this picture, his guards are shown executing Thomas Scott outside the walls of Fort Garry.

English-speaking Ontarians listened in horror to the stories told by anti-Métis leader John Schultz and his friends. In Toronto, a crowd of over 10 000 people heard Schultz and others denounce the execution. The stories painted Scott as a courageous hero. His execution was "murder"; the court-martial was improper, and so was its verdict and sentence; the Métis had no right to imprison or execute Scott.

French Canadians saw things differently. To them, Scott was a bigot who got what he deserved. Many in Québec supported the Métis, who shared a common language and Roman Catholic religion with them. Riel became a hero to Québec francophones and a tyrant to anglophones in Ontario.

Talking Again

Three negotiators left Red River for Canada in late March 1870 to bargain with the Canadian government. The delegates, led by Father Noel-Joseph Ritchot, worked tirelessly to achieve the goals of the colonists. On May 12 the final agreement was reached and on July 15, 1870, Manitoba became Canada's fifth province.

Sir John A. Macdonald sent troops on a "peace mission" to Red River. They travelled by ship, boat, canoe, and rough cart track from Collingwood, Ontario, to Fort Frances, Winnipeg, and on to the Red River Settlement.

How the Manitoba Act met colonists' requests	How the Manitoba Act did not meet colonists' requests
A new province, Manitoba, would join Confederation on July 15, 1870	Instead of a huge province, the Act created a tiny Manitoba and a large Northwest territory governed from Ottawa
Aboriginal Peoples' land rights were respected Land titles were guaranteed	Instead of granting Aboriginal Peoples and Métis large blocks of land, the 1.4 million acres [566 580 ha] reserved for them would be broken up into small parcels
Government would be conducted in English and French	No amnesty was granted to people who took part in the resistance
Courts would operate in English and French	
Schools would be separate for Protestant and Roman Catholic communities	

The troops from Canada arrived at Fort Garry in a drenching rain on August 24, 1870. Many were looking for revenge for the execution of Thomas Scott. No crowds welcomed them, and no Louis Riel awaited them. He had decided to leave the fort. By September 10, most of the troops had gone back to Canada, leaving a few from Ontario.

On September 6, 1870, Lieutenant-Governor Adams Archibald, a Nova Scotian, began his duties in the new Province of Manitoba. Two important issues remained: the amnesty, or pardon, requested by the Convention of Forty, and the settlement of the Métis land claims. Full amnesty was granted to all participants in the resistance except Louis Riel, Ambrose Lepine, and William O'Donoghue, a Métis leader. Settlement of Métis land claims was not final until 1996, 126 years later.

The Story So Far . . .

1 a) Why did the Métis sentence Thomas Scott to death?
  b) Why did Scott's execution cause such problems for the Red River Colony?
2 How successful were the colonists in achieving their goals for a new province?
3 Why would the Métis want an amnesty?
4 Who might not agree with the amnesty?

SUM IT UP!

In this chapter, we learned how rivalry between the North West Company and the Hudson's Bay Company was focused on events at Red River. Conditions in faraway Scotland had a big impact on the Canadian West when Lord Selkirk sponsored Scottish settlement around the Red and Assiniboine rivers. Families whose ancestors were Aboriginal and French or Aboriginal and Scottish joined these settlers. During the 1860s, the Hudson's Bay Company gave up control of Rupert's Land. A new country, Canada, declared an interest in adding the area to Confederation. When Canadian officials failed to consult the people who lived at Red River, residents of the colony resisted the Canadian takeover. In 1869 Métis leader Louis Riel and his followers formed a government at Red River and negotiated with Canada about joining Confederation. A peaceful settlement was upset when Métis guards executed Canadian Thomas Scott. Nonetheless, after tireless negotiations, Manitoba became Canada's fifth province.

THINKING ABOUT YOUR LEARNING

1. Why was there conflict at Red River in the early years of the Selkirk settlement?
2. Why did this conflict at Red River end with the merger of the HBC and the NWC?
3. List the groups at Red River in the 1840s. Describe how they made a living.
4. Why was the colony's isolation a problem?
5. What events outside Red River made change there inevitable in the 1860s?
6. Why did the Métis have the most to fear when Canadians began to move to Red River?
7. What actions did the Métis take to protect their claims?
8. Why might some historians consider Riel's execution of Scott a terrible mistake?

APPLYING YOUR LEARNING

1. This chapter includes many dramatic moments. Choose one and create a one-minute performance to tell the story. You will need to write a script, find actors, make some props, and put together some costumes. Record your minute on video, or present it to your class. Suggestions: Lord Selkirk's representative inviting Scottish settlers to join him; Colin Robertson persuading the settlers to return to Red River; Louis Riel and his followers stopping the Canadian surveyors.
2. Do some research to find out
   • what happened to Lord Selkirk
   • the state of the fur trade in Canada today
   • the state of the Hudson's Bay Company in Canada today
3. Name a person from the chapter whom you would like to meet. Explain your choice.

1 How did the travellers secure their horses?

2 How do you know this painting shows Métis?

3 From what you have learned in this chapter, how is this painting a valuable historical document?

4 Imagine you are one of these travellers. Write a letter or journal entry to describe what it is like to travel and camp on the prairies.

Paul Kane (1810-1871), Camping on the Prairie, 1846, oil on paper, 8¹/₈ x 13³/₈" (20.6 x 34.0), Stark Museum of Art, Orange, Texas

Paul Kane painted this picture, *Camping on the Prairies*, in 1845.

4 Develop a set of interview questions to ask Chief Peguis, Louis Riel, or Marie-Anne Lagemodière.

5 Write a newspaper account of fur trade rivalry between the HBC and NWC.

6 Create your own artwork to show fur trading between Aboriginal Peoples and HBC or NWC traders; the work of the voyageurs; or the buffalo hunt.

7 Make a model of a Red River cart or make a mobile to show who is who at Red River in 1860.

USING KEY WORDS

Write your own definition, using examples, for each of the following:
- pemmican
- merger
- resolutions
- provisional government

CHAPTER 6

King-George Men Move In

1778
James Cook lands at Nootka Sound

1842
HBC factor James Douglas builds post that becomes Victoria, British Columbia

1858–1860
Gold miners rush to the Fraser Valley and the Cariboo

1866
British Columbia and Vancouver Island colonies unite

1871
British Columbia enters Confederation; railway construction begins

SETTING OUR FOCUS

Take a look at the people in this photo. As you can see, they are all men. The chapter is mostly about men, but you will meet some remarkable women as well. The men — labourers, gold miners, surveyors, mounted police officers — will be mostly working outside, challenging the landscape of Canada, a landscape of rushing rivers, granite, mountains, valleys, swamps, and cliffs.

These particular men are building part of a railway. Their work is tough, dangerous, and dirty. They use mostly hand tools to shape rock and timbers. The railway track they are standing on links all parts of Canada, from sea to sea. It is part of the massive railway construction project to complete the "National Dream." These men are part of the rapid changes that all Western people, especially Aboriginal Peoples, experienced in their lives at this time.

Join the crew for a while. Slap some blackflies, pick a rock out of your boot, and enjoy a meagre meal of biscuit and tea. Try not to think about your aching muscles, the stinking bunkhouse, or your grumbling stomach. Tomorrow will be another day on the job — building Canada.

PREVIEWING THE CHAPTER

In this chapter you will learn about these topics:
- **the rush for gold in British Columbia**
- **why British Columbia joined Confederation**
- **the work of the North West Mounted Police in Western Canada**
- **treaties between Aboriginal Peoples and the Canadian government**
- **conflicts and changes in the West, including significant changes to the way of life of Aboriginal Peoples**
- **the construction of a great railway from Canada to the Pacific Ocean**

KEY WORDS

common property
Indian Act
negotiator
reserve
syndicate
terminus
transcontinental
treaties

1871–1877	1873	1874	1881	1885
Treaties signed between prairie Aboriginal Peoples and Canada	Pacific Scandal, Macdonald resigns	NWMP march west, police work begins	CPR Syndicate gets railway contract	Railway completed coast to coast

Europeans on the West Coast

For thousands of years the Aboriginal Peoples lived along the northwest coast of North America. Rapid changes began after European sailing ships appeared in the middle of the 1700s. In 1778 Captain James Cook and his men dropped anchor in Nootka Sound. The British sailors stayed a month, repairing their rotten masts, getting rest and fresh food, and trading with the Nootka people. They soon discovered that the sea otter pelts they got from the Nootkas were prized in China and brought huge profits. Within a few years, traders in ships from Britain, Spain, and the United States were competing for sea otter furs. Many Aboriginal Peoples died, stricken by diseases brought by the traders.

At the same time, fur traders and explorers travelled overland from the East to find furs, open trading posts, and make their way to the Pacific Ocean. North West Company (NWC) traders and their Aboriginal guides and paddlers struggled to open trade routes to the coast. In 1793 Alexander Mackenzie reached the Pacific, the first European to reach the coast from inland.

Ten years later, fur traders from the Canadas and Britain began to build posts in the interior of British Columbia, then called New Caledonia. The British government feared American expansion in the area, so it leased Vancouver Island to the Hudson's Bay Company (HBC). In 1849 Governor James Douglas of the HBC moved to Fort Victoria.

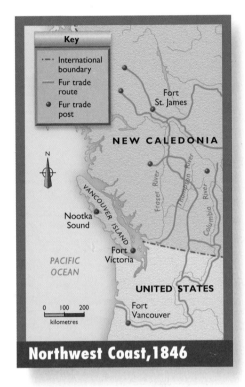

Northwest Coast, 1846

Key
- - - International boundary
— Fur trade route
● Fur trade post

Fort St. James

NEW CALEDONIA

N

VANCOUVER ISLAND

Fraser River

Thompson River

Columbia River

Nootka Sound

Fort Victoria

PACIFIC OCEAN

UNITED STATES

0 100 200
kilometres

Fort Vancouver

This illustration of Fort Victoria appeared in *The Illustrated London News* on August 26, 1848. The steamboat in the foreground was used by the HBC. Locate Fort Victoria on the map.

James and Amelia Douglas
A COUNTRY MARRIAGE

James Douglas, chief trader at Fort Vancouver in 1837, was furious. The object of his fury was the first chaplain to arrive at the busy Hudson's Bay Company post on the bank of the Columbia River.

Reverend Herbert Beaver and his strait-laced wife had arrived the previous September. Right away they had started causing trouble. They refused to have anything to do with the wives of the men who worked for the company. The reason? The couples had married in "the custom of the country" — the ceremonies had not been conducted in a church. How could they have been? Until the Beavers came, there had been no churches or ministers.

One of the women snubbed by the Beavers was Douglas's wife, Amelia. The two had married in the custom of the country while Douglas was a clerk at Fort St. James. Her father, a Scot, had been Douglas's boss; her mother was from the Dene Nation.

Douglas may have been especially sensitive to the snub because he, too, was the mixed-race child of a country marriage. His father, a Scot, had owned a plantation in British Guiana, known today as Guyana. There, he had married an African-American woman, and they had had three children. James, the oldest, had spent his first six years with his mother in British Guiana. Then his father took him to Scotland to be educated. He never saw his mother again.

Douglas swallowed his anger and asked Reverend Beaver to conduct a marriage ceremony. This was not an option for many of the other couples at the post. Most were Roman Catholics and Beaver was a Church of England minister. His attitude angered so many people that he soon left the post.

Still, the memory of this encounter with the priggish British couple may have had a lasting effect on Amelia. When Douglas was appointed Governor of Vancouver Island in 1851, and of mainland British Columbia in 1858, she chose to stay in the background. One of the couple's older daughters often took her mother's place at the official parties, balls, and other social events the Governor was required to give and attend.

Although she rarely appeared in public, Amelia — who became Lady Douglas when Queen Victoria knighted her husband for his accomplishments — never forgot her Aboriginal roots. Years later her grandchildren remembered her entertaining them at bedtime with legends and stories she had heard as a child at Fort St. James.

More people you could research are

Matthew Baillie Begbie

James and Amelia Douglas

John Helmcken

Maquinna

Catherine Schubert

David Thompson

The lives of the people who lived and worked in the area west of the prairies changed dramatically after 1858. Disease and conflict reduced the numbers of Aboriginal Peoples from 60 000 to about 25 000. An unidentified Aboriginal elder of the Seshahts voiced his concerns in 1860:

> *Our families are well, our people have plenty of food; but how long this will last we know not. We see your ships, and hear things that make our hearts grow faint. They say that more King-George-men [British people] will soon be here, and will take our land, our firewood, our fishing grounds; that we shall be placed on a little spot, and shall have to do everything according to the fancies of the King-George-men.*

The reason for this great change was gold.

The Story So Far . . .

1 What did Europeans who first visited the northwest coast hope to gain?

2 Why did the British government lease Vancouver Island to the HBC?

3 What fears did the Seshahts elder express? What do you think he might say today about the situation facing his people?

Rush for Gold

In 1857 a group of Aboriginal Peoples from New Caledonia sent about 800 ounces (about 23 kg) of gold to a mint in San Francisco to be sold. When the news leaked out, thousands were struck by gold fever. Miners from California boarded ships to take them north. Within a few months, about 30 000 people left their homes for New Caledonia.

The newcomers presented James Douglas with some big problems. How would he maintain law and order? How would he get people and supplies safely in and out of the gold fields? The British government named

Snippet

Calming Fears

As American miners flooded into the Cariboo, the Interior Salish people feared being forced onto reserves. This had happened to Aboriginal Peoples during the gold rush in the American Oregon Territory. The Salish were ready to fight to prevent this. Luckily, Governor James Douglas understood their concerns. On a visit to the Cariboo, he warned rowdy miners to respect the rights of the Salish.

him Governor of the mainland area, and renamed the colony British Columbia on August 2, 1858. A few workers came to help Douglas manage the colony, including Judge Matthew Baillie Begbie. He travelled across the colony to maintain the law and provide justice.

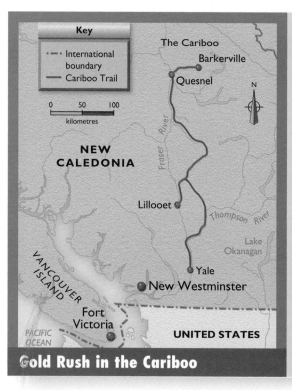

Key
- - - - International boundary
——— Cariboo Trail

0   50   100
kilometres

The Cariboo
Barkerville
Quesnel
NEW CALEDONIA
Fraser River
Lillooet
Thompson River
Lake Okanagan
Yale
New Westminster
VANCOUVER ISLAND
Fort Victoria
PACIFIC OCEAN
UNITED STATES

Gold Rush in the Cariboo

1. Estimate how far it was by trail and wagon road from New Westminster to Barkerville.

2. Compare the trails on this map with roads shown on a modern map of British Columbia. Which are the same?

3. Name the two main settlements in British Columbia in 1863. Name British Columbia's two biggest cities today.

Thousands of prospectors went up the Fraser River. Aboriginal Peoples' communities and lands were damaged as prospectors and miners moved into the Cariboo, ignoring Aboriginal rights. This was very different from the fur trade, where Aboriginal Peoples and traders worked as partners.

Farmers settled along the lower Fraser River. Cattle ranches and orchards blossomed in the Okanagan Valley. Sawmills produced lumber to build the houses, stores, and saloons in Yale, Lillooet, and Quesnel. In 1871 British Columbia joined the Canadian Confederation.

Far Left: **William Hind's painting of a miner panning for gold.**
Left: **Bill Phinney with a rocker**

Examine the two pictures showing miners working for gold.

1. Explain how these pictures fit into our chapter theme.

2. Which picture would you expect to be more accurate: the painting or the photograph? Explain.

The Cariboo Road was built from 1862 to 1864 to reach the gold fields to the north.

Take a look at the people in this photograph. They are making their way along the Cariboo Road to the gold fields. Step into the picture. Now, how do you feel so high up the side of this mountain? What do you see below you? Did you feel a little nervous when the other wagon and teams passed your wagon? Did you hope the ponies would not be spooked or slip? How uncomfortable are you — hungry? hot? tired? unwashed? Is it worth it to get to that gold? Talk with a partner about this, and then together present a short conversation that two of these travellers might have held.

1. What reasons can you think of to explain why the boardwalk was raised?

2. What services could a miner obtain, based on the signs seen in the photograph?

3. How does the photograph help us understand why the whole town was a fire hazard?

Snippet

Barkerville

One of the most successful miners in the Cariboo was a man named Billy Barker. A large town named after Barker sprang up to serve the miners working their claims on Williams Creek. Barkerville had saloons, restaurants, churches, stores, bars, a hospital, dance halls, a theatre, and gambling dens. Lots of miners won and lost fortunes in the card games.

The wooden buildings in Barkerville were so close together that a fire in 1868 roared down both sides of the street in minutes. Within a few days, people rebuilt their town.

The Story So Far . . .

1. Review Chapter 4. What persuaded British Columbia to join Canada?

2. Find out what happened to Barkerville when the gold ran out.

3. Why did people "rush" to the Cariboo country? Would you join a gold rush if you could? Why?

THE NORTH WEST MOUNTED POLICE

In 1870 the immense region west of Manitoba was home to Aboriginal Peoples, fur traders' families, and millions of bison and wolves. There were fewer than 50 000 people in an area about one quarter the size of North America. Food, especially buffalo meat, had become scarce during the 1860s. Buffalo hunters from Red River began to move farther west onto lands of the Cree people, pushing the Cree into the territory of the Blackfoot Confederacy. Warfare raged between Cree and

Firewater

Firewater was made from alcohol, chewing tobacco, red pepper, ginger, molasses, and water. Some traders included red ink.

Blackfoot in 1869, and hundreds died. Hundreds more died from smallpox during the 1870s.

The enemy of the Cree and Blackfoot was rapid change. Traders from south of the border crossed into Cree and Blackfoot camps looking for buffalo robes. In return they offered sickening concoctions of alcohol called "whisky." The traders built forts north of the 49th parallel with names like Whoop-Up, Whisky Gap, and Robber's Roost.

Buffalo hides were used to make belts to run industrial machinery in many factories in the Eastern United States and Canada. In the early 1870s, as many as 100 000 buffalo robes were shipped East each year.

By 1870 Canada was responsible for keeping peace in the West. Prime Minister John A. Macdonald had decided to create a police force for the West, but in 1873 the bill was still not law. Then, news of a massacre of Assiniboin people at Cypress Hills by whisky traders reached the East. Canadians demanded action. People feared that lawlessness on the Western plains would give Americans an excuse to move in. Within weeks, a force of men went west to bring law and order. They were called the North West Mounted Police (NWMP), later simply the Mounties.

The North West Mounted Police had the following responsibilities:
- End the illegal whisky trade.
- Patrol the United States–Canada border.
- End smuggling.
- Gain the respect and confidence of the Aboriginal Peoples.
- Preserve law and order.

In the autumn of 1873, the first 150 recruits of the NWMP gathered in Collingwood, Ontario. Some had been farmers, others bartenders, clerks, sailors, or police officers. Ahead of them was a challenging journey of 1400 km to Lower Fort Garry, and a winter in Manitoba preparing for their police work.

The Long March

On July 8, 1874, a procession of 300 recruits, 310 horses, 142 oxen, 114 Métis with Red River carts, 73 wagons, 33 cows, and 3 large field guns left Manitoba. On the wagons were six months' worth of sugar, tea, flour, bacon, ammunition, and food for the animals. It was a noisy column indeed. Soon the first of hundreds of problems struck: wagon wheels and axles broke regularly. Everyone had to stop for repairs. On September 10, Constable Fred Bagley wrote:

> No one seems to know where we are. Everyone glum and low-spirited. Future prospects gloomy. Cold wind and rain. Threat of snow. Camped on the open plain near a swamp. No water, no wood. No supper.

After three weeks, the column had travelled only 430 km. Commissioner George French split the group into two, sending the healthiest to Whoop-Up country. The others, called the "barnyard contingent," travelled north, their farm animals and horses slowly trudging across the prairie. They took 88 days to reach Fort Edmonton, after struggles with hunger, cold, mud, and insects.

Snippet

What's in a Name?

A lot, for some Americans in 1873. When they heard that Canada was planning to patrol the 49th parallel with an armed force called the Mounted Rifles, many were outraged with the warlike name. To appease them, Prime Minister John A. Macdonald asked for a draft of the Act creating the force. He crossed out "Mounted Rifles" and wrote in "Mounted Police." The Mounted Rifles Act became the Mounted Police Act.

The Route of Long March

Snapshot

Jerry Potts: Blackfoot First, Mountie Second

No one — European, Aboriginal, or Métis — wanted to tangle with Jerry Potts. Whether fighting in a barroom brawl or in a war party alongside the Blackfoot, his mother's people, the legendary Métis scout and interpreter always emerged unhurt. As a result, the Blackfoot believed that he had supernatural powers. Potts himself believed that his luck came from the charm he always carried inside his shirt — the skin of a cat.

Potts had much to offer the Mounties. Revered by the Blackfoot, he was an ideal go-between. Because he spoke English and several Aboriginal languages, he was able to promote understanding by explaining European ways to the Blackfoot and Blackfoot ways to the Europeans. His keen sense of direction helped him guide the Mounties across the rolling Western plains that, to eastern eyes, seemed empty of landmarks.

What did the Mounties offer Potts in return? The most important thing was an end to the whisky trade, which he believed was ruining his people. He also liked the Mounties' friendly approach, which was so different from the ruthlessness of the American cavalry south of the 49th parallel. Still, Potts' loyalties were always clear. The Mounties were never anything more than his employers. His people were the Blackfoot — and they counted first in his heart.

Snippet

The Scarlet Tradition Begins

To many Aboriginal Peoples of the West, American soldiers were the enemy. The blue-coated troops often treated them cruelly, but a British soldier in a red coat was different. This is why the Mounties decided their uniforms would follow the British military tradition. Someone in a scarlet tunic was more likely to be trusted by Aboriginal Peoples.

The Mounties struggled to "get their man" in this Henri Julien drawing of the trek west in 1874. They are crossing the Dirt Hills.

Winter was coming. Exhausted, shivering horses suffered from hunger and cold, so the men covered the animals with their own blankets. On September 10, they reached the place where they thought Fort Whoop-Up would be. Only the wind met them. In desperation Commissioner French rode to Fort Benton, Montana, to have supplies sent to the force. When the supplies arrived, a Métis guide, Ky-yo-kosi, known as Jerry Potts, was with them.

When James Macleod, guided by Jerry Potts, approached Fort Whoop-Up, a single trader opened the gates. The others had fled or were trading legally. The NWMP closed the whisky forts, built a base called Fort Macleod, and began patrolling the country. Their community quickly grew to include a saloon, stores, and even a hotel.

Web Connection

http://www.school.mcgrawhill.ca/resources

Go to the web site above to read Henri Julien's diary of his journey with the NWMP on the Long March. Go to History Resources, then to *Canada: The Story of a Developing Nation* to see where to go next.

Mounties on the Job

The Mounties' most important work involved keeping order. They patrolled on horseback or on foot, to end smuggling, stop whisky traders, and keep the peace. They soon earned the respect and trust of most people in the West. They delivered mail, provided medical services, took the census, and delivered relief supplies to Aboriginal communities. As well, they fought prairie fires, settled riots, and tracked down rustlers.

Here NWMP men are shown with Aboriginal scouts at Fort Macleod.

The Story So Far . . .

1 Why was a police force needed in the Canadian Northwest?
2 Why did NWMP officers have to be good horsemen?
3 Compare the jobs of the NWMP with the jobs of the RCMP. Make a comparison chart to explain your findings.
4 Explain how the legend of the NWMP grew.
5 Briefly describe the work of Jerry Potts, Ky-yo-kosi.

The Evidence Behind the Story

Most countries and peoples have stories, myths, and legends to explain past events. In Canada there is the legend of the invincible RCMP officers who "always get their man!"

The Mounties are a well-known symbol of Canada. They are often featured on postcards, on souvenir mugs, and on key chains. They are clearly visible when Parliament opens and look splendid in their scarlet tunics when newcomers swear allegiance to Canada at citizenship ceremonies. In fact during the last 125 years, they have starred in lots of novels and in many Hollywood movies, especially during the 1950s. During the 1990s, a popular TV program featured a Mountie acting just as legend suggests he should: calmly, honestly, politely, and cleverly, to "get his man" — the villain. He usually acted non-violently as well. This, too, fits the stories: Mounties are good-looking, tough, clever, and peaceful.

How did this legend arise? It has been around ever since those very first days of 1873, when the force began its gruelling trip west from Ontario. Newspapers in Eastern Canada were filled with tales of the heroic Mounties. The force had to fight cold, hunger, insects, icy rivers, and fierce winds. They trekked across the hot and dusty prairie, struggled across swamps and rivers, got lost, and suffered mightily; to bring law and order to the West. Here is what one historian says about the legend of the Mounties:

The most remarkable fact about the North West Mounted Police in this first generation was that it was loved and respected. The comment of an American train-robber, captured in British Columbia after a sizzling gun-fight, may serve as the expression of public opinion: "You may think it funny coming from me, but I certainly admire the way you boys do your work." The Mounties were an outstanding success.

Some people thought the trek west, which helped forge the reputation of the heroic and fearless Mounties, was an unnecessary waste of people and animals. The force should have prepared more carefully for their journey. They made foolish decisions, such as failing to provide water bottles and other blunders. After all, hundreds of Métis traders made journeys like theirs across the plains many times without mishap.

QUESTIONING THE EVIDENCE

A myth or a legend is a story that cannot be proven. Think of the legends of Laura Secord and Tecumseh. People enjoy and learn from them. Historical legends help people feel connected to their past.

1. What evidence would you need to show that a historical story is a myth or legend, rather than fact?
2. Use your understanding from language arts studies to explain why people like to have myths and legends to explain things.
3. In the past, people all over the world knew of the legendary Mounties. Do you think the Mounties have similar standing in Canada today? How do you know? Where have you learned about the Mounties? Does the knowledge you have support the legend?
4. Try to find some examples of the Mountie legend today; visit a souvenir shop and see what you can uncover, or see if you have any souvenirs at home. Report your findings.
5. Do some research on the RCMP today. Where do they work? What jobs do they carry out? What difficulties do they face? What changes has the force undergone during the last ten years?

TREATIES WITH THE ABORIGINAL PEOPLES

Plains Aboriginal Peoples faced a devastating upheaval in their way of life beginning around 1865. Over a 20-year period, the buffalo disappeared, settlers arrived, war and disease destroyed families, and railway trains crossed traditional lands. The people realized their old ways were gone.

Treaty-Making in the 1870s

Cree and other prairie people knew that the Canadian government had paid the Hudson's Bay Company for land in the West. They knew, too, that settlers would be coming. They saw that the buffalo were disappearing.

Cree Chief Sweetgrass described his concerns:

We heard our lands were sold and we did not like it; we don't want to sell our lands; it is our property and no one has a right to sell them. Our country is no longer able to support us. Make provision for us against years of starvation…we want you to stop the Americans from coming to trade on our lands.

As more settlers began to move into the West, Aboriginal Peoples pushed for **treaties** to settle issues of land and payments from the Canadian government. In 1870 Colonel Wolseley and his troops attempted to cross through Cree territories west of Lake Superior. The Cree agreed to let the troops pass through their lands, for a fee. In 1871, after some people tried to settle west of the Red River, the Aboriginal communities warned the settlers not to move onto land that was not theirs. A band of Saulteaux people led by Yellow Quill turned settlers back when they tried to move west of Portage la Prairie. It was time for treaty-making.

Huge piles of buffalo bones represented thousands of dead animals. The bones were picked up by early settlers and shipped east to be ground into fertilizer. Horns were made into buttons and combs. Hooves were turned into glue.

Marie Rose Delorme

WITNESS TO A DYING WAY OF LIFE

When the cart jolted to a stop, Marie Rose Delorme was the first to hop out. She wanted a few minutes to herself after spending a hot, dusty day in the covered cart with her older sister Elise and the babies, two-year-old Magdeleine and ten-month-old Pezzan.

It was June 1870. The Delormes were with a caravan of Métis families, following the 800-km Carlton Trail northwest to Fort Carlton on the North Saskatchewan River. From there, they planned to head for Fort Pitt. Then they would retrace the journey, arriving home in time to spend the winter in their log cabin near the Assiniboine River.

For the Métis, the trip served two purposes. Along the way, they would hunt buffalo. They would also barter their trade goods for furs and buffalo skins at Cree camps. The skins would, in turn, be traded when the caravan stopped at Hudson's Bay Company posts.

Marie Rose's time for herself was short. There was plenty to do as the families set up camp for the night. While the tipis were being put up, Marie Rose and Elise gathered dried buffalo chips for the cooking fire.

Helped by Elise, Marie Rose's mother cooked a supper of prairie chicken and bannock, a quick bread. The bannock was a treat. The flour supply had to last the whole trip, so it was used sparingly. After supper, many of the families gathered to drink tea, tell stories and play games.

Evenings were different when the men killed buffalo. Then, the caravan stopped for days and everyone worked from dawn to dusk. They skinned carcasses, smoked meat so it would keep in the summer heat, dried sinew for sewing, tanned hides, and made pemmican. Marie Rose preferred more relaxed evenings like this.

At sunup the next morning, the families started breaking camp. The scouts were already out on the trail. Their job was to find water and a place for the next night's camp. If they spotted Cree lodges where goods could be traded, all the better. They also kept a sharp eye out for buffalo and game.

Marie Rose did not know it at the time, but this hunt would be the family's last. Her father died soon after the Delormes returned home. Other families carried on for a few years, but they soon stopped making the annual trek. There was little point. The buffalo had disappeared — and so had a way of life.

More people you could research are

Marie Rose Delorme

Isapo-muxika (Crowfoot)

Ke We Tayash

Father Albert Lacombe

Maskepetoon

Mis Koo Kenew (Henry Prince)

In the summer of 1871, the Lieutenant-Governor of Manitoba spoke to the assembled Ojibwa about Treaty 1. As Queen Victoria's representative, he advised them that she wanted them to become farmers. He promised them land forever, with no intrusion by others. He also promised to respect hunting and fishing rights and to allow them to maintain their way of life. Promises such as these were not kept. In fact, they were not even included in the treaty. Many Ojibwa were unhappy with the results.

Treaty 3 involved the lands between the Selkirk settlement and Lake Superior. The Ojibwa did not waver in their demands for fair compensation. They wanted free passes on trains travelling through their territory, an end to liquor sales in their lands, farming equipment and animals, education, yearly payments, and large **reserves**. Reserves were areas of land set aside solely for their use. Government **negotiators**, the people who were sent to reach an agreement, agreed, and the treaty was signed in 1873.

Treaties 4, 5, and 6 were negotiated during the mid-1870s. The Cree and Assiniboin people were unhappy with many changes to their way of life. They complained about the money Canada had paid to the Hudson's Bay Company for Rupert's Land, arguing that this money was actually theirs. There were other complaints. As Poundmaker (Pitikwahanapiwiyin), a Cree chief, said "This is our land, it isn't a piece of pemmican to be cut off and given in little pieces back to us. It is ours and we will take what we want."

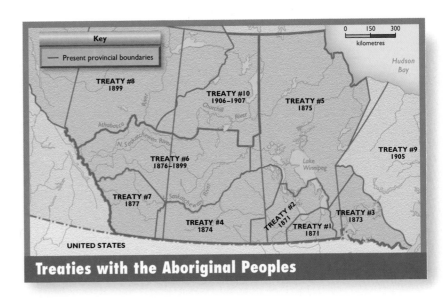

Treaties with the Aboriginal Peoples

Treaty 7 was the final agreement between prairie Aboriginal Peoples and the Canadian government. In September of 1877 thousands of horses, hundreds of members of the Blackfoot Confederacy, NWMP officers, and Canadian negotiators gathered at Blackfoot Crossing. They prayed, danced, traded, celebrated, bargained, and signed Treaty 7. The police kept order.

With the signing of Treaty 7, the lands of the prairies officially belonged to Canada. Canadian negotiators had achieved title to the Western lands, which could be sold or developed as the government decided. In return for giving up title to their lands, the Aboriginal Peoples negotiated reserve lands, annual payments, gifts of clothing, as well as rights to medical care, education, farm machinery, and relief from hunger. A law called the **Indian Act** described the rights and responsibilities of Aboriginal Peoples and the Government of Canada.

Blackfoot chief Isapo-muxika, called Crowfoot, signed Treaty 7. He praised the work of the NWMP among his people.

Taking a Look at the Treaties

What did the Aboriginal Peoples gain by the treaties? Did they know they had given up rights to huge areas of land? What did the Canadian government gain and give up? Did Canadian negotiators take advantage of the Aboriginal Peoples? These are questions that people have been asking ever since the 1870s. Here are some opinions:

• The idea of private property was new to some Aboriginal Peoples. They understood the idea of **common property**. Common property is used by all members of the community, but owned by none.

• Some Aboriginal Peoples did not realize they would be confined to reserves.

- Some Aboriginal Peoples understood they had given up use of the land for settlers to farm, but they believed they still had rights to water, timber, minerals, and fish.
- In return for continuing assistance from the government, some Aboriginal Peoples knowingly gave up their lands.
- In some cases, the spoken agreements between Aboriginal Peoples and government negotiators did not match the written agreements signed by each side.
- Language difficulties made some terms very difficult for both sides to understand in the same way.
- Government negotiators gave up much more than they had originally intended: rights to medical care, education, farm seed, and larger grants of land were not part of their plans until Aboriginal negotiators forced them to agree.
- Aboriginal Peoples thought of treaties as agreements that would be changed as conditions changed. Signing ceremonies were part of an ongoing relationship between the two sides.
- Europeans and Canadians thought of treaties as final settlements.

Although some Canadian negotiators and members of the NWMP kept detailed diaries of their observations at the treaty ceremonies, there are fewer Aboriginal records. We know that diaries are just the records of one person's observations and ideas. As one historian has written: "There will never be agreement on what the original parties did, let alone what they thought they had done."

Aboriginal Peoples suffered from hunger and upheaval in their lives during the 1870s and 1880s. Here they are shown receiving rations from an Indian agent.

While we cannot know what people signing treaties thought they were doing, we can learn what resulted for the people in the West. You will learn, in the next chapter, about frustrations, problems, and conflict that faced Aboriginal Peoples and settlers after 1877.

The Story So Far . . .

1 What reasons did Aboriginal Peoples on the prairies have for signing treaties?
2 What reasons did the Canadian government have for signing treaties?
3 Make a chart showing what Aboriginal Peoples gave up on one side, and what they gained on the other. Suggest some future problems that might occur for them.
4 Brainstorm and create a collage of words and pictures to show reasons for the treaties. Indicate which represent Aboriginal Peoples' perspectives and which represent the Canadian government's views.

BUILDING THE GREAT RAILWAY

The idea of building a Canadian **transcontinental** railway seems astounding. Think of the distances involved in connecting Halifax, Nova Scotia, with Vancouver, British Columbia. Think of the impossible stretches of mountains, forests, muskeg, and prairie to be crossed. A railroad across this land would be the world's longest and most expensive. In 1867 there were only about 3.5 million people in Canada. How could they dream of building such a railway?

Canadians wanted to demonstrate that they had the willpower, the strength, and the human ingenuity to finish such a project. They also wanted to make sure that American railways did not carry Canadian settlers and goods to the West, and Western products to the East. In 1871 Sir John A. Macdonald's government promised to build a railway to connect British Columbia with the Eastern provinces.

Pacific Scandal

Railways cost a lot of money to build. How could the government pay for the project? It did not have the resources and had to turn to private business interests. In 1873 Macdonald's government gave the railway contract to Hugh

Bridges and trestles had to be built to carry the railway tracks over rushing streams, wide rivers, and deep canyons.

Allan of Montréal and his American partners. Then the government decided that no Americans could control the project. Allan's partners reacted with fury. They accused Allan of buying the railway contract by paying to support the election of Macdonald's party in 1872. Soon newspapers had a startling story: telegrams stolen from Allan's lawyer's office safe seemed to incriminate Macdonald himself. One telegram said, "I must have another $10 000." Surely this meant Macdonald had asked Allan for campaign money and given him the railway contract in return. There was a parliamentary inquiry, and lots of screaming headlines in newspapers. Macdonald resigned in disgrace.

The new prime minister was Sir Alexander Mackenzie. His government did not push for the railway project to begin in a hurry. There was little money for such an immense job. Surveyors supervised by one of the most creative engineers in Canadian history, Sir Sandford Fleming, had to find and mark a route for the railway. For ten years, Fleming's crews worked tirelessly, whenever there was enough money to pay them.

Reflections

Surveyors worked in rough country, measuring and marking off routes for roads, boundaries, or railways. Put yourself in a surveyor's boots and write a few journal entries describing your work and the country you work in.

A decision had to be made: where would the western **terminus**, or end, of the railway be located? At this time, Vancouver was a village on the Pacific coast. In the summer of 1878, Prime Minister Mackenzie announced that Port Moody would be the Pacific terminus. Within months, Vancouver blossomed into a town and then a city.

This survey crew has just reached the summit of a pass in the Canadian Rockies. Their break time will be short.

Mackenzie's government decided to build a line in British Columbia from Port Moody to Yale, and from Fort William, Ontario, to Selkirk, Manitoba. The terrain posed terrible construction problems for the builders. West of Lake Superior, muskeg swallowed up trainloads of gravel, rails, and ties. Mosquitoes and blackflies plagued the workers. They laid only 100 km of track per year for seven years; and it was heartbreaking work. Endless kilometres of granite had to be blasted. Accidents involving nitroglycerine, the explosive used, killed or maimed many workers. Their task took courage and toughness; and lots of money.

After ten years, three big sections of the railway remained to be built, totalling about 3200 km of track. A company had to be found that would build and then operate the railway. This was not a job for a cash-strapped government.

The Story So Far . . .

1 Why did the Canadian government want to build a transcontinental railway?
2 Explain what the stolen telegram from Sir John A. Macdonald to Hugh Allan meant.
3 Discuss why the railway construction in the Canadian Shield was so expensive.
4 Write some newspaper headlines about the Pacific Scandal.

A big work crew stands still on their boarding cars for the photographer. These moving barracks were used on the prairies to save time setting up camps.

Getting on with the Job

In February 1881 Parliament agreed to terms with a Canadian company called the Syndicate to complete the railway project. (A **syndicate** is a group of companies or people who get together to get something done.) The contract included these terms:
- The Syndicate would build and operate the railway from Callander, Ontario, to the Pacific terminus.
- The railway would be finished within ten years.
- The Canadian Pacific Railway company (CPR) would get $25 million and 10 million ha of free land across the prairies. This land would be sold to settlers, the money staying in CPR hands.
- There would be no taxes on railway stations, grounds, or other buildings.
- The company would own railways that had already been built as part of the transcontinental system.
- No other lines could be built south of the CPR for at least 20 years.

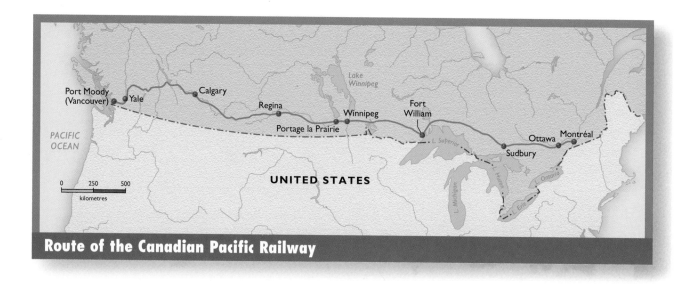

Route of the Canadian Pacific Railway

This contract caused many things to happen. The railway was completed in record time and towns sprang up along the railway line. On the other hand, many Westerners, especially farmers, came to resent the CPR for its monopoly, since the company could charge whatever it wanted to carry prairie grain to markets.

During the winter of 1882, the Syndicate hired a remarkable railway builder to get the job done. William Van Horne, an American, had many talents. He was a champion poker-player and rose-grower, violinist, artist, and collector of ancient Chinese porcelain. The Syndicate wanted him for one thing, however: to get the railway finished.

In the spring of 1882, a mountain of supplies was sent to Manitoba. Railway ties, rails, spikes, bolts, tools, 4000 horses, and 3000 workers were set to work. Each morning at dawn, the workers rolled out of their tents and had breakfast. Teamsters fed and watered the horses. Everyone worked for 5 hours, had a dinner break, and worked 5 hours before supper. Sometimes they worked evenings as well. Some spaced the ties, some placed rails, others fastened fishplates, bolts, and spikes. Still others built the stations that were spaced 12 km apart along the track.

In the autumn of 1882, construction on the prairies halted. The workers had finished 660 km of main line; set 1.5 million ties; laid 52 297 t of steel rails; and strung 1432 km of telegraph wire. People were riding trains between Winnipeg and Swift Current. The following year, the entire prairie section was completed; the steel rails were in Calgary.

Snippet

The Syndicate: Who Are These People?

Members of the Syndicate were wealthy men with connections to international bankers and financiers. Sir George Stephen was President of the CPR and the Bank of Montreal. His cousin, Donald Smith, had been the head of the Hudson's Bay Company and had negotiated with Louis Riel in 1870. Other Syndicate members included former fur trader, Canadian-born James J. Hill, who built railways in the United States, and bankers in Germany and France. They took on the project for one reason: to make money by carrying goods and people across Canada by train.

A track-laying machine puts down some track in Manitoba. Gangs of workers nailed in ties and rails carried forward by the machine. It was hot, dusty work.

The Story So Far . . .

1 Why was construction easier across the prairies than across the Canadian Shield?
2 What qualities would Van Horne need "to get the job done"?
3 What did the Macdonald government (and Canada) gain by the railway contract? What did the Syndicate gain?

Tough Going

The work in British Columbia was especially dangerous. An experienced American engineer, Andrew Onderdonk, was in charge of construction. His job was immense: get supplies and workers to the site, blast dozens of tunnels through the mountains, build 600 trestles and bridges, and do it within budget. There were not enough railway workers in British Columbia, so Onderdonk brought in about 7000 Chinese labourers. They were tireless, courageous, and indispensable. Hundreds were killed in accidents involving cave-ins, explosions, and falls down the enormous mountain cliffs. The Chinese workers were paid $1 a day and lived on rice, vegetables, and tea. They suffered from injuries and illness, and then hunger when they were laid off during the winter months. Some people in British Columbia treated them very badly, passing racist laws to discourage them from staying after the railway was finished.

Chinese railway workers were among the best on the CPR.

Pon Git Cheng

DREAMS OF GOLD MOUNTAIN

When opportunity came knocking, Pon Git Cheng of the village of Pinghong near Canton, China, was ready. Recruiters were signing up men to help build a railway in far-off British Columbia, Canada. Pon wanted to be one of them. It would be hard to leave his wife and three sons, but what choice did he have? The plot of land he farmed was too small to support his family. Taxes were high and there were no jobs. People were starving. North America — Gold Mountain — was a land of opportunity. Some Chinese people had made their fortunes in the California and Cariboo gold rushes. Maybe Pon, too, would be lucky. At the very least, he would be able to send money to his family.

Pon was just one of about 15 000 men who left China with the same hopes and dreams. They did not know that they were nothing but a source of cheap labour for the company that was building the railway. They also did not know that ahead of them lay prejudice, mistreatment, brutal working conditions, and even death.

Pon arrived in Canada in 1882. He was aged about 32. For the next three years, he worked from sunrise to sunset every day except when work stopped during the winter. For this he was paid $1 a day. Because he earned nothing when there was no work in winter, his wages totalled about $225 a year. The Chinese workers were forced to pay many expenses — tools, supplies, food, and rent. They also had to repay the cost of their passage to Canada. During a year of backbreaking work, the most Pon could send home was $40. In contrast, other labourers earned between $1.50 and $2.50 a day. Their living conditions were better and their work tools were free.

Pon and his countrymen became known as excellent workers. Their reward? The hardest and most dangerous assignments, such as building tunnels and working with explosives. So dangerous was the work and so harsh the living conditions that more than 600 Chinese workers had died by the time the railway was completed in 1885.

With the railway finished, Pon no longer had a job. He could not even return home. He could not afford the $70 fare. His only choice was to find another job and keep sending money to his family. He also saved a little, but it was many years before he managed to visit his home and bring two of his sons to Canada. Pon's dreams of Gold Mountain never came true in the way he had hoped, but his hard work and sacrifice did give his family a better life.

More people you could research are

Pon Git Cheng

Edward Mallandaine

Andrew Onderdonk

Delia Onderdonk

A. B. Rogers

William Van Horne

Go to the web site above to find more information and photographs on the building of Onderdonk's section of the railway. Go to History Resources, then to *Canada: The Story of a Developing Nation* to see where to go next.

Reflections

Suppose you are a railway worker in the Selkirk Mountains, north of Lake Superior, or across the prairies. Write a letter home about your work and feelings.

The railway builders faced a big obstacle in the summer of 1883. There was still no route between the prairie line and the end of Onderdonk's section. Completing the survey work and selecting a route required another legendary character. Major A. B. Rogers was a workaholic who thrived on danger and challenge. The CPR chose him to find a mountain route for the railway. Rogers drove his surveyors through a terrible ordeal to find the pass, now named after him, that became the railway route. Throughout 1884 and 1885, crews struggled to build bridges, trestles, and snow sheds and to lay track through the treacherous Selkirk Mountains.

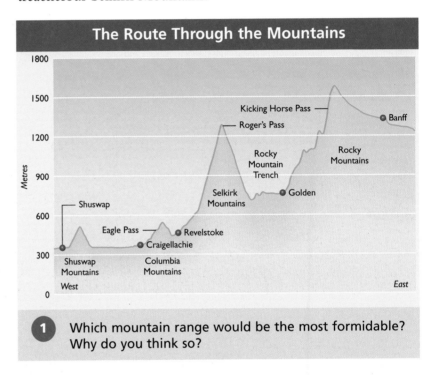

The Route Through the Mountains

1 Which mountain range would be the most formidable? Why do you think so?

Workers north of Superior faced challenges as fearsome as those of the Selkirk Mountains. The tough granite of the Canadian Shield yielded only to blasting — over $7.5 million was spent on dynamite and nitroglycerine for one 900-km stretch of track. By the spring of 1885, only a few gaps remained in the line between Montréal and Winnipeg.

Yet the CPR was in trouble. The company was out of money. Some workers had not been paid. Then some Western Métis and Aboriginal Peoples armed themselves to fight the tide of change, as you will learn in the next chapter. Troops from Canada were rushed to the Saskatchewan country on the brand-new CPR to end the Rebellion of 1885. A few gaps in the line north of Superior provided an opportunity for the Syndicate to ask the government for enough money to complete the line.

Web Connection

http://www.school.mcgrawhill.ca/resources

On November 7, 1885, a crowd of workers in their rough clothing and owners in their fine suits gathered high in the Selkirk Mountains. Donald Smith raised a spike maul and brought it down onto the spike — the last spike. His first attempt bent the spike. In went another. This time, he hit it cleanly. This was the end of a stupendous construction project — the massive transcontinental railway. After a moment, William Van Horne made a famous, short speech to the workers and owners: "All I can say is that the work has been well done in every way." Cheers rang across the canyons and echoed off the rocky cliffs. A photographer captured the scene for all of us to share more than a hundred years later.

Donald Smith pounds in the CPR's last spike at Craigellachie. The company could not afford a golden spike; an ordinary steel one did the job. This photograph is one of our history's most famous pictures.

The Story So Far . . .

1 List the special difficulties the workers faced in building the CPR line from Yale across the Rocky Mountains.
2 Research to find out more about the work of the Chinese on the railway. Find out where they came from; why they came to North America; and why many stayed.
3 Create a poster to attract someone to work on the construction of the CPR.

SUM IT UP!

In this chapter you met many people, especially men carrying hammers or axes. These people answered the call of the wealth of natural resources of British Columbia and searched for gold, or they worked on the huge transcontinental railway project. Some of the people experienced catastrophic changes in their lives, especially if they were Aboriginal. They found settlers, miners, or surveyors on their lands. They found whole communities sick and dying from smallpox or measles. They found themselves signing treaties that brought further changes — more settlers and more restrictions on their movement. Some of the people you met performed work of great skill or courage, whether they were Métis guides, Aboriginal leaders, Chinese railway workers, hardy surveyors, or NWMP officers. When our chapter began, Aboriginal communities of the northwest coast traded and lived as their ancestors had before them. Then came the European explorers, the fur traders, the gold seekers, the governors, and judges. Across the mountain barrier, police officers and government officials concluded treaties with prairie Aboriginal Peoples and brought law and order to the West. They were followed by thousands of workers who put together the great railway.

In our next chapter, you will see how the railway and the changes it brought affected the prairie peoples, and how Aboriginal Peoples and Métis joined together to fight the changes. As well, you will learn about another huge gold rush, this time to the Yukon. Change will keep coming faster and faster for the West.

THINKING ABOUT YOUR LEARNING

1. James Douglas is sometimes called "the father of British Columbia." Give reasons for supporting this title.

2. How did the gold rushes change British Columbia?

3. List the hardships that Chinese railway workers in British Columbia faced.

4. Why did the Canadian government set up the North West Mounted Police? In what ways was it a military force?

5. Do you think the Aboriginal Peoples had any choice about signing the treaties? Explain your answer.

6. Why was it important for the Aboriginal Peoples to have strong leaders like Poundmaker?

7　How do you think the knowledge of what was happening south of the border affected the treaties? You may need to do further research to answer this.

8　How would you explain the status of the RCMP to a visitor?

9　Write a point-form note of what you know about the lifestyle of the Métis and Aboriginal Peoples on the prairies before 1860, and how they were dependent on the buffalo and hunting. Then

(a) Write a paragraph to explain
- the problems they would have with the disappearance of the buffalo
- the skills they would need to take up farming
- the supplies they would need

(b) Was it realistic of the treaty-makers to expect them to take up farming? Why or why not?

10　Do some research to find three possible routes you might use to travel from Halifax to the Pacific coast in 1875. Show your findings using a map and drawings.

11　Survey classmates for opinions on why the opening of the CPR is seen as a turning point in Canada. Create a rating chart for the top ten reasons.

APPLYING YOUR LEARNING

1　Canadian ownership and Canadian routes for the railway were important to the Government of Canada. Why did they not want some parts of the route or ownership to be American? Are these concerns similar to some that Canadians have today about ownership of our industries, newspapers, or television and radio stations? Why do you think some people have these concerns?

2　Do some research and report on *one* of these topics: the CPR today; treaties today; the gold rush towns of British Columbia today.

3　Many moments of great drama occurred during the events in this chapter. Choose *one* of the following events to enact:
- Write and give a "last spike" speech.
- Write and enact a treaty-signing ceremony.
- Approach the gates of a whisky fort as a NWMP officer confronting whisky traders.

4　Write some questions to ask *one* of the following people in an interview:
- Amelia Douglas
- Andrew Onderdonk
- Sandford Fleming
- William Van Horne
- Chief Crowfoot
- Donald Smith

5　Create a magazine with feature articles, news stories, and illustrations for *one* of the following:
- building the CPR
- the NWMP's first ten years
- the treaties
- the Cariboo Gold Rush

6　Thousands of buffalo perished between 1870 and 1885. Why do you suppose no conservation measures were taken when it became apparent that the buffalo were near extinction?

USING KEY WORDS

Which of the key words are connected with which of the stories? Match them up (but do not write in this book!). Some fit more than once—some do not fit any! Be ready to explain your choices.

terminus	gold rushes in British Columbia
syndicate	treaties
reserve	British Columbia enters Confederation
transcontinental	building the CPR
negotiator	NWMP begins work

CHAPTER 7

Settlers, Rebellion, and Gold Again

1870
Manitoba joins
Confederation

1871
British Columbia
enters Confederation

1871–1877
Treaties signed
between Canadian
government and
Aboriginal Peoples

1872
Dominion Lands Act
passed

1874
Mennonites arrive in
Manitoba

1875
Icelanders arrive in
Manitoba

SETTING OUR FOCUS

Take a look at the artifacts in the photograph. They represent some of the stories you will be learning about, stories involving people on horseback using guns. One artifact is a Blackfoot pad saddle; the other is a gun sheath.

Métis people of the Canadian Northwest sat on pad saddles as they travelled on horseback. Family members spent days on these saddles as they rode into the buffalo hunt or guided trains of Red River carts.

The gun sheath uses Cree motifs. Guns will be used by Cree and Métis fighters, as well as by Canadian soldiers and NWMP officers. A rebellion against the Canadian government will end in trials and executions. Aboriginal and Métis people will see further change and loss as settlers arrive via the new Canadian Pacific Railway. Far to the north in the Klondike, NWMP officers, often without guns, will "get their man" — and preserve the peace.

Imagine that you can hold the gun sheath in your hands. Smell the smoked hide. Feel the smooth, hard beads in their perfectly sewn patterns. Admire the creative hands that made this artifact. Then remember what it was meant to hold — a rifle.

PREVIEWING THE CHAPTER

In this chapter you will learn about these topics:
- some reasons why newcomers came to settle the Prairie West
- immigration and settlement in the Prairie West by Chinese, Europeans, and Canadians before 1896
- conflicts and changes in the West, especially those involving Aboriginal and Métis people
- the causes, events, personalities, and results of the Rebellion of 1885
- the rush for the gold fields of the Klondike
- the work of the NWMP in the West and the Klondike

KEY WORDS

bloc settlement
homestead patent
land deed
pogrom
scrip
sourdough
speculators
title
township

1876	1881–1885	1885	1896	1898
Indian Act passed	Canadian Pacific Railway built	Métis and Aboriginal Peoples rebel. Riel executed	Gold discovered in the Klondike	Thousands join gold rush to Klondike

LOOKING FOR SETTLERS

Surveying the Prairies

Some Canadians in 1867 dreamed of a prosperous land stretching "from sea to sea" that included thousands of prairie farmers and ranchers. In 1870 the population of the Prairie West was about 50 000; in fact, the population of Aboriginal Peoples had declined, and few settlers lived outside the settlements around Red River. In the early 1870s, the Government of Canada began to make the dream a reality and prepare the West for settlers.

In 1872 the government passed the Dominion Lands Act to encourage settlers to move to the prairies to farm. Canada was competing for settlers with the American West, so the law was intended to be generous in helping newcomers.

Surveyors established baselines — their starting points — along the 49th parallel and at Fort Garry. From these lines, their measuring extended across the West. They divided the prairies into hundreds of **townships**, each six-miles square (9.7 km²), starting their numbering system at the Canada–US border. They divided each township into 36 sections, and each section into four equal parts, called quarter sections.

Within each township, land was set aside for farms, the CPR, schools, and the Hudson's Bay Company. Men over 18 years of age looking for free land could find plenty here; for $10 and a residence requirement of three years, they could obtain **title** to a quarter section. This meant that they became the land's official owners, with a document called a **homestead patent** to prove it.

This diagram shows how land was set aside in every prairie township. The CPR had the right to alternate sections within 39 km of the rail line.

1. Imagine your school is in the middle of a quarter section. Use a map of your community to estimate how much of the surrounding area the quarter section would occupy.

2. What problems could the township survey system present for early settlers?

A Prairie Township

Key

- Free homestead lands
- School lands
- CPR lands
- HBC lands

31	32	33	34	35	36
30	29	28	27	26	25
19	20	21	22	23	24
18	17	16	15	14	13
7	8	9	10	11	12
6	5	4	3	2	1

} Quarter section

} Section

0 mile 1
0 km 1.6

Farming the Prairies

The rich soils and hot summers provided good growing conditions, especially for wheat. There were risks in growing wheat, including a short growing season and the chance of early frost. Some areas were too dry unless farmers used special farming methods. Tough prairie sod was not easily broken up to plant seeds. Hand tools and small ploughs could not do the job. During the 1870s and 1880s, farmers, engineers, and scientists introduced improvements that made prairie farming more successful. Changes included

- the development of large steel ploughs to break the sod
- the invention of mechanical seed drills, reapers, and barbed wire to fence in cattle
- the invention of a flour-milling process to make white flour from hard spring wheat
- the development of Red Fife Wheat

Red Fife Wheat grew quickly and usually matured in time to be harvested before frost. The first crops were planted in the mid-1870s. Agricultural researchers continued to experiment with wheat, developing Marquis Wheat, a variety that resisted disease and matured sooner than Red Fife. By the early 1900s, the prairies had become the top wheat-exporting area in the world.

Improvements in farm machinery made wheat growing more efficient. A binder such as this could help harvest prairie grain.

The Story So Far . . .

1 a) What did the Canadian government do to prepare for settlement of the prairies?

b) The HBC ended up with one twentieth of the land (over 2.5 million ha). Refer to the statement by Chief Sweetgrass on page 167. Do you think he was justified in his opinion? Explain.

c) The CPR got 2590 ha for every 1.6 km of railway built. From what you know of the building of the CPR, do you think this was fair? Explain your answer.

2 List the changes that made prairie farming more efficient during the 1870s.

3 Why did the settlers need new methods of farming for the prairies?

SETTLERS FROM MANY CULTURES

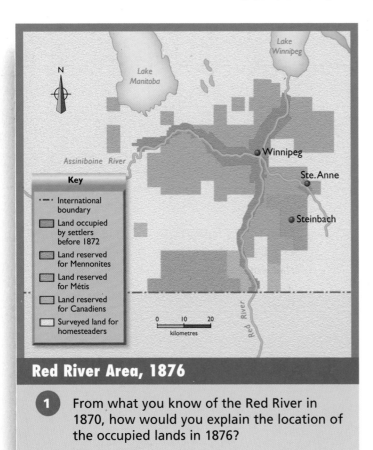

Red River Area, 1876

Key
- - - International boundary
- Land occupied by settlers before 1872
- Land reserved for Mennonites
- Land reserved for Métis
- Land reserved for Canadiens
- Surveyed land for homesteaders

1 From what you know of the Red River in 1870, how would you explain the location of the occupied lands in 1876?

Canadians today understand that our country is culturally diverse. Canada is home to people from many cultural and language groups. If you visited Winnipeg, Manitoba, about 100 years ago, you would have seen and heard evidence of cultural diversity there as well. In the following section of this chapter, you will learn about some of the groups that settled in the Prairie West before 1895.

The Mennonites

Among the earliest immigrant settlers in Manitoba were about 500 Mennonite families. The government invited Mennonite leaders in Russia to visit the new province, offering land and freedoms. Canada wanted experienced farmers; the Mennonites wanted to leave Russia. They were Christians who opposed war and violence. The Canadian government promised them freedom of religion and exemption from military service. As well they could live separately from other groups, speak German, control their own schools and maintain their culture.

In 1874 the first of 7000 Mennonites arrived. As skilful farmers, they had been very successful in Russia and brought cash and resources with them. They were settled in a **bloc settlement**; this means they were granted a block of adjoining townships so they could live near one another. The families lived in villages. Every family had a town lot and a house as well as outlying fields.

When we are putting together the stories of prairie settlement, we can use the records of settlers' memories. Mennonite pioneer Karl Reimer described his family's earliest struggles in 1874 in Manitoba. His account was written to celebrate the 60th anniversary of the Mennonites' arrival in the West. Reimer wrote in German, so the account below is a translation about the early days and the building of their house, a *semlin*. We are reading about something that is far removed from the original experience. Can we "trust" this information?

We bought the following articles in Duluth—a cookstove, an axe, a ham, and 5 lb [2 kg] of lard. Drove by rail to Moorhead and took the Red River steamer. . .
Pitched our tent and spent the night on shore (Sept 15, 1874). . . My brother [Abram]. . . and I found shelter in a Métis home.
When we reached Steinbach, each one's lot had been decided upon. On ours stood a large tree. Under it we pitched the ̇t. . . Then father hung the ham and his ̇n the tree and began to build.
̇as our father with his sick wife, ̇d eight children. . . under ̇ winter was at the door. ̇s follows: first we dug ̇feet [9.1 m] long, ̇ 3 feet [1 m] ̇ at the sides 3 ̇ two small ̇the earth. ̇et ̇trees ̇nd

Our food throughout the winter consisted of potatoes. . . , salt, black bread, and "prips" [a coffee made from barley]. . .

Mennonite homesteaders rest outside their sod and log hut. Large permanent homes soon replaced the Mennonite sod houses, but these were adequate shelters for the first winter in the West.

QUESTIONING THE EVIDENCE

1. How does the house in the photograph compare with Karl Reimer's description of a *semlin*?
2. How does his description help us understand more about prairie pioneer life?
3. What aspects of living in the *semlin* would you find most uncomfortable?
4. What other information about his early days do you wish Karl Reimer had also written?

The Mennonite communities grew and prospered as the farmers produced grain, milk, butter, cheese, and eggs. Enterprising Mennonites built a grain elevator, and a flour and feed mill to process the wheat and barley they grew. A sawmill, cheese factory, and metal works soon followed as the community expanded its population, businesses, and agricultural operations.

Sara and Johann Koop with their children in their garden. Women and girls had many housekeeping as well as barn chores. Men and boys did most of the field work.

Settlers of Other Cultures

Other groups settled in the Prairie West. About 2000 Icelanders moved to a large bloc of land near Gimli on the west shore of Lake Winnipeg in 1875. They were escaping from poverty and a natural menace: active volcanoes. They established a school, an Icelandic newspaper, and churches. Disaster struck in 1876, when a smallpox epidemic killed more than 100 people. Nature brought further heartache in 1877, when the Red River caused flooding in their communities. Many settlers moved out. Those who remained worked to develop a prosperous community.

Julia Scott

JACK AND JILL AND JULIA

Jack and Jill were 17-year-old Julia Scott's special responsibility. The two piglets, one male and one female, were precious. They were the breeding stock for a pig herd that would be started on the remote mission where Julia's family was about to begin a new life.

Julia's father, Reverend Malcolm Scott, was an Anglican clergyman. In 1886 he had agreed to help out at the church's mission at Fort Vermilion on the Peace River near the northern border of present-day Alberta.

The Scotts — Julia, her mother and father, and her younger brother, Osborne — had set out from Winnipeg on the long journey to their new home. The first leg had been easy. They had travelled to Calgary in relative comfort on the newly completed Canadian Pacific Railway.

At Calgary, they had loaded their belongings, including the crates carrying the piglets, into a horse-drawn wagon. They would spend the next two months making the arduous 1200-km trek north. Much of the first part of the journey would be overland. Then, at Athabasca Landing, north of Fort Edmonton, they would transfer their belongings to river boats. The boats would carry them up the Athabasca River, then west across Lesser Slave Lake. Then it would be overland again to Peace River Landing. There, they would build log rafts and float the final 480 km down the Peace River to Fort Vermilion.

At Red Deer Crossing, between Calgary and Fort Edmonton, the family had to ford the Red Deer River. River crossings were one of the riskiest parts of any journey. Wagons might get stuck or even overturn. People and goods could be swept away by the current.

At the crossing, the Scotts overtook the Lawrences, another family headed for Peace River country. One of the Lawrences' three heavy wagons was stuck in the river mud. Julia's father and other travellers quickly volunteered their teams and their muscle to help haul it free.

By this time, Jack and Jill could hardly be called piglets. They were starting to outgrow their crates. Before the families pushed on, 16-year-old Sheridan, one of the six Lawrence brothers, helped Julia build bigger crates for her charges.

Fourteen years passed before she met him again. When she did, the boy who had helped her build the new crates for her pigs was a prosperous rancher and businessman. The two fell in love and married. They started a family that grew to include 15 children and many grandchildren, great-grandchildren, and great-great-grandchildren. As for Jack and Jill, their descendants can still be found on hog farms throughout northern Alberta's Peace River country.

More people you could research are

Jacob Friesen

Mormon settlers

John Palliser

Julia Scott

Reflections

Put yourself in the place of a newcomer to the West between 1874 and 1895. Describe why you came to the West and comment on some of the things about your new life that have surprised you, and some that have disappointed you.

Jewish people in Russia faced terrible persecution because of their religion. During the early 1880s, the government and secret police in Russia began systematic **pogroms**, or officially approved persecution of Jewish families and businesses. They burned homes and shops, killing and terrorizing whole communities. When they were offered the chance to leave Russia, Poland, or Austria-Hungary, many Jews journeyed to the Canadian West. Many settled in Winnipeg, although there were also agricultural settlements.

Jews lived in a world where they were never sure of acceptance; most other prairie people were Christians. Yet some discrimination in Canada seemed preferable to the terror and pogroms of the old world.

After the treaties were signed, ranchers moved into southern Alberta. This photograph shows a round-up.

Snapshot

A Violent Mix

In 1892 prejudice mixed with fear to spark violence in Calgary. When a Chinese laundry worker came down with smallpox, he and his co-workers were placed in quarantine. This wasn't enough for some people. They used the dread disease as an excuse to try to drive Chinese people out of town.

Late in the evening of August 2, an angry mob started to gather. As the town constable looked on helplessly, the drunken mob went on a rampage through the Chinese neighbourhood. Fearing for their lives, some Chinese people took refuge in the home of a Methodist minister. Others rushed to alert the North West Mounted Police, then took shelter in the police barracks.

In the days afterward, the *Calgary Herald* kept feelings stirred up by supporting the rioters. The *Tribune*, on the other hand, spoke out against them. The threat of another riot continued for more than two weeks. During this time, the Mounties patrolled day and night, and continued to shelter Chinese people in their barracks.

Chinese immigrants to the prairies were originally railway workers. By 1885 about 15 000 Chinese, mainly men, lived in the West. After the CPR was completed and their contractors discharged them, most worked in laundry or restaurant businesses. Many Westerners were openly hostile to the Chinese. Laws openly discriminated against them.

The Story So Far . . .

1 Name the groups that settled in Manitoba during the 1870s.
2 Why do you think groups tend to settle together?
3 What advantages did Canada offer for groups like the Mennonites and Jews?

HARD TIMES FOR PRAIRIE PEOPLE

Métis in Trouble

In the early 1870s, Métis families in Manitoba had many concerns. Plagues of grasshoppers destroyed crops, and the buffalo herds were fast disappearing. Few had title to their lands, and many wondered if they would lose their farms as settlers from Eastern Canada moved in. These Canadians were often rude, racist, and insulting. Fights between Métis and newcomers broke out often in the taverns and the streets of Winnipeg.

Métis were supposed to be granted 1.4 million acres of land (nearly 600 000 ha) in Manitoba. The Government of Canada permitted the use of **scrip**, or pieces of paper valued at $160, for individual Métis to use to buy land. Instead, many Métis sold the scrip to **speculators** for a fraction of its value. Now they were required to obtain **land deeds** to their farms. Many lost both their land and the money they should have had, and decided to move west. By 1880 there were about 10 000 Métis people in the Northwest.

Settlements grew up around Fort Carlton, Batoche, Prince Albert, and St. Laurent. They included churches, farms, stores, mills, and a ferry service on the South Saskatchewan River. At St. Laurent a leader named Gabriel Dumont set up a community council. This seemed like a good beginning.

Snippet

Highway Robbery

The stagecoaches carrying people, mail, and goods between Calgary and Fort Edmonton were a tempting target for outlaws. On August 23, 1886, Alberta's first stagecoach holdup occurred when two armed men stopped the coach about 24 km north of Calgary and robbed the passengers. Though a posse of Mounties and civilian volunteers on horseback tracked the robbers west toward the Rocky Mountains, the thieves were never found.

This Métis family poses for a formal photograph in their Saskatchewan community in the 1880s.

Yet conditions were not happy for the Saskatchewan Métis. In September 1882 the people of Prince Albert district sent this Petition of Rights describing their problems to Sir John A. Macdonald:

> Sir: We the undersigned ... settled on the west bank of the Saskatchewan.... Great was our astonishment and perplexity when we were notified, that when our lands are surveyed we shall be obliged to pay $2.00 an acre [0.4 ha] to the Government.... We are poor people and cannot pay for our land....we consider it not asking too much to request that the Government allow us to occupy our lands in peace...by making to the Métis of the North-West free grants of land.

The North-West Territories was ruled at this time by a territorial government, made up of Lieutenant-Governor Edgar Dewdney and his council of five. Dewdney was not a popular man in the Northwest, partly for his refusal to consult with the people who were affected by his decisions. As well, government agents and surveyors did not speak French or Cree, which made communications difficult. In 1883 and 1884 requests flew to Ottawa asking for improvements.

Other settlers in the Northwest were equally unhappy. Many had chosen their homestead before 1881, expecting a railway nearby. They were angry that the new CPR was far south of their farms. As well drought, grasshoppers, early frosts, and low grain prices made farming very difficult. Settlers were unhappy that so many sections were set aside for the HBC and railways. They were further annoyed by the CPR monopoly. Settlers' petitions to Ottawa, like those of the Métis, were ignored.

Aboriginal Peoples in Trouble

There were about 20 000 Aboriginal Peoples in the Northwest by the mid-1880s. Their population had been reduced by disease and hunger. The Government of Canada, assisted by the NWMP, at times had to provide them with beef, flour, and tea. In 1876 the Government of Canada passed the Indian Act, a law that had an impact on all aspects of the lives of Aboriginal Peoples. Indian agents, non-Aboriginals chosen by the government, began to regulate people's lives.

Aboriginal Peoples were expected to become farmers. For this, they needed equipment and seed. When these were slow to arrive, Cree and government officials were equally frustrated.

Missionaries, NWMP officers, and settlers urged the government in Ottawa to prevent a disaster — people were starving. Conditions grew worse when the government decreased food shipments to the reserves in an attempt to force people to farm. Aboriginal Peoples driven by hunger became desperate.

Cree Chief Mistahimaskwa (Big Bear) wanted the people to unite to find solutions to their problems. His plan was to negotiate with the government. Other members of his large Cree community, led by war chiefs Imases (Little Bad Man), who was Big Bear's son, and Kapapamahchakwew (Wandering Spirit) urged the people to go to war.

Big Bear spoke to his people at a massive gathering at Duck Lake. They agreed to hold another council in 1885 to prepare demands for more territory and power. Big Bear had united the varied prairie Aboriginal Peoples, but his plans were political, not military.

Other Crees had different ideas. Warriors from Big Bear's band seized the HBC store at Frog Lake on April 2, 1885. Nine people were killed by the angry, hungry, frustrated Crees. Their leader, Wandering Spirit, explained the warriors' viewpoint:

Cree Chief Big Bear, Mistahimaskwa

The HBC sold this land to the Big Chief Woman (Queen Victoria)…; took money for it. Why did they do that? This land belongs to us. The Company did not own it. But they are rich because they got much money for something that was not theirs. We are not rich. We are poor. Often we do not have enough to eat. So we have taken back the land, and when it is sold again, the money will come to us.

These Cree people posed for the camera in their camp. Hunger and disease faced all Aboriginal communities on the prairies.

The attack at Frog Lake aroused fears of a violent uprising. People across the country demanded action by the Government of Canada. Now, war seemed probable.

The Story So Far . . .

1 a) List the Métis grievances. Which grievance described in the text and Petition of Rights do you think was most serious?

b) What grievances did other settlers have?

2 What did the Métis hope to achieve with their petition?

Métis Action

Métis patience was also running out. They remembered how the leadership of Louis Riel had succeeded in gaining entry into Confederation for Manitoba in 1870. A small group of Métis rode to Montana in June of 1884 to bring Riel to the Saskatchewan country. Together they would work to petition Ottawa for change.

Since 1870, Riel had spent time in mental institutions in Montréal, married, fathered several children, and worked in Montana. He now believed he was a religious prophet. His role in this rebellion would be very different from the one he played in Manitoba.

In December 1884, the Métis sent a petition to Sir John A. Macdonald's government. Here are concerns expressed by the Métis:

• Aboriginal Peoples are so reduced that settlers are compelled to give them food.

• Métis of the territories have not received 100 ha of land each, as promised in the Manitoba Act.

• Métis who possess land have not received patents (proof of ownership) for it.

• The North-West Territories (NWT) should have responsible government and representation in the federal Parliament. It has had a temporary government for 15 years.

• Saskatchewan should be organized as a province of Canada.

When the petition to Ottawa was not answered by the winter of 1884-1885, Riel urged resistance. With his military adjutant, Gabriel Dumont, Riel and the Métis captured a store of weapons at Batoche in March 1885. Days later, Métis fighters under Dumont's leadership defeated a troop of 100 men at Duck Lake. The Métis meant to be heard.

The Canadian government mustered the militia in Canada to go west and end the rebellion. Within two weeks, hundreds of soldiers in three columns were marching north from the CPR tracks toward the Saskatchewan country.

Métis led by Dumont fought with Canadian troops led by Major-General Frederick Middleton at Fish Creek. Dumont's natural skill in the buffalo hunt and his experience in battles in the United States made him a master of tactics. However, Riel always intervened to prevent Dumont from carrying out his plans. The Canadians regrouped to fight again.

Troops from Canada travelled west in record time via the CPR. Put yourself in this picture and imagine your discomfort.

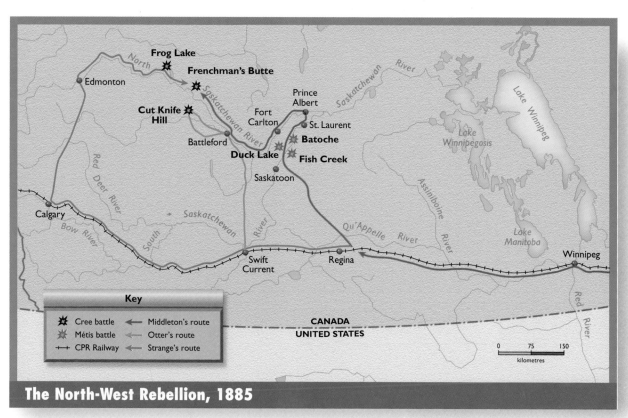

The North-West Rebellion, 1885

Key

✳ Cree battle   ← Middleton's route
✳ Métis battle   ← Otter's route
+—+ CPR Railway   ← Strange's route

CANADA
UNITED STATES

0   75   150
kilometres

Middleton's forces marched toward the Métis stronghold at Batoche, their central community. The battle here would be decisive for the Métis for generations to come. Their defences were strong but the courage of the Métis was no match for the superior numbers of the militia. About 300 Métis fighters faced the 850 troops led by Middleton. After four days of fighting, the Canadians charged the Métis trenches and drove Dumont's men back.

Dumont helped refugee Métis women and children. Then he slipped away, escaping to the United States. Riel surrendered to Major-General Middleton on May 15, 1885. Other Métis leaders and rebellious settlers were captured.

The Story So Far . . .

1 a) Brainstorm and make a list of reasons why the government did not answer the Métis concerns.
   b) What does the lack of response say about the government's attitude toward the Métis?
2 a) What did the Métis hope to achieve by inviting Riel to lead them?
   b) How did Riel damage the Métis cause?
3 How did the CPR affect the course of the rebellion?

Cree Action

To confront the Cree at Battleford, troops led by Colonel William Otter marched north from Swift Current. About 500 refugees were inside a small fort at Battleford, held there by Cree and Stoney warriors. When Otter's troops approached, the warriors left. Otter decided to attack Poundmaker's camp during the night, when the Aboriginal families were sleeping. Although surprised, the warriors soon surrounded Otter's troops at Cut Knife Hill. Poundmaker allowed the militia to escape, and then began to move toward Batoche. Before they reached the Métis settlement, they learned that the Métis had already been defeated. Poundmaker surrendered to Middleton to spare his people any further fighting and bloodshed.

Cree Chief Big Bear met General Thomas Strange's troops in a battle at Frenchman's Butte. The Cree warriors held off the attack, but they were weakened and left for the country farther north. Here they avoided the soldiers led by Strange for several weeks. On June 2, Big Bear walked into Fort Carlton and quietly surrendered.

The fighting was over. In all 53 soldiers had been killed, along with 35 Aboriginal and 50 Métis fighters. Over 115 had been wounded. The Métis nation had been defeated. The Cree plan to reopen treaty talks had been killed. Rebel leaders were in custody or exile.

Web Connection

http://www.school.mcgrawhill.ca/resources

Go to the web site above to find out more about the 1885 Rebellion and the people involved. Go to History Resources, then to *Canada: The Story of a Developing Nation* to see where to go next.

Troops led by Colonel William Otter travelled north from the railway to face Poundmaker's warriors. Here they are crossing a creek near Swift Current.

This famous photograph shows the court room in which Riel was found guilty and sentenced to death. He is standing in the centre of the picture, facing the jury.

After the Fighting

People in Ontario and Manitoba wanted the rebels punished. The rebellion had cost the government $5 million. Many people had given up their lives. Somebody had to pay.

In July trials began in Regina. The most newsworthy prisoner was Louis Riel. Although his lawyers urged a plea of insanity, Riel refused to consider spending his life in a mental institution. He was found guilty of treason and sentenced to death, despite the request for a reduced sentence by the jury. One juror explained:

> We were in sympathy with the Métis because we knew they had good cause for what they did....In recommending Riel to the mercy of the court, we did so because we considered that while the prisoner was guilty and we could by no means justify him in his acts of rebellion, at the same time we felt that had the Government done their duty and redressed the grievances of the Métis, as they had been requested time and again to do, there never would have been a second Riel rebellion, and no prisoner to try and condemn.

French-speaking Canadians denounced the death sentence. Some Québeckers felt that Riel was being punished because of his Roman Catholic religion and French language. Newspaper editorials, speakers at huge rallies, and petitions sent to Sir John A. Macdonald demanded that the execution not take place.

What would Macdonald do? He could commute the sentence, or let it stand. On November 16, 1885, Riel was executed. The outcry in Québec was loud, angry, and immediate. French-Canadian leaders vowed to work for the government's defeat. Macdonald's Conservative Party lost support in the province for decades. Many Ontario newspapers and speakers supported the execution. English- and French-speaking Canadians were divided and bitter. Events in the far-off Saskatchewan country had started a storm.

A group portrait taken after the fighting in 1885 includes Poundmaker (front right) and Big Bear with his youngest son (front left).

Gabriel Dumont

FIGHTING FOR HIS PEOPLE

Gabriel Dumont saw his friend Louis Riel for the last time in the woods outside the village of Batoche on the South Saskatchewan River. After the battle, their small force had scattered. Only a few men remained with them. The Métis and Aboriginal warriors were now fugitives. They had only their weapons and the clothes on their backs. To survive they needed food, blankets and horses. Dumont sneaked out of the woods to scavenge for supplies. When he returned, Riel was gone.

The area was crawling with troops. Their mission was to capture the rebels. Dumont was taking a risk by staying, but he would not leave until he was sure that Riel was out of danger. Besides, the veteran plainsman knew the area like the back of his hand. In better times, before the buffalo had disappeared, Dumont had been elected chief of the Métis hunters on the Saskatchewan River. So respected were his skills and courage that a priest told the troops searching for him: "You are looking for Gabriel? You are wasting your time. There isn't a blade of grass on the whole Prairie that he doesn't know."

Finally word reached Dumont that Major-General Frederick Middleton had promised Riel justice if he gave himself up. Desperately Dumont redoubled his efforts to find his friend. He wanted to tell Riel not to surrender, but he never got the chance. Riel turned himself in on March 15, 1885, six days after the battle ended.

With Riel in prison, it was time to flee. Mounted on stolen horses, he and one of his men headed south toward the US border. They were armed only with Dumont's favourite rifle, which he had named Le Petit. Still, the two knew they could count on receiving food and shelter from the Aboriginal and Métis bands they met along the way. Once in the United States, Dumont started planning to rescue Riel. He was never able to carry out his plan, however. Sure that the Métis would try something, the Mounties kept their prisoner under heavy guard.

After Riel's execution, Dumont joined Buffalo Bill's Wild West Show, travelling to US cities such as New York and Philadelphia and performing with stars such as Annie Oakley. It was not a life he enjoyed. When the Canadian government granted amnesty to those who had participated in the North-West Rebellion, Dumont returned to his homestead. He died there in 1906. Twenty-one years after the battle at Batoche, he was nearly forgotten, except by the Aboriginal and Métis people who quietly gathered to pay their respects to the man who had tried so valiantly to protect their way of life.

More people you could research are

Edgar Dewdney

Gabriel Dumont

Kapapamahchakwew (Wandering Spirit)

Mistahimaskwa (Big Bear)

Pitikwahanapiwiyin (Poundmaker)

The government was determined to prevent any further unrest among Aboriginal Peoples. Cree horses, guns and carts were impounded by the NWMP and Indian agents took on many powers on the reserves.

Aboriginal Peoples who wanted to farm were frustrated. The Indian Department limited reserve farms to small fields. Aboriginal farmers could not use expensive machinery to develop large wheat fields; they were forbidden to borrow the money needed to buy the equipment. Regulations forced them to use hand tools. When they failed to earn extra money because of the regulations of the Indian Department, the farmers themselves were blamed. By 1900 many had given up hope of success.

A Blackfoot farmer sows his crop by hand.

After 1885 most Métis people had left the Saskatchewan country, moving north and west into the bush country of the Peace and Mackenzie rivers. A gold rush to the Klondike in 1896 would find them again watching prospectors and miners trampling on their lands and their rights.

The Story So Far . . .

1 a) Why did Riel not plead insanity?
   b) What advice did the jury provide concerning Riel's sentence? Why?
   c) What was the reaction to Riel's execution?
2 Find out what became of
   a) the Aboriginal and Métis prisoners;
   b) the Aboriginal and Métis communities.

KLONDIKE GOLD, 1896

In 1896 three **sourdoughs**, or long-time prospectors, found gold in the Yukon at a place called Rabbit Creek. They shipped their nuggets off to Seattle, Washington, and within days, a huge gold rush was on. Dawson City was the goal of about 43 000 people in the years between 1897 and 1900. Treacherous rivers, towering mountains, frigid winter temperatures, vast distances, and great isolation challenged even the toughest gold seekers.

How difficult was it to get safely to Dawson City? If you were a prospective miner, you would face big challenges.

- Get and pay for a passage on a steamer to Skagway, Alaska. Watch out for crooks in Skagway.
- Outfit yourself to travel to Dawson. Follow a brutal trail over the mountains, then travel hundreds of kilometres down chilling rivers with killing rapids.
- Carry hundreds of kilograms of supplies on your back up the icy Chilkoot Pass. The NWMP will not let you start through the Pass unless you have enough supplies for one year.
- Build yourself a rough boat to carry your supplies down the Yukon River to Dawson. Expect to see many boats capsize and find the bodies of drowned gold seekers.
- If you decide to go overland from Edmonton be prepared to take two years to reach the gold fields — if you ever do. The route is marked with many graves.

Snippet

Sourdoughs

Veteran Klondike miners were called sourdoughs, probably because pancakes, biscuits, muffins, and bread made from sourdough formed such a big part of their diet. Rather than using yeast or baking powder to make the bread rise, the miners would save a piece of dough. This piece — called the sourdough — would become the starter for the next round of baking. The sourdough was often stored in a special kettle that hung on a nail above the warm stove.

Miners climb the Chilkoot Pass in single file carrying their supplies to the top. Huge piles of food and equipment sit at the bottom waiting to be carried across the Pass.

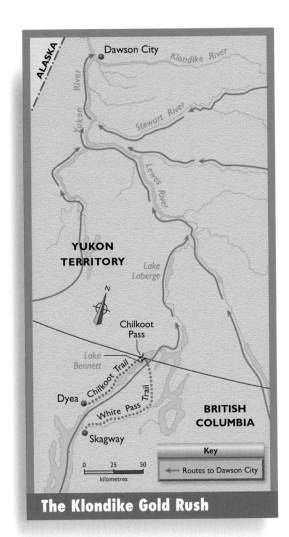

The Klondike Gold Rush

Reaching the gold fields was a terrifying ordeal for many people. Belinda Mulrooney travelled across the Chilkoot Pass in 1897. She describes part of the journey, and how she saved a woman's life:

If you start to freeze on the trail, you have the fight of your life on your hands. You want to lie down, for the snow looks just like a feather bed. I remember once … there was a …woman from Seattle lying in the snow. Her husband had gone ahead …and said for her to wait …, but she was impatient to be with him. She started in on her own, poorly dressed and with her own little sled.

When I came on her I said, "Come on. You'll have to get up and make an effort." She replied: "It feels wonderful." I …rolled her onto my sled. I had to tie her on good and hard…. Then I gave the sled a good kick down the hill to my camp.

Bill McPhee and another old-timer were huddled in my tent. . . I said, "I've got a poor woman here and I've got to thaw her out."

McPhee said, "Belinda, put her in here between us. She'll be as safe as if she was in God's pocket!" So I did, and when we got down safe to Dawson and she found her husband… she said, "Honey! Honey, come and take a look. These are the men I slept with on the trail!"

Miners operate a sluice, working to separate the gold dust and nuggets from the ore and mud they have dug out of their mine. Some struck it rich, others worked day and night with little success.

Martha Louise Munger Black
CONQUERING THE CHILKOOT

Martha Louise Munger stared at the distant, snow-covered mountain that lay between her and the Klondike. Soon she would leave Dyea, Alaska, to join the stream of people struggling over that mountain on the "worst trail this side of hell." Had she been foolish to leave her husband and two sons to follow her dream of finding gold — and adventure? Had her life as a society matron in Chicago, Illinois, prepared her for what lay ahead? Maybe the Klondike really was no place for a lady.

The 68-km Chilkoot Trail led straight up one side of the snow- and ice-covered mountain and straight back down the other. Munger felt a shiver of fear. Everyone knew that the bodies of 60 people buried in an avalanche three months earlier were still being dug out of the snow.

At noon on July 12, 1898, Munger set out on the trail with her brother George and her cousin Harry. They had been able to afford the $900 fee to hire packers to carry the heaviest of their goods over the mountain. By the end of the first day, the easy leg of the journey was behind them. The next day, they tackled the notorious Chilkoot Pass, the worst part of the trek. The melting snow made the steep, rock-strewn climb treacherous, especially for a woman clothed fashionably in the style of the 1890s. "I cursed my hot, high, buckram collar, my tight heavily boned corsets, my long corduroy skirt, my full bloomers which I had to hitch up with every step," Munger wrote later.

Finally they reached the summit. They passed through the customs post set up by the North West Mounted Police and entered Canada. Ahead of them was the trek down the mountain. "The most excruciating struggle of the whole trip," wrote Munger. "Down, ever downward. Weight of body on shaky legs, weight growing heavier, and legs shakier. Sharp rocks to scratch our clutching hands. Snake-like roots to trip our stumbling feet." Once on the other side, she felt a thrill of satisfaction. She had passed her first big test. She had conquered the Chilkoot! Although 18 000 men had already done it, she was only the 631st woman to finish the trek.

Although Munger did not know it at the time, she was expecting her third child when she made the dangerous trip. The following January her son was born. She also did not know that she would fall under the spell of the Yukon and adopt it as her home. Her two older sons would join her, and there she would marry her second husband, George Black. Perhaps her greatest achievement would come in 1935. Elected to represent the Yukon in the House of Commons, she would become the second woman member of Parliament in Canadian history.

More people you could research are

Martha Louise Munger (Black)

Faith Fenton

Skookum Jim

Robert Service

Sam Steele

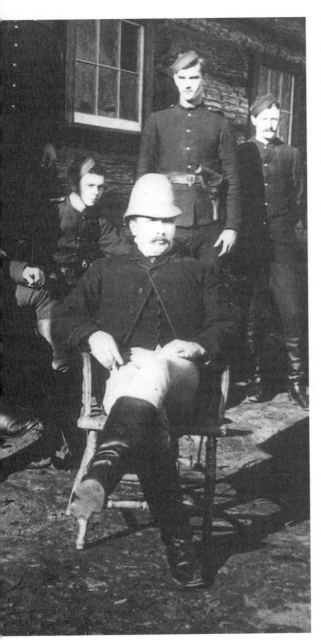

Sam Steele, a legendary figure, helped keep order in the Klondike gold rush. He later fought in the Boer War, and in World War I.

The Fortune Seekers

Who were these gold seekers? Most were everyday people from Canada, the United States, and Europe. Others were business people who profited from the needs of the gold seekers. They set up stores to provide equipment and food or sold horses or lumber to the prospectors. A third group was called "adventurers." They did not plan to do any gold mining unless it was in card games or other gambling ventures in the saloons of Dawson City.

The NWMP worked to preserve law and order in the Yukon. They also protected people from their own stupidity. Few realized the potential for disaster that lurked everywhere on the journey to the gold fields. The Mounties patrolled the passes and river passageways into the gold country, keeping on eye on everybody. When people built boats that were too flimsy for the swirling Yukon River, the Mounties inspected every boat before it could set off; too many people had already drowned in poorly built craft. In 1898 Sam Steele, a member of the NWMP, reported that every one of the 30 000 people who had passed down the Yukon River had been assisted by the NWMP.

Dawson City

Dawson City grew up almost overnight. Thousands of gold seekers arrived to make their fortunes. Most people in Dawson were men, but there were a few women. They included Nettie Fancher, a miner; Mary Thompson, who ran a hotel; Mrs. G. Lowe, whose businesses included laundry and fortune-telling; and Faith Fenton, a reporter for a Toronto newspaper. Many women worked in the numerous saloons, taverns, and dance halls. A woman describes her experience for us:

Web Connection

http://www.school.mcgrawhill.ca/resources

Go to the web site above to see more photographs of the Klondike gold rush. Go to History Resources, then to *Canada: The Story of a Developing Nation* to see where to go next.

My husband ... outfitted me with new clothing...then in the evening, he took me to a dance-hall. The place was filled with smoke, men were playing cards, roulette, faro, and other gambling games. Many of the men dressed in rough clothing. There were quite a few dance-hall girls, all in nice clothing.... It was rather wild in there, and I was scared and soon wanted to go home. I never went to a dance-hall again while in Dawson.

This 1899 photograph shows citizens of Dawson City celebrating July 4. More than seven of ten miners were Americans.

The Klondike gold rush was short-lived. By 1904 most people had left the area. The best creeks had given up their gold and new finds had been made in Alaska. The adventurers, the miners, the women, and children moved on.

The Story So Far . . .

1 List the challenges people faced to get to the Klondike.
2 a) Describe the role of the NWMP in the Klondike gold rush.
    b) How do you think the presence of the NWMP made this gold rush different from the Cariboo gold rush?
3 Dawson City at the height of the gold rush had electricity, running water, sewerage, and telephones. How do you think this made the gold rush different from the Cariboo gold rush?
4 Read the poem by Robert Service, *The Cremation of Sam McGee*. What evidence is there in the poem that cold weather plagued the Klondike gold seekers? Why was Sam happy at the end of the poem?

SUM IT UP!

The period between 1870 and 1890 brought change and catastrophe to the Aboriginal Peoples and the Métis of the West. Settlers, surveyors, railways, and farming changed their way of life. When peaceful means of solving problems that arose from these changes proved futile, they rebelled. Defeated by superior numbers of Canadian troops, Métis and Aboriginal leaders were executed or imprisoned. Many Métis moved into northern woodlands. Aboriginal Peoples tried to adapt to the new conditions and learn to farm but stifling regulations prevented them from successfully making a living from agriculture.

Other settlers were much more successful farmers. Groups of Mennonite and Icelandic settlers moved to Manitoba, followed by smaller numbers of people from Europe, China, and North America. The dreamers who looked for thousands of farmers, ranchers, and townspeople were still waiting by 1895 for the people to arrive. In one corner of the far Northwest, people were crowding in by the thousands. During the Klondike gold rush of 1898, tens of thousands of gold seekers took on the challenges of the harsh Northern environment in hopes of striking it rich. In a few years the fever subsided and people returned home. Still the dreamers waited for the homesteaders they knew should be settling on the prairies. You will learn about this in the next chapter.

THINKING ABOUT YOUR LEARNING

1. How did the Dominion Lands Act affect settlement patterns in the prairies?
2. What would be the advantages of a bloc settlement for a group like the Mennonites?
3. Create a flow chart to show the causes, events, and results of the Rebellion of 1885.
4. Look up the meanings of "rebellion" and "resistance." Why are the events of 1885 called a rebellion? What were the rebels rebelling against?
5. Why might the Indian Act cause conflict?
6. What were the hazards for people trying to reach the gold fields of the Klondike?

APPLYING YOUR LEARNING

1. View the 1999 television (CBC-TV) production of *Big Bear*. What perspective does the story take concerning the Rebellion of 1885? List five facts from the story. List five opinions. Who are the story's heroes? Who are the villains?
2. View the Heritage Minute "Louis Riel." Explain what has happened before the story told in the video.
3. Write a mini-biography for *one* of the leaders — military or political, Aboriginal, Métis, or Canadian — of the Rebellion of 1885. Put the biographies together in a class booklet.

1 Write a caption for this photograph to describe the scene.   **The Skagway Trail**

2 Select two people from the photograph and write an imaginary conversation between them.

4 Design and create a class web page for the Rebellion of 1885 or for the Klondike gold rush.

5 Should Macdonald have commuted the sentence of Louis Riel rather than allowing him to be executed? What sentence might have been appropriate?

6 Do some research on prairie ranching life before 1896. Present your findings in a mural, picture story, or video.

7 Create a newspaper or magazine for the Klondike gold rush.

8 Do some research to find out more about the technological changes in agriculture in this period. How did these affect prairie farmers?

9 Write a letter or memo to *one* of the following to warn them about what they may face and offer some suggestions for success:

prospective Klondike gold rushers; Aboriginal Peoples trying to start farms; Mennonites; Icelanders; Jews in Winnipeg.

USING KEY WORDS

1 Write a clue for three of the following words. Give your list of clues to a classmate to solve.
scrip
land deed
sourdough
homestead patent

2 Make up a tongue twister using the word *sourdough*.

CHAPTER

8

A Home in the West, 1896–1914

SETTING OUR FOCUS

Look at this poster. It was used to attract people to live in the West. In the years between 1896 and 1914, over a million people moved to the prairies — some to settle and homestead, some to work in the towns and cities, some hoping to earn money and then move on. The picture in the centre of the poster reminds us of the promise of prosperous farms, endless fields of rippling wheat, and a rich grain harvest. Maple leaves are a reminder that these fields are in Canada — not in the American West.

Suppose you were looking at this poster from communities in Norway, Russia, or the city of Toronto. Why might you be attracted to the Canadian prairies? What and who would you find there? How might you make your life better? What obstacles might you encounter?

PREVIEWING THE CHAPTER

In this chapter you will learn about these topics:

- **experiences of pioneer settlers in their first days on the land**
- **why people from many parts of the world moved to the Canadian prairies in the years from 1896 to 1914**
- **contributions of groups and individuals to the development of the Canadian West**
- **patterns of immigration and settlement on the prairies**
- **daily life for prairie people in towns and cities, as well as on farms, in mines and lumber camps, and on ranches**

KEY WORDS

baldheaded prairie
chain migration
communally
ethnocultural
freight rates
pull factors
push factors
soddie

1896
- Laurier government is elected in Ottawa
- Sifton becomes Minister of the Interior

1905
Saskatchewan and Alberta become provinces

1913
Largest number of newcomers ever, 400 870, arrive, many settling in the West

1914
Beginning of World War I ends massive immigration to prairies

THE WORK OF OUR OWN HANDS

1904

We reached our homestead at last. I'll never forget the desolate feeling that came over me, when, with the contents of our wagon out on the ground, we sat on a box and looked around, not a sign of any other human habitation or a road leading to one to be seen, nothing but bluff and water and grass. Then I realized that we were at the end of our journey, that this was to be our home, that if we wanted a house to cover us, a stable for our horses, a well for drinking water, it would all have to be the work of our own hands.

We pitched our tent and. . . set up the cookstove out in the open and built a table, and. . . a makeshift kind of stable. Then our thoughts then turned to the house. A cellar was dug, but we found that the cost of lumber would take all our money. . . We decided to put up anything with four walls and a roof. . .

We managed to stand the cookstove inside the opening of the tent, with the pipe out, but how we lived through those days and kept happy. . . is a marvel to me now. On one of the days I baked bread and. . . rolls when we heard someone outside. It was a man who had seen our tent from a distance, and had come over to see if he could beg or borrow some bread. He was

Prairie pioneers from Boston, Massachusetts, travelling to their homestead in Alberta pause for a photographer.

There were far more men than women on the prairies. Women's skills and hands were needed on farms. Few male farmers could succeed alone.

one of three men homesteaders, about a mile [1.6 km] away. They had only a sleeping tent and a camp stove, which they could not operate. . . in the rain. . .We wrapped up the rolls and told him that was all we had cooked and he started off. . . In about half an hour he was back again, lost. . .

We afforded a lumber roof and floor for our house, and two windows, but the walls must cost us nothing but labour. By this time there was a neighbour. . .who. . .came to help plow some sod for the walls. . .The sod was cut and piled up neatly for the walls and we were thankful to move into it and begin to make it as comfortable as possible. . .There were months during the winter when the blankets on our beds were held to the wall, tight with frost. We daren't try to move them for they were too precious to tear. . .

The Story So Far . . .

1   a) What does *desolate* mean? Why was the author feeling this way?
    b) Do you think this author is male or female? Explain your answer.
2   What qualities of successful pioneers do the author and partner in this story show?
3   How different were living conditions for the three single men who homesteaded nearby?
4   Why did these people use sod for the walls of their house?

Stepping Into the Picture

People who arrived by cart or on foot on the **baldheaded prairie** (the name given to the short-grass or treeless plains) faced a daunting task: they had to build a shelter quickly. Winds were constant. Prairie winters were very bitter with the threat of blizzards, high winds, and icy cold. Frost might come as early as mid-August, and winter would not be far behind. First homes were often tents, then **soddies**, homes made with sod walls, or log houses.

This is a picture of the Benson homestead on the baldheaded prairie in Alberta in 1910. The homesteaders have just ploughed the first furrow on their land. Imagine you are one of the people in this picture. Describe to a visitor what it is like living here, your hopes, your dreams, and your fears.

Push and Pull

Who are these pioneers? Where have they come from and why are they on the prairie, building stables and rough houses, and cooking with a wood stove out in the open? The people in the stories share characteristics with more than 1 million others who travelled to the West in the years between 1896 and 1914. They decided to move to the prairies, hundreds or even thousands of kilometres from their homes.

Two sets of factors worked to help them make that decision. These are called either **push factors**, or **pull factors**. They operate whenever people anywhere leave their homes and move to a new place. Some things push people away from their homes. Others pull them to a particular new place. During the years between 1896 and 1914, over 2.5 million people decided that they would leave their homes and move to Canada. Almost half of these people then moved to the Canadian prairies. The chart shows some of the factors that affected this huge mass migration of individuals, families, and larger groups.

Pushing People Out Of Their Homes	Pulling People To The Prairies
Persecution because of religion	Freedom from religious persecution
Persecution because of culture	Freedom to speak their own language
Farms too small or land too poor to make a living	Free land for homesteaders
High rents	Relatives, friends, and other members of their culture settled there
Heavy taxation	Cheap transportation and government help to get there
Inability to buy their own land	Safety and security provided by NWMP
Unemployment caused by technological change	Employment opportunities
	Advertising
	Transportation to move grain to markets
	New worldwide markets for prairie wheat
	Technological improvements in grains, farm machinery, and farm methods

Mayer Hoffer

SASKATCHEWAN HOMESTEADER

It was Passover when the train carrying Mayer Hoffer finally arrived at Hirsch, Saskatchewan, in 1907. "I was never so happy in my life as when I heard the conductor call Hirsch," Mayer wrote many years later. "I had reached the end of my journey and life lay ahead."

For the 17-year-old Jewish youth, the 14-day voyage across the Atlantic Ocean from Liverpool, England, had been hard. His ship, the *Siberia*, had once carried cattle. Their stalls had been converted into tiny cramped cabins. Some of the passengers must have wondered whether they were any better off than the cattle the ship had once carried. Terribly seasick, Mayer had spent most of the trip vomiting in the stuffy, smelly cabin that he shared with three other people.

Barely able to eat, he had been too weak to care when the alarm bells had sounded one night. The panic-stricken passengers were issued life belts and ordered up on deck. Mayer did not go. He was too sick. Luckily, the crisis passed and the order to abandon ship never came.

Once on dry land, he recovered quickly. Now he was in Hirsch, waiting to start a new life with his father and his brother, Israel. After Passover, Israel found him a job with a Jewish farmer. For $25 a month, he worked for this farmer until it was time for the Hoffers to start their own homesteads.

Each of them had filed for two quarter sections. Accustomed to the small, crowded farms of the old country, they were dazzled by the wide-open spaces of Saskatchewan. To gain title to this land, all they had to do was make a modest payment, then live on their farms for at least six months a year and build a home.

The Hoffers set out across the prairie to their homesteads with a wagon, a team of horses, a cow, and a calf. The wagon was loaded with groceries, lumber for building, an old range stove, a bed, a plough, a pail, a pickaxe and other tools, and a stoneboat. Into the stoneboat, which was a sledge on runners that could be hauled by horses, they would pile the rocks and stones they dug out of the soil. This was backbreaking work, but it had to be done to prepare the land for ploughing.

When the Hoffers arrived on their own land, the first thing they did was unload the wagon and turn it upside down. The overturned wagon would be their first home.

Although the tall grass of the prairie stretched around them as far as the eye could see, the Hoffers were not alone. "People were pouring into the district to start taking possession of the land," Mayer wrote. "Some came with small, young children; some came with quite grown children; some had money; others were poor. All came with a vision of the future before them."

More people you could research are

Isaac Barr

Johanne Frederiksen

Mayer Hoffer

Peter Veregin

John Ware

Everyone had different reasons for coming to the prairies. Some people were driven from their homeland by government-sponsored terrorism. For example, agents of the Russian secret police burned homes and imprisoned and killed people because of their religious beliefs. Other people were unable to make a living on their small farms in places like Ukraine, Norway, or Finland. English-speaking people left Britain expecting to prosper if they worked hard.

The Canadian government hoped to attract what they called "quality families"— experienced, hardy farmers who would work the prairie soil. Clifford Sifton, the dynamic federal Minister of the Interior, took responsibility for bringing in settlers and made it easier for people to homestead. There were posters in many languages, travelling road shows with examples of prairie products, and men with "magic lantern shows" who gave presentations showing pictures of the West. Canadian agents in the United States worked hard to attract experienced American farmers to the West. In 1903, for example, the Canadian Superintendent of Immigration reported the following:

All told, we had to deal with 114 124 requests for information by mail, in addition to many personal inquiries. We shipped to our agents in the US and Great Britain 575 cases, containing 637 578 pamphlets for distribution, our total output of literature being 1 313 909 separate copies.

Other factors acted to bring people to the prairies: as settlers moved in, there were many non-farm jobs in construction, railway building, and mining.

Travelling exhibits such as this "Girl from Canada" were designed to attract people to the booming prairies. This advertisement was used in Britain, but many were used in Europe and the US as well. What flag covers the girl? What decorations can you identify on the bicycle?

Clifford Sifton

SELLING "THE LAST BEST WEST"

As a student, Clifford Sifton was fascinated by science, a new subject on the curriculum. A brilliant scholar, he joined the science club at his college and became its president. He was also one of the first to take a special postgraduate science course. A career in science seemed like a natural choice.

Just one thing stood between the young man and this career choice: ambition. Science was so new that it was not considered quite respectable. And Sifton wanted a respectable career because his real ambition was to become a politician. That is why he decided to become a lawyer. In the 1880s a training in law paved the way to a political career.

Born in Canada West, Sifton had moved to Manitoba with his family when he was 13 years old. A childhood illness had affected his hearing, but he was determined not to let this interfere with his life. The family eventually settled in Brandon and that is where the young lawyer set up his office — and launched his political career. In 1888 he ran as a Liberal and was elected to the provincial legislature.

In 1896 the Liberal Party won the federal election and Wilfrid Laurier became Prime Minister. For Sifton, the timing could not have been better. His work had brought him to Laurier's attention. No one was surprised when the Prime Minister invited the ambitious young Liberal to join the federal cabinet as Minister of the Interior. Sifton jumped at the chance and was elected in the federal riding of Brandon.

It was as a federal politician that Sifton was to leave a lasting imprint on the West. As Minister of the Interior, he was responsible for the prairies and the North. The government wanted settlers on the prairies; Sifton set out to ensure that they came.

Years later he wrote that the kind of immigrant he hoped to attract was "a stalwart peasant in a sheepskin coat born on the soil, whose forefathers have been farmers for 10 generations, with a stout wife and a half-dozen children."

To achieve this goal, Sifton targeted certain groups. Catchy posters advertised the prairies as "The Last Best West." They were designed to lure American farmers north of the 49th parallel. Moreover, immigration agents were paid to recruit farming families from certain parts of Europe. To make settlement even more attractive, large blocks of land were set aside for groups such as Ukrainians, Doukhobors, and the British.

Although Sifton resigned in 1905 after a dispute with Laurier, this did not end his public career or his interest in politics. Still, he always considered the settlement of the West his greatest achievement.

More people you could research are

Wilfrid Laurier

Hugh John Macdonald

Frank Oliver

Ivan Pylypiw

Rodmond Palen Roblin

Clifford Sifton

Ukrainians

Ukrainians settled in large numbers in Manitoba. The first Ukrainian settlement began in 1896. Over the next ten years more than 31 000 Ukrainian settlers homesteaded on the prairies. Most had been farmers in their homelands in Eastern Europe and were comfortable working the soil. Many were disappointed when their land proved difficult, but they persevered. All relied on their families, schools, and churches to help maintain familiar ways.

Doukhobors

During the last years of the nineteenth century, members of a Christian religious sect called Doukhobors felt pressured and persecuted in Russia. These German-speaking people were pulled to the prairies in 1899 with the promise of religious freedom and exemption from serving in the army. About 7400 people moved to the prairies. They wanted to live **communally** on large blocks of homesteads with all group members sharing ownership of the property. This was frowned on by the Canadian government after 1906, which preferred individual family ownership of property. In 1907 large numbers of Doukhobors moved away to British Columbia or on to individual prairie homesteads.

People gather at a Ukrainian church in Vegreville, Alberta, in 1906. These settlers had been in the area about ten years when this photograph was taken.

African Americans

African-American families travelled to the prairies in hopes of homesteading to escape discrimination in the United States. The official policy of the Canadian government was to promote the settlement of Europeans and white people from Canada and the United States. Still, a small number of African-American families did become homesteaders, while others moved into prairie cities, especially in Alberta. Even though the total number of African-American families was small, some Canadians persuaded the government that African-American immigration should be limited. Despite this, there were success stories. Rancher John Ware and his family were among the African Americans who pioneered. Others recalled homestead stories of settlers working together regardless of the colour of their skin. African-American homesteader Thomas Mapp remembers:

John Ware was a well-known African-American rancher in Alberta. Here he and other family members and hired hands stop for the camera in the yard of his ranch near Brooks.

My neighbours came and helped me build my house. They didn't charge me; all I had to do was feed them. People in those days were more friendly than they are now.

British

Pioneers from England made up a substantial proportion of the newcomers who flooded into the prairies. Many came from towns and cities, others from rural areas. They set up the kinds of institutions that had served them at home: churches, clubs, sporting events, music halls, teas, and visits. Like other groups, they were drawn to settle in areas already occupied by other British people. Unlike other immigrants, language was not an issue for them: English was the language of the prairies. One large group, the Barr Colony, developed into the town of Lloydminster when it was settled by about 2000 British homesteaders in 1903.

Snapshot

Barr's Lambs

In 1902 Isaac Barr, a former clergyman, was a hustler with big ideas. Taking advantage of government policies that encouraged colonizers to bring settlers to the prairies, he came up with a scheme to lure settlers to what was then a remote area of Western Saskatchewan. By painting a rosy picture of the homesteading life, he recruited about 2000 British immigrants for the settlement, which he called the Britannia Colony.

When the group sailed for Canada in the early spring of 1903, things immediately started to go wrong. Barr broke promise after promise. By the time the settlers reached Saskatoon, many were sure that they were being fleeced. They started calling themselves "Barr's lambs."

At this stage, some settlers turned back. Most had little choice but to continue. They were out of money and could not afford to give up. As ox carts hauled them and their belongings westward from Saskatoon, they could only hope that the homesteads they had been promised would be waiting at the end of the long trek.

In fact, the pledge of land was one of the few promises Barr did keep. Still the angry settlers were glad to see him leave. Their final snub was to name the town that would become the hub of the community, Lloydminster, after Barr's assistant, George Exton Lloyd, who had helped them as much as he could.

These colonists moved from England to Saskatchewan in 1903. The Canadian government provided the tents, food, and wagons when the colonists reached the prairies.

School

Education was highly prized by many of the people who settled on the prairies. Children went to school as soon as there were ten students to attend. The government paid for buildings and teachers with money obtained by the sale of the reserved quarter sections in each township. English was the official language of the schools. Conflicts arose when some immigrant groups wanted their children to be taught in their native language, which in many cases was not English or French. Official French or bilingual education ended in 1916 in the West, after some people agitated for entirely English instruction in schools. Schools were regarded as a vital way for the new generation of Canadians to learn to be "Canadian."

Wood Lake School, Manitoba, in 1896. School was free and regarded by many prairie families as a way to help all newcomers become "Canadian."

The Story So Far . . .

1 Why do you suppose people tended to settle near others of the same ethnocultural group?

2 What potential problems did African-American homesteaders face?

3 Suppose a school was to be set up in a Ukrainian, Russian, or German community in the West.

  a) List three arguments in favour of having school classes conducted in the first language of the students in this community.

  b) List three arguments in favour of having classes in English only.

4 Do you think it is part of the job of schools today to help newcomers become "Canadian"?

SUM IT UP!

The years between 1896 and 1914 were a time of a great change on the prairies. Hundreds of thousands of homesteaders travelled from near and far to take up the challenge of farming. Many succeeded, turning the prairie lands into the "breadbasket of the world." Others moved to new towns and cities, building new lives in a fast-growing new world. People from Northern Europe, the United States and Canada, as well as China, settled in communities, some urban, some rural. They built schools, churches, shops, railways, homes, and barns. When their incomes improved, they built bigger and better homes, barns, and shops.

In the rough mining towns and lumber camps, workers from many cultures fought against tough conditions as they tried to earn a living. Winnipeg grew into the third largest city in Canada, after Montréal and Toronto. As the gateway to the West, it was a thriving, bustling centre, home to people from many cultures who had come to the land of new beginnings.

People came to find a better life, with hope for a more prosperous and independent future than they had in their homelands. They expected that conditions would improve — things would be better soon. The West became known by some as "next year country;" the place where people would prosper next year, when the crop would not be destroyed by disease, or the railways would not charge such high rates. When things did not work out, they moved again — maybe to a town or city, maybe to the United States, maybe back to Eastern Canada. All the time Western communities were changing.

THINKING ABOUT YOUR LEARNING

1. Put yourself into the boots of a prairie homesteader. Create a flow chart to show your journey from your home community to your first successful wheat harvest. What must you do after the grain is harvested?

2. Why did so many workers join harvest excursions? What role did they play in the development of the wheat economy?

3. The posters and pamphlets advertising the West promised riches and a good life to immigrants. The reality for many people was very different: a hard struggle that often ended in failure. Do you think the government advertisements deliberately misled people? Why might this be the case?

4. Make a mind map showing the role of the CPR in the West. You will need to include settlement, towns, jobs, mining, wheat, and moving people.

5. Write a list of interview questions for *one* of the people we have met in this chapter: the homesteader, Clifford Sifton, Theodore Strom, Gertrude Winter, Mayer Hoffer, the bachelor homesteaders, Cora Hind, the men doing their laundry, or a member of a threshing gang.

APPLYING YOUR LEARNING

1. Find someone who has immigrated to Canada, either recently or in the more distant past.
   a) Develop a set of interview questions to ask them about their experiences: deciding to come to Canada, travelling here, finding a home, finding work, learning English or French, and other aspects of their lives as "newcomers."
   b) Interview them about their experiences.
   c) Compare their experiences with those of the prairie newcomers about 100 years ago. What has changed for newcomers? What remains similar about the experience?

2. Research the role of the Dominion Experimental Farms and their work to improve prairie agriculture.

3. Research *one* of these groups that settled the prairies in the period 1896–1914: Ukrainians, Doukhobors, Finns, Norwegians, Germans, African Americans, or Russians.

4. Why did so many prairie people resent the CPR? Do some research to find out what they persuaded the Canadian government to do to improve the situation.

USING KEY WORDS

Make a word puzzle such as a crossword, word search, or other word challenge. Use these words:
- baldheaded prairie
- communal
- ethnocultural
- freight rates
- pull factors
- push factors
- soddie

Have a classmate try your puzzle.

UNIT 2

The West

CONNECTING YOUR LEARNING

UNDERSTANDING CONCEPTS

1 Explain some of the reasons for
   a) the Red River resistance in 1870
   b) the North West Rebellion of 1885

2 Create a chart showing similarities and differences for the conflicts in 1870 and 1885 between Métis and/or Aboriginal Peoples and the Canadian government.

3 Choose *one* of the following and explain at least two different points of view that people living at the time had about the event:
   • the early years of the Red River Settlement
   • execution of Louis Riel
   • signing of treaties by Aboriginal Peoples in the West and Canada

4 Explain briefly how each of the factors below led to settlement of the prairies.
   a) Homestead Act
   b) development of Red Fife and Marquis wheat
   c) end of good available land in the United States
   d) advertising campaign in Europe and the US of good land in Canada
   e) appointment of Clifford Sifton as minister responsible for immigration

DEVELOPING RESEARCH SKILLS

1 Plan and carry out a research project on *one* of these topics: the fur trade; Métis buffalo hunt; Doukhobor settlers; Selkirk settlers.

2 Write a mini-biography for *one* of the following. Be sure to explain how each contributed to the history of Western Canada.

Louis Riel	William Van Horne
Donald Smith	Isapo-muxika (Crowfoot)
Clifford Sifton	Sam Steele
Andrew Onderdonk	Peguis (William King)
Amelia Douglas	Poundmaker

3 Make a model of *one* of the following:
   a railway trestle; a prairie house; a Red River cart.

4 Find a song that tells something about settling the prairies. Explain how the song helps us understand more about the life of the settlers.

COMMUNICATING REQUIRED KNOWLEDGE

1. Create a mural to show *one* of these aspects of prairie life:
   Aboriginal Peoples; gold rushes; settlers; town or city life; NWMP.

2. Write a newspaper story about *one* of the following:
   prairie settlement; the Mounties' trek West;
   the Klondike gold rush.

3. Present a dialogue between *one* of the following:
   Louis Riel and Sir John A. Macdonald
   Sam Steele and a swindler in the Klondike
   family members who have just arrived on the baldheaded prairie

4. Create a poster to attract someone to one of the following:
   joining the NWMP   joining the Selkirk settlers
   building the CPR   becoming a fur trader
   settling the prairie   joining the Klondike gold rush.

APPLYING CONCEPTS AND SKILLS

1. Create a radio play about the execution of Louis Riel.
2. Create a poster, business card, or e-mail address showing
   information for one of the following:
   William Van Horne   Billy Barker
   Cora Hind   Jerry Potts
3. Create a plus/minus chart for *one* of the following:
   Selkirk settlers; creation of the province of Manitoba;
   prairie homesteading; Métis using violence in 1885; gold rush
   to Cariboo or Klondike.

CREATING A MIND MAP

For each category in the mind map below list statements that show
what role the topic played in the history of the West in this time period.

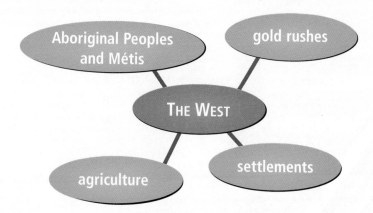

1876 1881 1914

1919

UNIT **3**

A Changing Society

THE BIG PICTURE

These are some of the stories you will read about in this unit:

- how the Industrial Revolution affected the everyday and working lives of Canadian people
- inventions and innovations in transportation and communications that changed peoples' lives
- how Canadian government policies affected Aboriginal Peoples
- the working conditions for Canadian people and how individuals and unions tried to improve these conditions
- the struggle of workers in the Winnipeg General Strike
- women who struggled to improve the position of women in society and win them the vote
- immigration policies and how they encouraged some people to come to Canada and kept others out
- what it was like for Canadian soldiers who fought in the trench warfare of World War I, and what they achieved
- how people in Canada supported the war effort at home
- conscription in World War I and how the issue divided the country

An Era of Change

1878	**1883**	**1891**	**1893**	**1896**	**1897**
Macdonald introduces the National Policy	Canada adopts Sandford Fleming's Standard Time	Sir John A. Macdonald dies	Canada's first electronic automobile appears	Wilfrid Laurier becomes Prime Minister	Canada's first gasoline-driven car for personal use appears

SETTING OUR FOCUS

The two photographs opposite show Main Street in Winnipeg, Manitoba. The top photograph was taken in 1879, the other in 1897. It is hard to believe it is the same place. How many changes can you see? What kinds of changes do you think have happened that you cannot see, for example, inside the buildings?

Imagine seeing the first streetcar or getting used to the huge poles and all those wires for telephones and electricity. In Halifax people came out at night to cut the poles and wires down — they thought they were ugly.

Almost every aspect of life changed in this era. Cooking and housekeeping, gardening and farming, transportation and communication, education, politics, medicine, business, sports, and art were all affected by some invention or new way of doing things.

How and why did all these changes occur? What effect did they have on the people of Canada? These are interesting questions. Try to imagine what it would be like if almost everything you do, see, know, and hear changed in the next few years!

PREVIEWING THE CHAPTER

In this chapter you will learn about these topics:
- the effects of the Industrial Revolution on Canadian society
- changes in transportation and communications
- the movement of people to towns and cities
- the National Policy and how it helped industries grow
- some individuals who helped change Canada

KEY WORDS

branch plants
depression
entrepreneur
globalization
industrialization
innovation
patent
rural
technology
urban

1901
Marconi receives the first wireless transatlantic signal in Newfoundland

1906
World's first radio broadcast by Reginald Fessenden

1911
Emily Carr exhibits "new art" in Paris

1914
World War I begins

1918
- World War I ends
- Women win the right to vote in federal elections

Charles Saunders was a scientist, musician, and scholar.

Emily Stowe had to go to New York to study to be a doctor since medical schools in Canada would not accept women before 1867.

Emily Carr was a writer as well as an artist.

TOWARD CANADA'S CENTURY

In 1904 Prime Minister Sir Wilfrid Laurier said that the twentieth century would be "Canada's century." Laurier's prediction did not seem unreasonable. Canada was full of amazing people at this time, all working to meet the challenges sweeping the young nation.

There was Charles Saunders, who developed Marquis Wheat, a hardy strain of wheat for the short growing season of the prairies. He was born in 1867, the year of Confederation. Sandford Fleming, born in Scotland in 1827, came to British North America at the age of 18 in the time of the Great Migration. As an engineer he crossed Canada by foot, snowshoe, dog-team, canoe, wagon, raft, and dugout. He was chief engineer for two of the most significant railway jobs in the young Canada: the Intercolonial Railway between Halifax and Québec City and the Canadian Pacific Railway from Ontario to the Pacific. As well, he created Standard Time, the idea of dividing the world into 24 equal time zones.

By 1867 Emily Stowe, born in 1831, was the first Canadian woman doctor to practise medicine. She then worked to open a Canadian medical college for women in Ontario in 1883. Emily Carr was born in 1871 and struggled with a "new art" that broke from the usual style of painting and defied the old way.

These were just four of the many Canadians who were meeting the challenges of the new age.

Signs of Change

In 1871 about one in six Canadians lived in cities or towns. Edwige Allard was a typical city dweller of the time. The wife of a Montréal carpenter, she looked after a large 0.4 ha garden. She grew enough beans, potatoes, onions, and root crops to feed her family of nine.

Ten years earlier Edwige might have kept pigs. The 1861 Census of Canada reported close to 3000 pigs in the city of Montréal, and historians think there were far more. By 1874 life in the city of Montréal had changed, and a bill to ban the keeping of pigs in the city passed quickly. By the turn of the century Edwige's large garden would not have been likely either. In 1901 one in three Canadians lived in cities or towns. Buildings covered land within the cities. No pigs were allowed, and there was no room for farm-size gardens.

Sandford Fleming
MARKING TIME

In 1876 Sandford Fleming, a civil engineer, decided to take a holiday in Britain. The trip would give him a much-needed break from his job of surveying routes for the Canadian Pacific Railway. His trip would trigger a revolution in the way the world kept time.

At his first stop in Ireland Fleming missed a train because of an error in the printed schedule. A typesetter had recorded the departure time as 5:35 p.m. The schedule should have read 5:35 a.m. Fleming had missed the train by 12 hours and was faced with a 12-hour wait for the next one. As he waited, Fleming thought about the mistake.

Instead of dividing the day into two identically numbered 12-hour periods, why not number the hours consecutively from 1 through 24, he wondered. This would prevent people from confusing a.m. and p.m.

This idea started Fleming thinking about another time-keeping problem. In Canada and other countries, clocks in major centres were set according to astronomical calculations made in each community. This meant that when it was 12 noon in Halifax, Nova Scotia, clocks in Moncton, New Brunswick, were set to 11:45 a.m. In Toronto, Ontario, they were set to 10:55 a.m. Train travellers had to reset their watches to a different time at every major stop along the way. Some people had even started wearing watches with several faces, each set to the time in a different community.

Dividing the world into 24 equal time zones would reduce the confusion, thought Fleming. Lines of longitude, or meridians, could form the dividing lines between the zones. If clocks everywhere in a particular zone were set to the same time, it would be easy to figure out the time anywhere in the world.

With typical energy and enthusiasm, Fleming started talking about Standard Time to anyone who would listen. In 1879 he presented the idea in a speech to the Royal Canadian Institute for the Advancement of Scientific Knowledge.

Soon afterward, the Marquis of Lorne, the Governor General, read the published speech. Lord Lorne was so interested in the idea that he sent copies to governments around the world.

Everyone liked the idea. Canada adopted Standard Time in 1883. Then in 1884 delegates from 25 countries met at the International Prime Meridian Conference in Washington, DC. They agreed to adopt international Standard Time, which is still in use today. The Greenwich Meridian, which runs through the Greenwich Observatory in London, England, was declared the standard for setting clocks around the world.

Fleming was knighted for his work and became Sir Sandford Fleming.

More people you could research are

Alexander Graham Bell

Charles Fenerty

Reginald Fessenden

Sandford Fleming

Abraham Gesner

Wallace Turnbull

1 List the five largest cities in each of the years shown.

2 In which part of Canada were the largest cities located in 1901?

3 a) What was happening to the growth of cities in
   i) the Maritimes?
   ii) the West?
   b) What explanations can you give for these trends?

Growth of Cities, 1871–1901

City	Number of People			
	1871	1881	1891	1901
Montréal	115 000	155 238	219 616	382 172
Toronto	59 000	96 916	181 215	209 892
Winnipeg	241	7 985	25 639	42 340
Vancouver	–	–	13 709	27 010
Hamilton	26 880	36 661	48 959	52 634
Ottawa	24 141	31 307	44 154	59 928
Québec	59 699	62 446	63 090	68 840
Halifax	29 582	36 100	38 437	40 832
Saint John	28 805	26 127	39 179	40 711

This change was only one of many. Others in the 30 years from 1871 to 1901 included:

- a 130 percent increase in the number of workers in manufacturing
- the value of output from manufacturing went up more than three times
- the length of rail lines laid went from 3200 km to 27 350 km

The Story So Far . . .

1 This assignment will be ongoing throughout this chapter. Choose either Charles Saunders, Sandford Fleming, Emily Stowe, or Emily Carr as an eyewitness of the period. Start to gather information on that person so that you can
   - prepare a report on that person's life and role in this era of change in Canada. Include any pictures you can find.
   - write imaginary journal entries as if you are this person, recording how you feel about the changes going on around you. For example, how do you feel about the growth of cities?

2 List the changes you have noticed so far. Beside each change, note what you think was the cause.

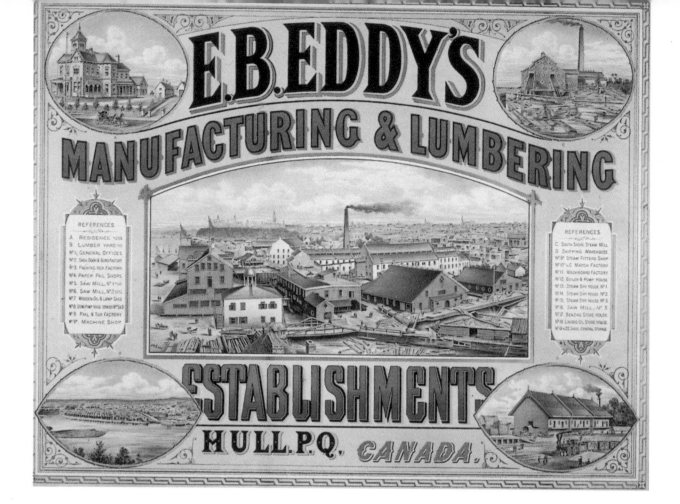

Full Steam Ahead

The changes that came with the Industrial Revolution were speeding up by the time of Confederation in 1867. The shift away from small pioneer farming communities where people lived off the land was well underway in Eastern Canada. In the larger towns, factories with machines run by steam engines were being set up. This shift to the use of mechanized tools and factories to produce goods is called **industrialization**.

The Industrial Revolution had started in Britain and the United States earlier than it did in Canada. Consequently the United States looked to Canada as a source of raw materials such as lumber and minerals for factories and as a market for their manufactured goods. This system had a few disadvantages for Canada.

The first problem was that raw materials sold for less than manufactured goods. The second was that most manufacturing in Canada in 1867 was done in small family-owned workshops. These workshops could not produce enough goods to compete with larger companies in the United States or Britain. This meant that Canada often spent more money on goods it imported, or brought into the country, than it earned from materials it exported, or sold to other countries.

E.B. Eddy's manufacturing plant and lumber mill at Hull, Québec, in the 1880s. People considered the smoke a sign of industry and wealth.

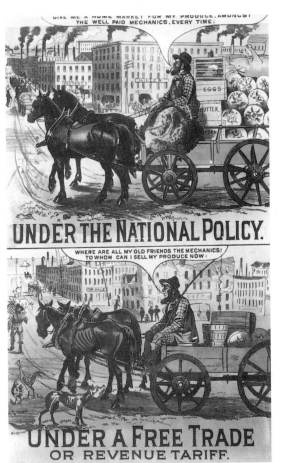

GIVE ME A HOME MARKET FOR MY PRODUCE, AMONGST THE WELL PAID MECHANICS, EVERY TIME!

UNDER THE NATIONAL POLICY.

WHERE ARE ALL MY OLD FRIENDS THE MECHANICS? TO WHOM CAN I SELL MY PRODUCE NOW?

UNDER A FREE TRADE OR REVENUE TARIFF.

This poster was used to help the Conservative Party win the election of 1891. What message do you get from this poster?

This could cause real hardship during a **depression**, or a period of economic slowdown. At these times other countries do not buy our raw materials, and we can not afford to purchase their manufactured goods.

Other countries were also becoming more closely linked as they exchanged more and more goods and services. This trend was a sign of the beginnings of **globalization**. With globalization, a slowdown in one country affected the countries it traded with. It seemed to some people in this age of change that Canada's infant industries needed protection so they could survive and grow.

In the 1870s there was a severe depression. Businesses could not sell their goods and were forced to lay off workers and some even closed. The Conservative Party, under Sir John A. Macdonald, fought the 1878 election on the idea of the National Policy. It included tariffs on imported manufactured goods to protect Canadian industries, the building of the CPR, and immigration to fill the Western plains. The Conservatives won the election, and conditions improved as the depression ended soon after.

Macdonald, of course, pointed proudly to the National Policy. His critics pointed to general prosperity worldwide, as well as good crops.

The Story So Far . . .

1 Draw a simple flow chart to show how the National Policy was meant to help Canada grow. You may want to refer to page 113 in Chapter 4.

2 The Industrial Revolution produced many lifestyle changes. Make a chart like the one below to give your opinion on these changes, and add to it as you read this chapter.

Change	Plus	Minus
People moved to cities	~	~

3 Write a letter by your eyewitness to a friend to say what you think about the changes taking place.

The Change in Manufacturing

The small family-owned workshops had all but vanished by 1900. As manufacturers made more money they were able to buy better machines to increase production.

Shoemaking is a good example of this change. In pioneer days skilled craftspeople known as cobblers made shoes individually by hand. Cobblers could make only about two pairs of shoes per day. They probably also made a few other small leather goods, farmed, and maybe fished or operated a little sugar bush if they lived in the country. With the development of sewing machines shoe factories replaced the cobbler. In a shoe factory a worker could make part of a hundred pairs of shoes a day.

This is what Olivier David Benoit, a shoemaker from Montréal, said to the Royal Commission on the Relations of Labour and Capital in 1889 when he was asked about the changes:

> The boot and shoe men of the old times could make a shoe or boot
> ... whereas today, as a general rule, all the men working in
> factories, especially in the large factories, are able to do only one
> kind of work, [such] as to set a heel or sew a sole, or set the
> uppers, because today perfected machinery has replaced hand work.

Shoes from the factories were less expensive. This meant more people could buy them.

Snippet

Boosting Industry

The National Policy caused grumbling. The wealthy did not like the 30 percent tariff on luxury items imported from the United States, for example. Still, the Conservatives' policy got results. In the first three years, the number of business failures decreased dramatically. During the same period exports were increasing. In 1878 the value of Canadian exports was $79 323 000. By 1896 this total had risen to $121 013 000.

A family-owned foundry in Montréal. Men poured molten metal into the boxes on the floor to make metal parts. Everything was done by hand.

Factories were usually set up in towns and cities where there were workers and transportation available. Toronto, for example, had a work force of 9400 employed by 530 manufacturers in 1871. By 1891, 20 years later, there were 26 242 workers employed by 2401 manufacturers.

Many skilled workers found their jobs taken over by machines operated by women or children, who worked to help families that could no longer earn a living from the land. By 1891 over one quarter of all manufacturing employees were women. So many children worked for wages that Ontario and Québec passed Factory Acts in the mid-1880s to ban the employment of boys under the age of 12 and girls under 14 years. Proof of age was a note signed by the child's parent, so you can imagine how well enforced these Acts were.

Only the highest paid workers could earn enough to support a family on their own. There were more and more poorly paid jobs for unskilled workers. On the one hand there was a growing economy that could pay for canals, railways, roads, and telegraph lines. On the other hand there were skilled people losing well-paying jobs.

The change in shoemaking from 1780 to 1880. Do you think the artist approved of the changes?

M930.50.5.262
1780. 2 pairs a day. The old style.
McCord Museum of Canadian History, Montréal.

M930.50.5.142
1880. 300 pairs a day. The new way.
McCord Museum of Canadian History, Montréal.

The Entrepreneurs

The changes in industry benefited enterprising people called **entrepreneurs**, who started their own businesses. Consider two men named Harris. One, James Harris, had set up a blacksmith shop in Saint John, New Brunswick, in 1825. Later he formed a partnership and turned his shop into a foundry, a factory to melt and mould metal, and began making parts for railway cars. During the 1880s James was able to finance a large factory, which produced more railway cars than any other firm in the country. Likely he lived in a lovely home like the one in Alberta.

Alanson Harris experienced a similar string of successes. He started as a sawmill operator in Brant County, Ontario. In 1857 he bought a foundry in Beamsville and made farm tools and

The Most Extensive and Best Appointed Establishment in Canada
FOR MANUFACTURING HARVESTING MACHINERY.

Works of The Massey Manufacturing Co., Toronto, Ont.

A Massey-Harris advertisement showing the main factory in 1881

A woman churns butter the old-fashioned way.

machines. Later he used the CPR railway system to ship his machines to the farmers of the West. In 1890 he merged his firm with his major competitor, the Massey Manufacturing Company, creating Massey-Harris. By 1891 Massey-Harris was Canada's largest corporation. You can imagine the type of home he must have lived in!

Stories such as these show the kinds of success that Prime Minister Macdonald and his supporters had hoped for as a result of the National Policy. Small shops became large companies. They grew with the help of the railway and protective tariffs. American companies started to set up **branch plants** here: Coca-Cola, Singer, Gillette, and Westinghouse to name a few. These American-owned factories made and sold their goods in Canada without paying tariffs.

The Story So Far . . .

1 Working in pairs, imagine one of you is a cobbler struggling because a shoe factory has opened in the next town, and one of you is Prime Minister Macdonald. As a cobbler, write a persuasive letter to the Prime Minister, expressing your dismay. As Prime Minister, reply to this letter explaining the purpose of the National Policy.

2 Not everyone was happy with the National Policy. Draw an editorial cartoon against the policy. Consider a shoemaker's point of view.

3 Draw a graph or illustration to show how much manufacturing grew in Toronto between 1871 and 1891.

Change on the Farm

Life on farms and the ways of producing foods and crops changed as well. Dairy farming is a good example. Before Confederation, women looked after the family cows. They milked them and made cheese and butter at home. Selling their products gave them a way to earn their own money. Even in towns, some families kept cows for milk and perhaps to earn some extra money or trade dairy products to friends, neighbours, and the general store.

In 1864 there was only one cheese factory, which was in Canada West. By 1871 there were 350 cheese factories in all Canada. By 1901 the value of Canadian cheese exports was $20.6 million, and it was Canada's largest single export. Men took over the industry, on farms and in the factories.

This mammoth cheese, 9900 kg, was made in Perth, Ontario, in 1893 for the world fair held in Chicago. It had to be sent there on a special train.

Machines had already replaced hand tools on most farms by 1867. Machinery had been first introduced in the 1830s. One example was the horse-drawn McCormick reaper used for harvesting grain. There were also mechanized hay rakes and mowers. Now they were replaced by power-driven machines. The first steam threshing machine, used to separate grain from the stalk or husk, was introduced in 1877 in Woodbridge, Ontario. Imagine the impact of a machine that could process more in a day than the average farmer could process in a year! Tractors run by gasoline-powered engines would change farming even more. These first appeared in the 1890s, but not many were used on Canadian farms until after 1920.

This progress came at a price for farmers. When they all had good crops, prices dropped. Farmers had to sell at that price or have no income. Some, who had borrowed from banks to pay for their seeds and machinery, did not make enough to repay their loans. Many farms failed and many farmers' children were lured to the city. By the twentieth century the new machines

Farms and Farm Sizes, 1871–1921			Urban and Rural Population, 1871–1921*			
Year	Number of Farms (thousands)	Area in Farms (millions of ha)	Year	Total Population	Rural (%)	Urban (%)
1871	368	15.3	1871	3 689 000	83	17
1881	464	18.2	1881	4 324 000	78	22
1891	542	24.3	1891	4 833 000	70	30
1901	511	25.5	1901	5 371 000	65	35
1911	682	44.1	1911	7 206 643	54	46
1921	711	57.0	1921	8 787 949	51	49

1 Working with a partner calculate the average size of a farm for each of the years shown.

2 Write a short statement to describe what was happening to farm sizes in this period.

3 In which two ten-year periods did population in Canada increase the most?

4 Draw a line, bar, or circle graph to show the trends in urban and rural population.

5 Numbers tell a story. List the ideas you get from these two charts.

*Urban population refers to people living in towns. Rural population refers to people living in the country, at this time on farms, in villages, and small communities.

Reflections

Imagine you are a member of a family that has struggled for 30 years to make a living on the farm that your grandparents cleared and settled. Crops have failed for two years in a row. Recreate a family discussion on whether to sell the farm or keep trying to make a living from it.

The Granger Collection, New York

Many emigrants from Québec went south to work in the facctories in New England.

meant fewer farms were meeting the national and international demand for food.

Some farm families prospered, others did not. Consider the fortunes of two farming families in Québec, the Alberts and the Etmanskis. Felix Albert had been born into a farm family in Québec. He farmed after he married and had a family. John Etmanski came to Québec as a child from Poland. He and his Polish immigrant wife, Mary Kiedrowski, eventually had 12 children. The family lived in a two-room dwelling, farming and lumbering some land.

In 1881 the Alberts gave up. Bad weather, wheat stem rust — a fungus that destroyed the wheat crop — and the low wages Felix earned in the nearby lumberyard convinced them to move to the United States. They were not alone. Estimates are that about 700 000 French Canadians from Québec did the same. On the other hand, the Etmanskis persevered with farming and lumbering. By 1895 they could afford to hire a Polish carpenter to build a large two-storey home on their property.

As you saw in Chapter 8, at first the new farming machines did not play much of a role in the everyday lives of poorer immigrants to the prairies. In her recollections, Ukrainian immigrant Maria Adamskova describes how she and her mother cleared land with a spade and an ax while her father began to build a house. During the same years that saw the first powered airplane flights and Ford's Model T car, Maria and her family dug, mowed, harvested, and raked by hand. Her father was not able to buy a reaping machine until more than three quarters of a century after it had first been introduced in Canada.

The Story So Far . . .

1 Create a visual to show the changes on farms. This can be a drawing, cartoon, or collage.

2 Over 1 million people left Canada for the United States from 1870 to 1900. Imagine you are one of these people. What reasons would you give to your friends for your decision?

3 What opinion does your eyewitness have about the changes in rural Canada?

Melvin Ormond Hammond

LEAVING THE FAMILY FARM

In 1890 14-year-old Melvin Ormond Hammond did not mind helping his parents with the work on his family's farm near Clarkson, Ontario. Although machines now helped farmers do some jobs like cutting, stooking, and binding hay and grain, the work was still very hard. When the time came to bind the grain into sheaves, for example, Melvin helped set up the binder. This chore took all day.

That summer of 1890, Melvin kept a diary in which he noted how he spent his time. On June 26, for example, he loaded, unloaded, and spread manure all day. Applying this fertilizer was essential if the farm was to produce healthy crops. On June 30 he picked 92 kg of strawberries. No one had yet invented a machine to take over this backbreaking job!

Melvin knew that he was helping to keep the farm going, and he did the work cheerfully. Still, as an only child, he worried about how his father and mother would manage when he left the farm. And he was determined to leave. He wanted to be a news reporter.

If Melvin's parents were disappointed that their son did not want to take over the farm, they did not show it. Many other boys his age had already left school, but they encouraged Melvin to get the education he needed to fulfil his ambition. They even allowed him to borrow one of the family's plough horses to make the long ride to high school in Oakville where he earned top marks.

When he graduated, Melvin became one of many young Canadians who were leaving farms to live in cities. He enrolled in a business college in Toronto. There, he learned shorthand and typing, considered essential skills for a news reporter.

Melvin landed an office job at a Toronto loan company, but this work did not appeal to him. His goal was still to work in the news business. Finally he got the opportunity he had been waiting for. He became the private secretary of the managing editor of *The Globe*, the Toronto newspaper that had been founded by George Brown. Within a year, he had joined the reporting staff — and abandoned the name Melvin, which he decided was not dashing enough. His by-line always read M.O. Hammond and, from then on, everyone called him by his initials only.

M.O. Hammond went on to have a distinguished career in journalism. For years, he was *The Globe's* parliamentary reporter in Ottawa, rubbing shoulders with the great and not-so-great in the corridors of power.

Although Hammond had become a confirmed city dweller, he never forgot his rural roots. For years, he planned his holidays so that he returned to the family farm to help his parents bring in the harvest.

More people you could research are

Robertine Barry

Kathleen (Kit) Coleman

Sara Jeanette Duncan

Melvin Ormand Hammond

Margaret Marshall Saunders

WE HAVE THE TECHNOLOGY

The invention of new machines was at the core of the changes that came with the Industrial Revolution. Sometimes an invention in one country was quickly adopted in other countries. The development of the steam engine is one example. It is also a good example of a **technology** that was put to many different uses — powering steamships, trains, farm machinery, early cars, and logging and mining machines.

Sometimes several different people thought of similar advances at the same time. The person given the credit as the inventor was the one who first applied for a **patent**, or got permission from the government to make, use, and sell an invention as his or her own property. Charles Fenerty of Nova Scotia, for example, developed the process for making newsprint from wood pulp. He did not publicize his discovery until after others had patented the process, so he lost inventor status.

Still others, like Alanson Harris, bought patents from other countries. That meant they held the Canadian rights for the production of other people's inventions here. Harris is credited with making **innovations** — changes and improvements — to several of the patents he bought.

Web Connection

http://www.school.mcgrawhill.ca/resources

Go to the web site above to find out more about Canadian inventions. Go to History Resources, then to *Canada: The Story of a Developing Nation* to see where to go next.

Snippet

Shedding Some Light

Two young Toronto men, Henry Woodward and Matthew Evans, knew they had an important discovery when they invented a light bulb in 1873. They continued experimenting but ran out of money. Discouraged, they sold their patent to wealthy American inventor, Thomas Edison. In 1879 six years after Woodward and Evans came up with the idea, Edison announced he had developed a light bulb and the names of the two Toronto inventors disappeared from history.

The Technology of Transportation

The change in land transportation from foot or horsepower to train had a huge impact in Canada. The train helped bind the nation. It inspired many Canadians to believe that technology could overcome all obstacles and change every part of life.

Electric streetcars were the first major users of electricity. Canada played a leading role in their development by demonstrating electric streetcar rides at the 1884 Toronto Industrial Exhibition (now called the Canadian National Exhibition). Imagine the shock of fair-goers who had arrived on foot, on horseback, or by horse and buggy!

Very few of these fair-goers could have even imagined the changes that would come with the car, the truck, the diesel tractor, and the airplane. For the average person then these innovations in transportation were interesting experiments. For most people they were unaffordable.

At first, many people were unimpressed by the noisy, expensive, and unreliable automobile. In fact, the phrase, "get a horse," became a popular cry against the car. Prince Edward Island even made automobiles illegal for a time. But the tide of change could not be stopped. Henry Ford established his first automobile branch plant in Canada in 1904. In 1920 the automobile industry in Canada made 94 144 cars and trucks and employed more than 8000 people. The price came down. Almost everyone could hope to buy the $300 Model T of 1921. Another effect of the cars was that people demanded, and got, better roads.

Snapshot

More Than a Passing Fad

In 1900 the McLaughlin Carriage Works in Oshawa, Ontario, sold 25 000 horse-drawn carriages in North America and around the world. But Sam McLaughlin, son of company founder Robert McLaughlin, was fascinated by a new invention — the horseless carriage.

His father dismissed the new machines as a passing fad. Sam was sure that they were here to stay. He and his brother George persuaded their father to try making automobiles as a sideline. They had one problem. The bodies could be made at the carriage works, but they needed a reliable engine.

McLaughlin contacted William Durant, owner of the Buick Motor Company in Flint, Michigan. Durant agreed to supply Buick engines for the McLaughlin cars and, in 1907, the first McLaughlin-Buick rolled out of the Oshawa carriage shop. McLaughlin's goal was to make 200 cars a year.

In the meantime, Durant was buying other American car-manufacturing companies, including Oldsmobile and Cadillac. In 1909 he merged these into a new company called General Motors. Then, in 1918, Durant bought McLaughlin's company. Though McLaughlin remained president, the family name disappeared when the new company was incorporated as General Motors of Canada.

This poster was part of an anticar campaign launched by the McLaughlin Carriage Works. What message is it giving about the car?

The Pictures Behind the Story

Faster and Faster

▲ An advertisement for the McLaughlin car

▼ The Silver Dart, designed and built by a team directed by Alexander Graham Bell, first flew in Canada in February 1903.

▲ Streetcars transformed cities.

Early telegraph equipment was portable and could be moved easily from one railway station office to another.

Steel-hulled steamships replaced sailing ships for transatlantic crossings. ▶

In the 1890s bicycles provided people with cheap tranportation. They also gave women more freedom to go out unescorted. ◀

▲ The first transatlantic radio signal was received by Italian inventor Gugliemo Marconi at Signal Hill, St. John's, Newfoundland, on December 10, 1901.

Free mail delivery to rural areas started early in the twentieth century. ◀

▲ An early telephone in the 1880s

Communications Changes

As early as the 1840s telegraph lines carried messages to link cities in Eastern Canada with cities in the United States. Imagine the difference the telegraph must have made. People were used to hearing the news months out-of-date. They had no way of sending or receiving urgent messages any faster than the speed of a horse or a ship.

It was not an easy task to string telegraph lines across the country, or lay the cables under the Atlantic Ocean. Once the lines were in place, a revolution in communications began. This was, perhaps, the first step in turning our world into a global village, where everyone can hear the news within minutes of it being reported if they have a radio. The communications revolution is not over yet.

The telephone, the invention of Alexander Graham Bell in 1876, was a huge advance in communications technology.

The invention of the radio took communications one step further and turned it into entertainment too. On December 23, 1900, Canadian-born Reginald Fessenden sent a voice message through the air, "One, two, three, four. Is it snowing where you are, Mr. Thiessen? If it is, telegraph back and let me know."

Film was becoming an important new medium in the early twentieth century. Mary Pickford, shown here on the right, was one of the early famous American stars. She was born in Toronto as Gladys Smith in 1893.

Fessenden went on to demonstrate the world's first musical broadcast in 1906. He eventually held 500 patents for a variety of inventions.

In 1919 the Canadian Marconi Company set up the world's first broadcasting station, XWA, in Montréal. Gradually barriers of distance were broken down, and the people of Canada were brought in contact with each other, and the world. The media age had begun.

The XWA broadcasting station in Montréal, which started broadcasting in 1919

The Story So Far . . .

1 Design a mural to demonstrate significant developments in the technology of transportation.

2 Many people were anticar early in the twentieth century, and many people are anticar now. Make two lists of reasons to be against the technology of the automobile, one for 1900 and one for now.

3 What would your eyewitness have thought of the changes in communication? Write an article or a letter to a newspaper editor.

In 1869 Timothy Eaton opened a store on Yonge Street in Toronto. The Eaton store had some policies that were quite unusual for the time.

- There would be no bargaining over prices. These were "rock bottom" and fixed prices.
- Cash only would be accepted. There would be no credit or barter.
- There was a money-back policy for unsatisfactory goods.

In 1884 Timothy Eaton introduced the Eaton Catalogue. The catalogue was sent to homes across the nation. In the early twentieth century it was often joked that the only book more popular than the catalogue across Canada was the Bible. The range and variety of goods offered was almost beyond the imagination before Eaton's existed. At one time it was even possible to order one-room cabin and one-room schoolhouse kits.

The store policies and the catalogue service were dramatic changes to the old way of shopping, where barter and credit systems were often used. The Eaton family continued to own and operate a large retail business until August 1999, when the Eaton stores were closed by bankruptcy.

Covers of the Eaton Catalogue

QUESTIONING THE EVIDENCE

1. Examine the Eaton Catalogue covers above. Imagine you are the graphic artist who designed the covers. Explain why you chose these particular images and words. Who and what are you appealing to? Would these covers be effective today?

2. Imagine you are a teen living on an isolated farm in Canada's new West in 1904. You are about to open a new catalogue. What are you hoping to find in it? What does your mother want to find? Your father? What interests your brothers and sisters? Write a diary entry about the excitement caused by the arrival of the catalogue.

3. Explain how these catalogue covers help you understand something about life in Canada in the early twentieth century.

World War I

Change speeded up during World War I from 1914 to 1918. The war effort at home included supplying millions of tons of food and millions of dollars worth of munitions. This was no small feat considering our population and that we only had one factory that could manufacture ammunition at the start of the war. On farms the use of machines increased. The Canadian government removed the tariff on tractors and arranged a deal for lower-cost tractors from an American company.

Ontario and Québec, already the most industrialized provinces, saw even more growth in industries. More and more people moved to the cities and towns for work. In British Columbia and Atlantic Canada, mining and shipbuilding were the industries most affected by the war effort. Metals were needed for shell casings, equipment, and ships. To keep up with the growth, towns had to provide better electric, water, and other services. Street and highway improvements were made at this time.

Social changes took place at this time too. Workers unions grew in response to low wages, long hours, and unsafe conditions. Women's demand for the right to vote and for changes in the laws that affected them grew. People began to demand that the government respond to the voters' needs.

The portrayal of society by artists and authors changed too. The works of "new art" artists like Emily Carr and members of the Group of Seven were unique. Canada's notion of entertainment was changed forever with the first Canadian viewing of a movie in Ottawa, in 1896. At first the "silent movies" were shown in community halls. Permanent movie theatres soon popped up across the country, the first in Vancouver in 1902. Sound was added to movies by World War I, just in time for wartime newsreels.

Recreation changed too. Better transportation made it possible for sports teams to travel to matches outside their community. Electric light meant that arenas, rinks, tracks, and gymnasiums could be open for extended hours year-round. Indoor sports became more popular, at least in the cities. Professional hockey and football became regular events in Canada, and sports coverage became a regular feature in Canadian newspapers.

Snippet

Canada's Claim to Sports Fame

James Naismith from Almonte, Ontario, developed today's game of basketball in 1891. He first introduced the game while he was a physical education teacher at the YMCA Training School in Springfield, Massachusetts. The Edmonton Grads were a women's basketball team formed in 1915, in Edmonton, Alberta. From 1915 until 1940 the Grads travelled over 160 000 km playing teams all over North America and Europe, winning 93 percent of their games.

William Peyton Hubbard

As the twentieth century dawned, the new technology of electricity was already promising to change people's lives. Debate raged over whether electricity should be controlled by private companies or the public. One of the most outspoken supporters of public ownership was William Peyton Hubbard, a Toronto politician.

At the time, electric lighting was nothing new. Streets in Toronto, Montréal, and Winnipeg had been lit by arc lamps since 1883. By 1890 cities such as Victoria, Vancouver, Halifax, Saint John's, and Moncton had done the same. Arc lamps could be used only outdoors, however. American inventor Thomas Edison had developed a light bulb for indoor use in 1879, but it would take a few more years to perfect a system for supplying homes with electric power.

It did not take long for businesspeople to see that they could make money from electrical energy. Soon, privately owned electric companies were competing with one another to supply power to homes. The companies had to apply to local governments for permission to install the poles and power lines that would carry the energy. A company that got this right won the contract to supply electricity to the community.

In Toronto and elsewhere, the awarding of these contracts sparked intense debate. The successful company would have a monopoly. On one side were those who believed that this was just fine. On the other side were people, such as Hubbard, who believed that electricity should be generated and distributed by a publicly owned utility. This, they said, would mean cheaper rates for customers.

This stand was typical of Hubbard. He was the first African Canadian elected to Toronto city council. He was a reformer, perhaps because he knew what it was like to be poor and suffer racial prejudice. Hubbard's mother and his father, an African-American slave who had been granted freedom, were of mixed ancestry. After marrying, they settled in Toronto, where Hubbard and his seven brothers and sisters were born. At the time, African Canadians often had trouble finding jobs that paid well, and life was sometimes hard for the large family.

Supported by many city residents, Hubbard and other city politicians waged a successful crusade. In 1908 they created a publicly owned company called Toronto Hydro to supply electrical energy to the city.

Unfortunately for Hubbard, the victory cost him his political career. Many of the voters were wealthy businesspeople who were against public ownership. In the next election, they campaigned against him and he was defeated.

Still, Hubbard must have felt a thrill of satisfaction on May 2, 1911. That was the day the switch was officially thrown to turn on power in homes across Toronto. His vision of a publicly owned utility had become reality.

More people you could research are

Thomas Ahearn

Adam Beck

Alanson Harris

William Peyton Hubbard

Hart Massey

Samuel McLaughlin

Land Reserved for Whom?

Most groups could point to some gains from the rapid development of Canada. However it was a strain on Aboriginal Peoples. Land on the reserves, which was supposed to be protected, was taken to make room for factories, roads, and railway lines. In 1906 the Indian Act, which was supposed to protect reserve lands, was changed to make their sale easier. During World War I the government even went so far as to withhold money until the Blood First Nation in southern Alberta sold off large chunks of their land. This was despite the fact that the number of Aboriginal soldiers involved in the war effort was much greater than their proportion of the general population.

It became increasingly acceptable for young women to take up sports. Here the young women's hockey team at Rossland, British Columbia, pose at the local ice rink.

The Story So Far . . .

1 Many historians have said that the train was the most significant advance in Canada during this era of change. Explain why you would or would not agree. What do you think was the second most significant advance?

2 Imagine a world without movies. Report how your eyewitness would react to seeing his or her first movie.

3 Research the story of Timothy Eaton and the Eaton stores. As a reporter in the nineteenth century write a news article on Eaton's and the new way of selling goods.

SUM IT UP!

It remained to be seen whether the twentieth century would be "Canada's century" but it could not be denied that the past half century had changed Canada completely. People were moving at an increasing rate from farms into the growing cities. Farms became larger although more work was done with fewer workers because of the availability of machines. Farmers depended for their income on the crops and produce that they grew and sold.

The people who moved from the land tried to find work in the cities. There the Industrial Revolution was transforming the workplace as factories replaced the crafts industries. In the early years many women and even children were employed in the factories; eventually laws restricting child labour were enacted. The Conservative Party brought in the National Policy to protect the infant industries. By the time of World War I Canada's industries had grown enough for the country to play a significant part in supplying munitions and other materials to the soldiers overseas. There was a huge division in wealth between the successful entrepreneurs and the labourers and workers who were employed by these people.

Change also came with the invention and adoption of new technologies, particularly in transportation and communications. Cars, telephones, and radio were all unknown at the time of Confederation. By the end of the period in 1920 they were becoming commonplace. Other inventions like electricity transformed cities and industries.

There was growth and lots of growing pains. The nation was not fully developed yet, but Canada's efforts and results during World War I, in particular, elevated its status as a nation.

The next chapter will take a closer look at workers in Canada and the labour movement. Further change, and conflicts, were coming.

THINKING ABOUT YOUR LEARNING

1. a) Explain why cities in Canada grew from 1867 to 1920.
   b) Make a time line of the changes you would have seen between 1867 and 1920. Remember to include details like inventions.

2. You are a reporter for *Your City Examiner*. You have been assigned to cover the Royal Commission on The Relations of Labour and Capital in 1889. Based on the responses of the shoemaker, write a front-page story. Do not forget the five Ws — who, what, when, where, and why.

3. Imagine you have been commissioned to design a book cover for a novel about life in the city. The year is 1900. Make up a title and design a book cover, front and back. Do not forget that the back of a book cover usually gives a brief synopsis of the plot or an excerpt from the novel.

4. Research *one* technological invention or innovation. Prepare a report on its development and the impact it had in this era of change.

5. Create a Trivial Pursuit-style game called *The Era of Change*. Some categories you might consider could be: inventions, inventors, innovations, growing pains, and dates.

6. Create an advertisement for one of the inventions or innovations mentioned in this chapter.

APPLYING YOUR LEARNING

1. Even the words we speak were affected by the Industrial Revolution. "Traffic jam" is one example of a new phrase. Working in a group, list as many other words and phrases as you can that come from the existence of the automobile.

2. Sometimes Canada honours significant people or events with a stamp. Design a stamp in honour of a person or a symbol from this time period.

3. We continue to experience technological change and innovation. Pick a recent technological development and prepare a short report on it and its impact on society.

4. What needs to be invented today? Draw or build a model of an invention or innovation that would be welcome now.

5. Finish your eyewitness report and journal.

6. Pick one of the "firsts" mentioned in this chapter and imagine you are there. How do you feel about what you have just seen or heard? What effects will it have on your life? Prepare to state your observations and reactions orally, as if to a group of friends you have just met at the general store.

7. Which invention or inventor would your eyewitness have detested? Write the journal entry they would have made about it.

USING KEY WORDS

A pictograph is a picture of an object that stands for a word or an idea. A school-crossing sign is an example. Draw a pictograph for each word of the following key words:
- branch plants
- entrepreneur
- globalization
- industrialization
- innovation
- rural
- technology
- urban

CHAPTER 10

The Working People, 1867–1920

1872
- Trade Unions Act makes trade unions legal
- Nine-Hour Movement begins

1873
Canadian Labour Union formed

1880s
The Knights of Labour try to organize workers

1884
Ontario Factory Act passed

1887
- Royal Commission on the Relations of Labour and Capital appointed
- Trades and Labour Congress (TLC) formed
- Factory Act ends employment of males under the age of 12 and females under the age of 14

SETTING OUR FOCUS

These men in northern Ontario are miners in the Porcupine-Cobalt area. They are marching to show their support for the trade union movement. The photograph was taken around 1910, and many of the men are recent immigrants, as you can see from the wording on one of the placards. Few workers in Canada belonged to trade unions, and most were seen as troublemakers. Would you have had the courage to walk with them?

At this time, wages in many jobs were so low that workers did not earn enough to support their families. If they were too sick to work, their pay stopped. During most of the period from 1867 to 1920, workers hurt on the job did not get compensation. When they were too old to work, they did not receive a pension. In this chapter, you will learn more about conditions for wage-earning workers, and the steps they took to improve those conditions.

PREVIEWING THE CHAPTER

In this chapter you will learn about these topics:
- what conditions were like for people in the workplace
- what part women and children played in the work force
- how workers organized themselves and the steps they took to improve their conditions
- what happened in the Winnipeg General Strike

KEY WORDS

capitalist
company town
craft union
general strike
Nine-Hour
 Movement
One Big Union
resource-based
 industry
shanties
strikebreaker
sweating system
sympathy strike
trade union

1894	1900	1914	1919
Labour Day made a national holiday	Federal Department of Labour created	Workmen's Compensation Act adopted in Ontario	• One Big Union formed • Winnipeg General Strike takes place in May-June

THE WORKPLACE

Safety on the Job

One of the major problems many workers faced from 1867 to 1920 was safety on the work site. Whether they worked in the **resource-based industries** such as farming, fishing, forestry, and mining or in the fast-growing manufacturing industries, the dangers were great. There were few regulations to protect workers, and few inspectors to enforce any regulations that did exist.

Workers in the forestry industry were in constant danger from falling trees and sharp cutting tools. One of the machines used in British Columbia to remove trees from the hill slopes was called the "widow maker." In the Ottawa Valley and along the rivers of the Maritimes, the greatest danger for workers in the lumber industry came when they had to break up log jams that developed as they floated the logs to mills or to gathering areas.

Web Connection

http://www.school.mcgrawhill.ca/resources

Go to the web site above to find out more about people, life, and logging in the West Coast forestry industry, and mining in Cape Breton. Go to History Resources, then to *Canada: The Story of a Developing Nation* to see where to go next.

Often one log would have to be moved to break a log jam. This engraving shows a worker risking his life to cut that log.

Coal mining was particularly dangerous. Some kinds of coal release gases that can easily catch fire. An underground coal gas explosion at Springhill, Nova Scotia, in 1891 killed 125 miners. Some miners were killed by the blast; others were poisoned by the toxic gases. A ventilation shaft linked two stopes, or working levels, in the mine, so the gases entered both stopes. These kinds of tragedies led to gradual improvements in safety.

Factories were no safer. Workers had no head or eye protection. Amendments to the Factories Act in 1904 specified that safety guards must be added to all dangerous equipment, but the penalties were too weak to make employers act. Most factories had poor ventilation and were dirty. Workers inhaled toxic chemicals in fumes and dust. Highly contagious diseases such as smallpox and cholera spread rapidly in these environments.

Horses and dogs were used in some Nova Scotia mines. They pulled boxcars loaded with coal along rail tracks to levels where it would be hauled to the surface. The animals lived in the mines.

MP-0000. 2082. 2 Workshop, International Manufacturing Company, Montréal, QC. 1914-1918. *McCord Museum of Canadian History, Montréal.*

Workers could easily get tangled in the mass of cables, pulleys, and belts that carried power to machines in factories. Accidents happened when the workers fell into the machines.

This is the testimony of John Gale, who had worked in a sawmill, to members of the Royal Commission on the Relations of Labour and Capital in 1887.

Q. I see that you have lost one of your arms?

A. Yes, my right arm.

Q. How did that occur?

A. It was an accident in a sawmill.

Q. How old were you then?

A. Between eleven and twelve years of age.

Q. Were there any other boys working there, at the time you met with this accident, about your age?

A. Yes.

Q. What were you getting at the time you worked there?

A. I was only getting 25 cents a day.

Q. What were you engaged at when you lost your arm?

A. Taking blocks way from the circular saw.

Q. These were large saws?

A. Yes.

Q. How large were they?

A. About 2 feet [60 cm] in diameter.

Q. Two feet through?

A. Yes.

Q. These other small boys, were they engaged in the same business as you were when you lost your arm?

A. Yes.

Q. Your employer did not do anything at all for you?

A. No.

Q. As you are now, can you earn your living?

A. No; not unless I learn something — not unless I get an education.

Q. Do you know of any other boys having received accidents?

A. Yes; about two months after a boy was working in the mill, where I was, and he got both his legs and arms taken off.

In 1884 the Ontario government passed the Factory Act that made it illegal for boys under the age of 12 and girls under the age of 14 to work in factories. Factories were defined as places with more than five employees. Most sawmills did not have enough workers to qualify as a factory.

I-78899, Circular saws, Wright, Bason & Currier Mills?, Ottawa River, ON-QC, 1872. McCord Museum of Canadian History, Montréal

The circular saw is shown in the middle of the picture

QUESTIONING THE EVIDENCE

1. **State three impressions that you have from John Gale's evidence of working conditions in the sawmill when he was a boy.**

2. **If you were a member of the committee, what recommendations would you have made to improve working conditions?**

3. **Suppose you were the owner of a mill that stressed safety where there had never been an accident.**

   a) **What would be your reaction to this testimony?**

   b) **Would you want to see any questions reworded? If so, which ones?**

   c) **Develop three additional questions you would want to ask.**

4. **Does the information that most sawmills had no more than five employees change your reactions to the actions of John Gale's employer? Explain.**

Living Conditions Away from Home

In the resource-based industries workers often had to live in isolated areas for large parts of the year. Their living quarters were supplied by the employers and were usually squalid and cramped. Workers in the forests in the winter lived in crude wooden cabins, called **shanties**, during the cutting season. The shanty was home to between 30 and 135 workers. Its dimensions were approximately 11 m by 12 m.

The cook was in charge of the shanty, keeping the fire going and cooking the food in a large fireplace. The fire was never allowed to go out as it provided warmth, light, and the heat for drying clothes. Meals of salt pork, tea, beans and molasses, and bread were served at 5.00 a.m., 12 noon (often a cold meal eaten at the work site), and 6:00 p.m.

In late March some of the workers left the shanties to return to their farms. They used their pay of up to $1.00 a day to buy supplies needed on their farms. Others stayed until it was time to drive the logs downstream.

Painting of a lumber camp shanty, 1879. These camps housed over 40 men.

Reflections

Imagine that you are a worker who lives in a shanty and works in the forest. Write a letter home telling your family about your life.

These men are railway construction workers in the bunkhouse where they sleep. Most are recent immigrants. They have just worked at least ten hours.

The bunkhouse shelters up to 60 men. It is a drafty shack built of logs. The poles on the roof are covered with tarpaulin and water often seeps through. No one walks on the unfinished sawn planks of the floor without their boots on. A wood-burning stove provides heat.

Imagine you are one of these workers. You will sleep tonight on a hay-filled mattress that you hope does not have lice or fleas. The smell from your fellow-workers' unwashed clothes fills the air. Talk to the other people in this group about why you are here and what you hope to gain from living and working in these conditions.

Snapshot

Always in Debt Alexander McGillvray, from Glace Bay, Nova Scotia, described to the Royal Commission on the Relations of Labour and Capital in 1887 what it was like to live in a company town.

Q. Look at this paper. That is the statement of your account for the month of July, 1887?
A. Yes.

Q. Making a total of $35.13?
A. Yes.

Q. Against this you were charged rent $1.50, coal 25 cents?
A. Yes.

Q. You are charged with oil 80 cents?
A. Yes.

Q. You are charged with powder $3.24?
A. Yes.

Q. You are charged with school 15 cents?
A. Yes.

Q. For doctor 40 cents?
A. Yes.

Q. For the tally 30 cents?
A. Yes.

Q. You are charged for store account $28.49?
A. Yes.

Q. So the credits and the debits for the month exactly balance making $35.13?
A. Yes.

Q. You received that month no cash?
A. No.

Q. Is it generally the case that at the end of the month no cash is coming to you?
A. On many occasions.

Company towns were most often built by mine owners, as mines were usually located some distance from existing towns and cities. These towns provided houses, schools, stores, and services for the workers and their families. The owners rented homes to the workers. They also owned the stores and they could set the prices for all the goods. Miners and their families were often deeply in debt to the owners.

The Story So Far . . .

1 a) Suggest why shanties and bunkhouses for workers were poor.
   b) Make a list of regulations to improve these living conditions.

2 In pairs, role play a meeting between an employer and a worker living away from home. The employer should explain why better housing is not provided, and the worker can explain why it is necessary.

3 a) What evidence is there to suggest that perhaps the owners in the company towns deliberately tried to keep their miners in debt?
   b) Why would it be an advantage for the owners to have the miners in their debt?

Earning Enough to Live

In 1914 the federal Department of Labour decided that a family of five needed to spend at least $14.59 per week on food, fuel, light, and housing. This was difficult even for skilled workers to earn. Highly skilled iron moulders in Hamilton, for instance, earned $19.25 for a 55-hour week. Many unskilled workers could not earn enough to maintain a family at the minimum standard. Labourers in manufacturing industries in Ontario averaged $12.21 per week. Women cotton spinners averaged $7.40 per week. Even skilled workers could not save enough money to get through a period of illness or unemployment. There was no government health plan. Unemployment insurance was not put in place until 1942.

Wages in Selected Industries, 1914	
Occupation	**Wage per Hour**
Iron moulder (Hamilton)	35 cents
Iron moulder (Toronto)	29 cents
Machinist (Hamilton)	32 cents
Labourer (average for Ontario)	21 cents
Cotton spinners (women)	13 cents

Sickness of the main wage earner could mean disaster.

The federal government became concerned about the number of children working for wages in the 1880s. In 1886 out of 43 511 workers in Canada's mills and factories, there were 104 boys and 69 girls under the age of 10, and 1263 boys and 823 girls between ages 10 and 14. Many of these children had no choice but to work long hours in unsafe conditions. Their families were so desperate for income that the children often used false documents, indicating they were older than they really were. Children could be punished at work for such things as shouting, laughing, or running. To be late or absent from work was an even worse offence. They were spanked, put in dark cellars, and fined for any behaviour the managers felt held up production. In 1892 Ontario passed the Truancy and Compulsory School Attendance Act, requiring all children aged 14 and under to go to school.

Cogwagee
THE CALEDONIA CYCLONE

To 12-year-old Cogwagee, the few kilometres between his home on the Six Nations Reserve and his school in Brantford, Ontario, felt more like a hundred. For the Onandaga boy, life as a boarder at the Mohawk Institute, the Anglican mission school for Aboriginal children, was an ordeal.

At home and at the band school he had attended when he was younger, he had spoken his own language. Now, his teachers made him speak English. They also urged him to abandon his longhouse religion.

The students were expected to work in the mission fields when classes were over for the day. As the middle child in his family, Cogwagee believed that he should be helping his mother, not the missionaries. Ever since his father's death seven years earlier, his mother had struggled to support the family on her small farm. Finally, Cogwagee had had enough. He ran away. His teachers caught and punished him. He tried again. This time, he made it to the farm of an uncle, who agreed to hide him. He never went back to school.

That summer of 1899 the boy turned 13 years old. Like many young people whose parents were poor, he spent his teen years working long hours at whatever low-paying job was available. His earnings helped support his family. Sometimes, he worked as a farm labourer; other times, he landed a job in one of the canning factories in nearby towns. As he travelled from job to job, he realized that many towns held annual field days. A long-distance run was often a featured event — and Cogwagee knew that he could run like the wind. Watching others collect the medals and merchandise offered as prizes started him thinking. The prizes might be another way of helping his family.

As a test, he entered the annual Victoria Day race in the nearby town of Caledonia. Halfway through the 8-km race, he had a big lead. Then he began to tire. Although another runner pulled ahead of him to win, he finished second and won a small prize. This was just the spark he needed. He started training. He ran every day, always striving to increase his distance and speed. The next year, he entered the Caledonia race again. He took a commanding lead right from the start and this time no one caught him. People started calling him the Caledonia Cyclone.

The victory was the first in a string that would make Cogwagee — also known as Tom Longboat — the most famous runner in Canada. The Caledonia Cyclone was only one of the admiring nicknames that headline writers would bestow on the man whose many wins would include the Boston Marathon in 1907 and the world professional marathon championship in 1909.

More people you could research are

George Beers

Cogwagee

Louis Cyr

Edward (Ned) Hanlan

George Orton

Youngsters would work at jobs like these selling newspapers, shining shoes, or delivering telegraph messages that could be done before or after school.

A typical day for a 14-year-old worker in a Québec textile mill in 1905	
5:00 a.m.	Get up, eat breakfast, walk to work
6:15 a.m.	Start work at factory
12:15–12:30 p.m.	Lunch break
12:45–5:30 p.m.	Work
6:30 p.m.	Supper
6:30–9:00 p.m.	Help with household chores
9:00 p.m.	Bed

The Story So Far . . .

1 Why would employers hire children to work in factories in the late nineteenth century?

2 Discuss why governments made school attendance for children compulsory.

3 Describe how you spend your typical day. Compare your record with the one for the textile worker. What has changed for 14-year-olds between 1905 and today?

Women Workers

Women in low-income families did not have many choices of work. They got the jobs men did not want, or jobs where the employer did not need men and wanted cheap labour. Their wages were often 40 percent less than the wages of men. Most women in the nineteenth century worked as servants, cleaning homes, and in clothing factories. The clothing industry in Québec employed thousands of women working at home or in small workshops. They were paid for "piecework," that is, for each piece of clothing they sewed. Many women owned their own sewing machines; others rented them. Many slaved for 60 hours a week, earning only a few dollars each week. This is why piecework was called the **sweating system**. The sweating system allowed women with young children to combine paid employment with housework and child raising.

For young women, domestic service, working in other people's homes, was less attractive than jobs in shops or factories. Domestic servants worked long hours for very low wages. Yet in the 1880s this was often the only kind of work that young women could get when they left their farms for the cities. Gradually job opportunities changed. In the early part of the twentieth century, the need for people to do clerical work began to grow rapidly. By 1920 clerical workers made up nearly 7 percent of the labour force. Women occupied up to 41 percent of all clerical positions in 1920, an increase from only 14 percent in 1891. Still, their wages were well below those paid to men in similar positions.

Young women dipping chocolates in an Edmonton factory.

RULES OF THE WORKPLACE

- Ten hours make up a day's work
- From April 1 to September 30, all employees working by the week must be to work at 7:00 a.m. and 1:00 p.m. Doors kept open 15 minutes later for piecework employees.
- No one is allowed to stop work during working hours.
- All employees to be searched before leaving factory.
- Loud or profane talking strictly prohibited.
- All employees wasting or dropping tobacco on the floor will be fined for each offence.
- No tobacco to be left on the tables after work.
- Anyone breaking these rules will be subject to a fine.
- Hair combing not allowed in the factory.
- No one allowed to leave the department.

These rules were for a cigar factory that employed mainly women.

Work in small groups to answer these questions:

1 Why would the cigar factory owner include each of these rules?

2 Pretend you are workers in this factory. Rank the rules from the most offensive to the least offensive. Be prepared to defend your ranking structure.

To work as a telephone operator in a clean environment was considered an improvement over factory work for young women.

Like many of the women workers who testified before the Royal Commission on the Relations of Labour and Capital, Elizabeth M chose to hide her identity. This is not surprising. Workers who spoke out risked being branded troublemakers or being fired. Workers who had been fired were often blacklisted by other factory owners. This could mean starvation for the families who relied on their wages.

As a teen, M told the commissioners, she had not wanted to cut short her schooling to go to work at Moir's chocolate factory in Halifax, Nova Scotia, but she had had no choice. Her father, a police officer, had been killed while trying to rescue a family from their burning house. Although he was a hero, his death meant that his pay stopped and his family was left with no income. To help keep the family going, M's three older sisters had gone to work at the chocolate factory. When M was old enough, they had arranged for her to get a job there, too.

She had spent her first two years training to be a dipper. The dippers — all of them women — sat at long tables. Their job was to dip the cream, fudge, and nut centres into the chocolate coating. The higher-paying job of bringing the centres to the women and taking away the finished chocolates was reserved for men. This kind of division of labour was not unusual in the late 1800s and early 1900s. Women were often barred from skilled, higher-paying jobs. For many women, the surest way of winning a pay raise was to do piecework. The more pieces they produced, the more money they would find in their weekly pay packet. This was M's plan. By the time she finished her apprenticeship, she was sure that she was fast enough to earn more as a pieceworker. But company managers tightly controlled the number of pieceworkers; they assigned her to lower-paying wage work. Disappointed, she wrote a letter asking them to reconsider. When they refused, she resigned.

For the next eight years, M worked as a clerk at shops around Halifax. Finally, she returned to work at Moir's. Why did she go back? At the factory, the work week was five days. In the shops, she had been required to work six days a week.

Elizabeth M was one of about 1800 people — only 102 of them women — who testified before the commissioners. Because she chose to remain anonymous, we will never know her identity. In the end, the Commission's report was ignored. Still, M's testimony — and that of the others who summoned the courage to speak out about their working conditions — has given historians an important record of factory life in the late 1800s.

More people you could research are

Helen Armstrong

John Flett

John Hewitt

William Lyon Mackenzie King

Elizabeth M

Alexander Whyte Wright

A few people had everything the workers dreamed of having. They were the **capitalists**: the owners of the factories, banks, stores, mines, and other workplaces. They had plenty of food, luxurious homes, and servants to make their lives as pleasant as possible. Their children attended the best of schools, had plenty of leisure time, and money to spend. Workers knew of these differences. They started to look for ways to improve their wages and working conditions.

1 What two groups are shown in the cartoon?

2 How does the cartoonist show the differences in standard of living between the two groups?

The title of the cartoon is "Collecting the Thanksgiving Dinner."

The Story So Far . . .

1 a) Suggest why employers preferred to hire women in factories wherever possible.

   b) Investigate the difference between the average for men's wages and women's wages today. How would you explain this difference?

2 a) Make a list of all the reasons why workers were unhappy with their situation. Rank these problems from the worst to the least. Be able to explain why you made these choices.

   b) What could these workers have done to try to improve their situations?

WORKERS ORGANIZE

The Beginnings of Trade Unions

Trade unions are organizations formed by workers who unite to improve their working conditions. They first developed in Britain and Europe, and many of the organizers of early unions in Canada were British and European immigrants. These first unions in Canada were small, local organizations that did not last long. Often they were against the law. In Nova Scotia, for example, in 1816 workers were forbidden by law from joining unions and could be sent to prison for doing so.

From the beginning, employers did everything they could to break trade unions. When workers asked to negotiate or discuss increasing wages or changing working conditions, the employer would often refuse, close the factory or workplace, and lock them out. Owners could fire workers who belonged to unions as there were many unemployed workers to take their place.

It is not surprising that trade unions grew slowly. When they did grow, they formed links with other unions. One of the first examples was the National Typographical Union, formed in 1852 by printers across the country. In 1863 a variety of different trade unions in Hamilton formed a Trades Assembly to deal with common concerns. Toronto **craft unions**, which were made up of skilled workers, did the same in 1871.

The Nine-Hour Issue

By 1871 the workers of Britain had managed to get a nine-hour working day in most of their industries. Evidence showed that many industrial accidents occurred during the last hour of the longer workday because workers became less careful when tired. Canadian unions and workers set the nine-hour day as their goal. The printers at *The Globe* made it a strike issue. All the printers at other Toronto newspapers joined them.

George Brown, the publisher of *The Globe*, organized the other newspaper publishers to take joint action against the strikers and the **Nine-Hour Movement**. Joining him in the fight were 17 publishers. The leaders of the strike were arrested and charged under a seldom-used law that made it illegal to form unions. Brown advertised for **strikebreakers** to take the jobs of striking workers. In response, 10 000 supporters marched in support of the strikers. The strike ended without workers winning the nine-hour workday; the leaders were tried and convicted of conspiracy.

On May 15, 1872, 1500 workers marched through the streets of Hamilton, Ontario. They were striking for a 54-hour work week and better wages. Do you think the people watching the march are supportive of the strikers?

Brown's action reminded the public that trade unions were still illegal and that their governments supported the employers. Later that year Parliament passed the Trade Unions Act, which made unions legal and removed the threat of future arrests for peaceful strikers. The unions had to register with the government and agree that they would be responsible for any property damage during a strike. Few chose to register.

Now union leaders turned their attention to creating a trade union that would be a voice for workers across the country. The Canadian Labour Union, formed in 1873, represented 31 unions. In spite of the name, only Ontario craft unions were represented. Other groups such as the Knights of Labour, an American union, started to form branches in Canada. The Knights of Labour wanted to have all the workers of each industry, whatever their skills, in one union. The craft unions were against this idea and in 1886 joined together in the Trades and Labour Congress (TLC). This split weakened the unions in the years to come. From 1880 to 1910 unions represented no more than 10 percent of paid workers in industries.

The Story So Far . . .

1   Why would employers want to stop trade unions from forming?
2   Strikebreakers were often used to end strikes in this period. From what you have learned so far, why would some workers be prepared to take a striker's job?
3   Who gained from the 1871 printers' strike: the publishers or the strikers? Support your opinion.

Conditions Worsen

By the early twentieth century the increasing number of strikes meant the federal government had to act to prevent a breakdown in relations between workers and employers. It set up the Department of Labour in 1900 to deal with some of the problems and passed the Conciliation Act, which gave the federal government the power to settle disputes if both workers and employers asked for their help. A long strike by railway workers across the country led to the Railway Disputes Act. This banned strikes on railways, because railways were considered essential services. By 1907 the government had similar powers to step in to settle disputes affecting mining, telephone, telegraph, and transport. William Lyon Mackenzie King, a future prime minister who was Minister of Labour, presented a report that exposed sweatshop conditions in factories that made military uniforms for the government. A law was brought in to ensure fair wages for federal government contracts. In 1914 the Ontario Workmen's Compensation Bill was passed. This meant workers injured on the job were paid a pension from government- and employer-funded insurance.

In 1906 streetcar workers in Winnipeg attempted to form a union. When property was destroyed by pro-strike citizens the mayor of Winnipeg called in troops. To workers it seemed that the government was siding with the employers.

By 1919 relations between employers and workers had worsened. Prices were rising, but wages were not. Men who had gone to fight in World War I returned home and could not find jobs. The government was doing nothing to help the many unemployed people.

Examples of Strike Actions

1909–1910	Strike in Cape Breton mines. United Mine Worker members were thrown out of their company-owned homes and banned from the company stores. Clergy who sheltered them were ordered to stop.
1912–1913	Strike in gold mines in Timmins. Thugs, armed with guns by the company, patrolled the streets. The Ontario government only ordered them to stop when someone was injured.
1912–1913	Strikes in coal mines in Extension, British Columbia. Strikers burned mine property and houses where strikebreakers were staying. Militia were sent in with guns; 200 strikers were arrested; one died in jail from lack of medical attention.
July 1918	Nation-wide strike of postal workers. Soldiers sent in to guard businesspeople who took over the mail sorting.

1 Choose one these strikes and find out more about why workers were on strike and if they made any gains by their actions.

Snapshot

Mining Black Gold

In the late 1800s coal was black gold for Robert Dunsmuir. As chief owner of Dunsmuir, Diggle and Company, he had grown wealthy from the profits of his coal mines. Known as the coal king of British Columbia, he ruled the company town of Wellington on Vancouver Island with an iron hand.

Dunsmuir's money-making strategy was simple — hire the cheapest labour possible, charge high prices at company stores where employees had to shop, ignore safety, and block attempts to form trade unions. Dunsmuir cut wages and raised the price of the powder the miners used to blast underground. Workers were paid by the weight of the coal they mined. When mine managers started short-weighing the coal by fixing the scales so they registered a lesser amount, the workers protested. Short-weighing was just another way of cutting wages.

In 1877 the workers formed the Miners' Mutual Protective Association and shut down the mine by going on strike. Dunsmuir hired strikebreakers and tried to evict the workers from their company-owned houses. When they refused to leave, he used his influence with the politicians at Victoria to persuade the government to call out the militia, which forced the miners back to work. In 1883 workers shut down the mine again. Again Dunsmuir crushed the strike. Though they failed to change conditions in Dunsmuir's mines, the strikes did signal the start of a long history of mineworkers' organization in British Columbia.

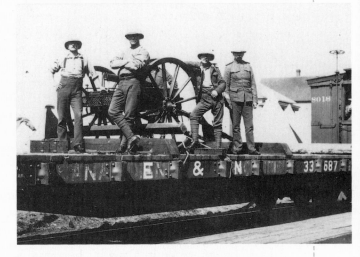

In 1913 the British Columbia government ordered the militia to quell a miners' strike at Extension after mine property was damaged. Here the soldiers are shown on their way to Extension with a machine gun.

The Story So Far . . .

1 Discuss why the Canadian government set up the Department of Labour in 1900.

2 Discuss why the federal government allowed troops to be used in strike situations.

3 Imagine you are taking part in a strike in the early twentieth century and troops are sent in to end the strike. Write a letter to the editor of a newspaper expressing how you feel about this action.

One Big Union

In March 1919 a meeting of Western labour leaders was held in Calgary. They did not agree with the Trades and Labour Congress that unions should be organized by crafts. Their purpose was to create **One Big Union**. The OBU would represent all workers, even unskilled workers who had not previously been members of unions.

Some factory workers and business owners, in particular, did not like the OBU because they thought it was a threat to society. In 1917 during World War I the corrupt government of Russia had been overthrown by a revolution led by Bolsheviks. The new leaders were Communists, who promised that the workers would soon run Russia. The delegates to the OBU convention sent greetings to the new government in Russia. Some people took this as a sign that the OBU was run by Communists, and advertised that joining the union would lead to a revolution like the one in Russia. Most Canadians were afraid of Communism.

The One Big Union was determined to have a say in the working conditions of Canadian workers. They thought **general strikes** were the way to make employers see that workers had power and must be listened to. A general strike occurs when all or most of the workers go on strike at the same time. The most important general strike in Canada's history was organized in Winnipeg in 1919.

The ONE BIG UNION is Bolshevism Pure and Simple

This is a reproduction of the headline of a poster put up by opponents of the One Big Union. What is Bolshevism?

WINNIPEG GENERAL STRIKE

Winnipeg in 1919 was the largest and busiest city in Canada's West. On May 1, 1919, 2000 building and metal workers, members of the Metal Trades Council, went on strike. The workers wanted higher wages (85 cents an hour), shorter hours (44 hours a week instead of 60), and recognition as a union. The employers refused to negotiate with the strikers.

The workers appealed to the Winnipeg Trades and Labour Council, which spoke for unions in the city. The Council asked all the city's union members if they would strike in sympathy with the metal workers on May 15. A vote was held: 11 000 voted for the strike; 600 voted against.

The workers formed a Central Strike Committee of their leaders to co-ordinate actions. At 11 a.m. on May 15, streetcars returned to the barns, and rail workers left their jobs. Within an hour telegraphers, telephone operators, and postal workers had left their posts. The trains continued to operate, but there were no express, freight, or baggage services. Newspapers were not published, and there were no milk or bread deliveries. The

12 000 strikers were joined by as many as 23 000 other workers. Essential services, such as light and water, were not affected by the stoppage and city police responded to the request of the Strike Committee and remained on duty to protect property.

Employers organized the Citizens' Committee of 1000 to act against the strikers. The leaders wanted to make sure that essential services were provided for the city. When the Strike Committee allowed bread and milk to be delivered in the city, the Citizens' Committee accused the strikers of trying to take over the government. They predicted that the general strike would lead to a Communist revolution in Canada. They urged the Canadian government to step in. Because they knew that the police favoured the strikers, they persuaded the city to fire the entire force and its chief. Untrained volunteers and hired substitutes replaced them at much higher rates of pay than the regular police force received.

Some veterans of World War I opposed the strike. Here they are meeting to listen to leaders of the opposition. Read the signs. Who do they say is leading the strike?

Workers in other parts of the country wanted to show their support for the strikers. They left their jobs in **sympathy strikes**. In Toronto nearly 12 000 workers walked off their jobs, and 10 000 went on strike in Vancouver.

After about a month some Winnipeg strikers were ready to go back to work. They could not afford to lose any more wages. It might have ended peacefully, but at this point the Canadian government stepped in. The Citizens' Committee had been pressuring the government to act to end the strike. In response, the government brought in extra members of the Royal North West Mounted Police. All public marches were banned by the mayor.

J. S. Woodsworth
CHAMPION OF WORKING PEOPLE

By the early 1900s Winnipeg's North End had become a slum. Poor people, many of them recent immigrants who could find work only at low-paying jobs, crowded into ramshackle houses that had been converted into filthy tenements. Malnutrition and disease ran rampant.

With his new wife, Lucy Staples, James Shaver Woodsworth arrived in the North End in 1904 – as superintendent of All Peoples' Mission, a Methodist Church charity set up to help North Enders. The young minister was about to enter the crucible that would shape his life. Much more than a church, the Mission offered classes to teach immigrants about Canada and help them learn English. It provided food, clothing, medical care, and legal aid to those who needed them. Special church services were conducted in immigrants' home languages and workers ran kindergarten classes, which were not offered in the city's schools, as well as a fresh-air camp.

As he and Lucy threw themselves into their work, Woodsworth became more and more concerned about the plight of working people. He became convinced that more than private and church charity was needed. To get at the root of the problem, he believed that society must change: competitive capitalism must be replaced by co-operative ownership.

By 1916 Woodsworth was working as director of the Bureau of Social Research, a government agency. With World War I raging, it looked as if the federal government was going to introduce conscription. Woodsworth, an ardent pacifist, published a letter opposing forced military service. When he refused to promise his employer to keep his views to himself, he was fired.

This was not the first time Woodsworth would stand firm in his beliefs. In 1921 he entered the federal election race under the banner of the Independent Labour Party. He won the riding of Winnipeg North Centre, and in 1933 he became the first leader of the newly formed Co-operative Commonwealth Federation (CCF), forerunner of today's New Democratic Party. His political career was devoted to advancing the cause of working people.

As World War II loomed, Woodsworth's pacifist principles were once again put to the test. When Canada declared war in September 1939, he was the only member of Parliament to speak against the action. Although his stand was unpopular even among his colleagues in the CCF, Woodsworth could do nothing else. To abandon his beliefs would have meant abandoning everything his life stood for.

More people you could research are

Ginger Goodwin

Daniel O'Donaghue

A. W. Puttee

R. B. Russell

J. S. Woodsworth

Bloody Saturday

On June 17 strike leaders were dragged from their beds at gunpoint and taken to Stony Mountain Penitentiary. Workers across the country were outraged. What laws had these people broken? On June 21 events came to a head when a group of soldiers, newly returned from World War I, decided that, despite the mayor's order, they would hold a protest march. They led the strikers down Main Street in Winnipeg. They were met by the Mounties swinging clubs and firing pistols. Two people died in the riot that followed. The volunteer police patrolled the streets armed with machine guns. The protesters were subdued but "Bloody Saturday," as the day was called, remained fresh in workers' minds across Canada and they became more determined than ever to obtain their rights.

Top: The protestors on June 21, 1919, overturn a streetcar in anger. Despite the strike, the cars had resumed service. Describe the protesters. How does the way they are dressed indicate they did not come to this site expecting violence?
Right: Mounted police charging the crowd of strike supporters

A week later the Central Strike Committee called off the strike. Seven members were convicted of conspiracy for plotting against the government and sentenced to prison for up to two years. Five were never brought to trial, and three were acquitted. One of the men arrested for publishing editorials supporting the strikers was J. S. Woodsworth, who went on to be a member of Parliament for the next 21 years. Three of the jailed men were elected to the Manitoba legislature while they were in prison.

After the Strike

For the strikers and trade union supporters, their efforts must have seemed to have gained them nothing.

- Many strikers and their families were deeply in debt because of the lost wages.
- To get their jobs back many strikers had to sign contracts that did not allow them to belong to unions.
- Many strikers no longer had jobs. Employers would not rehire them because they were considered to be troublemakers.
- The Government of Canada passed special legislation in July 1919 that allowed protesters suspected of violence to be searched, have their property seized, and face possible imprisonment. This law continued until 1936.

The city of Winnipeg did not benefit from the strike either. The industries involved lost business during the strike, some of it for good. The employers continued to pay low wages, and some historians believe the city's industries suffered because of this. The city accumulated a huge debt paying for the extra police force needed during the strike. The bitterness caused by the strike lasted a long time.

The government set up another Royal Commission to investigate the strike. The findings of the report supported the workers. It found that the strike was not an attempt to revolt as city officials tried to claim, but instead was a reaction to the differences in profits and living conditions between the working class and the owners who controlled the industries.

Different Points of View

Against the Strike	For the Strike
It was an illegal strike planned months in advance.	The right to strike is fundamental to the rights of workers.
It was not a strike but a Communist plot to overturn British institutions in Canada.	The workers had no choice. It was either strike or starve.
Law and order must be maintained.	Desperate measures were needed to make employers improve working conditions.

1 Summarize the different points of view expressed about the strike.

2 What would be your personal point of view concerning the strike if you were
a) a small business owner
b) a factory worker

The Story So Far . . .

1 Why did workers in Winnipeg go on strike?

2 What groups in Winnipeg were against the strikers?

3 Do you think a general strike, such as the Winnipeg General Strike of 1919, is a useful tactic for unions?

4 Do you think the strikers gained anything from the general strike?

SUM IT UP!

For most working people in the period between Confederation and 1920, hours of work were long and pay was low. Most people worked at jobs that demanded physical strength and stamina. Men built railways, planted and harvested crops, worked in factories, chopped trees, fished, and worked in mines. Women worked in their homes, in factories, and as servants. There were few laws to protect workers, or to regulate safety in the workplace.

Gradually, workers in factories and cities organized themselves into unions to improve their pay and working conditions. The union movement was split between organizers who thought that all workers in one industry should be in a single union and organizers who wanted unions organized by crafts. Strikes became the workers' ultimate weapon to try to force change. Progress was slow, but governments took their first steps in regulating the workplace and giving workers some protection.

The Winnipeg General Strike was the largest single effort by workers to try to improve their conditions. It ended with the use of the Royal North West Mounted Police against the strikers, which led to lasting bitterness. The leaders were imprisoned, and there was little improvement in working conditions.

THINKING ABOUT YOUR LEARNING

1 What were the major problems of the working people in the nineteenth and early twentieth centuries?

2 Why was it possible for employers to pay low wages?

3 Look at the visuals in this chapter and list those that show unsafe working conditions. Choose one of these, and describe how it shows unsafe conditions.

4 What did workers who joined trade unions hope to accomplish?

5 Why did it take courage to join a union in this period?

6 Look at the time line of the major events that affected Canadian workers from 1867 to 1920. How did these events improve the working conditions of workers today?

APPLYING YOUR LEARNING

1 Create a political cartoon to show the problem you consider to be the most severe for working people in this period.

2 Imagine you are a worker in one of the industries described in this chapter. Make a list of recommendations for improving workers conditions. Try to find out when these improvements were made.

3 Working in a small group, write a script and role play one of the situations described or shown in one of the pictures in this chapter.

4 Check the title of this book. Look up the meaning of the term developing nation. What visuals in this chapter show scenes that are similar to those in developing nations today?

5 Interview a union member about conditions of work and benefits today. Find out if he or she has ever been on strike, and if so, what the issues were.

6 Research to find out what the major labour issues are today, and whether any are the same as the issues that concerned workers between 1867 and 1920.

USING KEY WORDS

Complete the crossword puzzle to check if you understand all of the terms. Your teacher will give you a copy of the puzzle to write on.

Across

3. crude wooden cabins that served as living quarters for workers in the lumber industry

9. an industry based on natural resources

11. organization formed by workers who united to improve their working conditions

Down

1. a person who continues to work during a strike or takes a job to replace workers on strike

2. a union created in 1919 in Western Canada to represent all workers, even unskilled workers who had not previously belonged to unions

3. long hours at low wages on a piecework basis

4. attempt by workers to obtain a nine-hour working day

5. a strike by all or most of the workers in an industry or throughout a country or an area

6. a town built by a company for workers

7. shareholder or owner of a factory or important business

8. a labour union made up of skilled workers

10. a strike by workers not directly involved in a dispute to show support for other strikers

THE WORKING PEOPLE

The Struggle for Rights

1876

Indian Act is passed

1884

Indian Act is amended to outlaw Aboriginal cultural ceremonies

1885

Head tax of $50 is imposed on Chinese immigrants

1891

John J. Kelso founds the Children's Aid Society

1893

National Council of Women is formed

SETTING OUR FOCUS

These women are working on a farm in Manitoba in the early years of the twentieth century. It looks like backbreaking work. Look at the poles and wires in the background. This picture was taken in the era of change described in Chapter 9. Imagine you are one of the women. Already today you have made and baked the bread, prepared breakfast and lunch, gathered the eggs, milked the cows, made butter and cream, and scrubbed the clothes on your new scrub board. You need to pick the tomatoes, make dinner, look after the children and get them to do their chores, and darn your husband's good pants so he can go to town and vote tomorrow. You will be staying home at that time. As a woman, you cannot vote. You also have no claim to the farm unless your husband chooses to give you one. In this chapter you will see how women organized to change laws like these. Women were only one of many groups that were working to meet the challenges of the time.

PREVIEWING THE CHAPTER

In this chapter you will learn about these topics:
- **the changing role of women in this period**
- **some of the personalities that helped shape the changes in society**
- **the changing role for children in society**
- **the Indian Act and how it affected Aboriginal Peoples**
- **Canada's immigration policy at the time**

KEY WORDS

assimilated
boycotted
head tax
"no stoppage" rule
potlatch
prohibition
residential school
social activists
social movement
status Indians
suffrage

1904	1915	1916	1917	1918
Head tax on Chinese is raised to $500	Women gain right to vote and hold office in Manitoba, Saskatchewan, and Alberta	Women gain right to vote in Ontario and British Columbia	• Women gain right to vote and hold political office in Nova Scotia • Women gain right to vote federally	Women are allowed to run for office in federal elections and gain the vote in New Brunswick

THE GOOD OLD DAYS?

People today often romanticize life a century ago, saying life was simpler then. Was it? Imagine the year is 1889.

Nellie Mooney, who would become famous as Nellie McClung, was 16 years old. She began teaching in a rural school in Somerset, Manitoba. Nellie was one of the many young women who took up teaching as more children went to public schools. She knew she would be paid quite a bit less than a man, likely about half. During her first year of teaching, she received no pay at all because the area's crops had been destroyed by hail. The community could not raise the money for her salary. She had room and board with the local Methodist minister's family.

Nellie was young and energetic and at recess would play football with her students. Parents objected to this. Football was not a game for ladies. She continued to play. A few years later when she married the minister's son, Robert Wesley McClung, she had to give up teaching. Married women could not teach in the public schools.

Adelaide Hunter Hoodless was a busy mother of four young children in Hamilton, Ontario, in 1889. Then her youngest son, John, who was a year-and-a-half-old, died from drinking contaminated milk. She was devastated. When the doctor told her that John died because she had never been taught to cover his milk to keep flies off, she was furious. Why did the public schools not teach such life-saving information? Should not schools teach about new discoveries? Should public education be reorganized?

Above: Adelaide Hoodless with her children in 1887. Later she founded the Women's Institute, promoted the Victorian Order of Nurses, wrote a textbook on domestic science, and established a school to train teachers of domestic science.
Below: This clinic in Toronto instructed new mothers in infant care.

In Toronto hundreds of children worked on the streets as they had for years. They swept the pavements, polished shoes, and sold items like pencils, fruit, or newspapers. Families often depended on this income. John Joseph Kelso was one of these children. As an adult, in 1889, he petitioned the Toronto Police Commission to regulate the street trade with licences. These would prohibit children under the age of eight from working on the streets.

In British Columbia, in August of 1889, a Kwakiutl, Hemasak, was sentenced to six months' imprisonment for holding a **potlatch**. For Aboriginal groups of the Northwest Coast, a potlatch is an important traditional ceremony. The ceremony involves formal dances, songs, and the giving of gifts to guests. Hemasak knew that the Canadian government had passed many laws that affected his life, but did they really mean to forbid the traditional potlatch ceremony? His conviction was eventually overturned. The law against holding a potlatch had not said exactly what the ceremony was.

The Vancouver Trades and Labour Council was started to help labourers. It was also the centre of anti-Chinese activity, mainly because the Chinese worked for lower wages. Late in 1889 the council helped to work out an agreement between the city and a man who wanted to open a sugar refinery. The city agreed to give the owner tax breaks if he hired only white workers. Then the council **boycotted** Chinese laundries, refusing to use them and trying to stop other customers from using them. The council also made sure that a law forbidding

Snippet

A Kinder Society

J. J. Kelso was involved in founding the Toronto Humane Society in 1887, a charity organized to prevent cruelty to children — and animals. Its goals included rescuing children from vicious influences, preventing the beating of animals, adopting better horseshoeing methods, stopping drivers from overloading horse-drawn streetcars and wagons and working old horses, and encouraging everyone to practise and teach kindness to animals and others.

Chinatown, Victoria harbour, British Columbia. What, if any, advantages would there be to living together in groups, regardless of the poor standard of housing?

businesses to open on Sundays was strictly enforced against the Chinese. Then it put pressure on the federal government to increase the payment, called the **head tax**, that the Chinese immigrants had to make to land in Canada. By 1904 the head tax had been raised from $50 to $500. The Chinese community was almost helpless against this kind of activity as the Chinese were not allowed to vote in British Columbia.

The Story So Far . . .

1   Prepare a reply to someone who says that life in Canada was simpler for people a century ago.
2   Choose one of the people or groups mentioned in this section to study in greater detail.
3   Letter writing and petitions were two popular forms of protest in Canada in 1889. Imagine you are the person or group you picked in question 2. Write a letter or draw up a petition to protest your situation or an issue that affects you.

WOMEN'S STRUGGLES

In 1890 when a woman married she lost possession of her property and wages. All assets belonged to her husband. A married woman was not allowed to sign contracts. This made it difficult for her to carry on a business in her own name or without her husband's co-operation. A woman could not take her husband to court if he mistreated her. Children were considered the property of the father; a mother had no legal custody rights. In the West women had no legal rights of inheritance. There are records of at least one woman who disguised herself as a man after her husband died to make it easier for her to continue to raise horses and homestead on the prairies.

A woman's role was supposed to be as a dutiful wife and caring mother. The reality for many women, though, was quite different. Many women had to work for wages. In the 1890s in Montréal, for example, perhaps one third of all women over 40 years of age were widows who had to support themselves. In 1891 women held over 25 percent of all manufacturing jobs in Canada. Most servants, nurses, and schoolteachers were women. At the same time, popular magazines had covers that showed idealized mothers and children. They published articles that made claims like "Women's first and only place is in her home."

Snippet

Best-selling Author

In the 1890s many people still believed that writing was not a proper career for a woman. That is why Margaret Saunders decided to use her second name — Marshall — when she wrote *Beautiful Joe*, the story of a dog that is rescued from abuse. She believed that more people would read the story if they thought it was written by a man. Was she right? When it was published in 1894, *Beautiful Joe* became the first book by a Canadian author to sell more than a million copies.

This excerpt from the diaries of Lucy Maud Montgomery was written in 1905. It records her grandmother's situation after her grandfather died.

Uncle John and Prescott have been using grandmother shamefully all summer. In short, they have been trying to turn her out — Grandfather's absurd will put her completely in their power — the power of selfish, domineering men eaten up by greed. Grandmother told them she would not leave the home where she had lived and worked for sixty years and since then Uncle John has never spoken to her or visited her . . .

The situation of Lucy's grandmother was not unique. Lucy lived with her grandmother, who was in her eighties, so that she could look after her. She, too, could have been turned out of the family home.

QUESTIONING THE EVIDENCE

1. **What possible reasons might a man have for leaving his farm to his sons, rather than to his wife or daughters?**
2. **Script your version of the conversation Lucy's grandmother had with her son John about her leaving the farm.**
3. **What impressions do you get about society at this time from this excerpt?**
4. **Explain the reasons for valuing or not valuing a diary as historic evidence. Would your own diary or journal make good history at some point in the future?**

Lawyer Clara Brett Martin had to fight long and hard to be allowed to practise law.

Web Connection

http://www.school.mcgrawhill.ca/resources

Go to the web site above to find out more about one of the women mentioned in this chapter. Go to History Resources, then to *Canada: The Story of a Developing Nation* to see where to go next.

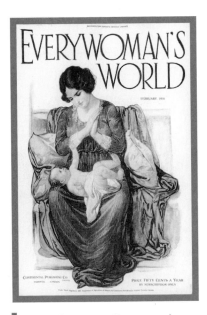

II-90561 Mr. Jackson and group fishing at waterfall, Lanark, ON 1889. *McCord Museum of Canadian History, Montréal*

Top: **Compare the magazine cover with the photographs at the beginning of the chapter and on page 275. How do you explain the contrasts?**
Right: **An 1889 fishing trip. Contrast the appropriateness of the clothing of the men with that of the woman and girl.**

Women had to struggle against a social order that was controlled by men. Some doctors claimed that a young woman's health would be damaged by higher education. Goldwin Smith, a Toronto journalist, wrote that the right to vote, or **suffrage**, for women would mean homes would suffer. Smith left his post at Cornell University in the United States in protest over the university's decision to admit women.

The Story So Far . . .

1   a) Identify the attitudes that society had about women and their place in society at this time.
    b) Discuss as a group whether any of these attitudes exist today.
2   How do you feel about the images portrayed on magazine covers today? Do some covers make you feel uncomfortable? Why? Do you identify with some covers? Why?
3   Create a display to depict the relationship between magazine covers and reality today.

Working Together

Women in Canada had always organized to help each other and those in need. Some middle-class women, because they had more free time, organized women's groups. These groups were part of a larger **social movement**. Many people were working together to make changes that would benefit society as a whole. They made people aware of issues such as prison reform, public health, and the need for better schools. Many groups were part of church-based groups doing volunteer work.

Some women's groups worked for equal rights. Women like Dr. Emily Howard Stowe, Dr. Eliza Ritchie, and Anna Leonowens were **social activists** who struggled against all the unfair laws and attitudes that discriminated against women. They were part of an international women's movement working for equality for women.

Reflections

Put yourself in the place of a married woman in Canada in the late nineteenth century. Write an article to a newspaper describing how you feel about your role in society and what you think should be done to change the situation.

Nellie McClung, Alice Jamieson, and Emily Murphy worked for women's right to vote.

Nellie McClung
CRUSADER FOR WOMEN'S RIGHTS

N ellie McClung was fuming. From her perch in the visitors' gallery on January 27, 1914, the popular novelist and mother of five children was listening to Rodmond Roblin, Manitoba's Conservative premier, address the all-male Legislature. He was explaining why it would be dangerous to grant women the franchise, or the right to vote, in provincial elections.

I believe that woman suffrage ... will break up the home; that it will throw the children into the arms of servant girls. The majority of women are emotional and very often guided by misdirected enthusiasms, and if possessed of the franchise would be a menace rather than an aid.

Roblin had challenged the women of Manitoba — but McClung and her fellow suffragists, including the journalist Cora Hind, were up to the challenge. The very next night, they rented a theatre and staged a mock sitting of the Legislature in which all the members were women.

The women overacted — to the delight of the packed house. But it was McClung, playing the premier, who turned in the most memorable performance. When a group of men pretended to plead for the right to vote, she responded in a perfect parody of Roblin. The audience howled with laughter as she said:

The trouble is that if men start to vote, they will vote too much. Politics unsettles men, and unsettled men means unsettled bills, broken furniture, broken vows and — divorce... If men were to get into the habit of voting — who knows what might happen — it's hard enough to keep them home now. History is full of unhappy examples of men in public life — Nero — Herod — King John...

Two years later women in Manitoba, British Columbia, Saskatchewan, and Alberta won the right to vote. By then the fiery feminist had moved to Edmonton with her family. In Alberta she was elected to the provincial Legislative Assembly, where she continued speaking out in favour of reforms that would place women on an equal footing with men.

McClung's best-known battle was still ahead, however. In the late 1920s along with Henrietta Muir Edwards, Louis McKinney, Emily Murphy, and Irene Parlby she would become one of the Famous Five. These five Alberta women would fight successfully to have women defined as "persons" in the eyes of the law and so be able to take seats in the Senate.

This battle, which became known as the Persons Case, would not be McClung's last. She continued crusading for women's rights until her death in 1951.

Other people you could research are

Nellie McClung

Louise McKinney

Agnes Campbell Macphail

Emily Murphy

Irene Parlby

Eliza Ritchie

Women of the Winnipeg Political Equality League gathered signatures on this petition to support granting the right to vote to women.

Two of the largest women's organizations at this time were the Young Women's Christian Association (YWCA) and the Women's Christian Temperance Union (WCTU). The YWCA was a major charitable organization. It helped train many working-class women, usually for work as servants in private homes. Adelaide Hunter Hoodless worked with the YWCA when she started her crusade for public health education.

Letitia Youmans founded the WCTU in Canada in Picton, Ontario, in 1874. She had been to the founding meeting of the American WCTU and was inspired to start a group like it for her home town. Like many women she had seen some of the tragic results of alcoholism. She told stories of drunken men freezing to death in snowdrifts or losing limbs because of frostbite.

By 1891 over 9000 women across Canada had joined local WCTU groups. The WCTU wanted **prohibition**, or a law to ban the sale or consumption of alcohol. They made little progress. Eventually many members believed they had to have the right to vote and hold political office if they wanted to change laws and society.

Snippet

The Temperance Movement

By the late 1800s people were blaming alcohol for all kinds of social evils — poverty, family breakdown, sickness, crime, and violence. The temperance movement reached a peak in 1915, when Saskatchewan became the first province to stop alcohol sales. Other provinces soon followed suit. The prohibition was short-lived, however. It was lifted after World War I. Since then, the movement has gradually died out.

Step-by-Step Progress

1872–1907	Married Women's Property Acts passes in all provinces except Alberta and Québec. This meant that a married woman's personal property and any income she earned were her own.
1873	British Columbia allows women property holders to vote in municipal elections.
1875	Mount Allison University grants a B.Sc. degree to Grace Lockhart, the first woman to graduate from a university in the British Empire.
1883	Medical colleges are established for women in Toronto and Kingston. Dr. Emily Stowe's daughter, Augusta, becomes the first woman to receive a medical degree in Canada.
1884	Women are admitted to the University of Toronto. Single women in Ontario who own property are granted the municipal vote. Married women in Ontario are allowed to sign contracts concerning their own separate property.
1897	Clara Brett Martin becomes the first woman to practise law in the British Empire, after Premier Mowat of Ontario pressures the Law Society of Ontario to admit women as lawyers.
1910	Alberta passes Married Women's Relief Act, entitling a widow to a court-assigned portion of her husband's estate if she has not been included in his will.
1916	Emily Murphy becomes the first woman magistrate in the British Empire – an appointment often questioned by lawyers since women were not legally considered "persons."
1916–1922	All provinces except Québec grant women the right to vote.
1917	British Columbia becomes the first province to pass custody laws, giving mothers the same rights as fathers over their children. The Military Voters Act gives the vote to women nurses serving in the war. The Wartimes Elections Act gives the federal vote to women who were related as wives, widows, mothers, sisters, or daughters to soldiers who had served or were serving with the Canadian or British military.
1918	All women who are citizens and over the age of 21 are given the right to vote in federal elections.

In 1893 the many women's organizations united to form the National Council of Women of Canada. Not all groups, or even all women, agreed with each other's aims. Adelaide Hoodless, for example, did not support the idea that women needed the vote. Yet working together in the National Council, the women were a powerful group. They learned how to attract publicity and speak in public. Their leaders put pressure on decision-makers, using letter-writing campaigns, petitions, parades, and delegations. In 1910 the National Council took up the cause of getting the vote for women.

An ambulance driver. The valued contributions of women to the war effort in World War I made it difficult to deny them the vote.

Gaining the vote was an important victory for Canadian women. The campaign had been long, but it was not over quite yet. Women were still not legally considered "persons," and that would not change until 1929. A host of other inequalities would be challenged throughout the twentieth century. Can you think of any recently resolved issues in the Canadian women's movement?

The Story So Far . . .

1 Go to an outside source to discover when women gained the right to vote provincially in Québec and Newfoundland.
2 If women were not "persons" until 1929, some of you might have grandmothers or other relatives who were not born "persons." Ask them how they feel about that.
3 Explain the connection between social reform and the women's movement during this time period.

THE CHANGING ROLE OF CHILDREN

Some of the women in the women's movement tried to change conditions for children. Emily Murphy campaigned for public playgrounds and school reforms. Nellie McClung worked for compulsory education and changes to the laws that unfairly affected women and children. Dr. Helen MacMurchy promoted infant health and welfare. She became chief of the Child Welfare Division of the Department of Health in 1919. Branches of the Children's Aid Society were set up. Child labour was gradually limited.

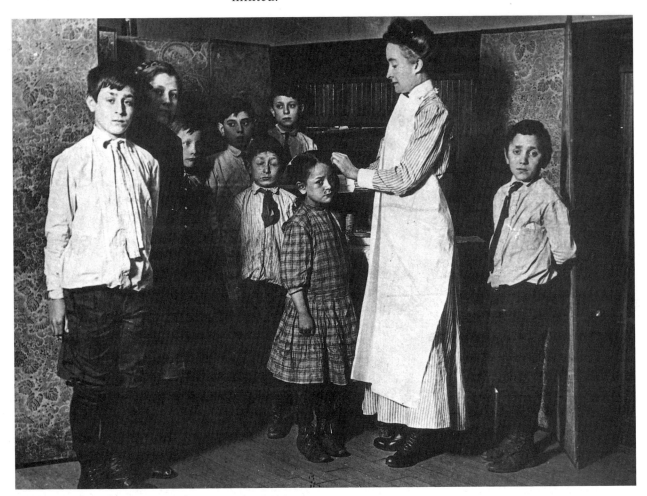

Students at a Toronto school are lined up for a routine check-up from the Board of Health nurse. How would you feel if you were one of the students?

Schooling

Under the BNA Act of 1867 education is a provincial responsibility. By 1905 all provinces except Québec had laws that provided for free schooling. By 1871 in Ontario, children under the age of 14 years were required by law to attend school. Reformers pushed for better teachers and for larger, better schools. There was such a demand for new schools that the T. Eaton Company sold a basic school-building kit in its catalogue of 1917–1918.

Children in rural areas often missed school whenever their families needed extra help with the farm work. The distance many children had to travel to get to school was also a drawback in some areas. Discipline was very strict in the schools, and some children avoided going to school if they could. By 1921 only 25 percent of teens over age 14 attended high school.

By the 1890s people wanted more subjects to be taught in schools. Physical education, military drill, singing, and training in subjects such as woodworking, domestic science, and art were added to the curriculum. Social reformers believed that children could be taught the "right way" to live. The "right way" included knowing about cleanliness, learning to garden, and technical and domestic training. Education began to be seen as key to improving one's life and surviving in the industrial age.

Domestic science for girls is an example of a subject that met these concerns. "Educate a boy and you educate a man, but educate a girl and you educate a family," said Adelaide Hoodless. Most people at the time accepted her message. Domestic science courses came to be taught in most provinces.

Snapshot

He Did Not Die in Vain

In 1895 the name George Everitt Green was a household word in Canada and Britain. The 15-year-old was making headlines not because of the way he lived, but because of the way he died.

George was born in London, England, to parents who were desperately poor. By the time he was aged 14, his father had died and his mother was penniless. She had no choice but to send George and his younger brother to a charitable home that took in poor or orphaned children and sent them overseas to work as farm labourers and servants.

Soon after they arrived in Ontario, the brothers were separated. George was sent to work on a farm near Owen Sound. Seven months later, he was dead. An inquest found that he had died of neglect and ill-treatment. The wounds on his emaciated body showed that he had been beaten. He also had tuberculosis and gangrene.

The woman who owned the farm was charged with manslaughter, but her trial ended in a hung jury. Although the case was dropped after this, George's terrible death was not in vain. People like J. J. Kelso took up the cause of child immigrants. As a result, several provinces, including Ontario, passed laws to protect these youngsters who were coming to a new country on their own.

Between 1864 and 1924 more than 80 000 home children were sent to Canada.

John Joseph Kelso
THE CHILDREN'S FRIEND

Eleven-year-old John Joseph Kelso needed to earn money. His father's low-paying job did not bring in enough to support the family. What was worse, George Kelso was starting to seek refuge in alcohol, placing even more strain on the unhappy family. To pay the rent on their rundown house and buy food, John's mother had already been forced to sell some of the fine furniture she cherished.

It was hard for his mother to give up the furniture. It was her last reminder that things had once been better for the Kelsos. As youngsters in Dundalk, Ireland, John and his eight brothers and sisters had lived comfortably. Each had a personal servant. Then their father's starch factory had burned to the ground. In an instant, the family had been plunged into poverty.

Planning to start over, the Kelsos had immigrated to Toronto. By 1875 the outlook was not bright. Unable to find a job that lived up to his expectations, John's embittered father was drinking away the family's hopes for a better life.

That was why John was pleased to see the help-wanted sign outside of a Toronto bookshop. Despite his youth, he talked the owner into giving him the job, which paid $1 a week. This was not much, but he knew that he would also earn tips for doing things like making deliveries and holding the door open for customers.

John was not worried about missing school, which he did not like much anyway. Children between the ages of 7 and 12 were required to spend four months a year at school, but the law was rarely enforced.

When he was aged 13, John stopped going to school entirely. He had moved from job to job, always trying to find something that paid more so that he could help his family. Finally he was hired as an apprentice printer at the Ryerson Press. He continued his apprenticeship at *The Mail*, one of Toronto's four newspapers.

As he watched the reporters at *The Mail*, John decided that he wanted to become one of them. To do this, though, he knew that he would need more education. He began spending all his spare time at the public library, trying to make up for the schooling he had missed.

With hard work and a bit of luck, John achieved his goal when he was 20 years old. As a young reporter, he often wrote about the plight of poor children in the city, but found that simply writing about it did not seem like enough. The misery of his own childhood drove him to do more, and he became the driving force behind the founding in 1891 of a charity dedicated to preventing cruelty to children. The first in Canada, it was called the Children's Aid Society of Toronto. This still was not enough for John. Nicknamed "the children's friend," he went on to play a key role in founding other children's aid societies across Canada.

More people you could research are

Adelaide Hoodless

John Joseph Kelso

Anna Leonowens

Clara Brett Martin

Letitia Youmans

A New Childhood

The view of childhood shifted between 1867 and 1920. For many families in 1867 a child was seen as an extra pair of hands for work. By 1920 a child had become someone to be protected. With more household appliances women were supposed to have more time to devote to their children's well being and upbringing.

This may have been true in some middle- or upper-class homes. For working-class and farm families, however, children were working members with adult responsibilities. Even in middle-class families, children rarely avoided work in some form or another. Living in a house with no electricity or indoor water supply and lots of grime from coal or wood fires meant work for every member of the family.

Children collecting waste coal from a rail yard. They probably used this coal to heat their homes.

There were efforts to help needy children. Some programs even removed children from one country to another. Thomas Barnardo of England devised a plan to send thousands of needy British children to homes in Australia and Canada. Unfortunately these well-intentioned plans did not always work. Many host families mistreated the children. One young girl in a child relocation program wrote back to her family in 1896:

> The people you let take me and raise as their child they would not sent me [sic] to school and mistreat me . . . I run [sic] away when I was 15 . . . I wish I could see you.

Amazingly, though, despite the blunders and the abuses, conditions for children did improve. Certainly some children benefited from better health and greater opportunity.

The Story So Far . . .

1. Make three columns on a page. In one column list the problems children could face during this time. In the second column list some of the solutions that were devised. In the third column state to what extent the solution seems effective.

2. With a partner, stage a conversation between John Joseph Kelso and Adelaide Hunter Hoodless about their goals for children.

A Catholic residential school in Canada North around 1890. What do you learn about these schools from this picture?

ABORIGINAL STRUGGLES

Just nine years after Confederation, the Indian Act of 1876 was passed. Under this Act, only Aboriginal Peoples who were registered with the federal government were to have the rights that came with the Indian Act. These people were known as **status Indians**.

The Act was meant to be temporary. The federal government expected the Aboriginal Peoples of the prairies to take up farming on their reserve land and live like the new settlers. Then they would give up their Indian status. They would be **assimilated**, or lose their separate identity in the community. Assimilation did not happen, and over the years many changes were made to the Act. These changes were made without consulting the Aboriginal Peoples.

Residential schools were another method the government used to assimilate Aboriginal Peoples. These schools were set up all over Canada. Aboriginal children who lived at these schools away from their parents were forced to give up their culture. The government gave responsibility for Aboriginal education to the major Christian churches in Canada.

On a typical day in the summertime, the boys and girls, some as young as six years old, got up at 5 a.m., tidied their living spaces, and then had lessons in the schoolroom until 7 a.m. Then they had breakfast and did chores until noon. They had dinner and some free time until 1 p.m., and then did more chores until 6 p.m. These "chores" were often hard, heavy labour. After supper they had more lessons until 8 p.m., when prayers were said and they went to bed. They were expected to be asleep by 9 o'clock.

All the children were given new names. The teachers thought their given names were too hard to pronounce. Besides, the missionaries and church leaders who ran the schools did not like the names. Children had to speak English — or French if they were in Québec — as soon as they arrived. They were forbidden to speak their native language and often punished if they did. They had to attend church and were taught the Christian beliefs of their caregivers. Children who had never been exposed to raised voices or physical punishment in their homes now faced both for not obeying the rules. We now know that many Aboriginal children were abused. Many were so homesick that they ran away.

Parents suffered, too, and some refused to send their children to the schools. They often fought to keep their families together but most had no choice. If they wanted their children to be educated to cope with the new society they had to send them to the residential schools. The uniforms, lessons, and strict rules were all part of the plan to get Aboriginal Peoples to give up their culture.

An Aboriginal man with three of his children who were in residential schools in Saskatchewan in about 1900

Snapshot

Destroying Aboriginal Traditions

In 1886 a year after the Northwest Rebellion, the federal government passed a new law affecting prairie Aboriginal Peoples. They had to obtain a pass to travel off their reserves. These passes had to be signed by the Indian agent and the local farming instructor, the official hired to show Aboriginal Peoples how to farm. The two had total control over where Aboriginal Peoples could travel. The law made Aboriginal Peoples prisoners on their reserves.

In 1895 another law banned the Sun Dance. This was a traditional gathering of Prairie Aboriginal Peoples. It was held at midsummer and often involved up to eight days of religious ceremony, feasting, and dancing. Officials wanted to stamp out the yearly festival. They said that it interfered with farming. One Aboriginal man was sentenced to three months in jail for holding a dance. Another, who was 90 years old, was sentenced to two months of hard labour. This sentence was reduced when people protested. Still, in 1906, the law was changed again to ban all Aboriginal traditional dances.

Traditional ceremonies like these were banned under the Indian Act.

Some of the schools trained Aboriginal students to work in domestic and unskilled labour. These schools were phased out beginning in 1907 when immigrants supplied cheap labour for these jobs. Education changed. Now the Aboriginal students were to be trained to make a living on reserves. Yet federal Indian agents often blocked the peoples' efforts. In one case the Ojibwa of Cape Croker in southern Ontario wanted to start a lumber mill. The Indian agent rejected the request but allowed non-Aboriginals to cut trees on the reserve.

The Story So Far . . .

1 Explain how the people who set up the residential schools thought they were part of social reform.
2 Imagine you are an Aboriginal child sent to a residential school. Explain the contrasts between the school and your home life.
3 Imagine you are an Aboriginal parent who has been forced to send their children to a residential school. Write a letter of protest to the Prime Minister.

Losing Land

As more settlers moved on to the prairies, the Canadian government began to eye the best Aboriginal lands. This land could not be sold unless the people on the reserves agreed. In 1906 Frank Oliver, the Minister of the Interior, made it easier to get consent from the Aboriginal Peoples. The law was changed so that instead of sharing only 10 percent of the money from selling land, the Aboriginal Peoples could share 50 percent. The Laurier government bought Aboriginal lands faster than ever before. Between 1896 and 1909 the government bought and then sold almost 300 000 ha for just over $2 million.

In 1911 Oliver changed the Indian Act again. Municipalities could take reserve land to build services like roads and railways if the federal government agreed. The government would decide how much should be paid for the land. As well, any reserve near a town of 8000 or more people could be moved. The reserve members would have no say in the decision. People on a Mi'kmaq reserve outside Sydney, Nova Scotia, appealed to a judge when the federal government decided to move their reserve. The judge ruled in the government's favour. He said the move was in the best interests of the public.

Snippet

A Bad Deal

In 1907 Frank Pedley, Deputy Superintendent of Indian Affairs, was in charge of the sale of the St. Peter's reserve near Selkirk, Manitoba. Local politicians claimed that his department bribed people on the reserve. They sold the land to the government for one fifth of its true market value.

Frederick Loft
A VOICE FOR ABORIGINAL PEOPLES

No matter how hard he worked, Fred Loft never seemed to get ahead in his job. He worked as an accountant at the provincial institution for the mentally ill in Toronto. Luckily, his wife, Affa, had a head for business. She bought and sold houses, took in roomers, and owned stocks. As a result, the couple lived comfortably and sent their two daughters to one of the best schools in the city.

Despite his low-paying job, Loft made a name for himself in the community. A regular churchgoer, he was a member of the militia, the Masonic Lodge, and the United Empire Loyalist Association. In 1917 he lied about his age — he was 56 years old at the time — so that he could join the army and fight overseas in World War I.

None of this seemed to matter to those in charge at the institution, even though Loft had been a hard-working employee for decades. The managers refused to raise his pay or grant him promotions. Why? Loft was sure that it was because he was a Mohawk. Born and raised on the Six Nations Reserve near Brantford, Ontario, he was proud of his heritage. He visited his childhood home often. He also lectured and wrote articles on issues affecting Aboriginal Peoples. His work was so respected that the Six Nations Council made him a Pine Tree chieftain. This was one of the highest honours of the Iroquois Confederacy.

Loft knew that status Indians who stayed on reserves had been denied the rights promised in treaties. His experience at work had also taught him that moving off the reserve would not mean the end of discrimination.

While Loft was serving overseas, he thought long and hard about ways to improve the lives of Aboriginal Peoples. Soon after arriving home in 1918, he founded the League of Indians of Canada. The League was dedicated to giving Aboriginal Peoples a voice as they pursued common goals. This included winning the right to vote, restoring reserve lands, lifting restrictions on hunting and trapping, improving educational opportunities, and trying to stop the destruction of their languages and customs.

Officials of the Department of Indian Affairs wanted nothing to do with this new organization. They saw it as subversive and did everything in their power to harass and discredit Loft. First they tried to revoke his Indian status. When this did not work, they threatened to lay criminal charges if he continued trying to raise money to fight for Aboriginal land claims.

Loft was growing older, and poor health prevented him from keeping up the work he had started. When he died in 1934, the League was already starting to fade into memory. It was a memory that never quite died, though. In 1968 Aboriginal Peoples across Canada revived Loft's vision when they formed the National Indian Brotherhood. This was the forerunner of the Assembly of First Nations, the national organization that speaks for Aboriginal Peoples today.

More people you could research are

Joseph Francis Dion
Pauline Johnson
Frederick Loft
Andrew Paull

Aboriginal Peoples Fight Back

Aboriginal Peoples opposed what was happening, but it was difficult for them to fight a powerful system in a different language. The most common way was to disobey by not sending children to school and continuing the potlatch and Sun Dance ceremonies. Letters were written — sometimes to officials, sometimes to newspapers. Aboriginal leaders organized. There was, for example, a Grand General Indian Council of Ontario. In 1906 the chief of the Capilano band of British Columbia travelled to England to petition King Edward VI. In 1915 the Allied Tribes of British Columbia was set up.

The Canadian government continued to believe that the assimilation of Aboriginal Peoples would be best. In 1885 the government had offered Aboriginal Peoples living east of Lake Superior the right to vote if they gave up their Indian status. Very few were willing to do this because once they gave up their status they could not get it back.

The wartime experiences of Aboriginal men heightened their political awareness and made many unwilling to accept treatment as second-class citizens at home.

After World War I Aboriginal service men were rewarded with the right to vote federally without losing their Indian status. All Aboriginal Peoples on reserves were not granted the right to vote until 1960!

The Story So Far . . .

1 a) What was the main purpose of the Indian Act of 1876?

b) Was it successful in achieving the goals of the government? Why or why not?

2 Imagine you are chief of the Capilano petitioning King Edward. What would you want the King to understand about the Aboriginal situation? What would you like him to do?

3 List the reasons the government could have for

a) opposing Frederick Loft's efforts

b) continuing to deny Aboriginal Peoples the vote

CHOOSING IMMIGRANTS

The 1901 census showed that 88 percent of Canadians were of British or French descent. Canadians with a British background were happy with Canada's mainly British-based culture. French-speaking Canadians were already worried about disappearing in a sea of English-speaking Canadians. They resisted the entry of any more cultures.

From 1867 to 1920 there were two ideas behind the Canadian government's immigration policy: large numbers of immigrants were needed to develop the country, and preference would be given to immigrants who would easily be assimilated.

Like other policies of the day, the ideas behind the immigration policy allowed for people to be treated differently based on their race or sex.

Most actions to keep people out were directed at people who were not European, although non-Christians were not welcomed either. Jewish immigrants were often refused housing and jobs on the basis of their religion. Russian Doukhobors had half their lands in Saskatchewan taken from them in 1907, even though they had been farming there since 1899. Their religion would not allow them to swear loyalty to the British Crown or serve in the military. There was discrimination too. In the Canadian West there were signs in shop windows reading "No British Need Apply." At the outbreak of World War I settlers from Germany and middle European countries were harassed, and some held in internment camps, as you will see in Chapter 12.

The title of this cartoon is "I want settlers but will accept no cuills." What does this cartoon say about the immigration policy in the early 1900s?

These people were not allowed entry to Canada for a variety of reasons: some suffered from mental or physical disabilities; others were classed as criminals or as being so poor that they would be a burden to society. Between 1903 and 1920 nearly 14 000 people were not allowed entry into Canada after arriving here.

Reflections

Put yourself in the place of a person who was not allowed to enter Canada. Write a letter to the local newspaper telling them your story.

Some of the policies included in the Canadian Immigration Acts of 1906 and 1910 were to
- accept European farmers
- accept some highly educated people from the United States and the United Kingdom
- accept orphaned children (home children) from the United Kingdom who will work in Canadian homes and on Canadian farms
- keep out non-Europeans
- refuse all immigrants from Asia
- refuse all people who are physically, morally, or mentally unfit
- refuse all people who are unlikely to fit in or adjust to life in Canada
- give preference to immigrants who can speak some English
- refuse all people who are likely to move into already crowded urban centres

The Asian Experience

Like other settlers, Asians came to Canada prepared to work hard to make a better life for themselves. Most met hostility and hardship. In almost every case, Asians were paid much less than European workers. Thousands of Chinese workers were lured to Canada to work on the Canadian Pacific Railway, where they earned low wages. Japanese immigrants, who started to enter Canada in 1877, worked in the fishing industry or farmed in the Fraser Valley. Like the Chinese, they were not allowed to vote or hold professional positions. The first South Asian immigrants

Passengers on the *Komagata Maru* wait to land in Canada.

were Sikhs from India, who arrived in British Columbia in 1903. As British subjects, these immigrants came with some advantages. Many could speak English and they understood English culture. Nonetheless, they, too, were discriminated against.

In time European workers wanted to keep out Asians who would accept the low wages and poor working conditions. In response, the Canadian government created policy barriers to stop these immigrants from entering Canada. The head tax, first imposed on Chinese immigrants in 1885, discouraged many who dreamed of bringing family members to Canada. By 1910 all Asians had to have $200 in their possession to enter Canada. For the Chinese, this would be in addition to the head tax.

A second hurdle was the **"no stoppage" rule**, passed on January 8, 1908. At the time Britain would not allow Canada to collect a head tax on British subjects from India who wanted to come to Canada. The "no stoppage" rule said that immigrants had to travel without stopping from their country to Canada. For South Asians from India this was not possible.

A few South Asians immigrated to Canada by going to the United States first and then crossing the border. Many of the earlier immigrants left Canada for the United States or India to be with their families. In 1919 the Canadian government allowed wives and children to join South Asian men who had immigrated earlier. The South Asian population in Canada fell to barely 1000 before the "no stoppage" rule was lifted in 1947.

Snippet

The *Komagata Maru* Incident

In 1914 Gurdit Singh, a Sikh leader, hired a ship, the *Komagata Maru*, to make a non-stop voyage from India to Vancouver. The ship arrived with 376 potential immigrants. Canadian immigration officials would not allow the men to get off the ship.

After two months of negotiations only 20 men were allowed to stay in Canada. The rest had to remain on the ship, which was escorted back to sea to return to India. This was the first official act of the recently formed Royal Canadian Navy.

The Story So Far . . .

1 List the ways that Chinese immigrants were discriminated against.

2 Even non-Asians thought the *Komagata Maru* incident was discriminatory, but the government felt justified in its actions. In groups, imagine and record public statements that could have been made by each of the following:
a) the Minister of the Interior
b) the Prime Minister
c) the president of the National Council of Women of Canada
d) Nellie McClung.
Make sure you can explain your choices of statements.

3 Imagine you are a wife, child, or parent waiting for your husband, father, or son to pay your passage to Canada. Write a diary entry that might have been written in your fourth year of waiting for passage.

Sum It Up!

The years between Confederation and World War I presented many challenges. Canadian society needed reform to adjust to the changes that came with industrialization and urbanization. Living and working conditions in cities needed improvement. Many social activists worked to bring about change.

Remember "the good old days" of 1889. By 1920 Nellie McClung could vote and women were being admitted to medical or law programs at Canadian universities. Adelaide Hoodless had successfully campaigned for the inclusion of domestic science courses, so that people were better educated about sanitation. Not as many children were working on the streets, and more were attending school. On the other hand, holding a potlatch was still against the law, Aboriginal Peoples had lost much of their reserve land and Aboriginal children still were sent to residential school. Fewer and fewer Asians made their way into the country and those who were here faced continued discrimination. There had been some progress, but there was still a long way to go.

Thinking About Your Learning

1. Think about the changes that were taking place in Canada at this time. Draw an editorial cartoon to show the effect of these changes on society.

2. Design a mural to show the effects of the Indian Act on Canada's Aboriginal Peoples. Do not forget to include the amendments to the Act.

3. You are a reporter for *Your City Examiner*. Your assignment is to write a "then and now" portrayal of one immigrant group mentioned in this chapter. A successful article will require research and interviews with people today. Do not forget the five Ws — who, what, when, where, and why.

4. October 18, 1929, was the day women were officially declared "persons." Design a Persons Day card for someone you know.

Applying Your Learning

1. Canada's Aboriginal Peoples continue to be controlled by laws that do not consider their unique place in Canadian society. Examine a recent area of conflict and explain how it could be resolved.

2. Design a stamp or coin to honour a significant Canadian woman and her unique contribution in Canada's past.

3. Métis and Inuit people were not originally included in the Indian Act. Choose *one* of

these groups and prepare a report on their history since Confederation.

4. A public education — social control or opportunity for all? Stage a debate on this topic. Your teacher will give you information about the rules and procedures of debate.

5. What social reform is most needed today? Write a letter to your member of Parliament explaining why this reform would make Canada a better place.

6. Prepare your report on the person or group you chose from The Good Old Days. In your written report include the questions you want answered and any visuals you can provide.

7. As a class, prepare a bulletin board display titled Immigration to Canada Today. Consider requirements, statistics, eyewitness reports of the new Canadian experience, assistance available, opportunities, and anything else that relates to present-day immigration.

8. Aboriginal Peoples have made a lot of progress in gaining respect in Canada, but many feel the battle is ongoing. Collect articles from newspapers and magazines that show the main concerns of Aboriginal Peoples today. You may wish to consult other sources including the web site for the Royal Commission on Aboriginal Peoples. Be prepared to share your findings with the rest of your class.

Web Connection

http://www.school.mcgrawhill.ca/resources

Go to the web site above to find information on the Royal Commission on Aboriginal Peoples. Go to History Resources, then to Canada: The Story of a Developing Nation to see where to go next.

USING KEY WORDS

Devise a game to play with the words in the Key Word list. Hint: Think of games like Charades or Pictionary or Mad Libs.

CHAPTER 12

Canada at War, 1914–1918

July 28, 1914
World War I begins

August 4, 1914
Canada joins World War I

October 1914
Canadian Expeditionary
Force lands in England

February 1915
First Canadian troops
arrive at the front

April 1915
Canadians fight at Ypres

SETTING OUR FOCUS

It is April 12, 1917. These are Canadian soldiers from the 29th Infantry Battalion crossing what was once fertile farmland in Northern France. Some of these soldiers have been in France for three years, surviving battle after battle. Others have been there a short time. Some will not make it back to Canada but will die themselves in the mud in the next few days. They are all young men, on their way to capture Vimy Ridge. For three years the Germans have held the ridge, but these Canadians will capture it, a feat no one thought possible. Today, looking back, some people consider this battle was a turning point in Canadian history. It gave the nation a feeling of pride and self-confidence.

Why was Canada involved in World War I in Europe? What kinds of sacrifices did the young nation make to fight in the war?

PREVIEWING THE CHAPTER

In this chapter you will learn about these topics:
- **why the Canadian government and people became involved in World War I**
- **the roles played by Canadian men and women in the war at home and abroad**
- **how issues such as conscription and internment of Canadians divided the nation**
- **the impact of the war on soldiers, their families, and Canada as a whole**
- **how the war helped Canada gain independence as a country**

KEY WORDS

allies
Armistice
Central Powers
conscription
convoys
enemy aliens
League of Nations
no-man's-land
patriotism
the front
trench warfare
Triple Alliance
Triple Entente
Unionist Party
Victory Bonds

April 1917	August 28, 1917	November 11, 1918	July 28, 1919
Canadians battle at Vimy Ridge	Conscription enacted in Canada	Armistice ends fighting	Treaty of Versailles signed

THE ROAD TO WAR

At the turn of the twentieth century, rivalry between major powers had already set Europe on the path to war. All the major countries were armed and prepared. Most people felt a war was inevitable.

By 1914 Europe was divided into two camps. On one side was the **Triple Alliance**, made up of Germany, Italy, and the Austro-Hungarian Empire. On the other side was the **Triple Entente**, an alliance among Britain, France, and Russia. Britain was the most powerful country in the Entente. It had support from the British Empire, which included Canada, Australia, New Zealand, India, and much of Africa.

1. Suggest why Germany and Austria-Hungary were also called the **Central Powers**?

2. Which countries were neutral in 1914?

3. Compare this map with a map of Europe today. What countries now occupy the area that was the German Empire and the Austro-Hungarian Empire in 1914?

Key
- Triple Entente
- Triple Entente allies
- Triple Alliance
- Triple Alliance allies
- Neutral states

Alliances in Europe, 1914

Note that although Italy was part of the Triple Alliance it remained neutral when war broke out until May 23, 1915, when it broke with the Triple Alliance and declared war on Austria-Hungary.

All that was needed was an incident to start the conflict. It happened on June 28, 1914. Archduke Ferdinand, the heir to the Austrian throne, and his wife Sophia were shot and killed by a Serbian nationalist. Within days World War I began.

As part of the British Empire, Canada was automatically at war with Germany the moment Britain declared war. Still the Canadian government had to decide how involved Canadians would be. Public reaction in Canada was strong: **patriotism** swept the country. Canada should support the British Empire. Great Britain and France were **allies**, and they were the homelands of the two largest ethnic groups in Canada. Germany's attack on neutral Belgium was seen as unprovoked aggression. Newspapers across the country, including those in Québec, came out in one voice encouraging Canadians to participate. No one expected it to be a long war.

Canadians Answer the Call

By August 12, 1914, less than ten days after Britain declared war, at least 100 000 Canadians had volunteered for the war. Why did so many join?

Of the first recruits 65 percent were recent immigrants from Britain and their ties to their old country were still strong. Another reason was that many men were unemployed, and the pay for a private was $1 a day with meals. Most Canadians had no experience of war and some were seeking the adventure of being in one.

The line-up outside the Jarvis Building in Toronto, which served as a naval recruiting station in 1914.

Recruiters were very selective about who could enlist. Women who tried to volunteer for overseas duty were automatically rejected. More than 3000 women, wanting to serve their country, joined the Canadian Army Nursing Services. Asians and African Canadians were usually turned down. The military leaders, all from the white majority, felt that their men might feel uncomfortable fighting next to people "different" from themselves and this would make units less efficient. At first Aboriginal Peoples were not allowed to enlist, but in the fall of 1915 this rule was lifted. One reason was that so many Aboriginals volunteered. On the west coast, the Canadian Japanese Association enlisted 227 men, who trained at their own expense and then volunteered their services. As recruitment numbers went down, the military became less selective and allowed Asians to serve.

Snippet

The Canadian Military Force in 1914

In 1914 the Canadian military consisted of 3110 regular soldiers. As well, there were 74 213 men who belonged to part-time local militia and who had an average training time of four days. The navy had only two outdated ships. There was no air force.

More than 3500 Aboriginal men served in the Canadian Expeditionary Force. Members of the File Hills Indian Colony in Saskatchewan posed with their parents before they left for England

Snapshot

Playing A Man's Part

When war broke out, some recruiting campaigns were aimed specifically at athletes. People thought they would make good soldiers. "Why be a mere spectator when you should play a man's part in the real game overseas?" trumpeted one poster. Marathon runner Tom Longboat was one of those who felt the pressure. In January 1916 he signed up.

Sent overseas, he was at first called on to compete in races against troops from other Allied countries. Finally Longboat was sent to France as a dispatch runner. Dodging enemy fire, Longboat had to find his way through trenches and shell craters and across barbed wire and muddy open ground. Wounded twice, he was also mistakenly declared dead once.

Longboat and other Aboriginal soldiers who served in World War I were given the right to vote. It would be more than 40 years before Inuit won the right to vote in federal elections, and more than 50 years before all Aboriginal Peoples were given the same right.

Longboat (on the right) in France during World War I

Enemy Aliens

In 1914 the Canadian government passed the War Measures Act. This Act gave the government sweeping powers to protect the lives of Canadian citizens. In response to public opinion—some even called it hysteria—the government began to take action against individuals with German, Austro-Hungarian, and other "enemy" backgrounds, who were considered a threat to the war effort. By the end of 1915 over 7000 men were locked away in 24 camps.

Another 80 000 people, all from Central Power nations, were classified as **enemy aliens**. Many lost their jobs. They had to report regularly to the police. Their foreign language newspapers were suppressed and censored and were forced to print bilingual columns. Their language schools and some of their churches were closed. Any who had become citizens of Canada after March 1902 lost the right to vote, and others were also denied Canadian citizenship until after the war ended.

Snippet

An Independent Decision

The council of the Six Nations Reserve on the Grand River in Ontario refused to join the war effort. The reason? As a sovereign nation, their Chiefs said, the Iroquois were not bound by Britain's declaration of war. They would enter the fighting only at the request of the British King. Despite this official stand, many residents of the reserve contributed to the war effort and many young men enlisted in the Canadian forces.

The internees were forced to construct camps if they did not exist. They also built roads, cut wood, cleared land, and built railways.

The Story So Far . . .

1 Imagine you are a young person in Canada in 1914. Discuss in a report what factors would influence your decision on whether or not you should join the Canadian Expeditionary Force heading for Europe.

2 Create a recruiting poster to attract young men to join the Canadian Expeditionary Force.

3 Create a political cartoon to show that even in times of war some Canadians were not treated fairly.

4 What extra powers did the government assume when the war started? Discuss whether these powers were needed.

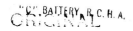

"C" BATTERY R.C.H.A.

ORIGINAL

ATTESTATION PAPER.

No. 349348

Folio.

CANADIAN OVER-SEAS EXPEDITIONARY FORCE.

QUESTIONS TO BE PUT BEFORE ATTESTATION.

(ANSWERS.)

1. What is your surname? — Bruce
1a. What are your Christian names? — David Alexander
1b. What is your present address? — 9 Bassett Street, Montreal, Que.
2. In what Town, Township or Parish, and in what Country were you born? — Montreal, Que.
3. What is the name of your next of kin? — Mrs. Jean Bruce
4. What is the address of your next-of-kin? — 9 Bassett St., Montreal, Que.
4a. What is the relationship of your next-of-kin? — Mother
5. What is the date of your birth? — 8th. August 1898
6. What is your Trade or Calling? — Clerk
7. Are you married? — No
8. Are you willing to be vaccinated or re-vaccinated and inoculated? — Yes
9. Do you now belong to the Active Militia? — No
10. Have you ever served in any Military Force?. If so, state particulars of former Service. — No 4 mths. McGill C.O.T.C.
11. Do you understand the nature and terms of your engagement? — Yes
12. Are you willing to be attested to serve in the Canadian Over-Seas Expeditionary Force? — Yes

DECLARATION TO BE MADE BY MAN ON ATTESTATION.

I, David Alexander Bruce, do solemnly declare that the above are answers made by me to the above questions and that they are true, and that I am willing to fulfil the engagements by me now made, and I hereby engage and agree to serve in the Canadian Over-Seas Expeditionary Force, and to be attached to any arm of the service therein, for the term of one year, or during the war now existing between Great Britain and Germany should that war last longer than one year, and for six months after the termination of that war provided His Majesty should so long require my services, or until legally discharged.

David Alexander Bruce (Signature of Recruit)

E.M. Hughes (Signature of Witness)

Date 12th. September 1916.

OATH TO BE TAKEN BY MAN ON ATTESTATION.

I, David Alexander Bruce, do make Oath, that I will be faithful and bear true Allegiance to His Majesty King George the Fifth, His Heirs and Successors, and that I will as in duty bound honestly and faithfully defend His Majesty, His Heirs and Successors, in Person, Crown and Dignity, against all enemies, and will observe and obey all orders of His Majesty, His Heirs and Successors, and of all the Generals and Officers set over me. So help me God.

David Alexander Bruce (Signature of Recruit)

E.M. Hughes (Signature of Witness)

Date 12th. September 1916.

CERTIFICATE OF MAGISTRATE.

The Recruit above-named was cautioned by me that if he made any false answer to any of the above questions he would be liable to be punished as provided in the Army Act.
The above questions were then read to the Recruit in my presence.
I have taken care that he understands each question, and that his answer to each question has been duly entered as replied to, and the said Recruit has made and signed the declaration and taken the oath before me, at Kingston, Ont. this 12th. day of September 1916.

William Sands (Signature of Justice)

M. F. W. 23.
600M.—2-16.
H. Q. 1772-39-841.

Every recruit had to answer the questions on this form.

Paperwork is needed for any organization. The Canadian military was no different. Volunteers for the Canadian Expeditionary Force, as the new army was called, were questioned at the place where they enlisted. Each recruit was asked the same questions, so the military had a personnel record of each solder. These were called attestation papers. The papers were completed in triplicate, and one copy accompanied the new recruit overseas. That copy was placed in the recruit's file at the Ministry of the Overseas Military Forces of Canada in London, England.

The attestation papers for all soldiers who served in the war are preserved at the National Archives of Canada.

QUESTIONING THE EVIDENCE

1. What information is gathered about the recruit in the attestation papers?
2. Explain why each piece of information was necessary.
3. Do you think it was necessary to have the papers completed in triplicate, or is this an example of too much paperwork? Explain your answer.
4. How could a historian use attestation papers?

The War Effort at Home

Most Canadians tried to get involved in the war effort. Women knitted socks, gloves, and scarves and made bandages. They raised money to send candy and extras to the soldiers and prepared packages to be sent overseas. School children collected scrap metal that could be used to produce equipment and munitions.

Women stepped into jobs left vacant by departing men. It became a common sight to see women working as streetcar conductors and in factories. The number of women in munitions factories alone exceeded 30 000. Between 5000 and 6000 women worked in civil service jobs, and others worked in banks and offices. Generally they were paid less than men, and they were expected to leave their jobs when the war ended.

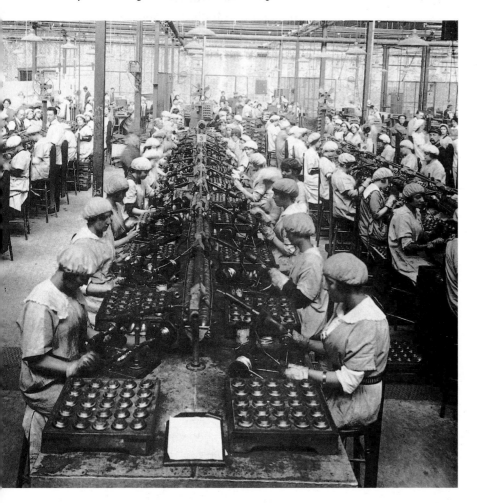

Women working in a munitions plant in Peterborough, Ontario. By 1917 one third of all the shells fired by the armies of the British Empire were manufactured in Canada.

By 1915 the Canadian economy was booming and everyone could find work. Factories filled orders for uniforms, military equipment, ships, airplanes, and artillery shells. More people joined unions, and wages rose, but not enough to keep up with the rising cost of living. The prices of food and clothing went up over 60 percent. Canada became an expensive place to live.

The war eventually led to shortages. The Canadian and Allied armies needed food. Canadian farmers tried to meet the challenge. Wheat production doubled, and meat exports increased by even more. There was a shortage of farm labourers, and older children were released from school to do farm work. Still farmers could not grow and harvest enough crops to meet the demand. In 1917 the Food Controller of Canada distributed an eight-page booklet urging families to save food.

A 1917 advertisement for Victory Bonds. Brainstorm as a group to list the messages this poster is giving the viewer about the soldiers at the front. How are the words on the poster an effective slogan?

City women like these shown were recruited to bring in the harvests.

By 1918 the war was costing the Canadian government about $1 million a day. In 1917 income tax was introduced as a temporary means of raising money to pay the country's war debts, but taxes brought in only about 15 percent of the revenue needed. The government issued **Victory Bonds**. The people who bought these bonds were actually lending the government money. In return they were guaranteed untaxed interest when the bonds matured. Banks, insurance companies, and wealthy Canadians purchased four fifths of these bonds.

The Story So Far . . .

1 Make a list of how the war changed life for soldiers' families; women who wanted to be in the work force; and children.

2 Discuss how wealthy organizations and wealthy Canadians could benefit from the war.

3 a) Why were there shortages during the war?
   b) Why did the cost of living rise? Who did this affect the most?

THE BATTLEFIELD

In early October 1914 over 25 000 men, 8000 horses, thousands of field guns, rifles, medical supplies, and other equipment were loaded onto transports and sent to Europe. Among those travelling with the troops were 101 female nurses. After training in Britain the 1st Canadian Division was sent to France in February 1915. In a short time they were engaged in **trench warfare**.

Artillery and horses being loaded at Montréal

Trench Warfare

The enemy troops faced each other in battle along a looping line called **the front** that stretched for almost 1000 km from the North Sea to Switzerland. Both sides built networks of trenches and tunnels to secure their positions and protect their soldiers. The finished trenches were at least 2-m deep, reinforced with heavy sandbags. Water collected in them and boards were placed on the bottom for men to walk on. There were firing lines, often dug in a zigzag pattern to make it more difficult for enemy fire to hit them. In some places enemy trenches were less than 110 m away. During the day when all was quiet the soldiers could hear the enemy troops.

Second and third trench lines were also built behind the front lines. These trenches were used to move supplies and troops to the front. A telephone communications network linked the trenches to each other.

Troops occupied the trenches in rotations, often spending a week or more at a time at the front line. Most of the night they

Reflections

Imagine you are a member of the Canadian Expeditionary Force on your way overseas. Write how you are feeling as you travel across the Atlantic toward the war. You might include why you joined the war and how you feel about war itself.

Snippet

Winnie-the-Pooh

A black bear from White River, Ontario, came to war with its owner, Captain Harry Colebourn. When he was called to the front lines Colebourn donated the bear, which he called Winnipeg, to the London zoo. Winnie, as she was nicknamed by adoring zoo visitors, is thought to be the inspiration for A. A. Milne's stories of Winnie-the-Pooh.

Snippet

Carrier pigeons were among the unsung heroes of World War I. At the height of trench warfare in 1915, Canadian signallers sent about 100 pigeons soaring into the air every day to carry messages between units. So vital were these winged messengers that a special pigeon service was created to handle the 20 000 birds used by Canadian signal companies.

worked fixing up the trenches, building more dugouts, and digging tunnels. Working parties repaired barbed wire or rebuilt trenches destroyed by artillery fire. Others went to collect food, water, ammunition, and other supplies from the reserve and communication trenches. Still others carried the wounded to field posts or buried the dead. Rations often ran out and it was dangerous to drink the water, which became contaminated easily. Meals often consisted of "bully" beef, or tinned corned beef, bread or biscuits, and hot tea. The men slept where and when they could. Often it was on their feet, slumped against the sandbags of the trench.

Here is how one veteran described what it was like to live in the trenches:

Trenches is too romantic a name....These were ditches....As time went by we had no garbage disposal, no sewage disposal — [we] became filthy. You threw everything you didn't want over the parapet....And if you ever stood at a place where...you could look at the trenches you saw this strange line of garbage heap wandering up hill and down dale as far as the eye could see. The smell ... in those dugouts was a sour, strange odour overlaid in winter by the smell of coke gas....

Steel helmets were given to the soldiers in 1916, after many losses due to head wounds. At first only 50 helmets were available per battalion, so they had to be shared.

1. About how wide is this trench?

2. How are the men spending their time?

3. List reasons why the men were not kept in the front line trenches for too many days when battles were not being fought.

I don't think it was possible to exaggerate the number of rats... Wherever you went, in daylight and at night, the whole place was squeaking and squealing with these huge, monstrous rats living on this garbage....

The tension never for one moment relaxed....You never knew at what moment one of those perfectly meaningless sounds ... would get you ....We had a thing called shell shock in our war .... It wasn't anything of the kind. It was just fatigue—not so much in battle as in these long intervals of living under these conditions...

These men at a rest camp are looking for lice in the seams of their clothing. Lice carried diseases such as typhus and trench fever.

The Story So Far . . .

1 What conditions in the trenches made the spread of disease a real threat?

2 Officials censored letters from soldiers from the front. Suggest why this was done.

3 From what you have learned, how likely was it that men at the front could control lice by following the suggestions of the army?

Between the two front lines of trenches was an open area called **no-man's-land**. Rolls of barbed wire stretched in lines across it. The sound of rifle and machine-gun fire filled the air whenever movement was detected in this unclaimed area. It was a very dangerous place to be.

Before an attempt to capture enemy trenches, the artillery fired shells into the enemy lines for days. Then officers ordered the troops to go "over the top." Here is how one veteran described his experiences on September 15, 1915:

The next morning, we were told we were going over the top at 5.06 in the morning.... A whistle started to blow, daylight was breaking, and the first tanks that ever roamed over no-man's-land came across the trenches.... We had to help one another over the front line trench. In the meantime the German artillery got a line on our trenches and they let us have it.... I saw a man wounded, scream like a horse....

Imagine you are one of these soldiers going "over the top." Describe what you see and what you feel as you cross no-man's-land.

Women mechanics repair aircraft.

Behind the Lines

Every fighting unit needed a field hospital to care for the wounded. By the end of the war, about one fifth of all Canadian doctors had joined the army, along with 2854 registered nurses, women ambulance drivers, and nurses' aids. Canadian researchers worked alongside them, trying to find treatments for new ailments such as poisonous gas burns and "shell shock," a mysterious illness that made men withdraw into themselves.

After a major battle, doctors and nurses worked around the clock trying to save the lives of wounded soldiers

Web Connection

http://www.school.mcgrawhill.ca/resources

Soldiers were not allowed to take photographs at the front, but Jack Turner's family sent him film. You can see his photographs and read about him at the web site above. Go to History Resources, then to *Canada: The Story of a Developing Nation* to see where to go next.

By the time she finished her long, overnight shift at No. 44 Casualty Clearing Station near the Somme River, First Lieutenant Katherine Wilson was too worn out to worry about her lifelong horror of insects. As she sank, exhausted, onto the thin mattress on the floor of her tent, she wanted only to sleep. She did not care about the bugs that seemed to be everywhere.

When war was declared, the young nurse from Owen Sound, Ontario, had been stirred by patriotism and a sense of adventure. Right away, she had volunteered to serve in the medical corps. Excitedly, she had donned her service uniform, an ankle-length dress of sky blue cotton that earned the nurses their nickname, bluebirds. She was proudest, though, of the two stars on the epaulettes. The stars signified that she was a First Lieutenant, the rank assigned to all nursing sisters. They were called nursing sisters because the first nurses to serve in war were women who belonged to religious orders. The white veil they wore on their heads was another reminder that they were carrying on a tradition started by nuns.

Now, three years later, Sister Wilson had no time to think about these traditions. Every day, ambulances brought a steady stream of wounded from the front just 8 km away. The job of the nurses and doctors at the clearing station was to stabilize the injured so that they could be transported to a base hospital farther behind the line. Too often it was a losing battle. Antibiotics were unknown. Soldiers whose wounds did not kill them outright often died when infection set in. Wilson estimated that, of the 48 patients on her ward at any time, only about 10 might live to see the base hospital. "What a ward of horrors!" she wrote.

One night, a badly wounded German prisoner was brought to the station. At first, Wilson balked at helping a hated enemy. Then her feelings changed. The soldier was little more than a boy. It was clear that he was terrified and barely clinging to life. She worked hard to save him, but he died just before dawn. "My heart felt sorry for a mother in Germany," she wrote later. "I wished that she might have known that a kindly priest had stood by her little boy until the last, and the nursing sister had nothing but pity in her heart. His helplessness and youth had wiped away all hate."

Although Wilson survived the war, married, and returned home, she found it hard to erase the memory of the horrors she had seen. "The casualty clearing station had left its mark," she wrote many years later. "Many hours I would lie awake thinking about my ward there. I could not make it a closed book."

More people you could research are

John McCrae

Margaret Clothilde MacDonald

Cluny Macpherson

Edith Anderson Monture

Georgina Pope

Katherine Wilson

In Flanders Fields

In Flanders fields the poppies blow
Between the crosses, row on row
That mark our place; and in the sky
The larks, still bravely singing, fly
Scarce heard amid the guns below.

We are the Dead. Short days ago
We lived, felt dawn, saw sunset glow,
Loved, and were loved, and now we lie
In Flanders fields.

Take up our quarrel with the foe:
To you with failing hands we throw
The torch; be yours to hold it high.
If ye break faith with us who die
We shall not sleep, though poppies grow
In Flanders fields.

Dec. 8, 1915

John McCrae, Canadian poet and doctor, worked in a hospital near the front. He wrote this poem not long before he died. It has become the best-known verse written in remembrance of those who died.

Web Connection

http://www.school.mcgrawhill.ca/resources

You can read about the life of John McCrae at the web site above. Go to History Resources, then to *Canada: The Story of a Developing Nation* to see where to go next.

The Story So Far ...

1 Why were people with occupations such as nurses, doctors, ambulance drivers, and postal clerks so important to the troops at the front?

2 Individuals who worked behind the front needed the same courage and daring as the men in the thick of battle. What evidence do you have to support this statement?

3 Why do you think *In Flanders Fields* has become a well-known poem? What does it say about the soldiers' sacrifice of their lives?

Battle of Ypres, 1915

The Second Battle of Ypres was one of the first horrific battles in which Canadian soldiers played a huge part. Some 6000 Canadians died in this battle. The attack began April 22, 1915,

Snippet

The Blue Puttees

Early in the war, puttees were part of the uniform of Canadian and British soldiers. Puttees were long strips of wool wrapped around the leg from ankle to knee. When the time came to outfit the Newfoundland Regiment, the supply of khaki-coloured wool had run out. Blue broadcloth was substituted — and the regiment got its nickname: the Blue Puttees. Later leather gaiters replaced puttees.

and lasted a week. Canadians had to face a new and highly dangerous weapon. About 100 000 Germans attacked, using poisonous chlorine gas. Canadians had to hold their own ground and try to recapture lost territory. Although thinly spread, and, at times, attacked from three sides, they held on against the German soldiers and fought them to a standstill.

Canadian, Dr. Cluny McPherson, created the first very primitive gas mask. Gas masks became required equipment for men and horses after the Battle of Ypres. How might the use of chlorine gas help troops capture enemy trenches? What natural conditions could make the use of gas dangerous to the user as well as the enemy troops?

Snapshot

The Ross Rifle Nothing Short of Murder

When they arrived overseas, Canadian soldiers carried the made-in-Canada Ross rifle. Excellent for target shooting, the Ross was loved by snipers. Yet it was a disaster in battle. It was 30 cm longer, 0.5 kg heavier, and more expensive than the British-made Lee-Enfield rifle. Even worse, it jammed easily and often seized when fired rapidly. "It is nothing short of murder to send our men against the enemy with such a weapon," one officer wrote angrily. Some Canadian soldiers started throwing away their Ross rifles and grabbing any Lee-Enfield weapons that British casualties dropped.

The Ross was the choice of militia minister Sam Hughes, who stubbornly refused to authorize a change in weapons. When the commander of one of the Canadian divisions armed his troops with Lee-Enfield rifles after the Second Battle of Ypres in 1915, Hughes was furious. The disagreement split the army's senior ranks. One general who supported Hughes threatened to punish any member of his division found carrying a Lee-Enfield. In the summer of 1916 the Ross was withdrawn. Canadian soldiers were finally armed with reliable weapons. Soon after the Ross went, Hughes went too. The Ross rifle fiasco was one of the reasons Prime Minister Robert Borden fired him in November 1916.

Battle of Vimy Ridge

Perhaps the most significant battle fought by Canadians was at Vimy Ridge in Arras, France. The Germans captured the ridge in 1914, and they held it for the next three years despite attacks from French and British troops. From the heavily armed position on the ridge, the Germans could controlled the surrounding area. On April 9, 1917, the Canadian Corps, under the command of the British officer Sir Julian Byng, accomplished what the others could not – they captured Vimy Ridge!

For the first time ever, four Canadian divisions fought as a team. Their attack was a model of planning, preparation, and training, and the Canadians gained more guns, more ground, and more prisoners than any previous British offensive. Many remembered the fierce noise of battle. One young signals officer, E. L M. Burns, described the noise: "Imagine the loudest clap of thunder you ever heard, multiplied by two and prolonged indefinitely."

From this time on the Canadian troops fought as a unit. They were respected as a fighting force by the enemy troops as well as by the allies. King George V knighted Canadian officer Arthur Currie after this great victory. Currie was soon promoted to Lieutenant-General, becoming the first Canadian-born commander of the Canadian Corps.

The Story So Far . . .

1 Most countries agreed not to use chlorine gas in warfare after World War I. Why was this decision made?

2 a) How long had Canadian troops been in the war when they fought at Vimy Ridge?
   b) Describe in picture, poem, or prose why the battle of Vimy Ridge was a great achievement for Canadian troops.

3 The British introduced tanks to help the foot soldiers. Complete some research to find out why these tanks were not particularly effective at first.

War at Sea and in the Air

Sea power was crucial in World War I. Britain and Germany both tried to stop goods reaching enemy ports by sea. Merchant ships travelled in large groups, called **convoys**, that included well-armed cruisers to protect the fleet. The main job of the

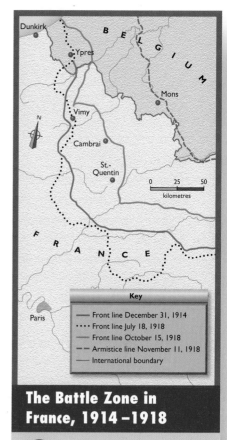

Key

— Front line December 31, 1914
· · · Front line July 18, 1918
— Front line October 15, 1918
- - - Armistice line November 11, 1918
— International boundary

The Battle Zone in France, 1914–1918

1 Use the scale on the map to estimate the distance between the front in December 1914 and October 1918 at its widest point.

2 What reasons would you give to explain why it was difficult for troops to advance and move the front?

Arthur Currie
GUTS AND GAITERS

By August 1918, Lieutenant-General Arthur Currie had moulded the 102 372 soldiers of the Canadian Corps into a crack fighting force. In the year since he had taken command after the victory at Vimy Ridge, his mission had been to create a mobile, well-trained, and well-prepared army that was ready to face any challenge. Now his troops had been handed that challenge. Just before dawn on August 8, 1918, they were in position near Amiens, France. Their assignment? They had been chosen with the Australian troops to spearhead an all-out attack on the German line.

Thanks to the Australian and Canadian fighting men, the plan was wildly successful. Crushing the German troops who stood in their way, the Canadians gained nearly 13 km that day. The Australians advanced more than 11 km. On the flanks of these "colonial" forces, the French moved ahead about 8 km, while the British gained about 5 km. In a war in which success had sometimes been measured in metres, this breakthrough was unprecedented. Canadians had led the way to the German army's greatest defeat. Although no one knew it at the time, this was the turning point of the war and marked the beginning of what would later be called the 100 days. This was the period — really only 96 days — between August 8 and November 11, 1918, the day the Armistice, or ceasefire, was declared.

There would be setbacks during those 100 days, but this was not the end of the advance. Before November 11, Canadian troops would meet and decisively defeat more than 50 German divisions, about one quarter of the total German forces on the Western front.

Currie did not start out as a professional soldier. Born in Ontario in 1875, he had migrated west as a teen and taught school in Victoria, British Columbia. Then he had changed careers, moving on to sell insurance and real estate. Like many young men, he had joined the militia, rising through the ranks to take charge of his regiment. Under his command, the regiment had won many prizes in militia competitions, bringing Currie to the attention of Ottawa. When war broke out, he was a natural choice to become a senior officer with the Canadian Expeditionary Force.

As an officer, Currie stood out from the crowd. He believed in careful preparation and training. He also championed the troops under his command, fighting to make sure that they were given the respect they deserved. The soldiers of the Canadian Corps returned this favour by giving their commander a nickname that showed their respect: Guts and Gaiters.

More people you could research are

Robert Borden

Henri Bourassa

Arthur Currie

Joseph W. Flavelle

Samuel Hughes

Royal Canadian Navy was to help Britain by escorting troops and supplies across the Atlantic. By the end of the war in 1918 there were 112 war vessels and 5500 officers and men in the Royal Canadian Navy.

Airplanes were a new technology in 1914. At first they were used for spying missions, flying over enemy territory to find out where the enemy was located, what weapons they had, and their troop movements. Pilots often took photographs that were studied back at home base. The cockpits were open so the pilots had an unobstructed view of the land below. The planes were poorly equipped for battle. The pilots' first weapons were hand-held rifles and pistols. These were quickly replaced by mounted machine guns. The next step was to arm planes with bombs to attack enemy lines.

War in the air was extremely dangerous for the flyers. A pilot whose plane was shot down had little hope of survival, as there were no parachutes. Watching an air battle from the air, Edward Foster noticed small specks falling from a burning plane. He explained the specks as "men who would sooner fall through the air than burn." Some 1563 Canadians died in the air war effort. One third of all the pilots in the British air services who downed 30 or more enemy airplanes were Canadian.

This photograph shows Billy Bishop, Canada's famous ace who won the Victoria Cross, in his plane with a mounted machine gun.

The Story So Far . . .

1 In a small group, brainstorm reasons why control of the seas was important in World War I.

2 What kinds of skills did a pilot need to fight in a combat in the war?

3 Visit a military museum or read descriptions of warfare in 1914–1918 to collect a story to share with the class.

CRISIS AT HOME

When the war began, nobody thought it would be so long or so terrible. By 1917 the number of volunteer recruits was not keeping up with the numbers of dead and wounded. This meant there had to be compulsory enlistment, or **conscription**, into the armed forces. Prime Minister Robert Borden knew conscription was not popular with some Canadians.

What a contrast to recruiting scenes at the beginning of the war!

Resistance was strongest in Québec, where Henri Bourassa led the anti-conscription movement. Writers in newspapers such as *Le Devoir* said that this was a European war and should be fought by Europeans. Enough Canadians had lost their lives. Many remember the actions of Hughes when he was minister of militia. He had angered many French Canadians by sending English-speaking recruiters to Québec, and by placing most of Québec's French-speaking volunteers in English-speaking regiments rather than forming separate regiments for these volunteers. He had also refused to put French-Canadian officers in positions of authority even when their qualifications were better than those of English-speaking Canadians. Most French Canadians, in Québec especially, vehemently opposed conscription.

Farmers were opposed. They felt they were already doing what they needed to do — growing food for the troops. Some people were pacifists who believed that violence of any kind, including war, was wrong. Quakers, Mennonites, Hutterites, and Doukhobors were the main pacifist groups. They had received the right to be excluded from military duty when they entered Canada as immigrants.

English-Canadian newspapers generally supported conscription. In their view Canada was taking part in the war and now must finish it. People opposed to conscription were helping the Germans and the Central Powers. Canadian men and women already overseas needed help. Conscription was not a choice but a necessity.

The country was divided on the issue, and in 1917 Prime Minister Borden called a general election to determine whether or not conscription would be put into place. Before the election, the government took steps to ensure its victory. It formed a coalition with other political party members who favoured a "yes" vote for conscription. This coalition was the

Nurses voting. One nurse, Ella Mae Bongard, recorded in her diary of December 9, 1917: "You may be sure I voted for conscription despite party politics for I don't want to see Canada drop out of the war at this stage."

Unionist Party. It passed a law that took away the vote of immigrants who might be against conscription and gave the vote to soldiers. For the first time women could vote, but only those with soldiers in their families. It also ensured that soldiers and medical corps overseas were allowed to vote on the issue.

After a bitter campaign that saw each side flinging accusations at the other, the vote was counted. The conscription side won. The soldiers' votes made the difference. The price of victory was steep, however. Borden and the Unionists won only three seats in Québec. It was Québec against the rest of Canada. The bitterness lasted for years to come.

The Story So Far . . .

1. What steps did the government take to make sure it would win the 1917 election?
2. Hold a public meeting in your classroom. Have opposing sides present arguments for and against conscription.
3. a) What previous issue that you have read about in this book divided Canada?
   b) From what you know of Canada today, what advice would you give Borden if you could talk to him before the election?

The Final Years

In 1917 Germany started all-out submarine attacks on any ships crossing the Atlantic Ocean with supplies for Britain. Faced with possible attacks on American shipping, President Woodrow Wilson declared war on Germany on April 6, 1917.

The entry of the United States into the war brought fresh energy to the tired, war-weary Allied forces. On the other side, the Central Powers were beginning to tire of the war and the many hardships it caused their soldiers and citizens. Turkey, Bulgaria, and Austria withdrew from the war because of citizens' attempts to overthrow their governments. Germany wanted the war to end as well. Finally they found their reason to surrender. The German Kaiser gave up his throne and fled Germany to neutral Holland. Without their leader there was no reason for the Germans to continue fighting.

At 10:55 a.m. on November 11, 1918 – five minutes before the Armistice took effect – a German sniper shot and killed Private George Price near the Belgian town of Mons. Price, of the 28th Northwest Battalion, was the only Canadian killed that day.

Snippet

Halifax Explosion

Halifax, Nova Scotia, was the chief Canadian port of the Royal Navy. On December 6, 1917, the Belgian Relief vessel *Imo* accidentally collided with the French munitions carrier *Mont Blanc*, which had nearly 2766 t of explosives on board. Fire broke out, and about 25 minutes later, fire reached the explosives. The resulting explosion destroyed a large part of the city, killing over 1600, injuring 9000, and leaving thousands more homeless.

Thomas Ricketts
FOR VALOUR

As the Battle of Courtrai raged on October 14, 1918, it looked as if 17-year-old Private Thomas Ricketts and the soldiers of the Royal Newfoundland Regiment's B Company might become victims of their own success. The Blue Puttees had pushed back the German line. In the process, they had advanced far ahead of the cover of their own heavy artillery. Now they were stranded, pinned down by withering fire from a German field gun. They could neither advance nor retreat. The platoon was being slaughtered. Their only hope of stopping the deadly fire was to get a Lewis gun, a light machine gun, close enough to attack the Germans from the flank. Then they might be able to flush them out of their nest.

When Thomas's platoon leader agreed to take on the dangerous mission, Thomas volunteered to go with him. As soon as they left cover, the enemy knew exactly what they were up to. Determined to foil their plan, the German gunners unleashed a hail of machine-gun and artillery fire at the two brave Newfoundlanders. As bullets whistled past the khaki-clad figures, exploding shells sent shrapnel flying everywhere. The noise was deafening. Miraculously, they were not hit. They ran stooped over, then threw themselves behind whatever flimsy cover was available. Every time they took cover, they fired a burst from the Lewis gun. As the Germans ducked, they leaped up and rushed forward another few metres. Gradually, they edged closer to the battery.

Their supply of ammunition was starting to run low. When they were still about 275 m from their goal, they ran out of shells completely. Thomas knew that he had to do something, or all would be lost. Dodging bullets and shells, he raced back to his company and loaded up with a fresh supply. Then he retraced his steps.

When the Newfoundlanders started firing the Lewis gun again, the Germans retreated to some nearby farm buildings. As they did, the soldiers of B Company leaped up and raced forward, seizing the battery. Without suffering any casualties, they captured four machine guns, one field gun, and eight German soldiers.

For his gallantry that day, Thomas, who had joined the army when he was only 15 years old, became not only the youngest Canadian but also the youngest person in the British Empire to win the Victoria Cross, Britain's highest decoration for bravery. The highly prized medal, which is cast in bronze and attached to a red ribbon, carries this simple inscription: For Valour.

More people you could research are

William Barker

William ("Billy") Bishop

Francis Pegahmagabow

Thomas Ricketts

Jack Turner

Five years to the day after the assassination that set off World War I, leaders and delegates met at the Paris Peace Conference in France to sign the treaty that formally ended World War I. The Germans were excluded from the discussions. They were simply presented with the final draft and ordered to sign. The Treaty of Versailles contained the following terms:

- Germany lost 10 percent of its territory and population, mainly to France and Poland.
- Germany was to pay for damages to France and Belgium.
- All troops and armaments were to be removed from the area between Germany and France called the Rhineland.
- The German army was reduced to 100 000 men.
- Germany was forbidden to build military aircraft, armoured vehicles, or submarines.

Canadian soldiers celebrate their victory.

The treaty also set up a new body, the **League of Nations**. Its aims were to foster peace through international discussion of issues rather than conflict. As well, an act of war against any member was an act against all members, and response from all could be expected. Canadian Prime Minister Robert Borden and three other Canadians served as part of the British delegation to the Paris Peace Conference and signed the Treaty of Versailles, independent of Britain. With this separate signing Canada made a definite statement that it would increasingly make its own decisions in foreign affairs.

The Story So Far . . .

1 Write a letter to your local chapter of the Canadian Legion suggesting how they can involve school children more in their observance of Remembrance Day. Mention in your letter why it is important for students to participate.

2 Imagine you are part of a family welcoming a returning soldier. Express your feelings in either a poem, a greeting card, or a picture.

3 a) What was the importance of Canada signing the Treaty of Versailles separately?

   b) How do you think the German people felt about the Treaty of Versailles?

SUM IT UP!

Canada followed the lead of Britain and declared war on the Central Powers in 1914. A huge number of volunteers enlisted to fight, although some were not accepted at first because of their race. The Canadian government passed laws that restricted and even imprisoned people who were from Central Powers nations. People at home supported the troops and the war effort. They worked in factories, increased food production, and bought Victory Bonds.

The combat at the front was fought over a small area of land. Thousands of men were killed and wounded each time an attempt was made to advance from the trenches onto enemy-held land. Canadian troops distinguished themselves in many campaigns, but especially at the Battle of Vimy Ridge. The loss of troops was so great by 1917 that the government decided to introduce conscription. An election was held that divided the country. The government won, partly by giving the vote to women who had soldiers in their families. The resentment and anger created by the issue lasted for years after the war ended.

The war speeded up the industrialization of Canada. Women took over jobs that had traditionally been done by men. Their role in society was changed forever. Workers were able to find jobs, although prices increased as fast or faster than their wages. Income taxes were introduced.

At the end of the war, Canada, because of its huge war effort, signed the peace treaty as an independent country, not as part of the British Empire.

THINKING ABOUT YOUR LEARNING

1. a) Explain why Canadians supported Britain and France in this war.
   b) Do you think Canadians would support a war like this today? Why or why not?
   c) How prepared was Canada to take part in the war?

2. How did the war affect working people in Canada? Think back to Chapter 10, and write a note explaining what happened to working conditions after the war.

3. There had been compulsory military training for young men in Germany for many years when the war started. Role-play a discussion among Canadian soldiers on the problems they might face in combat.

4. Create a skit to show how the position of women in Canada was affected by the war.

5. Over 8 million military personnel and 6 million civilians were killed in the war. Create a collage of words and pictures to explain the large numbers.

6 Both conscription and the treatment of "enemy aliens" divided the country. Which had the greater long-term effect? Write a position paper to support your viewpoint.

7 How did World War I help Canada gain recognition and independence?

APPLYING YOUR LEARNING

1 With a partner choose *one* of the people mentioned in this chapter who played a prominent role in World War I either at home or in the field. Research this individual and then prepare questions and answers to highlight the role the person played in the war. Be ready to share your interview with the class, with one of you conducting the interview while the other responds as the historical figure.

2 Imagine you are one of the Canadians serving overseas on leave in England. Create a postcard to send home to your family. On one side of your paper draw a scene that shows you in action or depicts a scene of life at the front or at sea. On the other side briefly inform your family about the picture they see on the front of the card.

3 Canada fought in many battles other than the two mentioned in this chapter. They included: Courcellette, Hill 70, the Somme, the Marne, Passchendaele, Canal du Nord, and Cambrai. Using the Internet and other resources, research and write about Canada's role and contribution in *one* of these other battles. Check out the resources available at www.schoolnet.ca/collections/courage/splash.html

4 Prepare the front page of a newspaper summarizing the Canadian contribution to World War I. Your newspaper should include articles, interviews, statistics, and pictures covering as many aspects of the war as possible.

USING KEY WORDS

On a copy of the Word Search below circle the key words.

Words to find:
name for members of the Triple Entente (6)
November 11, 1918 (9)
the Triple Alliance powers (7) (6)
forced military service (12)
fleets of merchant ships accompanied by ships of war (7)
Canadians who originally came from countries Canada was at war with (5) (6)
a world organization formed in 1920 to promote co-operation and peace (6) (2) (7)
land between two armies (2) (4)
love of and devotion to one's country (10)
a type of fighting that took place on the ground (6) (7)
Germany, Austria-Hungary, and Italy (6) (8)
Great Britain, France, and Russia (6) (7)
coalition party formed in Canada to support conscription during the war (8) (5)
a method of raising money in Canada during the war (7) (5)

T	X	C	O	N	S	C	R	I	P	T	I	O	N	T
A	R	M	I	S	T	A	C	E	D	A	Y	L	S	E
S	S	S	R	E	W	O	P	L	A	R	T	N	E	C
U	N	I	O	N	I	S	T	P	A	R	T	Y	E	N
E	O	F	F	L	Z	B	C	O	S	E	I	L	L	A
W	R	E	E	N	E	M	Y	A	L	I	E	N	S	I
N	O	M	A	N	S	L	A	N	D	U	T	R	A	L
S	N	O	I	T	A	N	T	O	E	U	G	A	E	L
L	I	P	P	A	M	N	E	T	H	W	Q	N	Q	A
A	R	R	R	C	O	N	V	O	Y	S	J	L	O	E
E	R	A	F	R	A	W	H	C	N	E	R	T	M	L
T	T	S	F	C	M	S	I	T	O	I	R	T	A	P
N	C	E	Z	F	V	A	T	X	D	K	N	E	L	I
E	H	V	I	C	T	O	R	Y	B	O	N	D	S	R
T	V	E	T	N	E	T	N	E	E	L	P	I	R	T

UNIT 3

A Changing Society

CONNECTING YOUR LEARNING

UNDERSTANDING CONCEPTS

1 Create a poster to show how *one* group or *one* individual contributed to the development of Canada between 1867 and 1920.

2 Choose the invention you think changed Canadian society the most between 1867 and 1920. Create an advertising campaign to promote the invention. Make sure you include its significance to the development of Canada.

3 Write a newspaper article to explain how social changes affected Canadian society between 1867 and 1920. Remember to include information about individuals who contributed to these changes.

4 Create a hanging mobile to illustrate the major conflicts and changes in Canada from Confederation to 1920. Each element of the mobile should include an illustration and a few words to identify the conflict or change.

DEVELOPING RESEARCH SKILLS

1 Choose *one* of the individuals mentioned in this unit and explain how that person contributed to change in Canada or the world.

2 Form a group in which some members act as workers in an enterprise such as a mine, a forestry company, or a factory in the late nineteenth century and three members act as owners. The workers and owners should present their priorities and concerns in a public meeting.

3 Take on the role of *one* of the following in World War I: a soldier, a fighter pilot, a female ambulance driver serving overseas, a nurse serving overseas, a farmer, a Ukrainian interned in a prison camp, a factory owner, a woman working in a munitions factory, a school child, a wife waiting at home. Research to find out more about the impact of the war on your character. Be prepared to share your findings with your classmates.

4 Choose a topic in this unit that you would like to learn more about. Make a list of questions you could use in researching this topic. Include factual, comparative, and speculative questions. Then use these questions as a research guide to discover more about the topic.

COMMUNICATING REQUIRED KNOWLEDGE

1. Imagine you were ten years old in 1867. In 1920 you are being interviewed and asked to talk about the changes you have seen in your everyday life? In society? In transportation and communications? In the workplace?

2. Design a web site or other computer-generated project to teach other students about the Women's Rights Movement in this period. Some topics you might include are inequalities in the work; force; inequalities in the home; actions by the movement leaders; personalities of the movement; significant changes.

3. Role-play a conversation between a government official who is putting in place the federal policy of assimilation of Aboriginal Peoples, residential schools, and the banning of traditional Aboriginal ceremonies and Frederick Loft.

4. Prepare an audiotape of a news report on *one* of the following events in World War I: the internment of "enemy aliens"; the awarding of the Victoria Cross to Thomas Ricketts; the federal election campaign of 1917 and the issue of conscription; the Battle of Vimy Ridge

APPLYING CONCEPTS AND SKILLS

1. Make a list of how technologies described in this unit changed peoples' lives. Then write an opinion paper to discuss the effects of changes in technology in your lifetime and on Canadian society today.

2. List the rights of workers today that workers in the late nineteenth and early twentieth century did not have. How did the efforts of individuals in this period help gain those rights?

3. As a class create a personality gallery of Asian and non-European immigrants who have made a significant contribution to Canada.

4. Why is it important to a historical inquiry to consider different viewpoints? Choose a local issue that is of concern in your community. Describe the different viewpoints held by various community members.

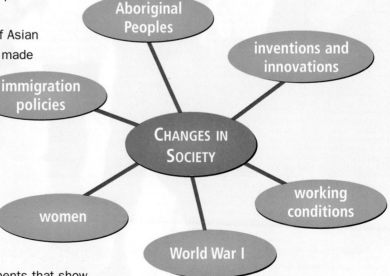

CREATING A MIND MAP

For each category in the mind map list statements that show what role the topic played in change in the period from 1867 to 1920.

The Story Today

1936
Canadian Broadcasting Corporation (CBC) is established

1949
Newfoundland joins Confederation

1959
Bombardier produces the first Ski-Doo

1973
Canada agrees to negotiate a treaty with the Nisga'a First Nation

SETTING OUR FOCUS

On April 1, 1999, hundreds of Canadians visited the tiny capital of Canada's new Territory of Nunavut. The Prime Minister of Canada, Jean Chrétien, and Governor General Roméo LeBlanc applauded a speech by Paul Okalik, the first Premier of Nunavut. Local groups put on a festival of singing, dancing, and drumming. Fireworks lit up the night sky.

Nunavut is the first new government to be formed in Canada in 50 years. The territory, with a 19-seat Legislature, gives the Inuit people a stake in their traditional homelands, Canada's Eastern Arctic region.

The story of Canada is ongoing. Our system of government allows for new provinces and territories. Such changes make us stronger. They are truly something to celebrate! Many other stories that began in Canada's past continue to be important today. In this chapter we will trace the recent history of five themes that you have studied.

PREVIEWING THE CHAPTER

In this chapter you will learn about these topics:
- Canada's new treaties with Aboriginal Peoples
- changing patterns of immigration and their impact on Canada's increasingly multicultural character
- Canadian leaders in science and technology and our adoption of new technologies
- the challenges of living next door to the world's most powerful nation
- efforts to strengthen the federal system and deal with Québec's need to safeguard its culture

KEY WORDS

Charlottetown Accord

Meech Lake Accord

multiculturalism

amending formula

veto

separation

1982
Canada brings its Constitution home with the adoption of the Constitution Act

1983
Canadian Space Agency is established

1988
Canadian Multiculturalism Act is adopted

1999
- Territory of Nunavut is established
- Nisga'a treaty is approved in House of Commons

ABORIGINAL PEOPLES

Canada's New Territory

In its early years, the Canadian government imposed conditions on Aboriginal Peoples that no other Canadians had to endure. Before 1920 Canada's Aboriginal Peoples appeared doomed to either assimilate or live on reserves without the rights of other Canadians. The reserve system still contributes to high rates of poverty, unemployment, and disease. But there are signs that the situation is changing.

The Inuit of the Eastern Arctic are one of Canada's Aboriginal Peoples who still hold title to their traditional lands. The Government of Canada opened negotiations for treaties with these peoples in 1973. The Inuit wanted their ownership of traditional lands to be recognized in a treaty. They also negotiated for a government separate from the Northwest Territories. They felt the territorial government in distant Yellowknife did not represent their interests. The issue was put to a territorial referendum, and the majority of people in Canada's North voted to create the Territory of Nunavut.

Both the Inuit land claim and the boundaries of the Territory of Nunavut were settled by Acts of the Canadian Parliament in 1993. Next, the residents of Nunavut voted to establish the capital at Iqaluit, a town of 4000 people on Baffin Island. Finally, in February 1999, the people of Nunavut held their first election for representatives to the new territorial government. The 19 MLAs chose Paul Okalik to be the Premier or leader of the new territory. Canada's newest territory occupies one fifth of Canada's total landmass, yet fewer than 25 000 people live there.

Celebrating the birth of Nunavut with traditional drumming

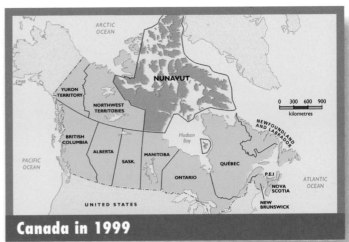

Canada in 1999

Righting Past Wrongs

The Nisga'a First Nation live in the valley of the Nass River in northwest British Columbia. They have lived there for at least 1500 years.

In British Columbia, when Europeans first came to settle, the government made few treaties with the Aboriginal Peoples. Usually, the newcomers simply took over the land. At the time, it was believed that Aboriginal Peoples would disappear, either by being assimilated or by dying from diseases.

Most of the land of the Nisga'a went to settlers, loggers, and prospectors. Aboriginal Peoples were allowed on their former lands only to fish and hunt. They were given a little land around their ancient villages as reserves.

British Columbia's Aboriginal Peoples have tried to get the governments of Canada and British Columbia to pay them for the lands they lost. Some took their case to court. Others have tried to get the government to negotiate a settlement. The Nisga'a were the first to follow this path of negotiation.

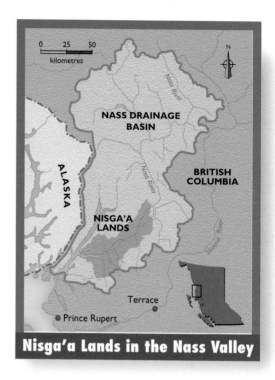

Nisga'a Lands in the Nass Valley

Nisga'a Steps to Settle Their Land Claim	
1887	Leaders travel to Victoria to meet with the Premier and are barred from the Legislature.
1913	Leaders take a petition to the highest court, the Privy Council in London, England. They ask for a treaty, a fair price for their land, and larger reserves. The requests are denied.
1915 and 1916	Delegates go to Ottawa to talk to the government about their claims. Their requests are denied.
1923	Delegates present their case before a joint committee of Canada's Senate and House of Commons. The committee says they have no right to claim land ownership.
1927	Government of Canada passes a Bill making it a crime for Aboriginal Peoples even to hire a lawyer to make a land claim.

This committee of Nisga'a people met in New Aiyansh in 1913 to prepare a petition to the Canadian Government.

In the 1950s a new generation of Nisga'a took up the claim. In 1967 they took their petition to the courts. Their lawsuit came before the Supreme Court of Canada in 1971. The Nisga'a asked the court to rule on two basic issues:

- Did the Aboriginal Peoples have title to (that is, own) the land when the Europeans arrived?
- If the Europeans did not conquer or buy the land, did the Aboriginal Peoples not own it still?

The judges were divided on the second question, but they agreed on the first. They ruled that Aboriginal Peoples were indeed the owners of their lands when the Europeans arrived.

At last, in 1973, the Government of Canada agreed to begin negotiating a treaty with the Nisga'a. The Government of British Columbia joined the discussions in 1990. In 1998 the two governments signed the first treaty made on the British Columbia coast since 1854.

In a speech to British Columbia's Legislative Assembly, Chief James Gosnell, president of the Nisga'a tribal council, said

The Nisga'a Treaty proves to the world that reasonable people can sit down and settle historical wrongs. It proves that a modern society can correct the mistakes of the past. As British Columbians, as Canadians, we should all be very proud. The Treaty proves, beyond all doubt, that negotiations — not lawsuits, blockades, or violence — are the most effective and most honorable way to resolve aboriginal issues in this country.

Web Connection

http://www.school.mcgrawhill.ca/resources

Go to the web site above to learn more about the Nisga'a nation and the treaty. Go to History Resources, then to *Canada: The Story of a Developing Nation* to see where to go next.

A VisionQuest and a New Beginning

When he was young, Roy Henry Vickers, an Aboriginal in British Columbia, wanted to join the Royal Canadian Mounted Police. Instead he became a noted artist. He also became an alcoholic. Years later, after Vickers got free of alcohol, he wanted to start a recovery centre for people addicted to alcohol or drugs. It was to be a place that would encourage their spirits to heal. The centre would be called VisionQuest, after a traditional spiritual quest, or search. Vickers talked to his friends in the RCMP, and the force agreed to help start a fund-raising project.

The VisionQuest campaign started with a journey. In the summer of 1997, 50 Aboriginal and Mountie paddlers travelled

1600 km, following age-old navigation routes. Vickers designed and built canoes along the lines of the traditional canoes of his father's people, the Tsimshian, but moulded of fibreglass and kevlar. He named his own boat *Many Hands*. It was black, with hands painted in red on the sides. The paddlers started on the Skeena River, travelling an average 50 km for 32 days, and ended in Victoria.

Long before they finished, they found that this journey had another purpose. At each Aboriginal village, they followed a traditional ritual and asked permission of the ranking chief to land. They held their paddles upright to signify their peaceful intentions.

In welcoming ceremonies the two groups made vows to end their many conflicts. The ranking officer of the RCMP said the Mounties were sorry for the times they had trespassed. One chief said it was the first time anyone representing the Canadian government had ever apologized to his people.

The Story So Far . . .

1 In what ways are the Nisga'a treaty and the Inuit treaty that set up Nunavut similar? How are they different?
2 a. How long did it take the Nisga'a to achieve a land settlement? Why do you think it took so long?
   b. What conclusions can you draw about the Nisga'a from this story?
3 Why was the VisionQuest an important event for all involved?

DIVERSITY ENCOURAGED HERE

The street signs in different areas of Toronto often reflect the cultural make-up of the local community. These street signs are on Spadina Avenue in the heart of Chinatown.

Canada is a large country with relatively few people. Immigration has helped the country to grow at critical points in our history. Today, the policy of encouraging immigration is changing the character of our country more than ever.

Toronto may be the city of the future. Nearly half the people who live in Toronto are immigrants from countries around the world. In becoming a meeting place for people of the world, Toronto has developed a unique character. Dozens of neighbourhoods reflect the diverse origins of its residents. There are more than 50 cultural neighbourhoods within the city's 632 km², among them Aboriginal Peoples, Portuguese, Greek, Caribbean, Spanish, Italian, Vietnamese, Chinese, Hungarian, Korean, Polish, Ukrainian, Russian, Tamil, and Indian. In Toronto, as in all of Canada, different races and cultures live side by side. The unique mingling of race and culture in Toronto has been called a "tapestry."

In a metropolitan area of more than 4.6 million people, racial conflict has been remarkably limited. Why is that? Social historians have studied Toronto's constantly changing neighbourhoods. They serve a valuable function. In a neighbourhood filled with people from their culture, people can shop and find services in their own languages. They can acquire the knowledge and skills needed to live and work in a Canadian culture, while still maintaining ties to their home culture. They can feel somewhat at home in a new land.

1 Where did most people come from in the period 1961–1970? Since 1991?

2 What reasons can you think of for these shifts?

3 What conclusions can you draw abut changes in Canada's immigration policies over the years?

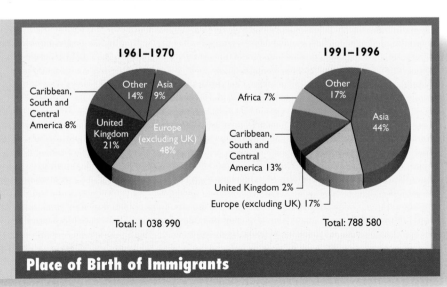

1961–1970
Caribbean, South and Central America 8%
Other 14%
Asia 9%
United Kingdom 21%
Europe (excluding UK) 48%
Total: 1 038 990

1991–1996
Africa 7%
Other 17%
Asia 44%
Caribbean, South and Central America 13%
United Kingdom 2%
Europe (excluding UK) 17%
Total: 788 580

Place of Birth of Immigrants

Except for Aboriginal Peoples, everyone in Canada has immigrated or is descended from someone who immigrated within the last 400 years. Over the years Canada has encouraged immigration to provide the work force necessary for the country's development — whether building canals, growing wheat, or working in high-tech factories.

For a long time, only people from a few European countries were allowed to immigrate to Canada. At times, the Canadian government has even passed laws to exclude people of different origins. Today, Canada encourages the immigration of all people with advanced skills and other valuable qualities. The result of these new immigration policies has been to create a country of great cultural diversity.

Canada's governments recognize that the country is made up of people of many different origins. In 1971 the federal

Web Connection

http://www.school.mcgrawhill.ca/resource

Go to the web site above to see a pictorial web site, designed by students, that tours multicultural storefronts in Toronto's neighbourhoods. Go to History Resources, then to *Canada: The Story of a Developing Nation* to see where to go next.

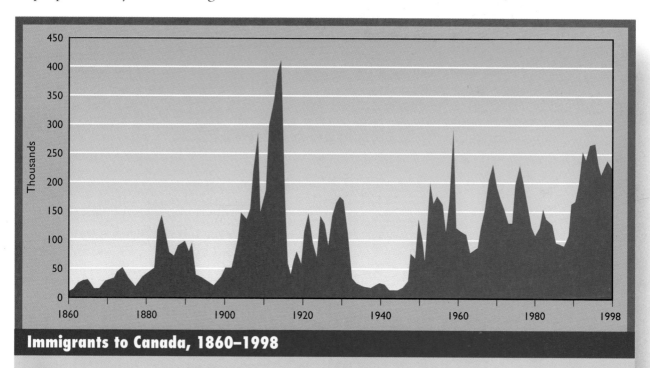

Immigrants to Canada, 1860–1998

1. a) What four years were the time of greatest immigration?
   b) About how many people arrived in these four years?
   c) Explain the reasons for this large migration.

2. What reasons can you give for the sudden drop in migration after these four years?

3. a) What is the trend in immigration from 1990 to 1998?
   b) How does the number of immigrants in this period compare with the number in past periods?

government announced a policy of promoting **multiculturalism**. In a multicultural society a number of distinct cultural groups exist side by side in one country. Canada's multiculturalism policy has three goals for our many peoples.

1. to foster a sense of belonging and attachment to Canada
2. to encourage active citizens who participate in shaping our future
3. to ensure fair and equitable treatment

In 1988 the Government of Canada gave multiculturalism the power of law through the Canadian Multiculturalism Act. It was the first country to do so.

The Story So Far . . .

1 Research ethnocultural community celebrations (for example, Chinese New Year) in your own community. Make a calendar for the local community to show these celebrations.

2 Do you think cultural diversity makes a community stronger, or not? Explain your answer.

CANADIAN TECHNOLOGY

Making History in Space

Canadian astronaut Julie Payette represented the Canadian Space Agency in the mission aboard the *Discovery*. Here she is working with Kent Rominger in space.

Developments in transportation mark the stages of Canada's development. First Aboriginal Peoples fastened birchbark over a wooden frame. Later the voyageurs navigated Canada's waterways in canoes to the farthest reaches of the land. Next the builders of canals, steamships, and railways brought millions of immigrants into the heart of the country, to settle and cultivate the land. More recently bush pilots opened up the vast northland. Today Canada's astronauts are pushing back the frontiers again.

Julie Payette was born in Montréal in 1963. When she was ten years old, she watched early astronauts driving a buggy on the moon. After that, she wanted to be an astronaut.

An engineer by training, Payette was researching computer speech in Montréal when she saw an advertisement for the Canadian Space Agency. She was one of 5300 applicants for four places in the astronaut program. Payette's dream of going into space came true in 1999. She was one of seven astronauts aboard the NASA Space Shuttle *Discovery*, which blasted off from Cape Kennedy, Florida, on May 29. She was the eighth Canadian astronaut to go into space.

The following day, *Discovery* docked at the *International Space Station*, orbiting 400 km above Earth. It was the first docking of a space shuttle with the new space station. The main purpose of the ten-day, 153-orbit flight was to leave more than 3 t of tools and equipment for people who would come later to work on the space station. Building the space station, Payette says, is like building a ship from scratch in the middle of the ocean in a storm. It will take five years to construct and is the most complex engineering project in history.

Astronaut Julie Payette operates the Canadian-built remote manipulator system (RMS) from *Discovery*'s aft flight deck. Television monitors give her two different angles of the cargo bay.

When asked what she felt were the best parts of her trip, Payette said the first was the chance to see Earth from above. The second was to operate the Canadarm.

This is something I've grown up with as a Canadian. It's part of our heritage. This technology has performed so well since the beginning of the Space Shuttle program.

The International Space Station is just a step in our normal progression as human beings. We have been pushing our frontiers all along. Our frontier today is space, and when we think about it, we haven't been that far. Why do we need to go further? Why do we need to explore? This has been part of our past, it's part of our present and it'll be part of our future.

Over long periods of time, we'll be able to do photo documentation of our environment from the International Space Station. We're now over 6 billion people who live, produce waste, use resources. We are changing the face of this planet and we've done more so in the last 150 years than we have ever done throughout our history. We've been conducting an uncontrolled experiment on our environment.

The Canadian-developed Canadarm is a 15-m-long "arm" used to work on the outside of the space station.

We need to continue observing and monitoring this very closely. It is our survival; the Earth is our only spaceship. It's the only place we have to live.

A Nation of Inventors

Canadians excel at inventing vehicles of transportation. The snowmobile is an outstanding example. Inventor Joseph Armand Bombardier grew up in Valcourt, Québec. When he was 15 years old, he created the first snowmobile from a sleigh, an automobile engine, and an airplane propellor. By the age of 19 he had his own service station. Then tragedy struck his family. The Bombardiers' second son Yvon developed acute appendicitis in the middle of a winter storm. All the roads were blocked by snow. Yvon died because his parents could not get him to a hospital. Before long, Armand had redoubled his efforts to invent a vehicle that could travel in the worst winter conditions.

A reconstruction of Bombardier's original auto-neige (snowmobile), designed and built when he was 15 years old

In 1937 Bombardier took out the first patent on a vehicle with tracked drive (like a bulldozer) that was steered by skis mounted on front. His first snowmobile could carry seven people inside a cab. That year he started a company, L'Auto-Neige Bombardier. Soon his invention was widely used by industry and schools. Bombardier kept working on the smaller version he had invented in his teens. The result was a machine he called "Ski-Dog." When a write-up misspelled the name "Ski-Doo," it stuck. The Ski-Doo went into production in 1959. Little did Bombardier know how popular his invention would become. The company he started in a garage is now Bombardier Inc., a large manufacturer of subway trains and other vehicles.

Canada is among the most advanced nations in the world in terms of technology. We are leaders in developing both transportation and communications technology. Canadians are at the forefront of the communications revolution. The results of this revolution can be found in most Canadian homes.

An early version of the Ski-Doo, the wildly popular miniature snowmobile that Bombardier introduced in 1959

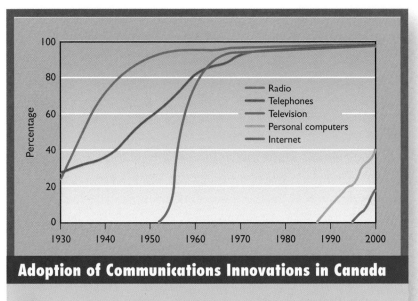

Adoption of Communications Innovations in Canada

The chart shows how communications media have become part of our everyday lives. Beginning at the bottom of the graph, each line shows increasing use over time. A device that has reached the maximum of 100 percent of households shows as a flat line. From the graph you can see how quickly each medium became popular.

1 When did radio become popular? Television? Which one became popular more quickly?

2 How popular is the personal computer and the Internet? Can you think of reasons why the computer is slower to become popular than television was?

The Story So Far . . .

1 Use your historical knowledge to explain possible reasons why Canadians are especially good at inventing ways of transporting and communicating.

2 Draw and label a diagram to show how teamwork is important in either paddling a canoe, building a canal, or operating a space shuttle.

3 In a few words, summarize Julie Payette's argument for going into space. What other reasons can you think of for exploring space? Can you think of reasons not to explore space?

HOW CANADIAN IS CANADA?

The Royal Canadian Mounted Police — what could be more Canadian? It is a symbol of Canada. Would it surprise you to know that a foreign company owned the rights to use images like this? In 1995 the Royal Canadian Mounted Police struck a deal with Walt Disney Canada Ltd., owned by the giant American entertainment complex, the Walt Disney Company.

Mounties on horseback have become a symbol of Canada.

The deal gave Disney the power to handle the licensing of all goods that showed Mounties or used their images. There was an outcry across the land. Many Canadians felt that our heritage was being sold to the United States. The arrangement ended in 1999, although the RCMP still gets money for the use of their image.

The United States has a big impact on all of us. It has been that way for more than 200 years. Our neighbour has nearly ten times our population. Most of us live within 400 km of the American border, now often called the world's longest undefended border. In the nineteenth century, American armies invaded Upper Canada during the War of 1812. You have read about the Fenian raids in the 1860s. Both these events had a big impact on our history.

The United States has affected many other aspects of our lives. Many businesses and factories in Canada originated in the United States. The North American Free Trade Agreement (NAFTA) has increased the trade links between the two countries. Every day, thousands of trucks and rail cars cross the international border carrying all sorts of Canadian goods for sale in the United States and US goods for sale in Canada. Many Canadian jobs depend on trade with the United States.

It is difficult to miss the impact of the United States on our lives when we think about culture. For most of the twentieth century the sounds and images of American popular culture dominated our radios, televisions, movies, and magazines. Some Canadians have been concerned about this. They think there should be more Canadian content on radio and television and at the movies. In 1936 the Government of Canada established the Canadian Broadcasting Corporation (CBC), operating in both English and French networks, to tell Canada's stories and play Canada's music. Today CBC networks on radio and television work to draw people from all parts of the country closer

1. What percentage of Canada's foreign trade was with the United States in 1986? In 1995?

2. Why is so much of Canada's foreign trade with the US?

3. Why might some people think it could be a problem that so much of Canada's trade is with the United States?

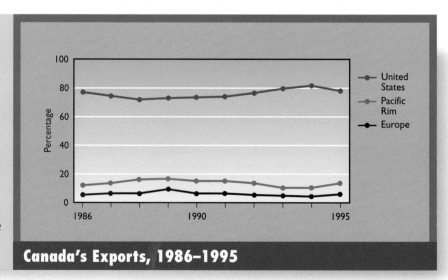

Canada's Exports, 1986–1995

together. The Canadian-Radio-television and Telecommunications Commission (CRTC) has the job of helping ensure that Canadian radio and television stations play Canadian music and tell Canadian news stories. Still, the American influence is great.

On average, Canadian watch more than 20 hours of television a week. Many children watch as much as five hours or more of television daily. About 70 percent of all viewing by English-speaking Canadians is American shows. French-speaking audiences in Québec tend to watch more shows made in Canada. Still, all Canadians watch lots of American television shows, and even more American movies. More than 95 percent of movies watched by English-speaking Canadians and 80 percent of those watched by French-speaking Canadians are American-produced.

What about the impact of the United States on popular music? Most of the compact disks sold in Canada are recorded by American musicians, although some Canadian musicians have found great success in the gigantic popular music industry dominated by Americans.

Canadians who love to read also find many examples of a large American impact. Only 25 percent of the hardcover books and less than 10 percent of the mass-market paperbacks we read in English are written by Canadian authors. About a quarter of magazine sales are of Canadian magazines.

Throughout our history our US neighbour has had a huge influence on Canadians. Will Canada be able to maintain a separate culture or will it be swamped by the powerful cultural influences coming from American television shows, movies, books, and magazines? What do you think?

The Story So Far . . .

1 a. List your 10 favourite films, books, TV programs, and
      songs. Then check to see how many of these are
      American.
   b. Do you think that your values as a Canadian are affected
      by such activities as watching American movies or
      television programs? Explain your answer.
2 What Canadian goods do you think people in the United
   States want? What American goods do you think Canadians
   want?
3 In groups, compile a list of things that are distinctly
   Canadian. Rank them according to their importance in our
   cultural life. Think of ways to protect their "Canadianness."

ONE NATION — OR MANY?

In a huge country with ten provinces and three territories, people are bound to hold different views. The Canadian Confederation is like a family that has disagreements. Keeping the family together can sometimes be a challenge.

Here are some recent issues that have caused dissension.

- Many people in Atlantic Canada feel that the federal government's management of fisheries in the Atlantic Ocean has resulted in great job loss.
- Many people in the Prairie provinces feel that Central Canada does not understand or want to help farmers who are hard hit by economic change.
- People in the northern territories feel left out of decision making in the "south."
- People in Québec believe that Confederation does not give the province enough control over its own destiny.

Throughout Québec's history, its people have been concerned about the survival of the French language and their distinct culture. In the 1960s, the province's elected governments began to develop a policy of *maîtres chez nous*, "masters of our own house."

The provincial government has pressed the federal government to give up control over such matters as health care and immigration. In fact, the Québec government has used this idea to take the province to the brink of **separation**, or independence, from Canada.

Québec took its first steps toward independence in 1976. The people of Québec returned the Parti Québécois, led by René Lévesque, to power in a provincial election. In 1980 Premier Lévesque held a referendum so that the people of Québec could vote on separation. The result was that 40 percent the people of Québec voted for separation.

René Lévesque, the leader of Parti Québécois, after his party's victory in 1976

This referendum pushed the federal government into action on a vital issue. Canada's supreme law, its Constitution, was the British North America Act. For years leaders of the federal and provincial governments had not been able to agree among themselves on a way to amend, or change, the Constitution. Any changes to the Act still had to be approved by the British Parliament.

In 1982 Canada brought home its Constitution. Parliament adopted the Constitution Act, which includes the 1867 British North America Act. The new Constitution included an **amending formula**, which says how Canada's Constitution can be changed — a vital part of any democracy. The premiers and federal government had long arguments about how to allow for amendment. Should the consent of all the provinces be required? Or the agreement of a simple majority of the provinces? Québec argued that it should have the power to veto, or block, proposed changes in the Constitution. Québec Premier Lévesque did not agree with the formula that was adopted in November 1981. As a result of that and other outstanding issues, Québec refused to sign the Constitution Act of 1982 into law.

Without Québec's approval, Canada's new Constitution was not complete.

The Meech Lake Accord

The federal government and the premiers of all ten provinces reached a new agreement in March 1987. Their proposed new Constitution was called the **Meech Lake Accord**, after the place of their meeting near Ottawa. They agreed that the changes to the Constitution would become effective only after all provincial Legislatures and the federal Parliament gave their support. The process was to be completed by June 22, 1990.

As the deadline approached, Newfoundland and Manitoba had not given approval. Elijah Harper, a Cree member of the Manitoba Legislative Assembly, used his power to withhold consent until the deadline had passed. In the eyes of Aboriginal leaders, the Accord did not give their peoples enough recognition. Harper's refusal helped to defeat the Meech Lake Accord. The failure of the Meech Lake Accord had far-reaching effects. In Québec, many people felt that the rest of Canada could never accommodate it. There were renewed calls for separation.

Elijah Harper holds a feather while running out the clock on the motion to accept the Meech Lake Accord, in June 1990. What do you think is the symbolic meaning of the feather? If you held the power to influence the country's future, what message would you want to send to people?

What Does Canada Stand For?

After the failure of the Meech Lake Accord, a Citizens' Forum on Canada's Future toured the country, listening to people's views on what Canada needed. In its report, the forum identified these values as being of importance to Canadians:

- belief in equality and fairness in a democracy
- belief in consultation and dialogue
- importance of accommodation and tolerance
- support for diversity
- compassion and generosity
- attachment to Canada's natural beauty
- commitment to freedom, peace, and non-violent change worldwide

1 Which of these values do you hold?

2 Rank these values on a scale of one to seven according to their importance to you. Then compare your ranking with the ranking of other members in your group.

3 Are there any other values that you would add to the list?

The Charlottetown Accord

Prime Minister Brian Mulroney and the premiers of the nine English-speaking provinces tried again to come up with a new Constitution after the failure of the Meech Lake Accord. For the first time these discussions included Aboriginal leaders. In August 1992 Premier Robert Bourassa of Québec joined the discussions in Charlottetown, Prince Edward Island. All the leaders agreed to new constitutional proposals. They decided that the new proposals, known as the **Charlottetown Accord**, would be put to a nation-wide referendum on October 26, 1992. The Charlottetown Accord failed to win a majority of votes. In Québec, 43 percent voted for it, while in the rest of the country, 46 percent supported it.

Meanwhile, the gulf widened between Québec and the rest of Canada. In 1994 the provincial election in Québec returned the Parti Québécois to power. The second referendum on separation was held on October 30, 1995. All of Canada watched as Québec voted. It seemed that the people of Québec held Canada's future in their hands. The voting was very close: 49.4 percent supported separation. The motion was defeated, by 53 000 votes.

Thousands of Canadians from across the country travelled to Montréal in the days before the 1995 referendum to show their support for federalism in the hope of persuading Québeckers to vote against separation.

Québec's push for separation from Canada raises several questions. The Parti Québécois maintains that a simple majority in a referendum is all Québec needs to leave Confederation. They propose to negotiate a new association with Canada after they declare independence. The federal government holds that a higher percentage of voters than 50 percent plus one will have to vote for separation in a referendum, and that Québec would have to negotiate a new relationship *before* they become independent. Aboriginal and English-speaking groups within Québec maintain that if Québec can secede, or withdraw, from Canada, then they can secede from Québec and remain part of Canada.

Canada's future may hang on the answers to these questions. It's a story that is still being written.

SUM IT UP!

Canada is a country with a long history that is still evolving. Many of the issues that concern Canadians today are the same ones that we have discovered in our study of our nation's history. The negotiation of a treaty with the Nisga'a illustrates how Canadians are working to correct the mistakes that were made with the Aboriginal Peoples in the past. Canada has long welcomed immigrants and refugees, and in the last 50 years we have opened our doors to many cultural groups. With immigrants now numbering one sixth of Canada's population, our country has adopted a policy of supporting multiculturalism.

For centuries Canadians have developed new technologies to solve our transportation problems, and in that tradition Canada played a prominent part in the space exploration program.

Canada's neighbour is the most powerful country in the world. The United States is our most important trading partner and we have benefited from this link. At the end of the twentieth century our ties to the United States are stronger than ever. Canada's cultural life includes such mass media as radio and television. Many Canadians are concerned with the dominance of American media and how it will affect our cultural values.

Canada's system of government includes both federal and provincial powers. The powers of the two levels of government are changing as the country seeks to accommodate the needs of Québec, Aboriginal Peoples, and the different regions.

THINKING ABOUT YOUR LEARNING

1. Summarize the steps that some of Canada's Aboriginal Peoples have taken to seek a settlement for the lands they gave up in the nineteenth century.

2. What examples would you use to explain to a visitor that Canada is a multicultural society?

3. Use the resources in this book and your own research to construct a time line to show the adoption of transportation and communications inventions and innovations in Canada.

4. Collect at least five news and magazine articles about the influence of the United States in Canada. Summarize each article in a few sentences to describe this influence according to the article.

5. Outline the major developments in Québec's

relationship with the rest of Canada since the 1960s.

APPLYING YOUR LEARNING

1. Construct an argument for or against treaties like the one made with the Nisga'a.

2. Collect news stories on Aboriginal issues. Then make a collage that puts these stories into categories such as land claims, housing problems, employment and any other issues that you identify.

3. Create a collage or other visual presentation of multicultural themes in Canadian society. You can find useable images in magazines.

4. Choose *one* of the following Canadian inventions and prepare a report on its inventor and the circumstances of the invention:
   McIntosh apple
   railway sleeper car
   foghorn
   five-pin bowling
   insulin
   snowblower
   zipper
   paint roller
   Jolly Jumper
   pictographs for public signs
   You may want to consult Roy Mayer's book, *Inventing Canada: One Hundred Years of Innovation*, published by Raincoast Books.

5. Research the influence of American culture in your community by compiling an inventory of television shows, radio shows, movies, music, advertisements, and other media. Keep track of which items are American, which are Canadian, and which are from other countries. Try to assess the time you are exposed to each item during the course of a day.

6. Research to find out more about Nunavut. Use these questions to help you get started:
   a. How many people live in Nunavut?
   b. What are the main settlements?
   c. How do people make a living?
   d. How has life changed in the past 50 years?
   e. What kind of government has been set up?

USING KEY WORDS

Match the terms with the definitions.

Charlottetown Accord	a constitutional agreement among Canada's First Ministers, signed in 1987 and requiring the support of the eleven Legislatures by June 22, 1990, to be adopted
Meech Lake Accord	a policy supporting or promoting the existence of a number of distinct cultural groups side by side within a political area
multiculturalism	a constitutional agreement among the federal government, the governments of the ten provinces, and the Aboriginal Peoples, signed in 1992 and requiring a referendum to be adopted
veto	to withdraw from Confederation
separation	a method for changing the Constitution
amending formula	the right or power to refuse consent

Glossary

A

abolitionists people who want to abolish or eliminate a particular law or custom, such as slavery

absentee landlords owners of land or property who do not live nearby and use agents to collect rent payments from tenant farmers. Much of Prince Edward Island was under the control of absentee landlords before Confederation.

allies supporters of the British Empire and those that fought against Germany and Austria in World War I

amending formula a method agreed on to change or amend the Constitution

amnesty a pardon for crimes

annexation take land as one's own, especially without permission, such as a movement to take over the colony of British Columbia by the United States

archives places, similar to museums, where documents of historical value rather than artifacts are preserved

Armistice Day November 11, 1918, the date fighting ended in World War I; now called Remembrance Day

assimilation absorb into the main group so as to lose an individual's or a group's separate identity

B

baldheaded prairie name given to the short-grass or treeless plains in the prairies

bloc settlement a block of adjoining townships set aside for settlement

boycotted refused to use a service as a protest against an action

branch plants factories set up by American-owned companies to make and sell goods in Canada so they would not have to pay tariffs imposed under the National Policy

C

cabinet minister an elected member of a political party appointed to the Cabinet, which determines government policy

capitalist a shareholder or owner of a factory, bank, store, mine, and other important business

cash crop a crop grown for sale, rather than for consumption on the farm

census an official count of the population

Central Powers the name given to Germany and Austria-Hungary and sometimes to their allies Turkey and Bulgaria during World War I

chain migration when one or more families settle in an area and are joined by others from their homeland

Charlottetown Accord a new constitutional agreement among the federal government and the governments of the ten provinces and Aboriginal groups, signed in 1992 and requiring a referendum to be adopted

charter a written grant by a government giving a group particular rights. The Hudson's Bay Company had a trading charter that gave them the sole right to trade in the area drained by rivers flowing into Hudson Bay.

citadel a walled city or fortress commanding a city

Civil War a war in the United States between the Southern states, the Confederacy, and the Northern states, the Union

Clergy Reserves land set aside in 1791 by Governor John Graves Simcoe for the support of a Protestant clergy

coalitions alliances between political parties

common property property used by all members of a community but owned by none

communal living together on large blocks of homesteads with all group members sharing ownership of the property

company town a town built by a company for its workers, the town is typically dominated by one industry or company

conscription the compulsory enlistment of people in the armed forces

Constitution the rules on how a nation should be governed

conventions meetings held by members of political parties to choose leaders and agree on policies

convoy fleets of merchant ships accompanied by warships

Corn Laws laws that guaranteed that no cheap wheat (called corn in Britain) would be imported to compete with that sold by British farmers

craft union a union made up of skilled workers engaged in the same occupation

crofters tenant farmers in Scotland

D

delegates people given power or authority to act for others

depression a period of economic slowdown

E

enemy aliens immigrants in Canada from the Central Power nations who were considered a threat to the Canadian war effort in World War I

entrepreneur enterprising person who starts his or her own business

ethnocultural group of people that share a common language and culture

F

federal system a system where there are two levels of government: a national or federal government, and a state or provincial government

federal union a system where a central government looks after larger national issues, and provincial governments look after local issues

Fenians a secret society formed to work to free Ireland from British rule, also known as the Irish Republican Brotherhood

free trade trade where there are no duties or taxes put on goods that are imported or exported

freight rates price paid to transport goods such as grain from the prairies by train

G

general strike a strike by all or most of the workers in a variety of industries that occurs at the same time

globalization countries linked through the exchange goods and services

H

head tax a tax levied by the federal government on Chinese immigrants landing in Canada

heritage buildings buildings of special historical interest that are preserved for future generations, usually marked with plaques

homestead patent document proving official ownership of a piece of land

I

identity who or what one is, and how one is distinct from another, such as the Canadian identity

Indian Act law describing the rights and responsibilities of Aboriginal Peoples and the Government of Canada

Indian status Aboriginal Peoples who were registered with the federal government, giving them rights that came with the Indian Act of 1876

Industrial Revolution the change from an agricultural to an industrial civilization, especially that which took place in England from about the middle of the eighteenth century to the middle of the nineteenth century

industrialization the shift to the use of mechanized tools and factories to produce goods

innovation a change made in the established way of doing things

L

la survivance the survival of the French-Canadian culture

land deed a legal document that shows who owns a piece of property

League of Nations an association of many countries, formed in 1919 to promote peace and co-operation among nations; the predecessor to the United Nations

Legislative Assembly a law-making body of elected representatives

Lieutenant-Governor the representative of the monarch in a province

M

Manifest Destiny the belief by many Americans that it was inevitable and right that the United States should take over all of North America

Maritime union the idea presented in 1864 by the political leaders of the four Atlantic colonies of British North America that they should join together

markets places where goods can be sold

Meech Lake Accord a new constitutional agreement between Canada's first ministers, signed in 1987 and requiring the support of the eleven legislatures by June 22, 1990, to be adopted

merger joining or combining of companies, such as the Hudson's Bay Company and the North West Company, to form a new company

Métis people of mixed European and Aboriginal descent

middlemen people who buy goods from producers for resale, such as Cree who traded with other Aboriginal Peoples to collect furs in exchange for trade goods

militia citizens who are trained to serve in the army in an emergency

monopoly the right given to a company to control trade in a certain area

motion a formal proposal for action in a meeting

multiculturalism a policy supporting or promoting the existence of a number of distinct cultural groups side by side within a country or province

N

National Policy The policy proposed by Sir John A. Macdonald in 1878 to spur development in Canada. The policy had three parts: tariff protection for Canadian industries, the settlement of the West, and the completion of the railway to the West

navvies labourers, usually immigrants, who built canals and railways

negotiator a person sent to reach an agreement in a dispute between groups

neutral not taking sides in a dispute

Nine-Hour Movement the attempt by workers in the 1870s to obtain a nine-hour workday

"no stoppage" rule a law passed in 1908 stating that immigrants had to travel directly to Canada without stopping in any other country

non-sectarian schools schools not connected with any religious denomination

Nova Scotia Party a political party led by Joseph Howe to oppose Confederation

O

One Big Union a union created in 1919 in western Canada that tried to represent all workers, even those who were unskilled, and unite the smaller unions

outport settlements scattered communities nestled around harbours along the rocky shores of Newfoundland

P

party platform the ideas and policies of a political party

patent a right given to a person by the government, making that person the only one allowed to make, use, or sell a new invention for a certain number of years

patriotism loyal support for the interests and rights of one's own country

pemmican a food made by North American Aboriginal Peoples from dried meat, fat, and berries

per capita grant a payment the federal government provided every year to certain provinces joining Confederation for every person living in that province

pogrom officially approved persecution of Jewish families and businesses

political deadlock a position in which it is impossible to act or govern because of a disagreement between political parties

political party an organization of people with similar ideas who unite to get their ideas adopted by the general population

populist party a political party that has the support of ordinary people

potlatch an important Northwest Coast Aboriginall ceremony involving the redistribution of possessions and wealth among members of the community

preferential tariffs the British policy of charging lower taxes on goods imported from British North America than from other countries

primary document something written or printed that gives a first-hand account

prohibition a law to ban the sale or consumption of alcohol

provisional government temporary government

pull factors factors that pull people to a new location to live

push factors factors that push people away from their location or homes

Q

quarantine station a location where passengers were isolated and checked for sickness after a long voyage

R

reciprocity a policy of free trade in some items between British North America and the United States. The Reciprocity Treaty was signed in 1854.

referendum the submitting of any matter to a direct vote

representation by population (rep by pop) each politician in the Legislature represents the same number of people

reserve area of land set aside by the government solely for use by Aboriginal Peoples

residential schools schools set up by the government and run by major churches for Aboriginal children, who were taught or required to give up their culture

resolutions formal decisions usually agreed upon by a group

resource-based industry an industry based on natural resources such as farming, fishing, forestry, and mining

responsible government a system of government in which the Cabinet or Executive Councilis responsible to the wishes of an elected Legislature

Rupert's Land a historical region of Canada consisting of all the land in the Hudson Bay drainage system, including part of present-day Prairie provinces, and present-day northern Ontario and Québec. The land was granted to the Hudson's Bay Company by Charles II in 1670.

rural having to do with the country, outside of urban areas

S

scrip certificate valued at $160 issued to the Métis to be used to buy land

secede withdraw formally from an organization such as a political federation

separation withdrawal of a province from Confederation

shanties crude wooden cabins that served as living quarters for workers in the lumber industry

shipway a structure close to the water's edge where ships are built and from which they are launched

social movement people working together to make changes that would benefit society as a whole

soddie a house made with sod walls

sourdough veteran Klondike miners

squatters settlers who did not hold title to the land they used for their home and fields

strikebreaker a person actively involved in trying to break up a strike, especially one hired to replace a striking employee

suffrage the right to vote

surveyor a person whose work is measuring or surveying land

sweating system use of low-paid workers who were paid on a piecework basis

sympathy strike a strike by workers not directly involved in a dispute to show support for other strikers

syndicate group of companies or people who form an organizartion to get something done

T

tariff a tax on goods that are imported

technology an invention or tool designed to deal with a particular problem

terminus end of a transportation route, such as a railway line

the Confederacy a group of 11 Southern states that seceded from the United States between 1860–1861 until 1865

the front a looping line of trenches that stretched for almost 1000 km in Europe where the enemy troops faced each other in battle in World War I

the Union a political organization that supported the federal government of the United States during the Civil War

timber ships ships built to carry timber from the colonies to Britain

title a piece of paper proving legal right or claim to ownership

township a prairie section of land, measuring 9.7 km²

trade union an organization formed by workers who unite to improve their working conditions

transcontinental across an entire country, such as the railway in Canada

treaties formal agreements between two or more peoples, nations, or countries; a number of official agreements between the federal government and certain Aboriginal bands whereby the Aboriginal People give up their land rights except for reserves and accept treaty money and other kinds of government assistance

trench warfare battles fought from ditches or trenches dug by soldiers on both sides during World War I

Triple Alliance an alliance among Germany, Italy, and the Austro-Hungarian Empire before the outbreak of World War I

Triple Entente an alliance among Britain, France, and Russia before World War I

U

Underground Railway a secret network of safe houses or "stations" that were used to help African-American fugitives from slavery reach the Province of Canada and freedom

Unionist Party coalition party formed in Canada to support conscription during World War I

urban characteristic of towns or cities

V

veto the right to refuse consent

Victory Bonds bonds sold by the government during World War I to help raise revenue for the war effort

W

ward a person in the care of a guardian or the government

Credits

NAC = National Archives of Canada

Page i Collection Canadian Museum of Civilization/V-B-424; **page v** NAC/C-073707; **page vi right** NAC/C-018737, **left** University of Washington Libraries, Alan Library, Photo by E.A. Hegg, Historical Photography Collection, **bottom** Provincial Archives of BC/PDP02612; **page vii top** Rogers Communications Inc., **bottom** Imperial War Museum/Q27255; **page viii left** Courtesy The Estate of William Kurelek and the Isaacs Gallery, Toronto, **bottom** Photograph courtesy of the Royal Ontario Museum, © ROM; **page ix top** NAC/C-001532, **centre** Toronto Reference Library, **bottom** NAC/K-40; **page x centre** NAC/C-008077, **montage at bottom – bottom right** Courtesy Bell Canada Historical Collection, **centre right end** NAC/ C-005945, **centre right** Glenbow Archives, Calgary, Canada/NA-2685-61, **bottom centre** NAC/C-0027791, **top right** Rogers Communications Inc., **top left** Courtesy of General Motors of Canada Limited, **centre left end** Toronto Reference Library/TEC1116.01, **centre right** NAC/PA-061741, **bottom left** NAC/PA-122236; **page xi top** Glenbow Archives, Calgary, Canada/ NA-1870-6; **Page 2** NAC/C-024369; **page 6** NAC/C-018743; **page 7** NAC/C-031183; **page 8 top** Michael J. Johnson/VALAN PHOTOS, **bottom** Kennon Cooke/VALAN PHOTOS; **page 11** National Archives of Canada; **page 13** NAC/C-005086; **page 14** NAC/MG24, B40; **page 18 top** NAC/C-006077. Reprinted by permission of CIBC, **bottom** Hudson's Bay Company Archives, Provincial Archives of Manitoba, 1987/363-R-2/T35B; **page 19 top** NAC/C-075911, **bottom** BC Archives/A-05056; **page 20 top** BC Archives/C-06124, **bottom** Toronto Reference Library/T16264; **page 24-25** CP Picture Archive/Fred Chartrand, **page 26** Toronto Reference Library/MTL2288; **page 29** Toronto Reference Library; **page 30** Courtesy the Estate of William Kurelek and The Isaacs Gallery, Toronto; **page 32** NAC/C-080319; **page 35** © Bettmann/ CORBIS; **page 36** NAC/C-019294; **page 37** NAC/C-069700; **page 39 top** NAC/C-003368, **bottom** The New Brunswick Museum, Saint John, NB; **page 41** NAC/C-008642; **page 43** Photograph courtesy of the Royal Ontario Museum, © ROM; **page 45** NAC/PA-124022; **page 46** NAC/C-005164; **page 47** Toronto Reference Library/T32034; **page 48** Courtesy of Dundurn Castle National Historic Site, City of Hamilton; **page 49** NAC/C-134167; **page 54 left** NAC/C-005962, **right** NAC/C-005961; **page 56** NAC/C-073707; **page 57** NAC/C-015494; **page 58** NAC/C-003160; **page 59** Public Archives of Nova Scotia; **page 60** NAC/C-029977; **page 61** NAC/C-006721; **page 62** Archives of Ontario/ S15071; **page 65** NAC/C-002813; **page 66** Archives of Ontario/S11831; **page 72** Queen's University Archives; **page 75** Courtesy Rogers Communications Inc.; **page 76** NAC/C-014246; **page 78** NAC/C-000733; **page 81** New Brunswick Museum, Saint John, NB; **page 83** NAC/C-011045; **page 84** NAC/C-095148; **page 86** NAC/C-049491; **page 88** NAC/C-001185; **page 89** NAC/PA-135072; **page 90 top** NAC/C-022002, **bottom** NAC/C-011351; **page 91** NAC/PA-012632; **page 92** New Brunswick Museum, Saint John, NB; **page 94** NAC/C-018737; **page 95** NAC/C-008252; **page 96** NAC/C-015021; **page 97** NAC/C-004393; **page 100** NAC/C-011508; **page 102** Public Archives of Nova Scotia/N-4149; **page 103** Public Archives of Nova Scotia/N-9476; **page 104** NAC/C-066507; **page 106** NAC/C-004572; **page 108** Glenbow Archives, Calgary, Canada/NA-1406-91; **page 109 top** Provincial Archives of BC/A-01222, **bottom** Provincial Archives of BC/1883; **page 110** Provincial Archives of BC/F-05095 (detail); **page 112** Robert Harris (1849-1919) Voting in Charlottetown, 1872. Collection of Confederation Centre Art Gallery & Museum, Charlottetown. Gift of the Robert Harris Trust, 1965; **page 114** NAC/PA-033465; **page 115** Glenbow Archives, Calgary, Canada/NA-1769-1; **page 116 top** NAC/C-006132, **bottom** Saskatchewan Archives Board/R-B3200; **page 117** Courtesy of the Public Archives and Records Office of Prince Edward Island, Acc#2320/38-1; **page 119** NAC/PA-128080; **page 124-125** Courtesy the Estate of William Kurelek and The Isaacs Gallery, Toronto; **page 126** Photo courtesy of the Royal Ontario Museum, © ROM; **page 130** NAC/C-002774; **page 131** NAC/C-001918; **page 133** Provincial Archives of Manitoba/ N9970; **page 134** Hudson's Bay Company Archives, Provincial Archives of Manitoba/N14645; **page 136** NAC/C-073663; **page 138** NAC/C-001932; **page 141** NAC/C-001937; **page 142** Photo courtesy of the Royal Ontario Museum, © ROM; **page 143** NAC/C-061461; **page 144** NAC/C-013965; **page 145** *Canadian Illustrated News*, January 1870; **page 146** NAC/C-001532; **page 148** NAC/PA-012854; **page 150** NAC/C-118610; **page 154** Canadian Pacific Archives/A11370; **page 156** Hudson's Bay Company Archives, Provincial Archives of Manitoba/P-397; **page 157 right** Provincial Archives of BC/A-1670 (detail), **left** Provincial Archives of BC/A-01229 (detail); **page 158** Provincial Archives of BC/PDPO2612, **page 159** Provincial Archives of

Railway 19/N13128, **bottom** NAC/C-016715; page 179 NAC/C-003693; **page 182 top** Collection Canadian Museum of Civilization/V-B-424, **bottom** Metis Gun & Sheath, AC 335, Glenbow Collection, Calgary, Canada; **page 185** NAC/C-030620 (detail); **page 187** Western Canada Pictorial Index Inc.; **page 188** Courtesy of Elizabeth Koop; **page 190** Glenbow Archives, Calgary, Canada/NA-2365-34; **page 192** Glenbow Archives, Calgary, Canada/NA-2631-7; **page 193 top** NAC/C-017430, **bottom** NAC/C-005101; **page 195** NAC/C-007683; **page 196** NAC/C-0006078; **page 197** NAC/C-005826; **page 198 top** NAC/C-001879, **bottom** Glenbow Archives, Calgary, Canada/NA-3205-11; **page 199** NAC/C-015282; **page 200** Glenbow Archives, Calgary, Canada/NA-127-1; **page 201** NAC/C-005142; **page 202** NAC/C-005394; **page 203** NAC/C-023354; **page 204** Glenbow Archives, Calgary, Canada/NA-294-1 (detail); **page 205** NAC/C-014258; **page 207** University of Washington Libraries, Alan Library, Photo by E.A. Hegg, Historical Photography Collection; **page 208** NAC/C-030620; **page 210** Glenbow Archives, Calgary, Canada/NA-470-1; **page 211** Courtesy of Saskatoon Public Library – Local History Room/Acc. No. LH3347; **page 212** Glenbow Archives, Calgary, Canada/NA-2543-1; **page 215** NAC/C-063256; **page 216** NAC/PA-027942; **page 218** Canadian Pacific Archives/NS12968; **page 219** NAC/PA-031489; **page 220** Provincial Archives of Manitoba; Agriculture Machinery 15/N10548; **page 221** Courtesy of Mike Egnatoff; **page 222** Saskatchewan Archives Board/R-B1781; **page 223** The United Church of Canada/Victoria University Archives, Toronto/93.049P/4796 N; **page 224** Glenbow Archives, Calgary, Canada/NA-404-1; **page 225** Provincial Archives of Alberta/B2626; **page 226** Provincial Archives of Manitoba; Jewish Historical Society/N20676; **page 227** Provincial Archives of Manitoba; Hind, E. Cora 1/N978; **page 229 top** Provincial Archives of Alberta/B2738, **bottom** Glenbow Archives, Calgary, Canada/NA-266-1; **page 230** NAC/K-40; **page 231** Provincial Archives of Manitoba; **page 236-237** Hudson's Bay Company-Corporate Art Collection; **page 238 top** NAC/C-033881, **bottom** Provincial Archives of Manitoba, Marquerite Simons Collection/C36/5; **page 240 top** NAC/C-009071, **centre** NAC/C-009480, **bottom** CP Picture Archive; **page 241** Canadian Pacific Archives/NS1429; **page 243** NAC/C-121146; **page 244** NAC/C-095470; **page**

245 NAC/C-058596; **page 247 left** NAC/PA-071362, **right** Provincial Archives of Manitoba, Foote 1491/N2438; **page 247** The Farm Museum, Milton; **page 248 top** Glenbow Archives, Calgary, Canada/NC-43-12, **bottom** NAC/PA-160539; **page 253** Courtesy General Motors of Canada Limited; **page 254 top** Courtesy of General Motors of Canada Limited, **centre left** Toronto Reference Library/TEC1116.01, **centre right** NAC/PA-061741, **bottom left** NAC/PA-122236; **page 255 bottom right** Courtesy Bell Canada Historical Collection, **centre right** NAC/C-005945, **centre left** Glenbow Archives, Calgary, Canada/NA-2685-61, **bottom left** NAC/C-027791, **top** Rogers Communications Inc.; **page 256** Archives of Ontario/F2082-1-2-10; **page 257** Canadian Marconi Company; **page 258** Eaton's Archives; **page 261** Provincial Archives of BC/B-8759; **page 264** Archives of Ontario/S13722; **page 266** The New Brunswick Museum, Saint John, NB; **page 268 top** NAC/C-000949; **page 269** Archives of Ontario/S3663; **page 270** NAC/C-038620; **page 272** The United Church of Canada/Victoria University Archives, Toronto/93.049P/3145N; **page 273** NAC/PA-001479; **page 274** Archives of Ontario/S13458; **page 275** Provincial Archives of Alberta/B1146; **page 276** Provincial Archives of Alberta/B1482; **page 278** The Vancouver Daily World, October 1912; **page 280** NAC/C-058640; **page 281** Provincial Archives of Manitoba, Winnipeg Strike Railway Strike1906/2/N15902; **page 282** Provincial Archives of BC/A-03159; **page 284** Provincial Archives of Manitoba, Winnipeg Strike 5/N12296; **page 285** NAC/C-055449; **page 286 left** Provincial Archives of Manitoba, Foote Collection 1696/N2762, **right** Provincial Archives of Manitoba, Winnipeg Strike/N12316; **page 290** Provincial Archives of Manitoba, East Kildonan – Farms 5/N12950; **page 292 top** NAC/PA-128887, **bottom** City of Toronto Archives/RG8-32-234; **page 293** NAC/C-023415; **page 295** The Law Society of Upper Canada Archives, Photograph Collection, P291; **page 296 left** Toronto Reference Library; **page 297** Provincial Archives of BC/B6791; **page 298** Provincial Archives of BC/B6789; **page 299** Provincial Archives of Manitoba, Events 173/3/N9905; **page 301** NAC/PA-001305; **page 302** Archives of Ontario/S15513; **page 303** NAC/PA-041785; **page 304** NAC/C-085881(detail); **page 305** NAC/C-085579; **page 306** NAC/PA-123707; **page 307 top** NAC/C-037113, **bottom** Provincial Archives of Alberta/B1004; **page 309**

NAC/PA-007439; **page 310** *Glenbow Archives,* Calgary, Canada/NA-5-16; **page 311 top** *The Daily Herald,* Calgary, January 1907, **bottom** NAC/PA-020910; **page 312** Provincial Archives of BC/D9118; **page 316** NAC/PA-001086; **page 319** City of Toronto Archives/SC-244-979; **page 320 top** NAC/PA-066815, **bottom** NAC/PA-001479; **page 321** Glenbow Archives, Calgary, Canada/NA-1870-6; **page 322** National Archives of Canada; **page 323** NAC/C-018734; **page 324 right** City of Toronto Archives/SC-244-640, **left** NAC/C-097750; **page 325** Queen's University Archives; **page 326** NAC/PA-002468; **page 327** Courtesy of the Public Archives and Records Office of Prince Edward Island, Acc. # 2767-145; **page 328** NAC/PA-000648; **page 329 top** Imperial War Museum/Q27255, **bottom** Public Archives of Nova Scotia/N-0300; **page 331** NAC/PA-003842; **page 332** NAC/PA-005001; **page 334** NAC/PA-001370; **page 335** NAC/PA-122515; **page 336 top** Queen's University Archives, **bottom** NAC/PA-002279; **page 338** Sgt. Thomas Ricketts, VC, Royal Newfoundland Regiment, AN 19910109-934, © Canadian War Museum; **page 339** NAC/PA-001332; **page 344** CP Picture Archive; **page 346** CP Picture Archive; **page 348** Provincial Archives of BC/D-07858; **page 349** Courtesy John A. Buis/VisionQuest; **page 350** Brian Sytnyk/Masterfile; **page 352** NASA; **page 353 top** NASA, **bottom** Photo courtesy of Canadian Space Agency © 2000; **page 357** © Paul A. Souders/CORBIS; **page 358** CP Picture Archive; **page 359** NAC/PA-141503; **page 360** CP Picture Archive/Wayne Glowacki; **page 361** CP Picture Archive/Ryan Remiorz

Text Credits

Page 7 Statistics research done by Charles Armour; **page 28-29** From *Immigration* by Ian R. Munro, John Wiley & Sons Canada Limited; **page 29 (bottom)** From *The Great Hunger* by Cecil Woodham-Smith, Harper & Row, 1962; **page 35** From *The Refugee or the Narratives of Fugitive Slaves in Canada* (Boston: John P. Jewell and Company, 1856); **page 65** From *Confederation Debates*; **page 138** From *Red River Settlement* by Alexander Ross, Smith, Elder & Company, 1856; **page 140** From *Women of Red River* by W. J. Healy, Peguis Press, 1967; **page 142** *The Toronto Star,* Nov. 8, 1988; **page 147** From *The North West: Its Early Development and Legislative Record* by E. H. Oliver, Vol. 11 (Ottawa: Queen's Printer, 1914); **page 158** From *Scenes and Studies of*

Savage Life by Gilbert Malcolm Sproat (London: Smith, Elder and Co., 1868); **page 166** From *The NWMP and Law Enforcement,* 1873-1905 by R. C. Macleod; **page 167** From *Looking Forward, Looking Back,* Vol. 1, "Report of the Royal Commission on Aboriginal Peoples"; **page 187** From *Historical Essays on the Prairie Provinces* by Donald Swainson, McClelland and Stewart, 1970; **page 192** From *The Petition of Rights,* 1884; **page 193** From *The Frog Lake Massacre: Personal Perspectives on Ethnic Conflict* by S Hughes, McClelland and Stewart, 1976; **page 198** From a speech by Edward Blake, House of Commons, March 19, 1886; **page 202** From *Klondike Women: True Tales of the 1897-1898 Gold Rush* by M. Mayer, Swallow Press/Ohio University Press, 1989; **page 205** From *A Pioneer Woman in Alaska* by Emily Romig, Caxton Printers, 1948; **page 210-211** From *Salt of the Earth* by Heather Robertson (Toronto: James Lorimer & Company, Publishers, 1974); **page 215** From a *1903 Canadian Superintendent of Immigration report*; **page 217** From *Salt of the Earth* by Heather Robertson (Toronto: James Lorimer & Company, 1974); **page 223** From *A Few Memories of When Calgary & I Were Young,* Glenbow Archives, Calgary Canada; **page 232** *Black Canadians, Their History and Contributions* by V. Carter (Edmonton: Reidmore Books, 1989); **page 245** From the *Royal Commission on the Relations of Labour and Capital, 1889*; **page 249** From *Nation: Canada Since Confederation* by J. L. Granatstein et al. (Whitby: McGraw-Hill Ryerson, 1983); **page 267, 271** From the *Royal Commission on the Relations of Labour and Capital, 1889*; **page 326-327** From the National Archives of Canada oral history tapes interviews conducted for the CBC radio series "In Flanders Fields" – Gregory Clark interview; **page 328** From audio recollections of George Hatch; **page 348** From Chief Gosnell's speech delivered to the BC legislature; **page 353** NASA

Index

abolitionists, 33
Aboriginal Peoples, 17, 108, 115, 128, 293, 306–310, 319, 346
  farming, 200
    land, 261, 308
    land ownership, 143
    population, 192
    property rights, 170–171
    reserves, 261
    traditions, 307
    treaties, 167–172
    voting, 310, 320
    World War I, 319
absentee landlords, 111
Act of Union (1841), 54
Ad mare usque ad mari, 85
African Americans, 229
agriculture: see farming
Albani, Emma, 86
Alberta
  Confederation, 116
  population, 115
Alberta Central Railway, 225
Allan, Hugh, 172–174
Allard, Edwige, 240
Allies, 318
American Civil War, 92
American Constitution, 84
American Revolution, 81
amnesty, 151
  Red River Rebellion, 151
Anglican Church, 56, 62
annexation, 108
Archibald, Adams, 151
archives, 14
Armistice, 334, 337
art, 259
Asians, 312–313
Assembly of First Nations, 309
assimilated, 306
assimilation, 310
Assiniboia, 132
Assiniboin, 130, 137, 162, 169
astronauts, 352, 353
attestation papers, 322
Austro-Hungarian Empire, 318

Bagley, Fred, 163
baldheaded prairie, 212, 219
Baldwin, Robert, 54, 57
bankruptcy, 258
bannock, 168
Barker, Billy, 161
Barkerville, 161
Barnardo, Thomas, 305
barnyard contingent, 163
Barr Colony, 230
Barr's Lambs, 230
Barr, Isaac, 230
Batoche, 191, 195, 196, 197, 199

Battle of Courtrai, 338
Battle of Ridgeway, 93, 94
Battle of Vimy Ridge, 333
Battle of Ypres, 331–332
Battleford, 197
Beamsville, 247
Beaver, Herbert, 157
Becker, Abigail, 41
Begbie, Matthew Baillie, 158
Bell, Alexander Graham, 254, 256–257
Belleville, 15
Bennett, Charles Fox, 104
Bibb, Henry, 60
Big Bear, 193, 197
bilingual, 107
binder-reapers, 220
Black 47, 32
black gold, 282
Black, George, 203
Black, Martha Louise Munger, 203
Blackfoot, 161, 162, 164
Blackfoot Crossing, 170
bloc migration, 228
bloc settlement, 186
Bloody Saturday, 286
Blue Puttees, 332
BNA Act, 83, 106, 108, 302
Bolshevism, 283
Bombardier, Joseph Armand, 354
Booker, Albert, 94
Booth, J.R., 38
Borden, Robert, 332, 335, 339
Bourassa, Henri, 336
Bourassa, Robert, 361
boycotted, 293
branch plants, 248
Brantford, 309
British Colonist, 109
British Columbia, 19, 85, 156
  Confederation, 108–109
  debts, 109
  discovery of, 156
  exploration, 156
  farming, 159
  fur trade, 158
  gold, 158–159
  population, 6, 108
British North America Act, 83, 97
Brown, George, 14, 58, 59, 62, 64, 66, 67, 68, 69, 74, 78, 79, 85, 96
Burns, E.L.M., 333
By, Colonel John, 12
Byng, Julian, 333
Bytown, 12, 64

Cabinet minister, 102
Caledonia Cyclone, 273
Calgary, 226
Canada
  immigration, 28
  population, 55
Canada East
  canals, 12
  culture, 10
  education, 56
  language, 10
  Legislative Assembly, 9, 54

  population, 6, 28, 55
  railways, 12
  religion, 10, 55, 56
  Royal Tour of 1860, 9–12
Canada West
  culture, 10
  education, 56
  farming, 16
  industry, 16
  language, 10
  Legislative Assembly, 9, 54
  lumbering, 16
  manufacturing, 16
  population, 6, 28, 55
  religion, 10, 15, 56
  Royal Tour of 1860, 12–17
  trade, 16
Canada's Century, 240
Canadarm, 353
Canadian Army Nursing Service, 319
Canadian Broadcasting Corporation, 356
Canadian Expeditionary Force, 334
Canadian Labour Union, 280
Canadian Marconi Company, 257
Canadian National Exhibition, 252
Canadian Pacific Railway Company, 174, 240
Canadian Radio-television and Telecommunications Commission, 357
canals, 43
  Canada East, 12
canot de maître, 130
canot du nord, 129, 130, 134
capitalists, 278
Cariboo, 158
  gold rush, 158
Cariboo Road, 160
Carlton Trail, 168
Carr, Emily, 240, 259
Carrier pigeons, 326
Carter, Frederick, 104
Cartier, George-Etienne, 10, 61, 64, 68, 74, 76, 77, 84, 87
cash crop, 37
census, 311
Central Powers, 318, 337
chain migration, 228
Charlottetown, population, 9
Charlottetown Accord, 361
Charlottetown Conference, 74, 75, 77–79
Charter, 17
Cheng, Pon Git, 177
child labour, 272
children, 302–305
  see also education
Children's Aid Society, 304
Chilkoot Pass, 201, 202
Chilkoot Trail, 203
Chinese, 190, 191, 293, 312
Chinese labourers, 176–178
cholera, 29, 31, 139, 268
Church of England, 56
Citadel, Quebec City, 10
cities, growth of, 242
Citizens' Committee of 1000, 284
Civil War, 79, 84, 92
Clear Grits, 14, 55, 59, 64

Clergy Reserves, 56
Co-operative Commonwealth
Federation, 285
coal mining, 266
coalition government, 68
coalitions, 61
coffin ships, 30
Cogwagee, 273
Coleburn, Harry, 325
colonist car, 218
Commission of Government, 118
common property, 170
communally, 229
communications, 256–257
Communism, 283
company towns, 271
Conciliation Act, 281
Confederacy, The, 79
Confederation, 73, 77, 91–95, 101
    Alberta, 116
    British Columbia, 108–109
    Labrador, 104
    Manitoba, 107
    Newfoundland, 104, 118–119
    prairies, 115
    Prince Edward Island, 111–112
    Saskatchewan, 116
Connell, Charles, 9
conscription, 335–337
conspiracy, 286
Constitution, 68, 83, 85
    amending formula, 359
Convention of Forty, 149, 151
Conventions, 55
convoys, 333
Cook, James, 156
Copping, Noel, 224
Corn Laws, 41
Council of Assiniboia, 144
Craft Unions, 279
crafts, 245
Cree, 128, 130, 137, 161, 162, 169, 193,
    197
Crimean War, 42
crofters, 132
Crowfoot, 170
culture, 101, 186–190
    Canada East, 10
    Canada West, 10
    prairie, 228
    Winnipeg, 226
Cunard, Samuel, 44, 45
Currie, Arthur, 333, 334
Cut Knife Hill, 197

Dafoe, John Wesley, 227
Daguerre, Louis Jacques Mande, 42
Daguerrotype, 42
Dawn settlement, 35
Dawson City, 201, 204–205
Dawson Road, 149
Dawson, Simon James, 149
De Cosmos, Amor, 109
Declaration of the People of Rupert's
Land, 148
delegates, 74
Delorme, Marie Rose, 168

Dene, 19
depression, 244
Dewdney, Edgar, 192
discrimination, 35, 177, 190, 227,
    228–229, 309, 311–313
domestic service, 275
Dominion Lands Act, 184
Dominion of Canada, 97
Douglas, Amelia, 157
Douglas, James, 19, 20, 156, 157, 158,
    159
Douglas, Thomas, 132
Doukhobors, 229, 311, 336
Duck Lake, 193, 195
Duke of Newcastle, 4, 15
Dumont, Gabriel, 191, 195–196, 199
Dunsmuir, Robert, 282
Durant, William, 253

Earl of Selkirk, 132
Eaton, Timothy, 258
economic depression, 113
Economy, 37
Edison, Thomas, 252, 260
Edmonton, 226
education
    Canada East, 56
    Canada West, 56
    children, 302–303
    prairies, 231
    Red River, 140
Edwards, Henrietta Muir, 298
Egnatoff, Mike, 221
elections, 55
Elgin Settlement, 34
enemy aliens, 321
entrepreneurs, 247–248
equal rights, 297
ethnocultural, 228
Evans, Matthew, 252

factories, 246
Famine Irish, 28, 29
Fancher, Nettie, 204
farming, 37, 141, 248, 266
    aboriginal peoples, 200
    British Columbia, 159
    Canada West, 16
    changes in, 248–250
    machinery, 253
    mechanization, 253
    numbers of farms, 249
    prairies, 185, 219–222
    Prince Edward Island, 9
    Red River, 137, 141
    sizes of farms, 249
    World War I, 324
federal system of government, 68
federal union, 79
Fenerty, Charles, 252
Fenians, 92, 93, 94, 95, 96, 356
Fenton, Faith, 204
Fessenden, Reginald, 256–257
fever ships, 30
Fife, David, 185
Firewater, 162

Fish Creek, 195
fishing, 266
    Newfoundland, 4
    Nova Scotia, 4
    Prince Edward Island, 9
Fleming, Sandford, 173, 240, 241
flooding, Red River, 188
forestry, 266
Fort Carlton, 191, 197
Fort Garry, 141, 149
Fort Pelly, 132
Fort Whoop-Up, 165
foundry, 247
Franklin, John, 18
Fraser River, 158
Fraser River Gold Rush, 19
Fredericton, 6
free trade, 40, 42
freight rates, 224
French, George, 163
Frenchman's Butte, 197
Frog Lake, 193–194
Front, the, 325
fur trade, 17, 128, 135
    British Columbia, 158
    posts, 129
    Red River, 137
    routes, 129

Gale, John, 267
Galt, Alexander, 46, 77
Garneau, Francois Xavier, 61
Gavazzi Riots, 57
Gavazzi, Alessandro, 57
General Motors, 253
general strikes, 283
German Empire, 318
globalization, 244
Globe, The, 58, 67, 251, 265, 279
gold, 158
    British Columbia, 158–159
    discovery of, 106, 108
    mining, 204–205
Golden Age of shipping, 39
Gosnell, James, 348
government buildings, Ottawa, 13
Governor General, 101
Grand Trunk Railway, 12, 47, 48, 61, 76
Grant, Cuthbert, 135
grass roots party, 59
Gray, John, 90
Great Coalition, 74, 87
Great Migration, 28, 92
Green, George Everitt, 303
Greenwich Meridian, 241
Grosse Ile, 30, 31
Group of Seven, 259

Halifax, 6
    population, 6, 242
Halifax Explosion, 337
Hall, William, 6
Hamilton, population, 242
Hammond, Melvin Ormond, 251
Harper, Elijah, 360
Harris, Alanson, 247–248, 252

Harris, James, 247–248
harvest excursion, 220
harvest gangs, 219
Haultain, Frederick, 116
head tax, 294, 313
Head, Edmund, 64
Henson, Josiah, 35
heritage buildings, 8
highway robbery, 191
Hill, James J., 175
Hincks, Francis, 48, 58, 59, 62
Hind expedition, 106
Hind, E. Cora, 227, 298
historical documents, 14
Hoffer, Mayer, 214
homestead patent, 184
homesteading, 213–218, 223
Hoodless, Adelaide Hunter, 292, 299, 301, 303
Hopkins, Frances Ann, 130
House of Commons, 83, 85
Howe, Joseph, 59, 90, 96, 102
Hubbard, William Peyton, 260
Hudson's Bay Company, 17, 20, 62, 106, 128, 132, 156
Hughes, Sam, 332
Humiliation Day, 313
hunting, Red River, 141
Hutterites, 336

Icelanders, 188
identity, 101
Imases, 193
immigration, 215, 311, 312, 350
    Canada, 28
    occupations, 36
    prairies, 217–218
import taxes: see tariffs
income tax: see taxation
Indian Act, 170, 192, 261, 306
Indian agents, 192
Industrial Revolution, 40, 243, 252
    transportation, 43–44
industrialization, 243
industry
    Canada West, 16
    Quebec City, 10
    shipbuilding, 39–40
    World War I, 259
innovations, 252
Intercolonial Railway, 90, 91, 240
Inuit, 346
inventors, 354
Irish Republican Brotherhood, 92
Isapo-muxika, 170

Jamieson, Alice, 297
Japanese, 312
Jewish immigration, 190
Jews, 311

Kane, Paul, 142
Kapapamehchakwew, 193
Kelso, John Joseph, 293, 303, 304
King, William Lyon Mackenzie, 280–281

Kingston, 15
Klondike Gold, 201–205
Knights of Labour, 280
Komagata Maru incident, 312

La Fontaine, Louis-Hippolyte, 54, 57
La survivance, 54, 84, 87
Labour Day, 279
labourers, 246
Labrador and Confederation, 104
Lachine Canal, 43
Lagemodiere, Marie-Anne, 133
Lajeunesse, Marie-Louise-Cecile-Emma, 86
land deeds, 191
land ownership, 184
    Aboriginal Peoples, 143, 261
    Prairies, 184
    Prince Edward Island, 111
language
    Canada East, 10
    Canada West, 10
Last Spike, 179
Laurier, Wilfred, 115, 216, 225, 240
Lavallee, Calixa, 63
Le Parti Bleu, 61, 62, 64
Le Parti Rouge, 55, 87
League of Indians of Canada, 309
League of Nations, 339
Lee-Enfield rifle, 332
Legislative Assembly, Canada East/West, 9, 54
Leonowens, Anna, 297
Lepine, Ambrose, 149, 151
Lévesque, René, 358, 359
Liberal-Conservative Party, 62
Liberals, 62
Lieutenant-Governor of Newfoundland, 4
Little Bad Man, 193
Lloyd, George Exton, 230
Lloydminster, 230
Loft, Frederick, 309
London Conference, 96
Long March, 163
Long Point, 41
Longboat, Tom, 273, 320
longhouse religion, 273
loose fish, 57
Lord Derby, 97
Lord Durham, 61
Lord Elgin, 41, 53
Lord Selkirk, 136
Lord Sydenham, 43
Lowe, G., 204
Lower Canada, 9
Lower House, 83
lumber gangs, 38
lumbering, 13, 266
    see also timber trade
    Canada West, 16
    New Brunswick, 6
    Ottawa Valley, 38
    prairies, 223
    Saint John River, 38

Macdonald, John A., 10, 15, 55, 61, 62, 64, 68, 74, 77, 81, 96, 101, 102, 103, 107, 113, 114, 148, 150, 162, 172, 192, 194–196, 198, 244, 248, 279
Macdonell, Miles, 134
Mackenzie, Alexander, 156, 173
Mackenzie, William Lyon, 58
Maclean, John Bayne, 227
Macleod, James, 165
MacMurchy, Helen, 302
MacNab, Allan, 48
maîtres chez nous, 358
Manifest destiny, 80, 81
Manitoba
    Confederation, 107
    population, 115
Manitoba Act, 107, 151
manufacturers, 246
manufacturing, 243, 245–246, 266
    Canada West, 16
Mapp, Thomas, 229
Marconi, Guglielmo, 254
Maritime Union, 74
markets, 111
Marquis strain (of wheat), 185, 240
marriage, 130
    custom of the country, 130, 157
Martin, Clara Brett, 295
Massey-Harris, 248
Maynard, Hannah, 110
McClung, Nellie, 292, 297, 298, 302
McCrae, John, 331
McDougall, William, 145, 147
McGee, Thomas D'Arcy, 59, 96, 97
McGillvray, Alexander, 271
McKinney, Louis, 298
McLaughlin, Sam, 253
McPherson, Cluny, 332
Meech Lake Accord, 359–360
Mennonites, 186, 187, 336
Meredith, Edmund, 89, 95
Meredith, Fanny, 89
merger, 136
Metal Trades Council, 283
Methodist Church, 56
Métis, 17, 107, 108, 115, 127, 131, 141, 145, 147, 151, 191, 194–196
    land claims, 151
Métis List of Rights, 147, 148
middlemen, 128
Middleton, Frederick, 195, 196, 199
military defence, 95
militia, 82
mining, 266
    Nova Scotia, 4
    prairies, 224
    World War I, 259
Mistahimaskwa, 193
Mohawk, 309
Mohawk Institute, 273
Molson, John, 44
monopoly, 17, 175, 224
Montgomery, Lucy Maud, 117, 295
Montreal, 53
    population, 12, 242
Moodyville, 109
Mooney, Nellie, 292
Morin, Auguste-Norbert, 58, 59
Mulrooney, Belinda, 202

multiculturalism, 350
Murphy, Emily, 297, 298, 302

Naismith, James, 259
Napier, Robert, 45
National Archives of Canada, 14
National Council of Women, 301
National Dream, 155
National Historic Sites, 8
National Indian Brotherhood, 309
National Policy, 113, 244, 245, 248
navvies, 43, 44
negotiators, 169
neutral, 81
New Brunswick
    lumbering, 6
    population, 6, 28
    Royal Tour of 1860, 6–9
    timber trade, 6
New Caledonia, 156, 158
New France, fall of, 10
Newfoundland
    Confederation, 104, 118–119
    fishing, 4
    Lieutenant-Governor, 4
    population, 28
    responsible government, 4
    Royal Tour of 1860, 4
newspapers, 58–59
Nine-Hour Movement, 279
Nisga'a First Nation, 347–348
no stoppage rule, 313
no-man's land, 328
non-sectarian schools, 56
North American Free Trade Agreement, 356
North West Company, 17, 128, 132, 156
North West Mounted Police, 161–166
North West Territories, 18–19
    population, 6, 115
    representative government, 194
    responsible government, 194
Northwest Rebellion, 307
Nova Scotia
    fishing, 4
    mining, 4
    population, 4, 6, 28
    Royal Tour of 1860, 4–5
    shipbuilding, 4
Nova Scotia Party, 102
Nunavut, 346

O'Donoghue, William, 151
occupations
    immigration, 36
    wages, 272
Ojibwa, 169
Okalik, Paul, 346
Old Tomorrow, 107
Oliver, Frank, 308
Onandaga, 273
Onderdonk, Andrew, 176–178
One Big Union, 282–283
one man, one vote, 54
Ontario, population, 6
Orange Order, 15, 16

Orangemen, 15
Orkney Islands, 134
Ottawa, 12, 64, 89
    government buildings, 13
    population, 242
    timber trade, 13
Ottawa & Prescott Railway, 15
Otter, William, 197
outport settlement, 104

Pacific Scandal, 172–174
pacifism, 285, 336
packet, 45
paddlewheelers, 44
Palliser, John, 17
Paris Peace Conference, 339
Parker, Eliza, 34
parklands, 219
Parlby, Irene, 298
parliamentary system of government, 55
Parti Québécois, 358, 361
Partridge Island, 32
party platform, 64
passenger liners, 44
patent, 252
Patriotes, 76
patriotism, 318
Payette, Julie, 352, 353
Pedley, Frank, 308
Peguis, 134
Peguis's Treaty, 136
pemmican, 128, 130
Pemmican Proclamation, 134
per capita grants, 77
Persons Case, 298, 301
Petition of Rights, 192
piecework, 275
pieceworkers, 277
pioneers, 213
Pitikwahanapiwiyin, 169
pogroms, 190
political deadlock, 64
political parties, 57
Pope, William, 74, 75
population
    Alberta, 115
    British Columbia, 6, 108
    Canada, 55
    Canada East, 6, 28, 55
    Canada West, 6, 28, 55
    Charlottetown, 9
    Halifax, 6, 242
    Hamilton, 242
    Manitoba, 115
    Montreal, 12, 242
    New Brunswick, 6, 28
    Newfoundland, 28
    North-West Territories, 6, 115
    Nova Scotia, 6, 28
    Ontario, 6
    Ottawa, 242
    prairies, 217, 223, 228
    Prince Edward Island, 6, 28
    Québec, 6
    Quebec City, 10, 242
    Red River, 147
    rural, 249

Saint John, 6, 242
Saskatchewan, 115
Toronto, 16, 242
urban, 249
Vancouver, 242
Winnipeg, 225, 242
populist party, 59
Port Moody, 173
potlatch, 293, 310
Potts, Jerry, 164, 165
Poundmaker, 169, 197
prairies
    Confederation, 115
    culture, 228
    education, 231
    farming, 185, 219–222
    immigration, 217–218
    land ownership, 184
    lumbering, 223
    mining, 224
    population, 217, 223, 228
    railways, 224
    religion, 186–190
    settlement of, 212–218
    surveyors, 184
    towns, 225
    travelling, 217
preferential tariffs, 37
    end of, 41
Presbyterian Church, 56
Price, George, 337
primary document, 14
Prince Albert, 191
Prince Edward Island
    Confederation, 111–112
    farming, 9
    fishing, 9
    land ownership, 111
    population, 6, 28
    railways, 111
    responsible government, 9
    shipbuilding, 9
    trade, 111
private property, 170
prohibition, 299
provisional government, 148
pull factors, 213
push factors, 213

Quakers, 336
quarantine, 31, 32
quarantine station, 30, 32
Quebec, population, 6
Quebec City, 89
    citadel, 10
    fall of, 10
    industry, 10
    population, 10, 242
    timber trade, 10
Quebec Conference, 82, 83–85

Railway Disputes Act, 281
railways, 46–49
    Canada East, 12
    impact of, 49
    prairies, 224
    Prince Edward Island, 111

unions, 49
Rebellion of 1837, 53
Rebellion of 1885, 115, 178
reciprocity, 41–42
Reciprocity Treaty, 42, 82, 92, 95, 111
recruiters, 319
Red Fife wheat, 185
Red River, 17
   education, 140
   farmers/farming, 137, 141
   flooding, 138, 188
   fur trade, 137
   hunting, 141
   land ownership, 143–144
   population, 147
   religion, 140
   transportation, 141
Red River carts, 127, 141
Red River Rebellion, 107
   amnesty, 151
Red River Settlement, 132, 134–135, 137
referendum, 104, 118, 361
Reimer, Karl, 187
religion: see also individual religions
   Canada East, 10, 55, 56
   Canada West, 10, 15, 56
   political dimension, 58–59
   prairies, 186–190
   Red River, 140
representation by population, 54, 74, 85
representative government in the North West Territories, 194
reserves, 169
   aboriginal peoples, 261
residential schools, 306, 307
resolutions, 145
resource-based industries, 266
   see also lumbering, mining
   living conditions, 269–271
responsible government, 53
   Newfoundland, 4
   North West Territories, 194
   Prince Edward Island, 9
   Vancouver Island, 20
Revolutionary War, 73
Ricketts, Thomas, 338
Rideau Canal, 12, 43
ridings, 55
Riel, Louis, 107, 133, 145, 146, 147, 149, 151, 194–196, 198, 199, 279
Rindisbacher, Peter, 139
Ritchie, Eliza, 297
Ritchot, Noel-Joseph, 150
Robertson, Colin, 135
Roblin, Rodmond, 298
Rogers, A.B., 178
Roman Catholic Church, 56
Ross rifle, 332
Ross, Alexander, 138
Royal Canadian Mounted Police, 166, 355
Royal Geographic Society, 17
Royal Tour of 1860
   Canada East, 9–12
   Canada West, 12–17
   New Brunswick, 6–9
   Newfoundland, 4

Nova Scotia, 4–5
Rupert's Land, 17, 62, 85, 108, 131
Ryerson Press, 304

safety, 266–268
Saint John, population, 6, 242
Salish, 159
Saskatchewan
   Confederation, 116
   population, 115
Saulteaux, 134, 137, 167
Saunders, Charles, 240
Saunders, Margaret, 294
schooling of children: see education
Schultz, John C., 143, 144, 148, 150
Scott, Julia, 189
Scott, Malcolm, 189
Scott, Thomas, 149, 151
scrip, 191
sea power, 333
secede, 84
secret ballot, 111
Selkirk Mountains, 178
Selkirk settlers, 137
Semlin, 187
Semple, Robert, 135
Senate, 83, 85
separation, 358
Seshahts, 158
Seven Oaks (battle of), 135–136
Seward, William, 80
Shadd, Mary Ann, 60
shanties, 269
shell shock, 329
shipbuilding, 7
   Maritimes, 39–40
   Nova Scotia, 4
   Prince Edward Island, 9
   World War I, 259
Shubenacadie Canal, 44
Sifton, Clifford, 215, 216, 227
Sihks, 312
Silver Dart, 254
Simcoe, John Graves, 56
Singh, Gurdit, 312
Six Nations Reserve, 309, 321
Ski-Doo, 354
slavery, 33, 79
slaves, 33
smallpox, 31, 132, 162, 188, 190, 268
Smallwood, Joseph, 118
Smith, Albert J., 91, 92
Smith, Donald A., 148, 149, 175, 178
Smith, Goldwin, 296
Smith, William, 109
social activists, 297
social movement, 297
soddies, 212
sourdoughs, 201
speculators, 191
Springhill, 266
squatters, 141, 143
St. Alban's raid, 82
St. Laurent, 191
St. Lawrence and Atlantic Railroad, 46, 48
Standard Time, 240, 241

Status Indians, 306
steamboats, 44
steamships, 45
Steele, Sam, 204
Stephen, George, 175
Stowe, Emily, 240, 297
Strange, Thomas, 197
strikebreakers, 279
strikes, 280–281, 283, 284
Strom, Theodore, 223
suffrage, 296, 298
Sun Dance, 307, 310
surveyors, 107, 173
   prairies, 184
sweating system, 275
sympathy strikes, 284
syndicate, 174

Tache, Etienne-Paschal, 83
tariffs, 37, 41, 90, 91, 113, 244, 245, 248
   preferential, 37
taxation, 90, 324
technology, 252, 352
   transportation, 252–253
   World War I, 335
telephone, 256–257
Temperance Movement, 299
tenant farmers, 132
terminus, 173
textile industry, 275
Thompson, Mary, 204
threshing gangs, 220
Tilley, Samuel, 90, 91, 92, 97, 102
timber ships, 29
timber trade, 37
   see also lumbering
   expansion, 38
   growth, 38
   New Brunswick, 6
   Quebec City, 10
title, 184
Todd, William, 132
Toronto, 16
   population, 16, 242
Toronto Humane Society, 293
Toronto Hydro, 260
Toronto Industrial Exhibition, 252
Tory Party, 62
townships, 184
trade, 90, 128, 162
   Canada West, 16
   Prince Edward Island, 111
trade unions, 279
trade war, 128
Trades and Labour Congress, 280
Trades Assembly, 279
transcontinental railway, 172
transportation, 43, 252
   see also canals, railways, steamboats, steamships
   Industrial Revolution, 43–44
   Red River, 141
   technology, 252–253
travelling on the prairies, 217
treaties, 167
   aboriginal peoples, 167–172
   property rights, 170

Treaty of Versailles, 339
trench warfare, 325–327
Trent incident, 81
Triple Alliance, 318
Triple Entente, 318
Truancy and Compulsory School
Attendance Act, 272
Trudeau, Pierre, 359
Tupper, Charles, 90, 95, 102
typhus, 29, 30, 31, 32

Ukrainians, 229
Underground Railway, 33–35
Union, the, 79
Unionist Party, 337
unions, 259, 279
    railway, 49
Upper Canada, 9
Upper Fort Garry, 147
upper house, 83

Van Horne, William, 174, 179
Vancouver, 109, 173
    population, 242
Vancouver Island, 20, 85
    responsible government, 20
Vancouver Trades and Labour Council,
293
Vickers, Roy Henry, 348
Victoria, 110
Victoria Cross, 6, 338
Victorian Order of Nurses, 292
Victory Bonds, 324
VisionQuest, 348
voting, 111, 301
    Aboriginal Peoples, 310, 320
    women, 296
    World War I, 337

wages and occupations, 272
Wandering Spirit, 193
war effort of women, 323–324
War Measures Act, 321
war memorials, 8
War of 1812, 81, 356
wards, 108
Ware, John, 229
Weir, Robert Stanley, 63
Welland Canal, 43
wheat, 185
Whelan, Patrick, 96
whisky, 162
whisky traders, 162
widow maker, 266
Wilson, Katherine, 330
Winnie-the-Pooh, 325
Winnipeg, 225
    culture, 226
    effect of strike, 287
    growth of, 226
    population, 225, 242
Winnipeg General Strike, 283–287
Winnipeg Grain Exchange, 225
women
    voting, 296
    war effort, 323–324

women workers, 275–278
Women's Christian Temperance Union,
299
Women's Institute, 292
women's issues, 294–296
Woodsworth, James Shaver, 285, 286
Woodward, Henry, 252
Workmen's Compensation Bill,
280–281
World War I, 259, 318
    aboriginal peoples, 319
    farming, 324
    industry, 259
    mining, 259
    shipbuilding, 259
    technology, 335
    voting, 337

Yellow Quill, 167
York Boats, 134
York Factory, 131, 132
Youmans, Letitia, 299
Young Women's Christian Association,
299